The
CHRISTIAN DOCTRINE
of
CREATION
and
REDEMPTION
DOGMATICS: Vol. II

EMIL BRUNNER

The
CHRISTIAN DOCTRINE
of
CREATION
and
REDEMPTION

DOGMATICS: VOL. II

Translated by
OLIVE WYON

Philadelphia
THE WESTMINSTER PRESS

First Published in Great Britain in 1952
By Lutterworth Press, London

PRINTED IN THE UNITED STATES OF AMERICA

9 8 7 6 5 4 3

PREFACE

DURING my last visit to the United States, which took place shortly after the publication of the first volume of the Dogmatics, a theological colleague expressed the desire that I would develop further the point of view contained in my book, *The Divine-Human Encounter (Wahrheit als Begegnung)*. He urged that he regarded this view as decisive for the development of theology, and that he wished me to expand it within the whole framework of Christian doctrine. I replied, that I had already made a beginning in *The Christian Doctrine of God*, and that what I had begun in that volume was being expanded in two later volumes.

In this second volume the reader will doubtless perceive still more clearly the logical significance of this point of view for the understanding of the Christian message. The discovery of the "I-Thou" truth in philosophy by Ebner and Buber is indeed, as Heim has put it, a "Copernican turning-point" in the history of thought. Here, however, our concern is not to try to combine the "I-Thou" philosophy with Christian theology, but to emphasize the importance of this truth, which is wholly derived from the Bible, for Christian thought. Hitherto this has never been done within the sphere of dogmatics. The present work is a first, and doubtless an imperfect, attempt in this direction. It shows, however, that it is only on these lines that Christian thought can be saved from the rigidity of ecclesiastical orthodoxy, and the results of Biblical criticism can be made fruitful for the shaping of Christian doctrine. For after the first promising beginnings of the "Dialectical Theology" in overcoming the sterile and false contrast between Liberalism and Orthodoxy, we are unfortunately back again at the point where this contrast dominates theological discussion afresh. The rediscovery of Biblical truth has again, as at the period of the Reformation, led to a rigid fundamentalism and confessionalism, which offers plenty of vulnerable points for rationalistic attacks from the intellectual Left Wing, and makes it appear as though criticism and convinced Christian thought were opposed. The doctrine of Creation and Revelation here offered is based upon the conviction that sound criticism and genuine Christian thinking are not incompatible. Those members of the Church who passively

accept what they have been taught as "revealed truth" seem
to be unaware of the fact that their view of "faith" is hampered
by an age-long tradition which has misunderstood the meaning
of "faith", regarding it not as "encounter" with the Living
Christ, but as the acceptance of "revealed truths".

The truth which broke through at the Reformation (though
later it was again obscured) of the personal character of faith,
as "encounter" with Christ, means liberation from the rigidity
and ethical sterility of orthodoxy, and sets us free to have a
faith which is based on nothing save the Love of God revealed
in Jesus Christ. This truth alone can preserve us from sterile
"theologizing" and from clericalism, and awaken in the Church
a missionary and pastoral spirit. This is the fundamental aim
of the present work. I now offer it to the reader's kind and
critical attention.

The fact that in spite of many health difficulties I was able
to finish this book before leaving Europe for my journey to
the East is due to the assistance of many good friends. Herr
Pfarrer Basler in Zofingen, and Fräulein Gertrud Epprecht,
Assistant-Minister in Zürich, have shared with me the labours
of proof correction, and my son, Dr. H. H. Brunner, Pfarrer
in Marthalen, prepared the Index. To all of these, and to
several others who remain anonymous, I tender my cordial
thanks.

EMIL BRUNNER

Zürich,
August 1949

TRANSLATOR'S NOTE

I wish to express my grateful thanks to all who have so
kindly assisted me with advice and information, as well as in
the labour of proof-reading; particularly to the following
friends: The Rev. W. D. Davies, D.D., the Rev. H. H.
Farmer, D.D., and Miss Mary Lusk, B.A.

O. WYON

CONTENTS

CONTENTS

PART 2

THE HISTORICAL REALIZATION

OF THE

DIVINE SELF-COMMUNICATION

CHAPTER I

THE CREATOR AND HIS CREATION

IN the first volume of this series, we dealt with the doctrine of God: the Lord, the Origin of all created things, who is Himself before all creation. There we were thinking of God as He is "in Himself", of His Being "before" all time, "before" history, and "before" revelation; because unless this were so, unless God exists—from everlasting—"in Himself", there would be no Creator, and no act of free creation. But we were only able to speak of Him who is "before all creation", and "before all revelation", on the basis of His revelation, not on the basis of any kind of philosophical speculation.

All that we have been saying about Him who is before all creation, and before all revelation, is based upon, and in accordance with the Scriptures. It is the divine revelation given to us in the Scriptures which constantly bears witness to the fact that God is "before all things", "before the foundation of the world".[1] At the same time we are aware of the fact that this word "before" does not denote "time"; for Time is itself the creation of God. Existence in Time is the way in which we—human beings—live, it is not the way in which God exists.

(I) THE ORIGIN OF CREATION

God stands "above" the world, because He is the Lord, because it is only through His Word that it exists at all; but we are well aware that when we say this, "above" is not a spatial expression, since God alone creates Space. The supramundane nature of God, which is part of His Being, does not tell us anything about the relation between the Being of God and the spatial existence of the world. These two words, "before" and "above", are both predicates of His Being as Lord. This is in direct opposition to the view of Greek philosophy and its later exponents, namely, that there is a correlation between God and the world, just as there is between left and right, i.e. that the one cannot be conceived apart from the other. We must drop this idea altogether, and try

[1] Col. 1: 17; Eph. 1: 4; 1 Pet. 1: 20; John 17: 24, etc.

to draw out the full meaning of the opposite conception. We are to think of God as the God who is "there", apart from the world, who indeed Himself posits the world, to whom the world is not His *alter ego*: and when we think of the world we must think of it as something which does not naturally, essentially, and eternally, belong to God, but as something which only exists because it has been created by God. If it were otherwise, God would not be the *Lord* of the world at all, but, so to speak, its double.

We have said, it is true, that God, as He is in Himself, is the reason why there is a world at all. God's being "-as-He-is-in-Himself" is at the same time the will to communicate Himself, His "being-for-us", before we come into being. It is because He is "for us" that we have been created; it is because He wills to communicate Himself, that the world exists. Hence we have been thinking, not only of the eternal Being of God, but also of His eternal *Will*, which precedes all created being as the ground of its existence, of His "decree of creation". It would be presumptuous to speak of this on the basis of our own thinking, how could a *man*—even the most gifted and far-sighted—be in a position to do this? But the Divine decree of Creation is the content of the divine self-revelation. "Things which eye saw not, and ear heard not, and which entered not into the heart of man, whatsoever things God prepared for them that love Him".[1]

It is no accident that, when man is thrown back upon his own methods of acquiring knowledge, he knows nothing of such a "decree of creation", the history of philosophy indeed—in so far as, consciously or unconsciously, it does not take the Biblical revelation into account—is silent on this point. But it is also no accident that the same original record of revelation which speaks of the divine plan of Salvation, also deals with the plan or decree of Creation; for how could God's purpose for the world not be His plan which precedes it?[2] How can the Lord of the world manifest His sovereignty without revealing to us that the world is grounded in His will, and, from the very beginning, has been ordered for this purpose? Not only the fact of the existence of the world, but all that is included in the fact of creation—the manner of creation and its purpose—is rooted in His Will as Creator, as that which precedes and establishes it.[3] We would have failed to give the phrase "the created universe" its Biblical content, unless

[1] 1 Cor. 2: 9 (R.V.)   [2] John 1: 1–3; Col. 1: 16; 1 Cor. 8: 6   [3] Eph. 1: 11

we had already dealt with the fact that the world is "rooted and grounded" in the nature of God, as Lord, and in His Will as Creator. In the following pages we now proceed to think out the meaning of this statement: that God, the Almighty Lord, is Creator, and that the world is His Creation. What does this mean?

(2) THE KNOWLEDGE OF CREATION

The theological statement: God is the "Creator of Heaven and Earth", brings this affirmation into the sphere of facts which are accessible to our natural knowledge. No other "heaven" than that which we know, no other "earth" than that upon which we live, is meant by this credal statement. The article of belief in the Creation unites (in a way about which we shall have to think further later on) the world which we know with the mystery of God. This world which we know, which everyone knows more or less, is God's creation. But while this article of belief in the Creation lights up the sphere of things with which we are familiar, what it says is not familiar. Of ourselves, we do not know that God is Creator, as we know the things of this world. This statement is not merely part of Natural Theology, in the sense of being a truth which a man can acquire for himself, but, like every other article of the Christian Creed, it is an article of faith; and that means, a statement based upon revelation.

When the words "Creator", "Creation" and "creature" are used by Christian thinkers, they mean what the Creeds say, in spite of the fact that there are non-Christian or philosophical statements which sound very similar. The fact that there are philosophical or religious expressions in other religions which, at first sight, seem to say the same thing is, however (as we shall see in a moment), not accidental; but whatever that may mean, one thing is clear from the outset: in the Christian Creed the Creator means the God of the historical revelation, the Father of our Lord Jesus Christ, the Triune God; and by "Creation" it means that event which is founded in the revealed divine decree of Creation.

Indeed, we must not ignore the fact that we have just mentioned, namely, that non-Christian thinkers also speak of the "Creator" and the "Creation". Yes, it is true that in almost all religions there *are* creation-myths of all kinds; there is the idea of a "Creator-Spirit" which, as it were, stands behind and above the polytheistic or animistic pantheon of the gods; there are theistic doctrines of Creation in certain sects within Hinduism: above all, there is the doctrine of the Creator in Zoroastrianism and in Islam; there are hints of the Christian doctrine of Creation in the *Timaeus* of Plato, and in the writings of the great Stoics, Epictetus, Cicero, Seneca, and Marcus Aurelius. These ideas exist, because God does not only reveal Himself through His Word in History, but also through His work in Creation, hence He leaves no man without a witness.[1] And yet, in spite of all the analogies and apparent similarities, all these ideas and suggestions are different from the knowledge of God the Creator, as it is attested in His historical revelation, because sinful man is not capable of grasping what God shows him in His work in Creation without turning it into something else.[2]

Just as the "Lord God" of the Bible, the Father of our Lord Jesus Christ, is not the same as the *Theos* of Plato or Epictetus, the *Rama* of the Sikhs, or the *Ahura Mazda* of Zoroastrianism, so also His existence as Creator and his creation of the world are not the same. Here the saying, *si duo faciunt idem, non est idem*, is supremely and peculiarly apt.

Unfortunately the uniqueness of this Christian doctrine of Creation and the Creator is continually being obscured by the fact that theologians are so reluctant to begin their work with the New Testament; when they want to deal with the Creation they tend to begin with the Old Testament, although they never do this when they are speaking of the Redeemer. The emphasis on the story of Creation at the beginning of the Bible has constantly led theologians to forsake the rule which they would otherwise follow, namely, that the basis of *all* Christian articles of faith is the Incarnate Word, Jesus Christ. So when we begin to study the subject of Creation in the Bible we ought to start with the first chapter of the Gospel of John, and some other passages of the *New* Testament, and not with the first chapter of Genesis. If we can make up our minds to stick to this rule, we shall be saved from many difficulties, which will inevitably occur if we begin with the story of Creation in the Old Testament.

Of course, I do not wish to deny the permanent significance of, and the absolute necessity for, the Old Testament account of the Creation—not only in the first two chapters of Genesis, but also in the Prophets, the Psalms, and in the Book of Job.

[1] Acts 14: 17; Rom. 1: 19   [2] Rom. 1: 21

In order to expand the somewhat scanty statements of the
New Testament we certainly need the weighty and enriching
testimony of the Old Testament; but in principle these statements are as introductory in character as the Old Testament
witness to the Messiah is to that of the New Testament.

Even the most intelligent exposition of the Old Testament
story of Creation which is offered as the basis of the Christian
doctrine presents modern man with numerous difficulties,
which cannot be removed by the most bold attempts at allegorizing the narrative.[1] At this point, to fall back into a
"Biblicism" which has already been abandoned in principle,
will have a peculiarly disastrous effect. In principle our belief
in the Creator is not bound up with the *narrative* of Creation
in the Old Testament. The truth which the story of the
creation of the world in six days contains is a powerful, and
eternally impressive, expression of the preparatory self-revelation of God in the Old Testament; but it is no more the
"canonical" form of the self-revelation of the Creator, than
Isaiah 9 is the "canonical" form of the Old Testament witness
to Christ.

(3) CREATION: NOT A THEORY OF THE WAY IN WHICH THE
    WORLD CAME INTO EXISTENCE

This becomes clear directly we ask the question: Where is
the meaning and the purpose of the divine Creation of the
world shown to us most clearly? It is characteristic of the New
Testament statements about the Creator and the Creation
that here the fact of Creation and the manner of Creation are
stressed far less than the reason why the world was created
and to what end; while the narrative of the Creation in Genesis
says nothing about this at all. It is true that a Christological
exposition of this Old Testament narrative of Creation may, to
some extent, fill the gap, but only at the cost of using arbitrary
and forced methods of exegesis. But if we start from the
decisive statements of the Fourth Gospel and the Epistles,[2]
the situation is immediately quite different.

Here certainly we are not given a narrative; there is no
series of events; everything is gathered up and concentrated

[1] In spite of the important truth of the exposition of the story of Creation
by Karl Barth, *K.D.*, III, 1, it is a great pity that the great Basel theologian
has presented his doctrine of Creation in the shape of an exposition of this
passage of Old Testament Scripture
[2] John 1: 1–3; Col. 1: 15, 16; Heb. 1: 2

at one decisive point: that God in, and through, the Logos, the Son, has created the world. If we keep *this* "record of Creation" before our eyes, then we do not need any lengthy system of argument to prove that it is totally different from all mythologies of creation, and also from all philosophical ideas of creation.

In the Prologue to the Gospel of John the Creation is mentioned in a way which we find nowhere else in the Bible; here it is clear that when a believer in Christ speaks of the Creation, he means something different from "explaining" why there is a world, or why things exist. In this witness to the Creation we are all addressed, and the meaning of our existence is defined. Here there is no question of confusing the Creation with a cosmogony. Here the Word which became flesh in Jesus Christ, and the Word of Creation, are one. In this Word of Creation the eternal decree, and in it also the purpose and the meaning of all existence become plain.[1]

To know the Creator thus, means to know, first and foremost, that God, because He is Sovereign Lord, is Creator. Thus from the outset this idea of Creation is clearly distinguished from all the various theories about the way in which the world came into existence. Before Israel knew Yahweh as *Creator*, it knew Him as *Lord*. Because He is absolute Lord He is Creator. It is not forbidden, and indeed it is inevitable, that, as human beings, on the basis of our knowledge of the world, we must ask questions about its origin, and certainly it is not unimportant that to-day leading physicists once more point to a divine reason as the basis of the world which they discover through science. But this has a very remote and indirect relation to the Christian doctrine of Creation. The Christian belief in Creation arises at the point where all Christian faith arises, namely, in the revelation of God in Jesus Christ. For there God meets us as the Lord, who, because He is Lord, is the Creator. Even faith in God the Creator is "truth-as-encounter"; the Lord who meets me in His Word, in His Word as Person—Jesus Christ, is LORD, absolutely; thus He who is "above" all and "before" all is the One who originates all things and is Himself originated by none; He is the One who determines all things and is determined by none. Even this truth is expressed in the form: "I, *thy* God and Creator", and not "HE, the World-Creator". This truth comes to man as a personal summons; it is not a truth which is the fruit of reflection; hence it is

[1] I Cor. 8: 6

truth which, from the very outset, makes me directly responsible. "I am the Lord thy God", the Creator; this means: "Thou art My property". This does not mean that I start from the idea that God is the Creator of the world, and then argue that since I also form part of the world I also recognize Him as my Creator, and then come to the conclusion that I belong to God. The way to the knowledge of faith is the very opposite: here, as everywhere in the Christian Faith, the "I-Thou" comes first; hence from the outset, and not later on, this truth has ethical force. For the fact that man belongs to God implies the whole truth of responsibility and of all moral obligation. In Jesus Christ we meet Him who addresses us as absolute Lord, and therefore as the Creator of all things: "I, thy Lord, the Creator."

This does not mean, however, that the truth of *my* creation precedes the truth that the *world* has been created. My Lord— that is, the Creator, absolutely, not only the Creator of my existence. Since in Jesus Christ I meet my Lord, I meet Him who is the Lord of the whole world. Since He reveals Himself as "my" Lord, He reveals Himself as the One who determines all things, and is determined by none. Schleiermacher's phrase "absolute dependence" is right, indeed it is excellent; only the way in which he expounds it is wrong. Here too we must admit that Schleiermacher was right in making a very clear distinction between the knowledge of this absolute dependence and any theory of a cosmogony.[1] If only he had taken this truth of "absolute dependence" seriously! But he could not do so, because his faith was not based on this personal encounter, because his faith was not based on the Word which addresses man personally. That is why this idea of "absolute dependence" is confused with the causality which runs through Nature,[2] with which it has nothing at all to do. For the idea of Creation means that I, together with the whole of Nature to which I belong, am absolutely dependent upon God, while He, on the other hand, is dependent neither upon me nor upon it.

(4) CREATION *EX NIHILO*

The truth that God is the One who determines all things and is determined by none, is the precise meaning of the idea of Creation as *creatio ex nihilo*. Creation "out of nothing" does

[1] *Glaubenslehre*, 36, 2   [2] *Ibid.*, 46

not mean, however,—as Gnosticism of all ages continually interprets it—that there was once a "Nothing" out of which God created the world, a negative primal beginning, a Platonic MÊ ON, a formlessness, a chaos, a primal Darkness. The "ex" of the *creatio ex nihilo* does not suggest any kind of "matter"—however vague and shadowy—but it means the fact that God alone brought the world into being. There never was a "nothing" alongside of God, as it were, but God alone. The Gnostic doctrine of "Nothing" is the final attempt to adapt the certainly incomprehensible mystery of Creation to that which we know from experience as a semi-creation, the formation of something; it understands the Creation as the moulding of a formless original substance.

This idea of Creation, as the shaping of formless matter, is the content of all creation *myths*, and we can even trace its influence on the Old Testament story of Creation. But the New Testament idea of Creation absolutely excludes any idea that any other force, save God, had any share in Creation. The idea of Creation expresses the truth that God assumes complete and sole responsibility for the existence of the world, and moreover it does not excuse the fact that it is finite, by suggesting the existence of a "nothing", an uncreated ὕλη, a MÊ ON, which—"unfortunately"—also played an anonymous part in the process, and is the reason for the imperfection of the world.

God is the One who absolutely determines all things, and is determined by none. He is conditioned by nothing, therefore, not even by a "Nothing". Were He to be thus conditioned He would not be Creator, but simply a demiurge. All that existed "before" all creation was God and His Word. The Creation has its foundation and its origin in God alone. "For He spake and it was done; He commanded, and it stood fast".[1] "In the beginning was the Word . . . all things were made by Him". This too is the meaning of the sublime story of Creation in the first chapter in the Bible! "God spake . . . and it was done." This magnificent presentation of the *creatio ex nihilo*, or—and it is the same thing—creation "by the Word", is still faintly coloured by a relic of the mythical idea of an original Chaos, an idea which in other passages in the Old Testament betrays still more clearly its polytheistic-mythical origin.[2]

To try to explain it away leads to an arbitrary process of allegorization, or (and from the theological point of view this

[1] Ps. 33: 9   [2] Ps. 74: 13, 14; 104: 6 ff.

is still more dangerous), to the idea of a nihilistic "danger" existing within God himself. It is precisely at this point that we see how important it is to start from the witness of the New Testament and not from that of the Old Testament. For in the New Testament the last vestiges of any ideas which would impose limitations upon God have disappeared. God alone achieved His Creation; He Himself, by His word. The explicit formulation of the idea of *creatio ex nihilo* appears for the first time in the literature of later Judaism, in the second Book of the Maccabees:[1] ἐξ οὐκ ὄντων ἐποίησεν αὐτὰ ὁ θεός.

This sentence could, of course, still be misunderstood in a Platonic Gnostic sense; but the formula used in the Epistle to the Hebrews: "that the worlds have been framed by the word of God, so that what is seen hath not been made out of things which do appear"[2] is unmistakable; so also is the phrase used in Rom. 4: 17: "God . . . who calleth the things that are not, as though they were." From this standpoint, as we look back, we may well say that this is also the real meaning of Genesis I, and of the witness of the Old Testament as a whole, as interpreted by the Prophets.

The words of the Second Isaiah:[3] "I form the light and create darkness", are to be understood as a protest against all mythical theories of a primal darkness. God alone creates the world with no other co-operating factor. That is the meaning of the Biblical words "create" and "creation".

This expresses something which is utterly beyond all human understanding. What *we* know as creation is never *creatio ex nihilo*, it is always the shaping of some given material. Fichte therefore was quite right when he said of the Creation that it is "something which cannot properly be imagined".[4] But he was not right in rejecting the idea of Creation on that account; but we can understand why this idea aroused his scorn as a philosopher. For a philosophy which is controlled by the belief that everything can be deduced by human reflection and thus assumes the absolute continuity of human thought, must be indignant about the "fundamental error" of the idea of Creation; because from the outset it presupposes the absolute discontinuity of human thought: God is over against the world, the world is over against God. God and the world are not bound together by any necessity; the world is the work of divine freedom. Fichte is an extremely logical thinker, with

[1] 2 Macc. 7: 28   [2] Heb. 11: 3   [3] Isa. 45: 7
[4] J. G. Fichte, *Ausg. Werke*, 5. 191

great intellectual energy. Since he constructs his system *a priori*, that is, entirely on intellectual grounds, he cannot admit the element of contingency. The idea of contingency itself is simply a philosophical formulation of the Christian idea of creation. It is therefore no accident that it is unknown to ancient philosophy.[1]

In point of fact, to "posit" a creation is, as Fichte says, philosophical nonsense; but the Christian Faith does not "posit" the idea of Creation, but accepts it as "posited" by God; this is a fact which we cannot grasp in thought, nor can we evolve it out of our own needs, but we have to accept it, through the Divine revelation, as "posited". Thus we now see the necessary connexion between *Creation* and *Revelation*. We can only speak of Creation on the basis of Revelation. From our point of view as human beings, on the basis of our own intellectual efforts, to speak of "Creation" is, as Fichte maintains nonsense, "the first criterion of the falseness of a doctrine". It is the same Word which created the world which also reveals to us the truth that the world has been created. The freedom of God can only be recognized in His self-mani-festation, that is, it can only be believed; the same is true of the Creation as the act of God's Freedom. These statements are confirmed by the fact that no philosophy—save that which begins with revelation and to which usually the very name of philosophy is denied—contains the idea of Creation, in the sense of *creatio ex nihilo*. Plato's Demiurge shapes the world, but does not create it; and Aristotle teaches explicitly the eternal co-existence of God and the world.[2] To the degree in which Western philosophy moves away from the Christian doctrine based on revelation, the idea of the creation of the world is replaced by the idea of the eternal correlation of God and the world.[3] Indeed, nothing else was possible; either human thought has power over God—and then God is no longer Lord, nor is He Creator; or God is Lord and Creator, and then human thought has no power over Him; then God can only communicate Himself and His Being as Creator by His own act, and man cannot reach this truth by his own thought, he can only accept it in faith. The Lord God, who alone *creates* the world by His Word, is also the Revealer, who alone *imparts Himself* to man through His Word.

[1] Cf. K. Barth, *Kirchl. Dogmatik*, III, 1, p. 5
[2] Cf. Gilson: *L'ésprit de la philosophie médiévale*, I. Ch. 3
[3] Cf. Pattison: *The Idea of God*, pp. 303 ff., and also Schleiermacher

(5) THE PURPOSE OF CREATION

This brings us, further, to another decisive element in the Biblical idea of creation, and above all in that of the New Testament. Creation by the Word is not only to be understood in an instrumental sense: God speaks, and it is done; it is also final. The Word by which, or in which, God creates the world is at the same time His plan for Creation, its meaning and its goal.

The fact of Creation has an actual aspect of power and an ideal aspect connected with its final purpose. The Creation is because God wills it; it has no other foundation. God's will is the *ratio sufficiens* of the Creation. The Creation is the work of the Divine Omnipotence. But it is not only the work of His Omnipotence but also of His Holy Love. God creates the world in absolute freedom, it is true, but there is nothing arbitrary about His action. His freedom is identical with His Love. God creates the world because He wills to communicate Himself, because He wishes to have something "over against" Himself. As the Holy God He wills to glorify Himself in His Creation; as the loving God He wills to give Himself to others. His self-glorification, however, is in the last resort the same as His self-communication. He wills so to glorify Himself that that which He gives is received in freedom, and rendered back to Him again: His love. Hence the revelation of this love of His is at the same time the revelation of the purpose of His Creation, and this purpose of creation is the reason why He posits a creation. The love of God is the *causa finalis* of the Creation. In Jesus Christ this ideal reason for the Creation is revealed.[1]

It is precisely because the Old Testament story of Creation does not contain this element that it cannot be the starting-point for the Christian doctrine of Creation. The Word by which Yahweh creates heaven and earth is a pure word of command which expresses His power, but it is not the Word which gives divine meaning to His Creation. The idea that the Messianic Covenant is the ideal basis of the Creation of the world is not yet expressed in the Old Testament story of Creation; it is only hinted at in the Prophetic writings. In the New Testament, however, it is clearly present; it is the same Word through which the world came into being, who "became Flesh" in Jesus Christ, in whom God makes known to us His

[1] That is the meaning of the passages already cited from John 1, Eph. 1, Col. 1, and 1 Cor. 8

Love and Grace, and in so doing, His purpose for the world. Indeed, He Himself, Jesus Christ, as the personal manifestation of God, is the Goal of the world, for whom, in whom, and through whom the world has been created.[1] It is indeed for this end alone that God has created the world; that in it He should manifest His glory and give Himself to His Creation; this is the meaning of the world, and this is its goal. It is the Logos who was in the beginning, through whom, in whom, and unto whom, all things have been created.

Greek philosophy also knows of a Logos, which makes the world a cosmos. It speaks of the Logos which permeates all existence and binds it into a harmony. It conceives the Cosmos as a work of art, as something actual through which the ideal shimmers. The Logos is the Beauty of the world, the world is the expression of the divine Logos. But this idea of the Logos-Cosmos is completely different from that of the Logos of Creation. God and the world stand alongside of one another, God is not "above" the world as the Lord; He is not "before" the world as the One through whose will alone it comes into existence. Logos and Cosmos are correlative expressions, the one cannot be conceived apart from the other. In Greek thought the world has already reached its goal, its goal is its immanent meaning from all eternity. The world is not a work of God, which has a beginning and an end. The beginning and the end here merge into one in the timeless present; the historical element is lacking, because the element of act, of the energy of the divine will, is absent. But the Christian idea means: that the purpose of the world is in God: that in it God wills His Glory; in it He wills to rule; and in it He wills to bring man—through His self-manifestation—into fellowship with Himself. The purpose, and therefore the fundamental meaning of the Creation, is the Kingdom of God. It is only from this point of view that we can understand what the world is, as Creation; and this purpose is revealed in Jesus Christ. From Him alone—and not from the Old Testament story of Creation which knows nothing of Christ—can we understand what God's creation of the world really means.

(6) CREATION: THE BEGINNING OF TIME

When we say that the world is God's world, we say that it had a beginning. Greek philosophy knows no real creation,

[1] Most clearly expressed in Eph. 1: 10

because it knows no beginning of the world. For it the world is co-equal and eternal with God. It knows no beginning to the world because it does not know the world as the work of the personal God.[1] When we say: The world has a beginning, we are uttering a paradox, namely that Time has a beginning. In positing the world God also posits Time. Just as He posits Space so also He posits Time. Time and Space are the fundamental constituents of the world as posited by God. This, however, means that Time and Space are finite, not infinite. We are not thinking here of Time and Space as conceptual but as they actually are. The Kantian antinomies refer to Time and Space which can be conceived, not to actual Time and Space. Whether these antinomies—namely, that Space and Time must be thought of at the same time as finite and infinite—are genuine antinomies or prejudices similar to that of the theory of Euclidean space, which is supposed to be an *a priori* truth, which can be proved—we can rightly leave to the philosophers to decide. From the standpoint of belief in the Creation we maintain the finite character both of actual Time and actual Space.

Time is, "since", and because, there is a world.[2] Of course, we cannot exclude the question: what was there "before" the world? To this question faith gives a twofold reply: Before Time there is God Alone: and "before Time" is a phrase which bears the imprint of our own temporal existence. Thought divorced from revelation cannot bear this paradox; either it eliminates Time by means of the idea of a timeless truth, or it eliminates the pre-temporal by the idea that "time alone exists".[3] That which truly exists, it says, is timeless, hence the temporal does not really exist. Or it says: the non-temporal is a mere product of the imagination, there is nothing but the temporal. But faith posits—or rather it is *given* to it through revelation—a beginning of time, through the eternal God. The temporal is just as much part of our creaturely existence as the finite. As we shall see later on, it would be a great error to equate the temporal with that which passes away, and hence to say that the temporal is a consequence of the Fall—that owing to the Fall, through sin, man falls into a temporal existence.[4] The temporal is the essence of that which is created; as creatures we are temporal, all is temporal.

[1] Gilson, *op. cit.*, p. 83   [2] Cf. *Confessions of St. Augustine*, XI, 13 ff.
[3] G. *Nur-zeitlichkeit*=that which is only temporal (TR.)
[4] K. Heim used to teach this. See *Glaube und Denken*, 1931, pp. 370 ff. But he abandoned this Gnostic view later on (cf. *Jesus, der Herr*, 1935)

When we say: "Time has a beginning", we are not, of course, saying that we know what this beginning is. When we begin with the Old Testament Story of Creation this constantly leads us to regard the chronology and the Six Days' work of creation of Genesis as an integral part of the divine revelation. But if we begin with the New Testament this danger does not arise. "In the beginning was the Word . . . all things were made through Him." This statement does not posit any point in time according to our chronology, as this beginning, although it is probable that the Genesis view of the universe was also that of John. The finite character of Time, the fact that time has a beginning, does not mean that we know this brief beginning, or that we shall ever know it. Possibly so far as Time is concerned, the position may be like that of Space, at least since Einstein. Space, so the physicists say, is finite but unlimited. To-day they are inclined to speak in a similar way about Time. When we maintain, therefore, that the world has a beginning, in and with Time, in any case we are not in opposition to the modern knowledge of physics.

The fact that Time has a beginning is just as important as the other fact, that it has an end. Its end coincides with the end of created existence. This end, however, is not "nothingness", but it is the Goal which is both the end and the completion of the created universe. God Himself is the End of Creation, but this does not mean that He will be once more without a creation, as at the beginning; but it means that He will glorify Himself in the Creation, and give Himself to it, in such a way, that it will shatter the framework of the created universe as we know it.

The temporal is also connected with "becoming". Here, for speculative thought, the position is the same as it is with Time: either, that which "becomes" does not truly exist, but, as in Plato, it is a blend of being and non-being, or the tide of "becoming" swallows up everything in its path, and God and Truth are submerged. The Biblical revelation takes into account a created world, which is determined by the law of "becoming". The laws of "becoming" belong to God's world of creation and are not the result of the Fall. With the other orders of creation, the New Testament also regards "becoming" as belonging to God's creation.[1] The Story of Creation in Genesis, however, lays particular stress on this fact, since it represents the fruitfulness of all living things, continually

[1] Mark 10; 1 Cor. 11, 8 ff., 15: 47

reproducing their own kind, as the content of the Divine Command of Creation.

(7) IS *THIS* WORLD THAT WHICH GOD HAS CREATED?

We have now already opened up a whole group of questions in which our natural knowledge of the world and the communication of the divine revelation impinge upon one another or permeate each other. We must therefore first of all put the fundamental question: What kind of world did God create? This question, which at first sounds strangely in our ears, has exercised the mind of Christendom since the days of Marcion, and must still do so. For the more fully we ascribe—in our doctrine of Creation—responsibility to God for that which is created, the more disturbing is our view of the actual reality. Can this world, so full of meaningless, cruel suffering and death —be God's Creation? On the other hand, what meaning would the doctrine of Creation have, if it did not mean that God has created what we call "Heaven and Earth", this world with all that it contains? The belief in Creation is indeed, as we said at the beginning, intended to connect the world with which we are familiar, with the God who transcends the world. There are, however, two extreme views, which have arisen in the history of Christian thought, which we must reject from the outset: one that is wrongly pessimistic, and one that is wrongly optimistic.

(a) The erroneous pessimistic view, formulated first of all by Marcion and the Gnostics, maintains that this world, as we know it, cannot be the work of God the Creator. God created a good world, but the world with which we are familiar is not good, thus it is not the work of the God who is Perfect Love, revealed to us through the Gospel of Jesus Christ. However it came into being—and there are several Gnostic theories about this point—in any case it is not the creation of God.[1]

(b) The mistaken optimistic view, on the other hand, maintains that the world as we know it is identical with the Divine Creation; thus it finds itself forced to attribute what we call "sin" to the Creator, and to assert the impossibility of a distinction between Creation and Sin.[2]

In the light of the truth of Scripture neither view is tenable;

[1] For Gnostic speculations of this kind in modern theology see Althaus, *Die christliche Wahrheit*, I, pp. 190 ff.

[2] The most extreme modern champion of this view is E. Hirsch, *Schöpfung und Sünde*

both theories constitute an attack upon the foundation, the heart, of the Biblical doctrine of revelation.

First of all, we must certainly admit that the Old Testament does seem to be very near to the second view. It is true that the Genesis story of creation is immediately succeeded by the story of the Fall, of the divine curse upon man, who has become sinful, and on the ground which he cultivates, the story of man's expulsion from Eden, in which God had placed him; but no cosmic inferences are drawn from this story of the Fall. Above all: in the rest of the Old Testament there is no reference to this story of the Fall. It is true that Sin and Creation remain distinct; sin is the human denial of the divine order of creation; but the creation as a whole is not further affected by sin. Apart from the evil in men's hearts, and in their actions, everything in the world is God's creation: the course of the stars, the changing seasons, the form and the life of plants and animals—even of wild animals[1]—the human body in its relation to the soul, the series of human generations, birth and death—all this is, as it is, and takes place in this way, because, and as, God has appointed it, from the standpoint of His creation.

Even if Evil and Sin are not the work of God, but are rebellion against His order, yet these negative forces do not alter the structure of the world; this familiar world—with the one exception of Evil—is God's creation.

Even in the New Testament, the structure of the world, especially of the world of nature and the happenings of nature, are admitted to be created by God; even, too, the fundamental constitution of man, his psycho-physical unity, the fundamental elements of social life,[2] are recognized as the Divine creation; in the New Testament, however, the universal power of sin is emphasized much more strongly than in the Old Testament; further, the connexion between death and sin on the one hand, and between the sin of the individual and the sin of Adam in the Fall on the other, is admitted; and, further still, the belief is expressed that in a general way this earthly historical world is under the sway of demonic-satanic forces. This world may be the creation of God, but figuratively speaking, it is overshadowed by anti-divine forces, both within and outside of man, so that it is impossible to equate it absolutely with the creation of God.

But in this emphasis on the negative element the New

[1] Ps. 104: 21   [2] Matt. 6: 30; 10: 30; 1 Cor. 15: 46 ff.; 11: 9 ff.

Testament never goes so far as to question the truth itself: that God, the Father of Jesus Christ, is the Creator of *this* world, of *this* heaven and *this* earth, that the natural orders of this world are God's orders of creation, that even the structure of human existence, in its permanent elements, which are independent of freedom, that is, in those "constants" which are independent of historical change, is to be regarded as derived from God's creation.

The Church was therefore quite right, even in her earliest conflicts with the Gnostics, and with Marcion, to reject all dualistic views which denied the fact of the divine creation of this world as we know it—and to do so in no uncertain terms. Its decision was accepted everywhere until recently, even after confessional divisions had taken place. In accordance with the view of the New Testament, the Church stands firmly by the statement: "factorem coeli et terrae, . . . visibilium et invisibilium . . . per quem omnia facta sunt". It sternly rejects all depreciation of material and natural existence, which is necessary from the standpoint of a Platonic "spiritual" point of view. In this connexion the Old Testament story of Creation, with its evident emphasis upon the concrete things of Nature, in all their variety, has done yeoman service. It is true that it has also led theology astray beyond the frontiers of legitimate religious knowledge into the sphere of Natural Science, and it has had to pay dearly for this in recent days.

(8) THE INDEPENDENCE OF THE CREATION

The fact that God "called the world into existence"[1]—this expression is genuinely and exclusively of Biblical origin—means that He has created something Other than Himself, "over against" Himself. This means that non-divine, creaturely existence, and even all that is material and destined to pass away has been freed from the odium of standing in opposition to God. This puts both an unreal "spirituality",[2] and the Monism which is so characteristic of speculative thought, out of court. Thus Space and Time, Matter and the causality of Nature, the burden and inertia of things, and the fact that all living creatures are connected with the earth, cease to be

[1] The reference is to Rom. 4: 17; Moffatt translates the closing words of this verse thus: "A God who makes the dead live, and *calls into being what does not exist*" (TR.)

[2] I.e. a way of thought which regards "the spiritual" as all, and ignores the meaning of the Incarnation (TR.)

regarded as contemptible, disgusting, or unreal. Creaturely being, which is quite different from God's Being, is not set in opposition to God on account of this "otherness". God *Wills* this Other, it is He who has established it as the wholly other. It is His will that a second existence, and indeed a very varied and many-sided second existence, a world of very varied creatures, should be over against Himself. The fact that God and the world are not identical, which Monism fears and detests, has lost its terrors. A world which is not God exists alongside of Him.

This, however, means that God does not wish to occupy the whole of Space Himself, but that He wills to make room for other forms of existence. In so doing He limits Himself. He limits Himself by the fact that the world over against Himself is a real existence. Hence the maximum of the divine self-limitation is equally the maximum of actual "over-againstness" —the free position of that being who is "over against" God, and is therefore able to answer the Word of the Creator in freedom. Yes, indeed, this is precisely the ultimate, and the real meaning of the divine Creation of the world. In the full sense of the word, God can only glorify Himself and impart Himself where a creature in freedom gives His word back to Him, *the* Word which He addresses to it, the word of love. Now we begin to see what a large measure of self-limitation He has imposed upon Himself, and how far He has emptied Himself, in order to realize this aim, to achieve it, indeed, in a creature which has misused its creaturely freedom to such an extent as to defy God. The κένωσις, which reaches its paradoxical climax in the Cross of Christ, began with the Creation of the world.

This being who stands "over against" God—who is the actual purpose of God's Creation, is a creature which may, can, and must pray to Him, a creature, moreover, to whom God pays so much attention that He listens to his prayer. I say this now in anticipation, because only thus can we perceive how seriously God acts in His self-limitation, and how far real Biblical thinking is from all forms of Monism and monergism.[1]

In itself the New Testament does not suggest (as in the Story of Creation in Gen. 1) the graded variety of the created forms of life. This is simply included in the word "all", in the statement of the fact of Creation. But the whole wealth

---

[1] Among modern dogmatic theologians A. V. Oettingen presents this view most strongly; cf. index under "Selbstbeschränkung", *L.D.*, 11, 2

of the creaturely forms of existence, which surround the life of man and constitute His world, are included in this word "all". Here, however, the expansion of the witness of the New Testament by that of the Old is of great significance, in spite of the fact that it also raises many problems. The story of Creation in the Old Testament lays emphasis upon the fact that God has placed man in a world of nature with a great many aspects, which presents itself to our observation as a graded hierarchy of forms of existence, which, from purely material existence through the plant world to the lower and higher forms of animal life, finally reaches its zenith in Man.

Why we should consider this graded hierarchy of forms of life from man's place in the universe as a theological undertaking, to be not only justified, but commanded, will be explained later on. The Old Testament story of Creation leaves us in no doubt whether this graded hierarchy is rooted in God's will as Creator. This hierarchy of created life corresponds to the greater or lesser distance from the human way of existence. It is the hierarchy which is determined by the degree of freedom or unfreedom, which leads from the minimum of freedom in the sphere of matter to the maximum of freedom in Man, which, for its part, has its essential characteristic and its theological significance in the fact that Man may and should answer the divine Word in freedom.

(9) ANALOGIA ENTIS?

The world created by God, as limited, dependent being, is fundamentally different from the Being of God. All the differences within created existence, living and dead, free and un-free, human and non-human, are insignificant, in comparison with the uncreated Being of God and created being, between God and the world. Those differences are relative, this is absolute. And yet this creature, as the work of the Creator, who wills to glorify and communicate Himself in it, is not without some resemblance to the Divine Being. God manifests Himself in His works in Creation, for in them He manifests "His everlasting power and divinity".

In the material world there is a mathematical order which bears witness to the thought of the Creator. Here there is life which is a reflection of Him who is Himself the true Life; in the material world there is the mystery of the whole of organic life, with its wonders of nature—seeing eyes, hearing ears, a purposeful organization which indicates a creative planning spirit behind it all;[1] there is the marvel of spontaneity and freedom, which is a picture of Him who is Himself unconditioned, absolute freedom. Above all there is Man, whose unique quality is described in Scripture by the phrase "created in the Image of God". As Man represents the maximum of freedom in the sphere of the visible creation, so also his whole being represents a maximum of parabolic similarity, which exists in spite of the absolute dissimilarity between creaturely being and the Being of God.

Hence it is most ill-advised, and inevitably leads to serious inconsistencies, to take the view that the idea of the *analogia entis*—common to the whole Christian tradition—must be rejected as specifically Catholic, Neo-Platonist, and therefore a "foreign body" in Christian theology. Whatever the Creator makes bears the imprint of His Creator-Spirit in itself; hence it is to some extent "similar" to Him and is therefore a "parable" or "analogy". The idea of the *analogia entis*, like that of the Revelation in Creation, from which it is derived, cannot be severed from the Biblical doctrine of Creation. How fundamental it is for all theological statements comes out in the fact that we preserve this element of analogy in two constituent elements of all Biblical theology: in the idea of the *Word*, and in that of the *Person*. The fact that man can speak is similar to the fact that God speaks; the fact that man is Person, is an analogy to the Being of God as Person.[2]

The misgiving aroused by a certain *use* of the principle of Analogy in medieval, and later Catholic theology derived from it, is fully justified; but this misgiving should not extend to the principle itself, but only to this particular use of it which, in point of fact, is not based upon Biblical, but upon Neo-Platonic foundations (Bonaventura), and thus becomes the principle of Natural Theology.

This particular use of the idea of Analogy presupposes the inviolable character of human knowledge, in accordance with the fact that man has been created in the image of God; it does not take into account the fact that God's revelation in Creation, as such, taken by itself, is not sufficient to lead sinful man to a true knowledge of the Creator. It overlooks the fact that wherever man has tried to know God by his own efforts, on the basis of that which is at his disposal as a creature among other created beings, he has never attained his goal. The natural "knowledge" of God is actually no knowledge

[1] Ps. 94: 9   [2] Cf. the *Appendix* on the Problem of Analogy, pp. 42 ff.

of the True God, but it is always inevitably a mixture of true knowledge and the deification of the creature. Sinful man cannot help interpreting the glimpses of the Creator in the creation in a wrong way: in polytheism, pantheism, Deism, agnosticism, and atheism. His inward eye is not a clear mirror in which God's revelation in creation is reflected in its truth, but it is one whose sight has become dimmed by sinful anxiety and sinful arrogance, sinful optimism and sinful pessimism. Natural Theology is therefore not, as that medieval doctrine believes, a reliable basis for Christian theology, but a very contradictory phenomenon, in which both truth and error, divine revelation and human delusions are involved.

This does not, however, make Natural Theology a negligible quantity. Though it may not be the basis, it still is a very important part of Christian Theology, especially in the doctrine of Man. It is a sign of divine revelation in Creation that men can never cease to speak about God and to think about Him in one way or another—even if in a wholly negative manner— and thus to produce theologies. Each of these "theologies"— even at the lowest level—contains an element of divine revelation. Each of these theologies—even at the highest level—also contains the element of sinful corruption and delusion, that dissolving ferment which transforms the wine of the divine revelation into the vinegar of idolatrous representations of God.[1]

When, however, through God's Word the "inward eye" of man is really enlightened, then he is also enabled to see the divine revelation in Creation, as it really is; then he is able to understand the *analogia entis* aright, and to praise God the Creator in the works of His Creation. Christendom has indeed never allowed this truth to be taken from it; the prayers and hymns of all churches, all over the world, have at all times praised God, not only for His revelation in His Word, but also for His revelation in His Creation; this has produced what I used to call—wrongly, in a misleading phrase—a "Christian natural theology". Similarly, Theology has always held fast to the truth that there are created "analogies" to the Creator, and that *for this reason* we may speak of God in human terms, as a God who "sees" and "hears", "thinks", and "wills", "speaks" and "acts".

For this reason, and for this alone, Christian theology is not

[1] See the Appendix (in Vol. I of this *Dogmatics*) on the "Natural Knowledge of God", pp. 132 ff. (E.T.)

a negative one, whose main thesis is that negations alone are fitting to describe the Being of the Creator; but it is a positive theology which rests upon the truth that there *is* a relation of similarity between God's being as Person and the being of man as human, thus between the Being of God and the being of His creatures, which makes the use of such human, parabolic language legitimate.

The substitution of an *analogia fidei* for the *analogia entis* is based upon a misunderstanding which it is easy to explain. Quite apart from the fact that the traditional use of the phrase means something wholly different—namely, the rule that the Scriptures must be expounded in the light of the Creed (or Confession of Faith)—the *analogia fidei*, in this new sense, pre-supposes the *analogia entis*. When we say that we can only speak of God aright because God has spoken to us in His revelation, we have already made the tacit admission that there is a fundamental analogy between what "speaking" means in the divine and in the human sense. Speech, even when it is God who "speaks", is the form in which reason communicates with reason, person with person, . . . primarily analogous to the process in the intellectual and spiritual sphere, and not primarily to the process in the natural physical sphere of creation.[1]

The principle of the *analogia entis* is also, manifestly, the presupposition (which must always be taken into account) of that theology which denies this, and denies the principle of analogy itself; therefore, because it wishes to deny this, it is also forced to deny the revelation of Creation recorded in the Scriptures. The *analogia fidei* cannot replace the *analogia entis*, because at every point the *analogia fidei* presupposes the *analogia entis*.

(10) THE ORDER OF CREATION

Another controversial problem of a similar kind is that of the *orders of creation*. It is most intimately connected with the revelation in creation. God has given to that which has been created—to *all* that has been created—a certain definite order which, because it has been created by Him, is the expression of His will. The way in which a creature has been made is an expression of the divine will. This is an idea which seems to be especially important for the Biblical truth of creation, and

[1] K. Barth, *K.D.*, I., 1, p. 138

it therefore recurs frequently. "Praise Him, all ye stars and light. . . . He hath made them fast for ever and ever: He hath given them a law which shall not be broken."[1]

What we call the "laws of nature" are God's orders of creation. This, and this only, is the way in which God has ordered the world. God is a God of order, not of disorder; He works according to law and not in an arbitrary manner. It is true that with this idea we enter a sphere where religious truth and natural knowledge—for instance, scientific knowledge— interpenetrate one another, and here we need to speak very carefully. But the fundamental idea, that there are constants in nature which have been created by God, lies outside the sphere of controversy, and is not disputed by anyone who has any respect for the truth of the Bible.[2]

Thus to know something of such forms of life, and such orders, is to know part of God's creation, and thus of the will of God. Kepler was not mistaken when he thanked God that through the discovery of the laws of the rotation of the earth he had been able to see a little way into God's workshop, and to see something of His Wisdom. It is the God of revelation, not of any philosophy or mythology to whom Kepler offers his thanks; here he is accomplishing an act of legitimate "Christian natural theology". Because Kepler knew the God revealed in Jesus Christ, and meant Him and no other, his praise went in the right direction, and did not go astray, and the order of creation which he learnt to know became to him a concrete instance of the legitimate knowledge of God.

The idea of the "order of creation" interests us particularly as the principle of social ethics. In the human sphere there are certain natural constants, which at the same time belong to the sphere of human freedom and decision. For instance, God has so created man and woman that their sex union can only be accomplished according to the purpose which He has laid down for them in the monogamous permanent marriage. It is part of the very way in which God has created man and woman, in the unity of personal-being and the sex-nature, that only monogamy corresponds to the destiny given to man by God. Therefore Jesus Himself bases the indissolubility of marriage upon the order of creation.[3] Why the "monos" in monogamy is so essential whereas in other circumstances, for

[1] Ps. 148: 3, 6 (Prayer Book version)
[2] For the significant use Jesus makes of the order of creation, cf. Mark 10: 1 ff.
[3] Mark 10: 1 ff.

instance, in friendship, it is not essential, cannot be understood save in the light of the truth that God has created sex. In creating man and woman God has appointed a definite order for the sex relation, an "order of creation". The same is true of the relation between parents and children, and thus of the Family. Marriage and the Family are orders of creation, and, indeed, precisely in the similarities and inequalities which these involve. Thus the question can never be put thus: Are there orders of creation which constitute an ethical standard? but only: What are they? and which orders are *merely* due to human convention? How far the principle of the order of creation extends for the formation of a social ethic cannot be discussed here. Here all we need to do is to stress the fact that this principle as such—whatever its validity and its limits may be—is a central idea in the Biblical doctrine of Creation, as indeed it has always been so used by the Theology of the Church at all times. It is not difficult to show that if one transgresses this law in ethics one does not go unpunished, and also the other fact, that it can easily be misused. But *abusus non tollit usum.*

(II) NATURAL KNOWLEDGE OF THE CREATED WORLD

Since God creates a world, He creates something which is not God, namely, the world. In so doing He creates the sphere of things, which, in principle, He places under the control of human natural knowledge.[1] God has given man reason, in order that he may learn to know the world, and to find himself at home in the world. This world is, it is true, the creation of the Triune God, whom none can know through the intellect as such. But, as the sum-total of *things* of all kinds, it has been given to man's reason. The legitimate sphere of reason is: the things of the world. Whether men know God or not, they can in any case know the things of this world; and that means, to know them aright. Even a man who does not know God properly can have a vast knowledge of the things of this world. For instance he may be an eminent scientist, or a great linguist, or a great mathematical genius. Thus, without knowing anything of the true Creator, man may know the orders and laws of the Creator, without knowing whose laws they are. Obviously, what Euclid, Aristarchus or Archimedes found to be valid for all time in the sphere of mathematics and physics, they learned

[1] Gen. 2: 19; Ps. 115: 16

to know independently of the state of their knowledge of God. We do not know, and at the moment we are not concerned to know, what they thought about God. They succeeded in knowing one part of the world, a section of the order of creation, without knowing the Creator.

Thus it is possible to over-estimate, as well as to under-estimate, the blinding of the intellect by sin. We have indeed no right to assert, as some pessimists do, that sinful man as such, cannot know *anything* aright. This kind of pessimism is out of touch both with the Bible and with experience. On the other hand, an optimism which ignores or denies the significance of sin is equally unjustified. In the one case, as well as in the other, an undifferentiated general statement is wrong. Rather, it is necessary to make a distinction between knowledge of the world and knowledge of God. Sin does not hinder men from knowing the things of the world, the laws of nature, the facts of nature, and man in his natural, historical and cultural manifestations. But the more we are dealing with the inner nature of man, with his attitude to God, and the way in which he is determined by God, it is evident that this sinful illusion becomes increasingly dominant. The more closely a subject is related to man's inward life, the more natural human knowledge is "infected" by sin; while the further away it is, the less will be its effect. Hence we find the maximum of sinful blindness in the knowledge of God itself. Hence mathematics and the natural sciences are much less affected by this negative element than the humanities, and the latter less than ethics and theology. In the sphere of natural science, for instance—as opposed to natural philosophy—it makes practically no difference whether a scholar is a Christian or not; but this difference emerges the moment that we are dealing with problems of sociology, or law, which affect man's personal and social life. In the doctrine of God, however, this difference becomes a sharp contradiction. Greek wisdom and philosophy has achieved valid work in the most varied spheres of knowledge, and even the theologians who have been most faithful in their adherence to the Bible—such as Luther and Calvin—have admitted this fact. On the other hand, between the different forms of Greek metaphysics and the Christian doctrine of God there are contradictions which cannot be reconciled. The same is true, in my opinion, of modern science and philosophy. The more that science and philosophy are self-critical on the one hand, and the more purely theology is aligned to real faith on the other side, the less will be the possibility of conflict.

Not only secular science and philosophy, however, but Christian theology also, may fail through lack of self-criticism, and, in point of fact, this has often happened. For centuries, Christian theology has been greatly to blame for the fact that it conceived the Biblical picture of the world, which in essentials is simply that of the Ancient World, as the content of the divine revelation. This made the Bible the infallible textbook of natural science and historical science. The conflict with science therefore became unavoidable, and the war between science and theology had to end with the pitiable defeat of theology. Theology forgot to make that critical distinction between that which is the object of natural knowledge of the world through reason, and that which, by its very nature, can only be the content of divine revelation. It forgot that the Church bears this "treasure" (of revelation) in "earthen vessels"; it confused the vessel and the content, the knowledge of God and the knowledge of the world.

This is particularly true of all the religious truths connected with the creation of the world; because here there is a subject which, on the one hand, can only be understood from the standpoint of revelation, and on the other hand, by the use of methods applied to all natural knowledge. The so-called "Mosaic" story of Creation is not only a wonderful testimony to the divine revelation, but it is also the product of a very primitive view of the world. Hence it tells the story of Creation with the aid of conceptions which, without ceasing to be vessels of divine revelation, are such that their intellectual outlook is in conflict with modern knowledge. The Biblical story of Creation is bound up with the picture of the world current in antiquity, which no longer exists for us. The failure to distinguish between a particular world-view and religious truth has made ecclesiastical theology first the enemy, and then the laughing-stock of science. At the present time theology as a whole usually fails to recognize the significance of these facts for modern man. This whole conflict might have been avoided if the Church had known how to make a distinction between the vessel and its content, between the view of the world and the statement of faith. Since even down to the present time the Church is still out-of-date on this point, we must try to give at least in outline some indications for the solution of this problem; the fact that it has been neglected

for far too long, has been, and still is, a serious hindrance to
the faith of countless men and women.

(12) NATURAL KNOWLEDGE AND REVEALED KNOWLEDGE

First of all, however, we must look at a purely theological
problem, which concerns this dualism of scientific knowledge
and religious knowledge, or knowledge derived from revelation.
The world as created by *God* can only be known through God's
revelation: but as *created* by God, it is the sphere of legitimate
natural, or scientific, knowledge. How are we to understand
this twofold character of knowledge, without destroying the
unity of knowledge? The unity is given to us in the idea that
just as the world is based upon the Creator-Logos, so also our
natural knowledge, in all its activities, ultimately presupposes
the Creator-Logos. Even natural knowledge, which is acquired
through the senses and the intellect, is not simply something
"profane"; in so far as it wills and grasps Truth, it is something
sacred. Valid knowledge is based upon a principle and a
criterion of validity which is not simply a fact of the world,
but is of a divine character. The idea of Truth, and the obligation to be genuine and sincere, which is fundamental in all
serious pursuit of knowledge, points to an ultimate ground of
Truth. The human reason, by means of which we distinguish
true and false in the sphere of natural or scientific knowledge,
is no more based upon itself than the world which it knows is
based upon itself. The world is based upon God's thought and
will in Creation, in the fact of its existence, in its content, and
in the manner in which it is created; likewise the reason through
which we know it, is derived from God's truth. Through the
Creator, the world, and the knowledge of the world, are
destined for each other. Both are rooted in the Logos of
Creation; from it they derive both the objective basis of
existence and the subjective basis of knowledge. This Logos
of Creation, however, is no other than He who in Jesus Christ
became Man and thus revealed to us His secret.

Hence all that is taught in accordance with Scripture about
the revelation of God in the works of creation, is to be understood "Christologically". There is no other revelation in
creation save that which derives its being from the Eternal
Son or the Logos. "For in Him were all things created . . .
through Him and unto Him . . . and in Him all things hold
together." Thus all the "orders of creation" which are given

to us men as the norm of our action are "orders" which have been created through the Logos-Son, therefore they are all ordained and subordinated to His goal, His plan and purpose for the world. As then we believe in the Creator revealed through Christ and in none other, so we also believe in no other revelation in Creation, and in no other "orders of creation", than those which have their ultimate basis, their meaning and their end in Him.

Further, the reason and the knowledge which it acquires finds its ground and its purpose in the Son. The capacity of man to *know* is one aspect of that quality of "being made in the Image of God" which constitutes the nature of man. Precisely those elements of—natural—knowledge which are different from merely animal ways of getting one's bearings, and from wild flights of the imagination, namely, transcending, and critical strictness, strict objectivity and logical argument, belong to that "fact of being made in the image of God" which differentiates man from the rest of the creation, and gives him the consciousness of possessing a particular dignity and a special destiny. For this reason alone can science be the service of God, and for this reason alone so many of the greatest scientists have been able to regard their work as the service of God and their knowledge as the gift of God. Therefore in the mind of a Christian scientist there is no conflict between his faith in Jesus Christ and his scientific work which is based on, and controlled by (very strictly) the work of the intellect; on the contrary, he is aware of an ultimate unity between the two aspects of his life, although, it is true, a certain duality of knowledge does exist. The knowledge of the world and the things of the world is reached in other ways than those which lead to the knowledge of God and His plan for the world. "He has given the earth to man"; the words "replenish the earth and subdue it" are the Magna Carta of all secular knowledge as well as of all the achievements of technics and civilization. It is thus that the J redactor understood it who makes the history of man begin with the fact that God gives permission to man to name the animals. God gave this permission, and with it He gave man the capacity to make use of it.

Just as God has created a world which is not Himself but a second entity, over against Himself, so also has He given to man, as a human being, a reason which is capable of understanding what is in the world. Therefore according to the will of God there is a "natural knowledge", which really knows, that is, finds the real truth, even if this truth is never the final and complete truth, but one which is ever being discovered afresh, and the knowledge thus gained is never final and complete, but is always growing, and ever purifying itself with its own criticism, and transforming it. Precisely the man who believes in Christ will always be on his guard against two errors: the danger of denying, in a sceptical way, the possibility of true knowledge, and, on the other hand, of transforming the knowledge he has acquired, uncritically, into an absolute. Sin betrays its influence in the sphere of knowledge in two directions: as sceptical despair of knowing and as uncritical dogmatism. And the experience of the present day shows how both elements can dwell side by side in the same person, and can give their colour to one and the same generation.

It cannot be the work of dogmatics, but must be left to a Christian philosophy to develop these fundamental insights further, to examine more exactly the theological presuppositions of natural rational knowledge, and to show, on the one hand, its God-given possibilities, and, on the other hand, the limitations to which it is subject, due to creatureliness on the one hand, and to sin on the other. To a world proud of its intellectual powers, and sceptical, it will emphasize the basis and the limitations of natural knowledge; to an uncritical orthodox theology it will have to exercise the critical office of a watchman, in order that in the name of revelation a knowledge of the world be not offered as the inviolable divine revelation, and that which God has left for the natural knowledge of man to explore be not restricted to the sphere of a mistaken Biblical authority. This last point is especially important in connexion with the Creation story in Genesis.

(13) THE BIBLICAL VIEW OF THE WORLD AND SCIENCE

The Old Testament story of creation gives us the story of God's creation in connexion with a definite picture of space, of time, and still more definitely, of the beginning of all forms of life which have ever been and are unalterable. At all three points the position of modern knowledge forces us to abandon this view and to replace it by other ideas.

(a) The view of Space. For the Bible the world-space is no bigger than a bowl inverted over the diameter of the Earth. The modern astronomer measures space in terms of which the unit is the "light-year"; light travels at the rate of 186,000 miles a second. Thus in measuring star distances he calculates in "light-years", or millions and millions of miles. Thus the picture of Space has been expanded millions of times over.

(b) The same is true of the view of Time. For the man of the Bible the world—reckoned from to-day—is some six thousand years old. Modern science gives the age of the earth—which again is only one fragment of the age of the world of the fixed stars—as some milliards of years, and the age of the human race as some 200,000 to 500,000 years. Thus the time during which the world has already existed, according to our present knowledge, is a million times greater than that which it was for the man of the Bible, and until recently for the Church.

At one point, however, the most recent science seems to confirm the statements of the Bible, and possibly this point is far more important than all the others that have been mentioned: the world has a beginning. The idea of Greek philosophy of a world with no beginning is—so it seems—clearly in conflict with modern scientific knowledge. Real Time is not infinite like time which has been thought. Likewise real Space is not infinite like space which has been thought. Whether we are really justified in equating the beginning of the world posited by science or to be thus attained with the beginning of the world posited by faith, must I suppose remain an open question.[1]

(c) The destruction of the Biblical view of time and space which began with Copernicus, has, as is well known, led to protracted and heated discussions between the protagonists of Theology and of Natural Science, in which Theology came off very badly. In importance, however, these controversies were far outstripped by the changes at the third point, in the view of the constancy of the forms of life and existence at one time established by God. The Bible assumes that the plants and animals with which we are familiar are part of the unalterable original state of the world as God created it. The findings of Natural Science of the present day force us to give up this idea entirely. Whatever may be our attitude towards the theory of evolution or even to Darwinism, at one point the discussion has been closed for ever, namely, that most of the forms of life which now exist did not formerly exist at all,

[1] In addition to the standard work of Bavink (*Ergebnisse und Probleme der Naturwissenschaften*, 8, 1945), cf. the writings of the physicist C. F. v. Weizsäcker, *Zum Weltbild der Physik*, 1945, and *Geschichte der Natur*, 1948

that many of those which used to exist no longer do so, and that between the earliest and the present-day forms of life—plants and animals—there were very many others, so that those which now exist prove to be one of the many worlds of forms which followed each other in orderly progression. We would be well advised once for all to abandon the contemptible habit of taking refuge behind the hypothetical character of these results (of scientific research)—this dirty trick of a lazy apologetic—and to acknowledge the results of scientific research which all scholars accept because they are based upon proof, and to admit that they are obligatory also for us. There are plenty of hypotheses left . . . and none of these scientific results affects ultimate questions at all. For, as we have already said, these questions are only raised by the *narrative* of the Creation in the Old Testament, but not by the truth of the Biblical account of Creation. Only at one point does this scientific knowledge give us any serious difficulty, and that is in the doctrine of man. Hence our further discussion should deal with the doctrine of man.

(14) *CREATIO CONTINUA*

On the other hand, however, scientific truth concerning changes in forms of life calls our attention to a genuine and ancient *theological* problem, the question of *creatio continua*. There is, as we have already seen, a central religious concern in the statement that the created world had a beginning in Time. To predicate eternity, "without beginning" of the world as well as of God, makes the world the *alter-ego* of God, and God the double of the world. This idea deifies the world and de-spiritualizes God; inevitably it is pantheistic. God alone is from everlasting, not the world. Beginning in Time belongs to the existence of the world, to the Creation. But this cannot mean that God's activity as Creator is limited to this beginning in Time. Once more, it is the one-sided orientation towards the *narrative* of Creation which favours this prejudice, and has tended to colour the doctrine of a *creatio continua* with pantheistic suggestions.

Certainly the danger of Pantheism lurks in the background. The danger-zone has already been entered when Creation and Preservation are identified with one another. For anyone who does not admit the distinction between the creation and the preservation of the created world does not take the fact of creation seriously. The relation of God to that which He has created is not the same as His relation to that which is yet to be created. That which has been created stands actually "over against" God. Henceforth, through the action of God it has an independent existence, even though this independence be a limited one. It depends on a divine thread of preservation above the abyss of nothingness; at any moment God can let it fall into nothingness. But to preserve that which has been created does not mean continually to create it anew; to claim this would mean that it has an actual existence for God, that it has an existence of its own. Theological monergism is already the beginning of Pantheism.

Now the recognition of a divine preservation of the world, as distinct from His creation, does not exclude the truth that God is still actively and creatively at work in a world which He has already created, and which He preserves. If we indulge in a little mild allegory we may interpret the creation of the world in six days thus: the series of creative acts of God, which has been planned in a clear succession of periods (whether of days or of millions of years) contains at least one aspect of the doctrine of a *creatio continua*, plurality in Time, the ordered series of acts of creation. The more we take into account the fact that the various forms of life did not all arise at the same time, as we certainly must do on the basis of our present knowledge, the more unavoidably are we led to this thought. God did not create everything at once; He is continually creating something afresh.

This idea is not alien to the Bible. It appears even at a most important point, where the individual—such as Job or a Psalmist—recognizes himself in the presence of God, as having been created by Him. The Psalmist does not say: "Thou, O God, hast created Adam and from him I am descended", but "Thou hast knit me together in my mother's womb".[1]

The Either-Or of dogmatic theologians between "Creationism" and "Traducianism",[2] is a pseudo-problem. I, this human

[1] Ps. 139: 13 (R.V. Marg.)

[2] *Creationism:* the doctrine that God immediately creates out of nothing a new soul for each member of the human family, while for the human body there was but one creative *fiat*

Traducianism: maintains that both the soul and body of the individual man are propagated. It refers the creative act mentioned in Gen. 1: 27 to the human nature or race, and not merely to a single individual. It considers the work of creating mankind *de nihilo* as entirely completed on the sixth day; and that since that sixth day the Creator has, in this world, exerted no strictly creative energy (TR.)

being, am evidently both a product of my ancestors and a new creation of God. We must assign the continuity to the preservation, the new element to the creation of God, whereby the question may remain open whether or not as a whole and apart from man each individual as such, in spite of all continuity and explicability of its elements from its antecedents, is something new. This must in any case indubitably be claimed for the human person. Every human being is a new creation of God; every one is an original, and none is a product of a series, although in its cultural manifestation the originality may be very slight. Each human being is not only an individual but a person, and therefore directly related to God as its Creator.

Hence there is no difficulty in bringing creation and evolution into agreement with one another, particularly if we take into account an *évolution créatrice*, as indeed even science must do in the face of the facts. Yet this agreement must not be confused with identity. Evolution, even creative evolution, is a phenomenon which we are able to observe, something which is in the foreground of empirical fact, something which the botanist and the zoologist can establish over and over again in his researches. . . . But he can never thus prove Creation. Creation remains God's secret, a mystery, and an article of faith, towards which the fact of creative evolution points, but which is never contained within it. What the scientist himself interprets, on the basis of his empirically established positions, as creative evolution, he believes, praying, to be God's creation.

At this point we return to the beginning of our observations. The Christian statement on Creation is not a theory of the way in which the world came into being—whether once for all, or in continuous evolution—but it is an "existential" statement. In His revelation the Lord meets me, my Lord, as the Creator, as My Creator and the Creator of all things. In so doing I become aware that I who know that I am the servant of this Lord, am His servant, His property, because all that I am and have I have from Him, because not only I but all that is, has been created by Him. I, together with my world, am, O God, Thy creation; therefore I too am included in the aim of creation, which in the same Word through which all was created is revealed to me. As the one, however, to whom this Word is *spoken* in order that he may hear it and obey, am I singled out and distinguished above all other creatures. The following chapters will deal with this subject.

APPENDIX TO CHAPTER 1

(A) ON THE HISTORY OF THE DOCTRINE OF CREATION

FOR the preservation of the Christian doctrine of Creation the Old Testament was of immeasurable importance. The Church had to meet the difficulties raised by Gnosticism on two fronts. She defended both at the same time, the Old Testament and the doctrine of Creation, and in so doing, the unity of God as Creator and Redeemer. Irenaeus is the great figure in this fight for existence. It was he too who, in complete accordance with Scripture, showed the way to the later tradition, in the emphasis he laid upon the *mundi factor vere est verbum dei* (*Adv. haer.* V. 18, 3) and in so doing firmly established the unity of the Logos of Creation and of Redemption. On the other hand, not only the Gnostics, but Apologists like Theophilus and Justin Martyr presupposed matter which God had not created (ὕλη ἀγέννητος); their view found some justification in the description of Chaos "without form and void" in Gen. 1: 2. The Biblical doctrine of Creation was again endangered by the theory of Origen: namely, that God was Creator from all eternity, and that before the creation of our world He had created others (*De princip.*, III, 5); still more dangerous was his theory that the καταβολὴ κόσμου already presupposes the Fall, and thus that the world as we know it arose out of a fallen creation. But the most serious intrusion of Platonist dualism into his thought is his doctrine of the pre-existence of human souls who have been imprisoned in a material body, as a penalty for the Fall. With the discrediting of Origen in the Orthodox Church this theory, which was incompatible with the Biblical doctrine of Creation, was finally rejected, having already been attacked by Methodius.

Augustine introduced the very important doctrine that the world was created *with* Time. *Id ipsum enim tempus tu feceras nec praeterire potuerunt tempora antequam faceres tempora.* God eternally precedes all that has been created (*Confessions*, XI, 10 and *Civ. Dei.* VII, 30, XII, 15 ff.). For a time this secured the Biblical doctrine of Creation, until it was again disturbed by Neoplatonist ideas—not the restrained Christian Neoplatonism of Augustine—but by the fully developed views of men like Dionysius the Areopagite and John Scotus Erigena (where the theory is only faintly tinged with Christian thought).

John Scotus starts with the idea that, in God, being and action are identical.[1] This denies the act of Creation with which Time begins. His pantheistic doctrine was rejected by all ecclesiastical theologians; on the other hand, the thought of St. Thomas Aquinas, that God is the Original Cause of all things (*dicendum quod Deus est prima causa exemplaris omnium rerum*, P. I, *quaestio* 44, *art.* 2) does contain features which suggest "emanation" theories;[2] this is probably due to his Aristotelian doctrine of entelechy. Mystical thought (e.g. Eckhart) is always, of course, at variance with the Biblical doctrine of Creation, since it is forced to maintain the nothingness of all creaturely existence. The creaturely as such is something negative, something which cannot be recognized. The Biblical view of Creation comes into its own again with the Reformers, especially with Calvin, whose whole theology is not only based upon the Creation as the obvious truth, but who makes it also the direct and central point of reference for all his theological statements. And yet he too, like Luther, often verges on pantheism; Luther's idea that "all creatures are masks of God" beneath which He hides Himself, and in the world reigns and moves so wonderfully" (*W.*, 30, I, 136) may be compared with Calvin's statement in the *Institutes* (I, 5, 5): "I admit that the expression, 'Nature is God', may be piously used, if dictated by a pious mind."

There is a tendency to monergism in the thought of all the Reformers, due to their desire to protect the truth that God alone can pardon the sinner by His Grace, which, however, endangers the Biblical idea of Creation, and threatens to destroy human freewill and responsibility. While here there is the danger of ignoring the relative independence of the creature, in the theology of the period of the Enlightenment, influenced by Deism, the opposite tendency predominated. Here creaturely independence was emphasized at the expense of permanent dependence on the Creator.

In this period, however, wholly different problems in the doctrine of Creation began to emerge: the criticism of the Old Testament story of Creation which, up till that time, had been

[1] "That inasmuch as every creature is a participation of Him who alone exists of Himself, all Nature may be reduced to the one Principle and Creator and creature may be regarded as one." Copleston, *Hist. of Philosophy*, Vol. II, p. 121 (TR.)

[2] "We have to think not only of the emanation of some particular being from some other particular being, but also the emanation of the whole of being from a universal cause, which is God, and it is this emanation we call by the name of creation" (*S. Theol.* Ia. q. 85, a, I) (TR.)

accepted more or less without thought as revealed truth, and the discussion with the new view of the world opened up by natural science. Suddenly the other side of the theological relation to the story of Creation in Genesis became visible. At the present day we can scarcely imagine the heat engendered by the controversies between the champions of the Bible and their scientific opponents, due to the shattering of faith by the revolutionary discoveries of natural science. How tenacious was the unfortunate confusion of Biblical faith with the Biblical picture of the world can be seen in the fact that even a scientist like Cuvier felt it necessary to construct a synthesis between the new discoveries of science and the Old Testament narrative (*Discours sur les révolutions du Globe*, 1812). As late as 1857 a geologist of repute, Hugh Miller (*The Testimony of the Rocks, or Geology in its bearings on the two theologies, natural and revealed*) tried to harmonize them, and on the fundamentalist side similar attempts have been made, and still are being made, with the aid of the most unfortunate methods of allegorical exposition of the text of Genesis.

In a certain sense even Karl Barth's extremely allegorical exposition of the creation of the world in six days (*K.D.*, Vol. III, I) which is the form in which he casts his theological doctrine of Creation, must be reckoned in that category, although his purpose is not that of apologetics. In spite of the fact that we consider it absolutely necessary on theological grounds to abandon the *story* of Creation (as given in Genesis) yet it cannot be denied that in its main features the cosmology of Genesis I and that of scientific knowledge do not absolutely contradict each other. Even Haeckel (*Natürliche Schöpfungsgeschichte*, p. 35) has borne this witness: "Two great and fundamental conceptions in the theory of natural development meet us in this hypothesis of Creation in the Mosaic record with surprising clarity and simplicity: the idea of differentiation and the idea of progressive evolution, or perfecting. We can honestly pay our tribute to the magnificent understanding of Nature of the Hebrew legislator, without admitting that this is a divine revelation". Possibly this reflects the fact that the "Mosaic" revelation of God's Creation contains elements of imperishable truth, in a picture of the world which is in itself primitive.

There is little new to record in the history of modern theology on the doctrine of Creation. The theology of Schleiermacher and Ritschl was a mistaken reaction against the confusion of cosmology and the doctrine of Creation, since both represent the view that the Christian Faith is not concerned with a doctrine of Creation, since the emphasis on the absolute dependence of the world upon God is the only concern of faith (cf. also Kaftan, *Dogmatik*, 1897, pp. 227 and 242). The severance from the Mosaic story of creation has been accomplished gradually, but without clear systematic knowledge of the necessary Christological, and therefore New Testament, starting-point. Karl Barth's doctrine of Creation constitutes a great step forward on account of its logically worked out Christological tendency, which, however, owing to the return to the exposition of the Creation of the world in Six Days, and the allegorical method which this entails, has not achieved all it should have done.

(B) THE BELIEF IN CREATION AND THE SCIENTIFIC THEORY OF EVOLUTION

The heat of the controversy between Natural Science and Theology is only intelligible when we remember that for a thousand years or more the Old Testament was the basis and the authoritative source of scientific and historical knowledge. The "*diluvium*", the Flood, as the description of a geological epoch, is the last testimony to this fact. So long as some sections within the Church continue to regard the doctrine of Verbal Inspiration as the standard of faith, scientists will never believe the theologians when they say that long ago they gave up regarding the Biblical view of the world as a Divine revelation. The efforts to construct an apologetic —still being made in some parts of the Church—which will achieve a synthesis between the "Mosaic" view of the world and modern scientific knowledge, can, of course, only convince the scientists still more that the theologians are not being honest when they make the above statement about revelation and science. Hence we cannot say too strongly that the Biblical view of the world is absolutely irreconcilable with that of modern science, just as the world view of Aristotle cannot be reconciled with that of modern science. I would only add, that the world view which the Bible gives us has nothing to do with Divine Revelation.

On the other hand, the purely concrete question does arise: How can the scientific theory of Evolution be combined with the Christian belief in Creation? First of all, we will try to answer this question in the form of an analogy: How can we combine the chemical analysis of a painted canvas with the aesthetic judgment of this canvas as a work of art? Obviously the two are not mutually exclusive, because the two subjects are on different planes. Where the chemist only sees the various elements of a chemical mixture, the artist sees a significant whole, an expression of mind and spirit.

So this world, whose different successive states are described by the various natural sciences (astrophysics, geology, etc.) and are causally connected, is for faith a work of the Divine Creator, Creation. Just as the judgment of the art critic does not question the analysis of the chemist, but on the contrary, presupposes it, without bothering about details ("with certain chemical ingredients called 'colours', the artist has been able to say this or that"), so the conviction of the Christian believer is not shaken by the scientific description of the scientist; without troubling himself about details he takes it for granted. God has created the world in such a way that to scientific knowledge His Creation represents a series of definite stages, in a definite causal connexion. The Creation is the invisible background of Evolution; Evolution is the visible foreground of Creation. Faith alone grasps that invisible aspect; science grasps this visible aspect. Evolution is the mechanism of creation; creation is the spiritual source and the Final Cause of Evolution.

In the scientific view of Evolution, however, there are points which suggest that behind the mechanical, causal series, there lies a mystery; namely, the points where we cannot directly explain the "consequence" from its "antecedent". Thus from the point of view of pure causality it is unintelligible —and in the highest degree improbable—that the highly complicated organic material with which life is connected, can have been formed out of accidental combinations of non-organic molecules of matter (Lecomte du Nouy, *The Destiny of Man*). Thus, too, from the purely causal point of view, it is not intelligible how a divided organism can regenerate itself, how cells can "vicariously" take over the functions of other cells. The whole development of the organic takes place in a way which is contrary to the Law of Entropy. Everywhere in the sphere of the organic we come upon facts which we are forced to explain in the sense of an *évolution créatrice*.

The most important point of "discontinuity" is the emergence of the human spirit, which cannot be understood from the point of view of instinct, nor of mere sensation; this human

spirit appears with the principle which is lacking in the whole
of sub-human life, the law of norms, the creative idea, the
meaning of the whole, etc. Here we are dealing with the facts
which we mentioned above under the title of the "supra-
causal". (On this see the brilliant remarks of Bergson in his
Évolution Créatrice, which is still valid, though often not known
nor understood by many modern scientists: see also the excellent small book by Max Scheler, *Der Mensch im Kosmos*.)

At bottom, we are here confronted by an epistemological
problem. Anyone who understands what a valid thought is, in
comparison with a mere association of ideas—and all assertion
of truth is based upon this distinction—sees at once that the
causal explanation is not adequate. For the true statement is
not explicable in causal terms. That which can be logically
established cannot be (causally) *explained*, and vice versa.
(Husserl's *Logische Untersuchungen*, Vol. I, are as valid to-day
as they were thirty years ago.)

So far as science is concerned, especially where there is a
tendency to make too hasty an interpretation of scientific
results in their effect on one's general outlook on life, we
must stress the fact that the truths discovered by modern
science do not in the very least shake either the Christian
faith in God, the Creator, or the doctrine of man as created
in the Image of God (rightly understood); on the other hand,
where a very rigid traditional theology is concerned, we have
to stress the fact that modern science (and this means the
theory of Evolution) ought not to be opposed in the name of
religion. In such circles, we still hear it said that the theory
of Evolution is a "mere hypothesis"—and, indeed, a hypothesis
which ought to be rejected from the religious point of view.
For, after all, the theory of Evolution simply means that the
world has reached its present state in a very natural way,
developing out of earlier and different conditions, throughout
vast tracts of time. Anyone who admits that there was once a
world in which there was not yet an Earth, an earth upon
which there once lived plants and animals which are different
from those we now have, a time when there may have been
mammals but no human beings, tacitly accepts the theory of
Evolution. How this process of Evolution took place, and
what was the part played in the process by the principle of
selection, the survival of the fittest, etc., are questions which
natural scientists can discuss as much as they like among
themselves. The theory of Evolution ought not to be identified

with a theory of mechanical causality, or with the Darwinian principle of Selection, either on the theological or on the scientific side. The principle of "Creative Evolution", that is, the appearance of new forms of life which cannot be explained in causal terms, and the significance of non-mechanical factors are to-day admitted by scientists of high standing. That theory of Evolution which believes that everything can be explained in causal terms, exists to-day less in the brains of scientists than in those of theological apologists—as that which they oppose—and in the minds of popular materialistic philosophers —as that which they absolutely believe. Anyone who exposes his mind to the whole impact of contemporary scientific views and tendencies which are provided in the works of Bavink (*op. cit.*) and Neuberg (*Das Weltbild der Biologie*) is aware, on the one hand, that to-day everything is once more in flux, but also that, on the other hand, some fundamental features of modern science are firmly established, as compared with the ancient view of the world.

(C) ON THE DOCTRINE OF THE *ANALOGIA ENTIS*

Since Karl Barth's vehement attack on the *Analogia entis* ("I regard the *analogia entis* as an invention of Anti-Christ, and I believe that on this account it is impossible to be a Catholic". *Preface* to *K.D.*, Vol. I, I, p. viii), this conception, which previously had not aroused much interest, has now become a main theme of theological discussion. Before we ourselves plunge into this discussion, one or two points must be first established.

The reader of Barth's *Dogmatics* might easily be tempted to think that this doctrine of the *Analogia Entis* was already familiar to Catholic theology, and that it had long been regarded as one of its fundamental doctrines. This, however, is not the case. So far as I know, the first person to use this expression was the Jesuit religious philosopher Erich Przywara in his book (which appeared in 1932) under the title of *Analogia Entis, Metaphysik*. The phrase may be recent, but the thought behind it—the principle of Analogy—has long played an important part in Catholic doctrine; yet none of the Reformers, and no later Protestant writers who were loyal to the spirit of the Reformation, have ever treated this subject as a point at which the paths of Protestant and Catholic theology diverge. The idea that this is so is a new argument, first used by Karl Barth.

Since then, it is true, it has been taken up by several theologians, and not least by the Jesuit theologian and philosopher Urs von Balthasar, who—in a series of articles in *Divus Thomas, Analogie und Dialektik*, begun in 1944, No. 2—agrees with Barth's view, and then, for his part, from this standpoint attacks Reformation theology, which he sees carried to its logical conclusion in the teaching of Karl Barth. Before this, another Swiss Catholic, J. Fehr, in the same journal, published an article on *Revelation and Analogy*, with the same purpose (*D.Th.*, 1937, No. 3), while G. Soehngen—*Analogia fidei*—adopts a more mediating position in *Catholica*, 1934, Nos. 3 and 4. Although it may seem strange that a central theological conception, from which the whole contrast between the Catholic and the Reformation point of view can be deduced, in spite of its decisive importance, had not been perceived by previous theologians, we are forced to agree with Karl Barth, that it is at this point that—perhaps more clearly than anywhere else—the ways of Roman Catholic and Protestant theology diverge. Thus concentration on the doctrine of the *Analogia entis* as the decisive distinction between Catholic and Protestant thought was really the achievement of Karl Barth, which proves how sensitive is his feeling for what really matters in theological thought. What Karl Barth understands by the *principle of Analogy* is the parting of the ways.

Here, however, we have a repetition of what happened a few years ago, on the occasion of the controversy about Natural Theology: Barth's "surgical" temperament—and also his genuinely "medical" insight into the seriousness of a disease—drives him not only to cut out the malignant growth but also a great deal of healthy tissue as well, in order to be quite sure that the evil has been eliminated. Thus Barth rejects not only the Catholic—or, to be more exact, the Neoplatonist element in this doctrine, but he also rejects the Biblical principle of analogy, and indeed every kind of possible analogy in created existence; in so doing he not only contradicts his own theology, which, like every other theology which is not satisfied with mere negations, lives on the principle of Analogy.

Thus we ought to make a very clear distinction between the *analogia entis* as the principle of Natural Theology, and the Biblical idea that created existence, and man in particular, because he bears within himself the "image" of the creating God, can—in a parabolic way—"reflect" God, in order to express God's revealed Being, and His revealed relation to Man.

Barth means something of this kind when he speaks of an *analogia fidei*; here, however, he uses this phrase in a quite different sense from that in which it had previously been used in dogmatics: namely, the hermeneutical rule, that difficult passages in the Scriptures ought to be interpreted in the light of the Creed, the *"analogia fidei"*. Here are Barth's own words: "Thus we do not oppose the Catholic doctrine of the *analogia entis* by denying the concept of analogy; but we say that the analogy in question is not an *analogia entis*, but according to Rom. 12: 6 the ἀναλογία τῆς πίστεως, . . . *analogia fidei*" (*K.D.*, I, i, p. 257).

Barth, however, ignores the fact that this analogy which he uses inheres as such in all existence created by God, and is not an addition created by faith. We can only speak of a "Word" of God, of a "thinking" or "willing" of God, because the divine speech—in spite of all dissimilarity—still is similar to human speech, just as divine personal being is similar to human personal being—in spite of all dissimilarity—so that in both cases we may use the same word, "speech", "person". Indeed, it is on this that all expressions are based with which the Bible designates God's Being and Action, which philosophers always describe as "anthropomorphisms". In point of fact they are not "anthropomorphisms", because this similarity actually exists, having been made by God. Even Barth acknowledges this in his writings: "Speech, as the speech of God, is the form in which reason communicates with reason, person with person . . . primarily *analogous* to what happens in the spiritual sphere, and not primarily analogous to the process in the natural and physical sphere of creation" (*K.D.*, I, i, p. 139).

Without this similarity between the human process which we call "speech" and "word", and the divine process which we describe in these terms, we cannot speak of God at all. The Bible speaks of God so simply and "anthropomorphically", and not in an abstract manner, so personally and not impersonally, because God reveals Himself to us in the Scriptures as Person, and because at the same time He reveals man as having been created in His Image. So long as Barth wholly rejected *this* concept of the *Imago*, he could not admit that he himself used the *analogia entis*. Since then, however, Barth's thought on this point has changed. He now admits this "structural" concept of the *Imago*, which is found only in the Old Testament; he distinguishes it from the concept of the Reformation (and, may we add, of the New Testament), as the element in the Image of God which cannot be lost, as opposed to that which can be, and has been, lost (*K.D.*, III, 1, pp. 206 ff.). And now in this connexion the previously prohibited concept of Analogy reappears. The *Imago Dei*, in the sense of Gen. 1, the "over-againstness of I and Thou" he calls "the analogy between God and man" (p. 207). And Barth asserts that *this* element in man as "made in the Image of God, has not been lost, as we see from the legend of the Fall" (p. 225). This is exactly what I said in my pamphlet, *Natur und Gnade*, some time ago. I am happy to know that this controversy, which caused so much discussion, may now be regarded as settled. We may now expect that Karl Barth will look at the whole problem of Analogy from a new angle, without in the very least retracting his criticism of the Catholic principle of the *analogia entis* as the basis of the *theologia naturalis*.

For the fundamental principle of the *analogia entis*, which is basic in medieval theology, especially as adopted by Bonaventura, which serves as the foundation of a rational *theologia naturalis*, is not derived from the Biblical idea of Creation, but from the Neoplatonist theory of emanation; it comes from the school of the most influential doctrinal authority of the Middle Ages, Dionysius the Areopagite, to whom Bonaventura refers more frequently than to any other "master". This, however, is not the place to discuss the highly complicated statements of the Catholic defenders of this Principle of Analogy. The significance for theology and for the Theory of Knowledge of the principle of analogy in our sense and the impossibility of rejecting it, has been worked out excellently by Ed. Burnier in his work, *La Parole de Dieu et l'analogie de foi dans la dogmatique de Karl Barth*, in the volume entitled *Bible et Théologie*, Lausanne, 1943.

CHAPTER 2

MAN AND CREATION

(1) THE SIGNIFICANCE OF ANTHROPOLOGY

THE Christian doctrine of Man is of particular, indeed, we might also say of incomparable, importance, from two points of view: (a) as a subject of common concern in discussion with the unbelieving world; (b) as the basis of social ethics. Knowledge of Man is the common theme and the common concern both of secular and of Christian (theological) wisdom. Apparently at least, we can ignore God; we cannot ignore man. The question: What is God? may be regarded as unanswerable, or out of date, or uninteresting, but no one would say the same about the question: What is Man?[1] Thus Man is the favourite subject of the philosophers—at least since Socrates—as well as of the psychologists and the poets. The exhortation γνῶθι σεαυτόν on the portico of the Temple at Delphi, frequented by people seeking and receiving enlightenment from those who had wisdom to impart, is still relevant. Down to the present day there is scarcely any other subject about which there are more contradictory views and theories of our empirical world than this, which is so close to us, and seems so familiar.

The first question we have to answer is this: From the point of view of the Christian Faith, is it any use discussing this particular subject with those who do not take the Christian position? For the moment we would answer that even the Apostle Paul ascribes a certain knowledge of himself to the "natural man", who has not been influenced by revelation;[2] and indeed, that in point of fact, all preaching of the Gospel—whether rejected or accepted in theory—presupposes and allows for this natural self-knowledge. All pastoral or missionary discussion aims at self-knowledge and makes use of natural psychological knowledge of the nature of Man. Of course we must recognize that there *is* an anthropology based on natural science which is quite independent of the Christian Faith, and there *is* a psychology, which, at least in part, is not affected

[1] K. Heim, in his latest work, *Der Christliche Glaube und die Naturwissenschaft* (1949), has brought this out very well
[2] I Cor. 2: 4

either by faith or unbelief, a knowledge of facts about man
which the Christian must weave into his picture of man like
anyone else, if his picture is to be a true one.

This positive statement must be balanced by the negative
statement, that nowhere so much as in the sphere of self-
knowledge does sin blind men to the truth, and cause so many
hindrances; further, that before he is stripped bare in the light
of revelation man does not want to be exposed to the light,
but either he thinks of himself in naturalistic terms, which
provide him with convenient excuses, or he sees himself in a
romantic idealistic light.[1] Hence it is part of the genuine
Christian experience that only the man who has been influenced
by the truth of Christ is honest with himself, because he alone
dares to look the naked truth in the face. For both these reasons
we can see why the process of becoming a Christian must begin
with "entering into oneself", and yet can only be accomplished
by "going out of oneself", and thus why the form of "conversation" is necessary for Christian knowledge. Only in "conversation about yourself" can "you" become a Christian.

The second point, which gives the doctrine of man its
peculiar significance, is the fact that all political, social and
cultural development presupposes an "anthropology"; that
every political or social theory, and every social or political
postulate stems from a definite anthropology. Behind Liberalism, behind Totalitarianism, behind Communism, there is
always a certain view of man, each of which is an alternative
to the Christian doctrine of man, just as, on the other hand,
particular social, political or cultural postulates are deduced
from the Christian view of Man. The ideas of Rousseau in the
Contrat Social, and the ideal of the "classless society" of
Marx, are consequences of their "anthropology". The Totalitarian State bears its own logical fruit in the negation of
original human rights and in the non-recognition of the dignity
of man. The latest politico-social developments have again made
men aware of the fact that Western culture and civilization is
based upon certain anthropological axioms which arise out of
Christian doctrine. This is one reason why anthropology is of
such vital importance for the relation of the Christian Church
to its environment. This may indeed justify the intensity with
which—even within the sphere of dogmatics—this subject is
being discussed at the present time.

[1] This is a leading idea in the *Pensées* of Pascal, and in the earlier works of
Kierkegaard

(2) HAS THE DOCTRINE OF THE PRIMITIVE STATE ANY SIGNIFI-CANCE FOR THE MODERN WORLD?

The standard doctrine of the Church, from the time of St. Augustine onwards, connects the theological truth of man's creation in the Image of God and the fact that he is in rebellion against his Divine destiny, by means of the idea of the "primitive state" or man's existence in Paradise, presented, moreover, as an historical fact. In classical theology this means an existence which, in spite of its qualitative difference from our present world of time and space, belongs to the history of this earth, and is thus to be localized somewhere upon this earth which we know, and at some time in the history of mankind. What justification there is for supporting this belief by an appeal to Chapters 2 and 3 of Genesis and the testimony of the Apostle Paul, will be explained later on. For modern man this possibility no longer exists. This is not a question of "believing" or "not believing"; the position is this, that for everyone, however "orthodox" or even "funda-mentalist" he may be in thought, the possibility has dis-appeared of reproducing the views of an Augustine or of the doctors of the Church who followed in his steps. The picture of Time and Space in which these thinkers moved has irrevocably been swept away, even for the most orthodox people. Just as when we now look up into the starlit heavens we no longer see the sky which the ancients saw, but a heaven with infinite spatial depths and constellations millions and millions of times larger than the earth, so also the world of Time in which we live—in which even the most orthodox person lives—is no longer the time-world of an Augustine or a Luther. This change has taken place for good and all; it is our destiny; our faith or our unbelief has no effect upon it; it cannot be altered, just as the earth which is shaped like a ball and not like a plate is our destiny, and no faith or unbelief can alter it.

Thus the man who wants to "hold firmly to the historicity of the story of Adam" is doing something quite different from what he thinks he is doing. He thinks he is preserving the faith of his fathers; in reality he is doing something quite different; he is trying to include in the modern picture of Time and Space, a process which belongs to a quite different picture of Time and Space, which he cannot possibly reproduce. Thus he is not "conservative", but quixotic and reactionary. He is attempting the impossible: to combine the views of Time and Space which cannot be combined. The figure of "Adam" in Paradise which results from this effort is in any case very different from that of the ancients; it is an impossible centaur, a mixture of elements from the ancient and the modern view of the world. It is not possible to place the Augustinian "Adam in Paradise" in a post-Copernican world of Time and Space without turning *this* "Adam in Paradise" into something wholly different. It would only be possible to remain true to the "Adam" conception of the ancient world, if we could give up all effort to co-operate with the changes in the view of Time and Space which have been taking place for four hundred years—and this, in point of fact, is simply impossible. This change, as has already been said, is our destiny; it affects us all, whether we are believers or unbelievers. This possibility could only exist for a human being who was actually still living in this ancient world of Time, that is, for one who had never heard of Copernicus, or who rejects *all* scientific knowledge outright as "godlessness". On the other hand, the combination of the modern view of Time and Space and the ancient one of "Adam in Paradise" is an indisputable *quid pro quo* which can only injure the reputation of the faith of the Bible and of Theology among all people who possess a strong feeling for Truth.

The "Adam in Paradise" of the ancients was a human being historically connected with the history of the people of Israel. That is the reason for the genealogies from Abraham back to Adam and from Abraham onwards to David, and then to Jesus. On the other hand, "Adam" is the man who, chronologically, was contemporary with the Six Days of Creation; that is, he was the first of mankind, which is only a few days younger than the world. Through the middle term "Adam in Paradise" the chronological history of Israel is indissolubly connected with the story of the beginning of the cosmos in absolute continuity. The world of Adam is not older than Adam and his human race; Adam in Paradise is the last of the living beings created by God not subject to change. The conception of "Adam in Paradise" is indissolubly connected with the Six Days of Creation. The Primitive State in Paradise is what it is through the fact that it participates in this original character of the creation of the Cosmos.

Hence if we try (as the orthodox apologists of our day try to do) to combine the idea of "Adam in Paradise" with a view of the world in which millions of years precede the existence of man, in which the species come and go, with a history of the earth, in which the last epoch is preceded by the Mesozoic and the Palaeozoic, and in which, during the last epoch of Neozoic, at the end of the Tertiary Epoch, or in the Quaternary—more than one hundred thousand years ago— and Neozoic man, as a quite new phenomenon, appears in the form of the *homo primigenius*—then this man, however passionately one may assert it, cannot possibly be the same as "Adam in Paradise", even if all the theological attributes of the figure of Adam are transferred to him. For here the essential elements are lacking: the visible chronological continuity with the history of Israel on the one hand, and the simultaneity of Adam with the Creation of the world on the other. To equate the Neanderthal Man with "Adam in Paradise"—an attempt which is being made to-day, even by European theological university professors—merely produces an impossible bastard conception, composed of the most heterogeneous and incongruous views.

The historical figure of Adam of the ancients, and the pre-Copernican view of Time and Space are inseparable. When one disappears the other vanishes too. Theoretically there are three possibilities:

(i) Fidelity to the conception of the "Adam" of the ancients with the abandonment of the whole modern view of the universe; (ii) a compromise in the form of an attempt to combine the Copernican view of the world with a conception of "Adam" as an historical figure; and (iii) the surrender of the ancient view, which is necessarily involved in the acceptance of the change brought in by Copernicus, with the abandonment of the second or compromise form, which has become inwardly impossible. Anyone who has once seen this situation clearly, has no choice left. He admits that the third alternative is the only possible one. This means, however, that we can no longer teach that man, as created by God, is descended from "Adam in Paradise", and the Primitive State. The primitive state of Paradise as part of earthly and temporal history, as its first, brief section, is no longer a tenable idea.

But if this abandonment of the ancient view of "Adam" should mean the surrender of the distinction between human existence as created by God, and that of sinful man, and the surrender of the idea of the Fall, which separates the two from each other, this would mean nothing less than the shattering of the foundations of the whole Biblical doctrine of Man, and indeed of the whole Biblical doctrine of revelation and of salvation. When we realize how much is at stake, we can at least understand the contortions of Fundamentalist theology, which, in themselves, are most unfortunate. Over against a theory of Evolution which sweeps away all ideas of Creation and of Sin, Fundamentalism, in spite of its curious aberrations of thought, is absolutely right. If, on the one hand, we maintain that we cannot think in Copernican terms without giving up the *story* of Adam, then, on the other hand we must also say: that we cannot believe, in Christian and Biblical terms, without holding firmly to the distinction between Creation and Sin, and therefore the idea of a Fall. To give this up means to abandon the Biblical faith as a whole.[1]

In this dilemma, some recent Theology has taken a bypath which, at first sight, was tempting. The view that Adam was an historical figure is given up—that is, one no longer says: once upon a time upon this earth, and within human history there was a place called "Paradise" and a first man called "Adam", who is connected with Abraham, through a few links in the Old Testament genealogy, and thus with the beginning of the history of Israel. Those who take this view posit a "pre-existent" Adam, and a meta-historical, or transcendental Fall of this "Adam", thus combining Platonist and Kantian ideas with the Biblical truth of the first human being, created by God, and fallen away from God. In so doing they wipe out the difference between such a transcendental view of Adam and the Augustinian, historical, view by describing the Genesis story as a "legend", or something of that kind. The gain is evident: all the impossibilities connected with a view of "Adam" as an historical figure have been eliminated, and this view does not clash with the modern view of time and space. But the price which we pay for this solution is too high: it leads us into a "platonizing" view of Creation as a whole, which must have a disastrous effect on the doctrine of Sin and the Fall. More will be said about this later on. In any case, this metaphysical theory cannot base itself upon the Bible, for the Bible certainly does not mean such a transcendental figure of Adam—neither in the version in Genesis nor in the teaching of St. Paul—nor a transcendental Fall of man. Some of us for a time followed this bypath; but we must describe it as a speculation which is foreign to the message of the Bible as a

[1] This applies to the book by E. Hirsch, *Schöpfung und Sünde*

whole, and in essentials it contradicts it. This, however, imposes upon us the difficult task of gaining a fresh view of the theological content of the doctrine of the Primitive State, without the use of the story of Adam, and without metaphysical speculations about a Primitive State and the Fall, couched in transcendental terms.

Thus we are confronted by the very difficult theological task of formulating the distinction between the nature of man in accordance with Creation, and as sinner, and the idea which this involves of the Fall of Man, without using the thought-form of an historical "Adam in Paradise" and of the Primitive State.

(3) THE STARTING-POINT

As we shall see, we shall do justice to this postulate by holding firmly to our theological canon, namely: that in all theological statements about the divine revelation we must begin with Jesus Christ, as the Word of God Incarnate, and that we are not bound by any Biblical passages taken in isolation, and certainly not by isolated sections of the Old Testament. Here too the method which has already proved fruitful in the doctrine of Creation will show us the way out of a difficulty which has only arisen out of a mistaken view of the Bible, and for the same reason is constantly repeated.

As, in the doctrine of Creation, we gave up any idea of starting from the Old Testament account of Creation, and decided to begin with the New Testament witness to Creation in the Prologue to the Gospel of John, so we must do the same here with the doctrine of Man. When we do this, we shall see that the difficulties caused by the idea of the Creation of the world in Six Days, the idea of a Primitive State, and of an "Adam in Paradise", vanish into thin air. Thus we see that fidelity to this theological principle, which we believe to be sound, sets us free from problems caused by the fact that we had been, theologically, on the wrong line. This conclusion is confirmed by the fact that this view lessens the tension between the modern and the ancient view of the world; in fact, it is now seen that the change of outlook does not really affect the fundamental Biblical truth, and it certainly does not need a prominent place in our discussion. In so doing it is, of course, understood—as we saw in the previous chapter—that we shall gain a great deal of truth from the testimony of

the Old Testament in spite of its mythical form. Thus we shall
not gather up all the anthropological statements of the Bible
and set them out, in order, as is usually done, so as to
construct Christian anthropology as a doctrinal whole, but we
shall start from the centre, from the revelation of God in
Jesus Christ; we shall then ask ourselves what this teaches us
about man; then we shall introduce particular statements
about man from the Old and the New Testaments, interpreted
in the light of this central truth, in order to complete and
confirm it.[1]

Our Christo-centric method would be misunderstood, however, if we were to deduce from it that the first thing we have.
to do is to establish a doctrine of the Humanity of Christ. To
look at man *in the light* of Jesus Christ is not the same thing
as knowing Jesus Christ. Here our concern is with anthropology, not with Christology, even if this anthropology, like
every other doctrine within Christian dogma as a whole, must
have a Christological foundation. Jesus Christ as the Word
of God Incarnate is here not the object, but the source and
norm of truth.[2]

(4) MAN AS CREATURE

To meet God the Lord means that we acknowledge that we
are creatures. It may seem tautological to say: To know God
the Creator means to know ourselves as creatures. But this
tautology expresses the truth: that the knowledge of God as
Creator, and the knowledge of ourselves as creatures, are
correlative truths. We cannot know the one without the other.
Since God the Lord meets me in Jesus Christ I know that He
is Creator, and that I am His creature. And conversely: I only
know that I am a creature in this encounter. There may be a
general sense of religious "creatureliness",[3] it is true, a sense
of weakness, of transience, of nothingness. But to the extent
in which this "divine" is not the real Creator I do not know
myself truly as a creature. Not every feeling of impotence and
nothingness means knowledge of one's nature as a creature.
I know that I am a creature because I know of the Creator,

[1] Excellent material for this procedure is provided by (a) Eichrodt, *Das
Menschenverständnis des Alten Testaments*, and (b) Kümmel, *Das Bild des
Menschen im Neuen Testament*
[2] This second way, here rejected, is taken by Karl Barth, *K.D.*, III, 2,
but it does not lead to any result which contradicts my main argument
[3] Cf. Otto, *The Idea of the Holy*

and I know of the Creator because I know and recognize the fact that I am a creature.

This knowledge of, and this recognition of, our "creatureliness" is not something we can take for granted. The more that man is able to distinguish himself from the rest of creation, the more he becomes conscious of himself as subject, as an "I", to whom the whole world is Object, the more does he tend to confuse himself with God, to confuse his spirit with the Spirit of God, and to regard his reason as divine reason. The "I" philosophy of India, the Greek doctrine of the divine νοῦς, and modern Idealism, all confirm this statement. It is only the man who has not yet become aware of his nature as a spiritual being, who still regards himself as one object among many others, who thinks it is easy to reject the temptation to become like God. The man who has no spiritual view thinks it is ridiculous that man could possibly confuse himself with God. But the more fully developed man becomes in mind and spirit, the more clearly he makes a distinction between persons and things, the more is he inclined to identify the human and the divine Subject. Indeed, from Heraclitus onwards, Western philosophy—when untouched by materialism—has made repeated attempts to achieve this identification, while Indian philosophy has not hesitated to go all lengths—in its pantheism. Further, where man *thinks* God by his own efforts, and does not meet the God who reveals Himself, in the last resort he cannot help achieving this identification, although he may qualify his theory in many directions. It is only the encounter with the Living God which eliminates this error.

It is not—at least not primarily—the fact that the human Self is connected with a material body, like that of the lower animals, which makes clear the absurdity of the illusion of divinity. The desire to deify the Self has always made short work of this fact of the connexion with the body. The body, the animal nature with the senses, does not belong—so they say—really to "me" at all. It is a prison into which I have somehow or other fallen, a tomb, a shadow, a "double", a relic, an illusion; in short it is not the "true Self" which is the spirit. Thus it is not the perception of the connexion with the body which impels man to recognize that he is a creature, and not the Creator, but conversely, it is because he admits his "creatureliness", that he knows, in faith, that the body is really part of him, and is not an alien addition. He becomes aware of his creatureliness not through the perception of his corporeality, but through the fact that God, when He confronts him as Lord, claims him wholly for Himself. As a creature "I" belong wholly to God; I am not independent and free, but I am a being who is derived from, and made for, God. This perception of what it means to be a "creature" does not deny our freedom, but it springs from the fact that our freedom is founded in God, and is limited by that. The belief in Creation does not deny that man is different from the world; rather it acknowledges this when it says that man has been created in the Image of God; this means however, that we cannot speak of our "creatureliness" without dealing at the same time with the truth that man has been created in the Image of God.

(5) THE IMAGE OF GOD AND CREATION

This truth also must be understood from the point of view of the New Testament, and not primarily from that of the Old Testament; that is, we must start from the Centre. In Jesus Christ God meets me as the One who imparts Himself to me in freedom, since as Holy Love He claims me wholly for Himself. It is as such that He reveals Himself to me. But the fact that He so reveals Himself to me means that He also at the same time reveals myself to me: that is, He shows me my relation to Himself. He is the One who wills to have from me a free response to His love, a response which gives back love for love, a living echo, a living reflection of His glory. I cannot meet the holy loving God in Christ without knowing this about myself. Once more, both are correlated and connected; to be aware of the holy Loving God, and to be aware of the fact that my nature is created by God, comes to the same thing. It is thus, and not otherwise, that I am intended to be by the Creator. This generous will which claims me, of the God who wills to glorify Himself, and to impart Himself, is the cause of my being, and the fundamental reason for my being what I am, and as I am. Now we must go into some particular points in greater detail.

(a) God, who wills to glorify Himself and to impart Himself, wills man to be a creature who responds to His call of love with a grateful, responsive love. God wills to possess man as a free being. God wills a creature which is not only, like other creatures, a mere object of His will, as if it were a reflector of His glory as Creator. He desires from us an active and spontaneous response in our "reflecting"; He who creates through the Word, who as Spirit creates in freedom, wills to have a "reflex" which is more than a "reflex", which is an answer to His Word, a free spiritual act, a correspondence to His speaking. Only thus can His love really impart itself as love. For love can only impart itself where it is received in love. Hence the heart of the creaturely existence of man is freedom, selfhood, to be an "I", a person. Only an "I" can answer a "Thou", only a Self which is self-determining can freely answer God. An automaton does not respond; an animal, in contradistinction from an automaton, may indeed *re*-act, but it cannot *re*-spond. It is not capable of speech, of free self-determination, it cannot stand at a distance from itself, and is therefore not *re*-sponsible.

The free Self, capable of self-determination, belongs to the original constitution of man as created by God. But from the very outset this freedom is limited. It is not primary but secondary. Indeed, it does not posit itself—like the Self of Idealism—but it is posited; it is not *a se* but *a Deo*. Hence although man's answer is free, it is also limited. God wills my freedom, it is true, because He wills to glorify Himself, and to give Himself. He wills my freedom in order to make this answer possible; my freedom is therefore, from the outset, a responsible one. Responsibility is *restricted* freedom, which distinguishes human from divine freedom; and it is a restriction which is also *free*—and this distinguishes our human limited freedom from that of the rest of creation. The animals, and God, have no responsibility—the animals because they are below the level of responsibility, and God, because He is above it; the animals because they have no freedom, and God because He has absolute freedom. Man, however, has a limited freedom. This is the heart of his being as man, and it is the "condition" on which he possesses freedom. In other words, this limited human freedom is the very purpose for which man has been created: he possesses *this* "freedom" in order that he may respond to God, in such a way that through this response God may glorify Himself, and give Himself to His creature.

(*b*) Now, however, it is of the essence of this responsible freedom that its purpose may or may not be fulfilled. This open question is the consequence of freedom. Thus it is part of the divinely created nature of man that it should have both a formal and a material aspect. The fact that man must respond, that he is responsible, is fixed; no amount of human freedom, nor of the sinful misuse of freedom, can alter this fact. Man is, and remains, responsible, whatever his personal attitude to his Creator may be. He may deny his responsibility, and he may misuse his freedom, but he cannot get rid of his responsibility. Responsibility is part of the unchangeable structure of man's being. That is: the actual existence of man—of every man, not only the man who believes in Christ—consists in the positive fact that he has been *made* to respond—to God.

Whatever kind of response man may make to the call of the Creator—in any case he does respond, even if his reply is: "I do not know any Creator, and I will not obey any God." Even this answer *is* an answer, and it comes under the inherent law of responsibility. This formal essential structure cannot be lost. It is identical with human existence as such, and indeed with the quality of being which all human beings possess equally; it only ceases where true human living ceases—on the borderline of imbecility or madness.

In the Old Testament, the Bible describes this formal aspect of human nature by the concept of "being made in the image of God". In the thought of the Old Testament the fact that man has been "made in the Image of God" means something which man can never lose; even when he sins he cannot lose it.[1] This conception is therefore unaffected by the contrast between sin and grace, or sin and obedience, precisely because it describes the "formal" or "structural", and not the "material" aspect of human nature. Then how is it possible to perceive reflected similarity in this formal likeness to God? The similarity consists in being "subject", being "person", freedom. Certainly, man has only a limited freedom, because he is responsible, but he *has* freedom; only so *can* he be responsible. Thus the formal aspect of man's nature, as a being "made in the image of God", denotes his being as Subject, or his freedom; it is this which differentiates man from the lower creation; this constitutes his specifically *human* quality; it is this which is given to him—and to him alone—and under all circumstances—by Divine appointment.

The New Testament simply presupposes this fact that man—in his very nature—has been "made in the image of God"; it does not develop this any further. To the Apostles what matters most is the "material" realization of this God-given quality; that is, that man should really give *the* answer which the Creator intends, the response in which God is honoured, and

[1] Cf. the article on εἰκών (by V. Rad) in Kittel's *Th. Wb. z. N.T.*, II, pp. 387 ff., and also K. Barth, *K.D.*, III, I, pp. 224 ff.

in which He fully imparts Himself, the response of reverent, grateful love, given not only in words, but in his whole life. The New Testament, in *its* doctrine of the *Imago Dei*, tells us that this right answer has not been given; that a quite different one has been given instead, in which the glory is not given to God, but to men and to creatures, in which man does not live in the love of God, but seeks himself. Secondly, the New Testament is the proclamation of what God has done in order that He may turn this false answer into the true one.

Here, therefore, the fact that man has been "made in the image of God" is spoken of as having been lost, and indeed as wholly, and not partially lost. Man no longer possesses this *Imago Dei*; but it is restored through Him, through whom God glorifies and gives Himself: through Jesus Christ. The restoration of the *Imago Dei*, the new creation of the original image of God in man, is identical with the gift of God in Jesus Christ received by faith.[1]

The *Imago Dei* in the New Testament, "material" sense of the word, is identical with "being-in-the-Word" of God. This means that man does not possess his true being in himself, but in God. Thus it is not a fact which can be discovered in man, something which can be found through introspection. It is not the "Thou" of Idealistic philosophy, but it is the "I" derived from the "Thou". Hence it cannot be understood by looking at man, but only by looking at God, or, more exactly, by looking at the Word of God. To be true man, man must not be "himself", and in order to understand his true being he must not look at himself. Our true being is *"extra nos et alienum nobis"* (Luther); it is "eccentric" and "ecstatic"; man is only truly human when he is in God. Then, and then only, is he truly "himself".

From the standpoint of sinful man the *Imago Dei* is existence in Jesus Christ, the Word made flesh. Jesus Christ is the true *Imago Dei*, which man regains when through faith he is "in Jesus Christ". Faith in Jesus Christ is therefore the *restauratio imaginis*, because He restores to us that existence in the Word of God which we had lost through sin. When man enters into the love of God revealed in Christ he becomes truly human. True human existence is existence in the love of God. Thus also the true freedom of man is complete dependence upon God. *Deo servire libertas* (Augustine). The words "Whose service is perfect freedom" express the essence of Christian faith. True

[1] 2 Cor. 3: 18; Rom. 8: 29; Eph. 4: 24; Col. 3: 10

humanity is not genius but love, that love which man does not possess from or in himself but which he receives from God, who is love. True humanity does not spring from the full development of human potentialities, but it arises through the reception, the perception, and the acceptance of the love of God, and it develops and is preserved by "abiding" in communion with the God who reveals Himself as Love. Hence separation from God, sin, is the loss of the true human quality, and the destruction of the quality of "being made in the Image of God". When the heart of man no longer reflects the love of God, but himself and the world, he no longer bears the "Image of God", which simply consists in the fact that God's love is reflected in the human heart.

Since through faith in Jesus Christ man once more receives God's Primal Word of love, once more the divine Image (*Urbild*) is reflected in him,[1] the lost *Imago Dei* is restored. The *Imago Dei*, in the sense of true humanity—not in the sense of formal or structural humanity—is thus identical with the true attitude of man in relation to God, in accordance with God's purpose in Creation. Your attitude to God determines what you are. If your attitude towards God is "right", in harmony with the purpose of Creation, that is, if in faith you receive the love of God, then you *are* right; if your attitude to God is wrong, then *you* are wrong, as a whole.

It is evident that our thought will become terribly muddled if the two ideas of the *Imago Dei*—the "formal" and "structural' one of the Old Testament, and the "material" one of the New Testament—are either confused with one another, or treated as identical. The result will be: either that we must deny that the sinner possesses the quality of humanity at all; or, that which makes him a human being must be severed from the *Imago Dei*; or, the loss of the *Imago* in the material sense must be regarded merely as an obscuring, or a partial corruption of the *Imago*, which lessens the heinousness of sin. All these three false solutions disappear once the distinction is rightly made.

(c) The process of making this distinction aright, however, is made more difficult by the fact that in both instances the fact that man has been made in the Image of God is conceived not as a self-existing substance but as a relation. And this is the most important point to grasp. Responsibility is a relation; it is not a substance. If, on the contrary, as in the Catholic

[1] This is precisely what is said in 2 Cor. 3: 18

tradition, the *Imago Dei* is conceived in the formal structural sense as the endowment with reason, as creative freedom, then Man possesses the Image of God *in himself*. *This* view of the *Imago Dei* is the gate by which a pantheistic or an idealistic deification of man can enter. Man then possesses the divine reason in himself; his spirit is then a "spark" from the Divine Spirit. He has "divinity within himself"; *"est Deus in Nobis"*. Then the Divine element in man, and the destiny of man, will consist in this participation in the divine reason; then man will only need to become aware of this divine reason within himself, by making a clear distinction between it and that other lower part of his nature, which is non-divine, the body. The result of this erroneous conception of the *Imago Dei*—as substance and not as relation—is a mistakenly "spiritualized" view of man and his destiny.

It is, however, difficult for us to combine the ideas of "structure" and "relation". And yet it is the distinctive quality of human existence that its "structure" is a "relation": responsible existence, responsive actuality. The Biblical testimony on this point is ruthlessly logical; man is the being who stands "before God", even if he is godless. The fact that man, misusing his freedom and denying his responsibility, turns his back on God, does not mean that he no longer stands "before God". On the contrary, he stands "before God" as a sinner; he stands before God in a wrong attitude, hence he is "under the wrath of God". We shall be dealing with this point later on; here all I want to do is this: to make it clear that the loss of the *Imago*, in the material sense, does not remove responsibility from man; he still stands "before God", and he is still a human being. Only human beings can be sinners; to be a sinner it is necessary to possess that quality which distinguishes man from the animals. The loss of the *Imago*, in the material sense, presupposes the *Imago* in the formal sense. To be a sinner is the negative way of being responsible.

(*d*) We must note, however, that necessary as it is for us to think of the *Imago Dei* with this distinction between the formal and material aspect, from the point of view of the divine Creation it does not exist. God calls man into existence in order that he may respond to Him aright—not in order that he may respond wrongly or rightly. Man is not destined to choose between faith and unbelief, obedience and disobedience; God has made man in such a way that he can respond as God wills Him to do. A certain freedom of choice, which makes this response possible, only becomes visible when the wrong response has been made. Formal freedom, severed from material freedom, from existence in the love of God, is already a result of sin. Man ought to know nothing of this freedom save in the form of the generous love of God. The fact that he is aware of this freedom of choice is already the effect of sin, and of separation from his connexion with God.[1] We shall be seeing later that this is the origin of the contrast between the Law and the Gospel. Responsibility, severed from the generous grace of the Creator, can only be understood as legal responsibility. Legal responsibility is therefore already a result of the false autonomy of man, and has a correlative relation to it.

From the side of God, therefore, this distinction between the "formal" and the "material" does not exist; it is not legally valid. But it does exist—wrongly. This means that when we look at the *Imago Dei* from our angle, that is, the angle of sinful man, it necessarily appears under this twofold aspect of the "formal", that is, the responsibility which cannot be lost, and the "material", lost destiny, lost "existence in the love of God". This is why, when man meets God in Jesus Christ, he must hear both the Law and the Gospel—the Law which makes him responsible for sin, without, however, making him able to fulfil it, and the Gospel, which gives him existence in the love of God, without law, through faith.

(6) MAN AS EMBODIED SPIRIT

It is a well-known fact, at least within the Christian Church, and among readers of the Bible, that the Bible understands man as a whole, as an entity consisting of "soul" or "spirit" and "body". The Biblical view leaves no room for the dualistic notion that though the "spirit" (or "soul") is of divine origin and divine in character, the body on the other hand is something lower and inferior. But it is less well-known *why* the Bible takes this view. Whence comes this dignity given to the body as something created by, and therefore willed by God? We have already suggested the answer to this important question, when we said how difficult it is for man to understand himself as a "creature". The man who does not know the Creator is always trying either to deny God, or to regard his

[1] This is the theological meaning of the prohibition of the knowledge of good and evil—addressed to Adam in Paradise

physical nature as something which does not really belong to him, in order to be able to maintain the divinity of his "real" spiritual nature.

The natural man is always either an Idealist or a Materialist; an Idealist who regards his spirit as part of the divine Spirit; a Materialist, who, owing to his corporeal nature, regards himself merely as a "more highly developed animal", and denies his higher eternal destiny. It seems to him impossible that body and spirit[1] can come equally from God.

In point of fact—how can he possibly understand this? Of himself, he cannot know the Creator. The Creator only permits Himself to be known through revelation as the Lord who meets man. As the Lord who meets man, however, He is One who claims me in the totality of my existence, who claims me as I am, body and soul. If He is the Creator of the *World*, He is also the Creator of the *body*. The God whom man invents for himself has no relation to the material world and to human corporeality. From the point of view of faith in the Creator, the material body, and matter as such, are the distinctive marks of the created, as opposed to the uncreated existence of the Creator. The physical nature of man is therefore the sign, the concrete expression of the creaturely nature of man, of the fact that he is not God. But the fact that man is not God does not mean that he is without God. Man as soul-and-body has therefore been created to glorify God; hence, conversely, the highest self-communication of God is the Incarnation of the Word in a man of flesh and blood. For one who meets the Incarnate Word of God, it is no longer possible to despise the body, and to regard his spiritual nature as divine, but his physical nature as something foreign to God. For him, the body is "the temple of the Holy Spirit".[2]

The relation of body and soul is determined by the divine revelation in the Incarnate Word. Indeed, the fact that man has been made in the image of God implies that the body is equally the means of expression, and the instrument, of the spirit and the will. The body, this definite body, has been given to man by the Creator, in order that in it he may express his higher calling and make its realization concrete.[3] The body which God has created for man is full of the symbolism of his

---

[1] Here, and in other places in this chapter, "spirit" (*Geist*)="personal being" (TR.)

[2] 1 Cor. 6: 19   [3] 1 Cor. 6: 20

divine-human destiny, and is admirably suited for its realization.

The spirit, on the other hand, is that aspect of human nature by means of which man can perceive his divine destiny and, knowing and recognizing this, can receive it, and transmit it to the body, as the instrument through which it is accomplished. The spirit receives the Word of God, as it is the Spirit[1] of God which speaks to it within the human spirit. The Spirit of God "beareth witness with our spirit that we are children of God." It is significant that this passage suggests that the actual "place" where God reveals Himself to man, and the place where man realizes his responsibility for sin, is not the "spirit", apart from the body, but the "place" where "spirit" and "body" are one, that is, the "heart". This is in harmony with the fact that God's Word never comes to us as a purely spiritual word, but is always mediated to us through physical means as a spiritual message, as a word that is spoken with the lips, and that the perfect revelation of God took place through the Incarnation of the Word. It is not in an abstract spirituality, but in a spirituality of faith, connected with the body, that man receives the divine self-revelation. As He is the God who wills to reveal Himself *through* the world, and in the world, so He creates a creature in His likeness, which by nature is a unity of body and soul. The divine love in its self-revelation can only be received by "the heart", by the heart which is destined to love. This throws a light also upon the fact of sexual polarity.

(7) THE POLARITY OF SEX

"Male and female created He them"—this is directly connected with the main statement: God created man in His Image. It is going too far to assert that the male and female existence of humanity is identified with the *Imago Dei*.[2] Sex polarity is indeed not the distinctive element in man which differentiates him from all other creatures. The fact that the human pair are not simply male and female, but are husband and wife, presupposes that the twofold character of sex is not in itself the distinctive human element, but that it is one strand in this element. But there is truth in this conception, to this extent, that this sex polarity belongs not only to the nature which has been created by God, but also to the *Imago Dei*. This is not

[1] Rom. 8: 16 [2] As K. Barth does: *K.D.*, III, 1, pp. 206 ff.

understood so long as the *Imago Dei* is sought in man's reason, and is not understood as relation.[1]

But if we understand responsibility as existence determined by the fact that man has been created in the Image of God, this means that in the purpose of Creation man's existence consists, from the formal point of view, in existence-for-love, and from the material point of view, in existence-in-love. Thus the distinctively "human" element, as such, does not appear in the individual; for existence-in-*community* is part of true humanity. Hence from the outset man has not been created as an isolated being, but as a "twofold" being;[2] and not simply as two human beings, but as two beings who necessarily belong to one another, who have been created for this purpose, and whose whole nature is ordered in this direction, that is, as two beings who cannot *be*, apart from each other. In the older version of the Creation story (J) this is explicitly stated: "It is not good for man to be alone".[3] The Creation of Man is not finished until the partner is there. In the later version (Gen. 1) the twofold Creation is presupposed from the outset, and follows immediately on the definition of man as made in the Image of God. Because God is Love, because in God's very Nature there is community, man must be able to love: thus "man" has to be created as a *pair* of human beings. He cannot realize his nature without the "Other"; his destiny is fellowship in love.

This twofold character of man in the Creation Story is in contrast to the world-wide myth of androgyny. The latter is necessarily connected with rational thinking, for which the ultimate and supreme truth is UNITY, just as the fact of the two sexes is necessarily connected with the God who wills community. Either community or unity is the final supreme truth. The God of the Biblical revelation is the God of community; the God of rational philosophy is the God of unity. It is no accident that Plato's *Symposium* accepts the myth of androgyny. Androgyny belongs to the thought of Platonism, and sexual polarity to Christian thought.[4]

[1] The fact that here K. Barth, in this connexion, even admits an *analogia relationis* (p. 219) gives me special satisfaction, for the distinctive being of man consists in this relation

[2] See *Der Mensch im Widerspruch* (1937), pp. 95 ff.

[3] Gen. 2: 18

[4] It is therefore no accident that the gnostic thinker, Berdyaev, accepts the androgynous principle, and conceives the fact of the two sexes as the result of the Fall. *Die Philosophie der Freiheit des Geistes*, p. 238

8

888

888

Androgyny is the ontological basis of narcissism. Within the sphere of speculative thought love is always, in the last resort, self-love, because the final end sought is unity. Within the sphere of Biblical thought love is never narcissism or self-love, because love is always self-communication, the will to community. *Agape* presupposes the "I" and the "Thou" over against each other; narcissism, androgyny, presupposes thought which aims at unity; it presupposes the elimination of anything opposite; it presupposes the identity of object and subject. It is not aware of the "over-againstness" of the "I" and the "Thou". In the sphere of Biblical thought, only man in the dual form of the "I" and the "Thou" is the man who has been "made in the Image of God".

Sexual polarity, however, as such, is not itself the "I" and the "Thou". It is only a picture of the purpose of Creation, and the natural basis of the true "I" and "Thou". Sexual polarity is therefore not intended for eternity[1] whereas the "I" and the "Thou", the communion and the fellowship of the Kingdom of God, is certainly intended for eternity. Hence sexual polarity is not itself the *Imago Dei*; it is, as it were, a secondary *Imago*, a reflection of the Divine purpose, and at the same time the natural basis of true community. Sexual love indeed is not itself the love at which the Creator aims, but it foreshadows true love, and is also its natural presupposition. It does so in two ways: (a) the human race in its physical reality is derived from it; and (b) by it man learns what love is, as it were, in a preparatory school. Hence the sexual quality and function of man is full of the symbolism of true community. The love between the sexes, the love of man and woman, is the earthenware vessel in which true love, *agape*, is to be contained; it can therefore be thrown away when the course in the preparatory school has achieved its end.[2]

(8) INDIVIDUALITY

Sexual polarity also involves the existence of individuality; not the fact of being an individual, for this is given with the fact of being a self, but the fact of *being other*. In the Bible individuality is never a subject for consideration, but it is everywhere presupposed, and it is observed in a masterly manner. Individuality is part of creaturely bodily existence.

[1] Matt. 22: 30   [2] Eph. 5: 25 ff.

The ancient statement of the philosophers: *principium individuationis est materia,* is wrong, from the point of view of Biblical religion. *Principium individuationis est voluntas Dei creatoris.* God Himself gives to every human being his own face, as he created Adam as man and Eve as woman. As in sexual polarity, so also in the individual, "otherness" or the creaturely incompleteness of the individual is expressed. The richness of human existence cannot be known in any individual, it can only be seen in the fullness of individualities. And just as sex as a whole needs completion, so also does individuality. Because men are unlike they need one another. Individuality is the natural presupposition of community; the natural fact that we need each other, is, so to speak, the natural form of community. We need one another, hence we come together, and we work together. This fact is of immense importance for social ethics. Like androgyny, the equalitarian view is in harmony with rational thought; like sexual polarity the nonequalitarian view corresponds with Biblical thought. From the point of view of Biblical thought we have to take into account both facts: the differences between individuals and the similarity of men, due to their common humanity. As created in the Image of God all men are equal; created as individuals, they are unequal. The need for completion, due to inequality, is the natural form of that true community, of *agape* (ἀγάπη) which belongs to the truth that man has been made in the Image of God. These statements contain the characteristic principles of Christian social ethics.

(9) MAN'S DOMINION OVER NATURE

It is a very significant feature of the Old Testament Creation narrative that all other creatures are called into existence by the commanding word of the Lord, but man, as it were, by a divine decree: "Let us make man in our image, after our likeness." This clearly differentiates the creation of man from that of all the other creatures. It is not human arrogance to believe that he is the crown, the goal of creation. He is so— not only because he is the last in an ascending series, but because, by his very nature, he has been appointed for this. For in man alone can God truly glorify and communicate Himself, because here alone can His love be received by an answering love, because here alone can His Word be answered with a free response. It is foolish to imagine that the greatness of the universe is a counter-argument to this "childishly anthropocentric" way of thinking. What has a *quantum* to do with a *quale*! Man, who through his mind can think the universe, discover its laws, and estimate its extent, is greater than the universe. This Idealistic statement is not contradicted by the Bible; it only needs to be modified. The true greatness of man is not his reason, by which he learns to know, but it consists in the fact that he has been made for communion with God and his fellows. This includes the superiority of the Subject over the Object, but not the opposite.

Hence the fact that in the Creation Story man is represented as having been made to dominate the lower creation, should not be equated with the fact that he has been created in the Image of God—although this mistake is often made—but it should be conceived as its consequence. Because man, and man alone, has been created in the image of God, and for communion with the Creator, therefore he may and should make the earth subject to himself, and should have dominion over all other creatures. The call to create civilization which this involves is not indeed the essence of real humanity, but it is its necessary presupposition. Man is only capable of realizing his divine destiny when he rises above Nature and looks at it from a distance. The man who lives purely on the "natural" or instinctive level cannot lead a truly "human" life. Even the fact that he walks "upright" shows that he is called to this "elevated position". He is exalted above Nature in the fact that he *knows* it—the naming of the animals occurs in the J narrative—and that he *uses* it. Man has been called by God as *Homo faber*, and the creator of civilization, although this does not fully express his quality as man.

Man's decisive position above Nature, however, is attained in the fact that he does not worship it as divine. Man's distance from Nature presupposes that he knows God as the Creator of the World, as the One who stands above the whole creation. So long as man regards Nature as divine—(as is the case throughout the pagan world)—he is not really its master, he has not really risen above it, and he is also not really capable of being truly human. When, as is the case to-day, he falls back into the habit of treating Nature as divine, inevitably he will once more lose his humanity. On the other hand, how-ever, man also loses his true human quality when he believes that this consists in his mastery of Nature, in his civilization, or even in his technics. Civilization—in the broadest sense—

is no guarantee of "humanity" (*Menschlichkeit*). On the contrary, where it is not subject to a Higher Power, it becomes perverted into something inhuman.

This can be seen from the order of the statements about the *Imago Dei* and the mastery of Nature. The former *must* come first; the latter follows naturally from it. Man does not become human through culture and civilization. But civilization and culture become human when the man who creates them is truly human. The true human quality of man, however, is rooted in his relation to God, in the acceptance and realization of his destiny for love and for eternal life. When, instead of this, man seeks his supreme end in culture and civilization, and puts this in the place of God, and turns it into an absolute, the germ of inhumanity has been introduced into his life. A civilization and culture which has severed its connexion with God, and thinks more of achievement than of persons, necessarily becomes inhuman. It loses its true centre, and thus disintegrates into sectional spheres and sectional interests, each of which comes into conflict with the others, and tries to develop itself at the cost of the rest. True civilization and true culture can only develop where the cultural creation and activity is directed and ordered from a centre which transcends culture. A culture or civilization which is indifferent to morals and religion is bound to degenerate. Religion and morality, however, are identical, where the God of Holy Love is known as the foundation of all being, and His will as the norm of all morality; that is, where man knows himself to have been created by God for love, and for communion with the God of love, in faith in Jesus Christ.

Upon this foundation alone, also, will man use his mastery of Nature aright; only thus will he be preserved from a selfish, arrogant exploitation of Nature—which is a perversion of his powers. Man is not called to an absolute, arbitrary mastery of Nature, but to a mastery of Nature which remains under the order of the Creator, and therefore honours and loves the created universe as God's creation.

(10) THE QUESTION OF THE IMMORTALITY OF THE SOUL

Almost the whole of the Christian tradition in the realm of doctrine regards the immortality of the soul as the distinctive feature of man's being as created in the Image of God. Recently, on strongly Biblical grounds, the correctness of this view has been contested; it is now maintained, in vigorous terms, that the idea of immortality is derived from Platonism, and is not an element in Christian thought. In this question too we see how necessary it is to interpret the *Imago Dei* as *relation* and not as *substance*, as something which is part of man's nature. Then we can resolve the contradiction, which exists where the whole doctrinal tradition seems to be opposed to the witness of the Bible.

It is true that the doctrine of the immortality of the soul as a *substance*, is of Platonist, and not of Biblical origin. It is a result of the view that the human spirit is essentially "divine". But if we start from what God has given us in His self-revelation, this idea of an immortal soul is replaced by the truth of man's destiny for eternal communion with God. The essential destiny of man is not substantial immortality, but eternal life. This eternal destiny is, however, to this extent, part of the essential structure of man, in that what man is, can never be understood apart from his relation to this destiny. Man never ceases to be a being created for eternity, even when he misses his true destiny by turning away from God and from his eternal destiny. Just as man does not cease to be a responsible being when he sins, so too he does not cease to be a being destined for eternity.

Just as sin deprives man of true humanity, true responsibility, and the love of God, so also sin deprives him of that eternal life for which he has been destined. As a sinner he lives no longer in the love of God, but he comes under the divine wrath. This divine wrath, however, does not destroy his eternal destiny. In depriving himself of eternal life he brings upon himself eternal destruction. "Anyone with whom God speaks, whether in wrath or in mercy, the same is certainly immortal. The Person of God who speaks, and the Word, show that we are creatures with whom God wills to speak, right into eternity, and in an immortal manner" (Luther).[1] The future of man remains in the hands of the Creator; his eternity is not due to the indestructible character of his "soul-substance", but to the divine will. In Jesus Christ this will of God is manifested as destiny for eternity. The fact that this "destiny for eternity" cannot be lost is evidently of such a character that it is decided positively or negatively as faith or unbelief.[2]

[1] See *WA.*, 43, 481
[2] Further detailed discussion belongs to the realm of Eschatology; cf. Althaus, *Die letzten Dinge*, pp. 92–110

(II) NATURAL SELF-KNOWLEDGE IN THE LIGHT OF REVELATION

It is the nature of an "object" that its being is independent of what people think about it. Conversely, it is the nature of a "subject" that its being cannot be severed from its knowledge of itself, and what it wills itself to be. Since man is both object and subject, he is capable of misunderstanding himself, sometimes in one direction, and sometimes in the other. If man understands himself simply as an "object" among other objects, this misunderstanding leads to naturalism, and in extreme cases to materialism. If, on the other hand, man understands himself exclusively as "subject", then he falls into the error of Idealism, which leads in extreme instances to Theopanism, the theory of identity. If man does not understand himself in the light of his encounter with the living God, there is nothing left but to understand himself on one side or other of his nature—in both instances, however, in his own light, that is, not in that of his relation to the Creator.

The most primitive and in a certain sense the most modern conception of man is naturalistic, the self-understanding of man as a natural being among other natural beings, as an animal among animals. Primitive man makes no distinction between the world of nature by which he is surrounded and himself, thus he makes no distinction between animals and human beings. He believes himself to have animal ancestors, whom he reveres as his totem. Similarly the modern follower of Darwin regards man as a mere member of the series in the evolution of mammals. Man is "only" a more highly developed mammal. This view is, of course, not without a *fundamentum in re*; man *is* indeed actually to be found as an object through the observation of Nature, and as a living being very similar to the higher mammals, which is in genetic connexion with the animal world. This "objective" way of thinking, however, does not do justice to the fact that this view describes one side of man's nature only; because that which differentiates man from the animals is not something concrete which can be seen "objectively"—unless we think of the human spirit which finds "objective" expression in civilization—but a reality which is only perceived as the result of a process of thought.

It is true that the phenomenon of human culture (or civilization) is an objective entity, which clearly differentiates man from the animal creation; but this clear distinction, and indeed the whole significance of civilization, can, as experience shows us, be so interpreted, that man is not clearly differentiated from the animals, but only in some degree. Similarly, the anthropology of the present day based on natural science emphasizes the profound physical differences between human beings and animals;[1] but, again, these differences are of such a character that according to the way in which they are interpreted are only relative; they are differences of degree, not of principle.

It is not possible to convince a man who thinks in this "objective" way that his view is wrong. This will only become clear to him when he becomes aware of the fundamental difference between Object and Subject. When this has taken place, then he may incline to the opposite conception, that is, he may understand man from the point of view of a principle which does not appear in the vocabulary of a Naturalist—namely, as the bearer of "meaning" or "Logos" or "reason". It was Greek philosophy which first made this discovery—already adumbrated in the myth, and in art—and expressed it with intellectual clarity. It emphasizes the fact that man does what no animal can do: he speaks, he shapes significant forms, he enquires into the meaning of life, he asks: what is right? what ought man to do? He goes beyond what is required for his own life, and creates a spiritual world of his own. But when he reflects on the laws which govern this development, he finds that he does not create this spiritual world, but he discovers it. He perceives that the divine "Logos" is the foundation of his own spiritual life. He understands his spirit, his reason, as a share in the divine reason, and this share in the divine reason constitutes his true quality as man. Logically, the final result is to equate the human and the divine subject with one another. From this point of view, man as object, man as a physical creature with an animal nature, is only an unreal, illusory, unnatural human being. True humanity consists in setting the spirit free from its bondage to nature, in developing the purely spiritual man, shaping man in accordance with his identity with the divine principle of spirit.

Both these anthropologies, since man began to reflect upon himself, are in conflict with one another, and neither the one nor the other has been able to gain the victory. Both are right and both are wrong. It is true that the attempt is frequently made to find a synthesis—a synthesis which the non-reflective

[1] Cf. Portmann, *Biological Fragments for a Doctrine of Man*

man somehow always constructs, which he only states, however, as the "givenness" of both spirit and nature, reason and instinct, without being able to give the reason for or the root of this connexion. Where the attempt is made in the realm of thought it always ends in a system of compromise, which is unable to do justice either to the spiritual side of man's nature or to his natural side.

We are now in a position to say why this is so. From the standpoint of thought man is unable to limit his "spiritual nature", that is, to prevent himself from identification with the divine spirit, nor can he understand the fact that body and soul belong to each other. Both are only possible where man understands himself not in his own light, but in the light of the creating Living God, where he sees himself to be a "body-mind" being, a responsible creature of God, thus where his Self is not an independent entity derived from himself alone, but one which, in dependence upon God, and derived from Him, has a relative freedom, freedom understood as the freedom of responsibility. Thus his creaturely connexion with this body is not a degrading bondage to something foreign to his nature, but is a barrier of "creatureliness" which God Himself has established. Both Naturalism and Idealism are partial truths, and, as such, untruths, misunderstandings, which necessarily arise where man does not understand himself in the light of God, but tries to see himself in his own light.

From this standpoint then, we can understand the fact (already mentioned in an introductory way) that anthropology, the self-understanding of man, is and must be the real place for discussion between the Christian Faith and non-Christian thought. Pascal was the first to place this discussion between faith and unbelief in this sphere, in the Doctrine of Man. It was Søren Kierkegaard who placed his intellectual genius at the disposal of this discussion, and thus became the founder of the Existential Philosophy. It is the task of a genuine Christian science of "eristics" to carry this discussion a stage further. In the realm of theory it does what every true sermon does in its practical application to the individual hearer: it shows man, who cannot avoid desiring to understand himself, that he can only understand himself truly and realistically when he understands himself in the light of faith in the Creator revealed in Christ.

(12) MAN, CREATED BY GOD

From the standpoint of Jesus Christ, then, how can we conceive the man who has been created by God? All that we have been saying hitherto may be summarized in the following statements: In Jesus Christ we know ourselves to be creatures of God, who, in contrast to His other creatures, have been created not only *through* the Word, but *for* the Word and *in* the Word of God. We have been created as "body-soul" persons, whose personal being is based upon their responsibility, and whose responsibility is derived from the call of God. This call of God, however, is to be understood in the light of Jesus Christ, not as a purely categorical imperative or a moral law, but as the call of God to communion with Him the Creator, and through Him to communion with men. The true human quality which is due to this call of God is existence-in-love and is received in faith. The creation of God, true human existence, is an act of God, which can only be completed in the answering act of man. Man has been so created that he must answer, whether he will or no, either by responding to or reacting against the divine will of the Creator.

This "Either-Or", however, is not that of the divine Creation; it is only as a result of the wrong answer, which is the result of sin, that this "Either-Or" confronts us as an alternative. From the standpoint of the divine Creation freedom is not freedom of choice between two possibilities, but it is freedom in the love of God, the freedom of absolute dependence. Likewise the distinction between a formal-structural responsibility which cannot be lost, and the responsibility which finds its fulfilment—materially—in existence in love, is such that it can only be derived from the false decision, from sin.

In God's Creation man is created not only *for* love, but *in* the love of God, which fills his whole life. Original existence in the love of God, and its counterpart, existence for eternal life, is not a mere ideal, or a categorical imperative, but it is the God-created *nature* of man. When man decides against this divine destiny he is in opposition, not only to an ideal destiny, but also to his own nature, and this self-contradiction is now within himself. Man can, it is true, as an unbeliever and a sinner deny or misinterpret this contradiction but he cannot get rid of it. In the midst of sin, he has within himself, as his nature, the original divine creation, which he contradicts by his wrong choice, but which also is always in opposition to him who thus distorts the truth of his being.

This is the truth which lies behind the mythical idea of a Primitive State in Paradise. Jesus Christ, in the parable of the Prodigal Son, replaces this Paradise myth[1] by the simple idea that man was originally "at home" with the Father, from whom he separated himself, in false independence. The view that there was once an original historical Primitive State, in which man lived wholly obedient to the Creator's will, till through temptation from outside there arose in him the evil will, or false independence, and he "fell", and the Paradisal Primitive state came to an end—this mythico-historical conception, almost inevitably, is the form which expresses, whether we want it or not, the contrast between Creation and Sin. But faith is not concerned to preserve this "historizing" element as "historical fact". Wherever this became the theological tradition, from the time of Augustine onwards, and where theological emphasis is laid upon the "historicity of the Primitive State", not only does this cause a disastrous conflict with the scientific view of history, but it also gives rise to theological ideas which cause great confusion in the understanding of faith and sin. In the light of Jesus Christ there is not the least ground for this view, which treats the doctrine of Creation as an historical affirmation, any more than there is for the "historizing" conception of the Creation of the world to be regarded as "the *History* of Creation". The beginning of the world and the beginning of man, in the sense of the Creation, cannot possibly be measured by our chronological "this-world" standards. The contradiction between the Creation and Sin, fundamental and implicit in the Christian revelation, has no connexion with a statement of its empirical origins, nor should it be identified with a transcendental theory of origin and of empirical reality. However, both the true meaning of the statement about the Creation, and the danger which menaces it, of interpreting it either in the categories of empirical history, or of philosophical transcendentalism, can only become quite clear in connexion with the doctrine of Sin.

---

[1] The word "myth" is to be preferred (in spite of its ambiguity) to "legend" (which Barth suggests), because "legend" refers to historical fact

APPENDIX TO CHAPTER 2

(A) ON THE HISTORY OF THE DOCTRINE OF THE *IMAGO DEI*

FIRST of all, in contrast to the traditional doctrine of the Church, we must stress the difference between the conception of the *Imago Dei* in the Old Testament, and that of the New Testament. In the Old Testament the doctrine of the *Imago* is only mentioned three times in the Book of Genesis (Gen. 1: 26 ff., 5: 1, 9: 6) and in the Apocrypha, in the Book of Wisdom 2: 23, and in Ecclus. 17: 3. In the decisive passage, Gen. 1: 26, the idea is expressed by two words which are similar in meaning: *Tzelem* and *Demuth*. According to the latest lexicographical researches of Köhler (*Theol. Zeitschrift*, Basel, 1948, pp. 16 ff.) *Tzelem* means figure (or form) *statue*, and indeed suggests the upright position of man (but this is not proved). The passage should be translated thus: "We will make men in our form who look like us"; this "likeness", however, is to be understood as "mere likeness" and not as real similarity. Nevertheless, according to Köhler, there is here a suggestion of something which differentiates man from the rest of creation, and brings him "nearer to God". We must not assume, however, that the author of Genesis 1 regards the upright position as the one element which constitutes the uniqueness of man. To him it is a symbol of that which distinguishes man as a whole, and this again is understood as a certain likeness to God, even if it be remote.

The idea of Karl Barth, that this means the polarity of the sexes—that man has been created as "man and woman"—will scarcely find favour with exegetes, in spite of the brilliant way in which this idea is worked out (*Kirchl. Dogm.*, III, I, pp. 206 ff.), and the light that it throws upon the right understanding of the *Humanum* in man's relation to God. For, of course, we cannot understand the meaning of the *Imago* concept of Gen. 1: 26 by means of lexicographical considerations alone. The theme, we might even say the thesis, which it presents is not exhausted by the linguistic exposition. The thesis is this: that there is something which differentiates man, as God's creature, from the rest of the creation, and sets him apart, and that this distinctiveness is based upon a—certain, remote—similarity to God. The upright position, of which, according to Köhler, P is thinking, is certainly, even for him, only one element in that quality which distinguishes man from the rest of creation; in principle, it therefore includes everything which can be described as "specifically human". In whatever way the content of this *humanum* may be understood in greater detail—one thing is clear in the Old Testament: Something is meant which distinguishes man, always and for ever, which is not affected by the contrast between sin and faith. This formal structural idea of the *Imago* is also mentioned in two passages in the New Testament: 1 Cor. 11: 7 and Jas. 3: 9. Without the word being mentioned it is also suggested by Acts 17: 28.

This Old Testament formal concept of the *Imago* is contrasted with the material concept of the New Testament, which presents the content of the idea; this is explicitly suggested in Rom. 8: 29, 2 Cor. 3: 18, Eph. 4: 24 and Col. 3: 10. Implicitly, in addition we must reckon all that the New Testament says about being "like unto God" (or that we should, or may become or have become "like Him"). Here the word "likeness" means something which sinful man, by the very fact that he is a sinner, no longer possesses; which, however, is given back to him in the new life he receives from Jesus Christ. Thus here what is meant is not "human nature" as such, but the complete fulfilment of man's destiny; in the language of the present day this means: not the (formal) fact of being responsible (which we cannot lose), but the actual (material) fulfilment of responsibility, living in love (in the love of God), which is the same as being "in Christ", living as the "Children of God", etc.

So far as I know, Luther was the first, and the only person, to notice that there are these two fundamentally different conceptions of the *Imago* in the Bible; he defines the distinction as the *imago publica et privata* (*WA.*, 42, 51). Actually the Fathers and the medieval theologians did distinguish the two ideas, but from the point of view of exegesis they were mistaken in dividing them between the two words *Tzelem* and *Demuth* in Gen. 1: 26, whereas Luther understood these two expressions aright as an ordinary instance of Hebrew parallelism. The fact that the Bible actually contains a twofold conception: a formal one which concerns "structure", and a material one which concerns "content", was never clearly perceived by the theologians of both confessions; hence, on both sides their criticisms have been wide of the mark. In point of fact, if the "structural" idea of the *Imago* be meant, then the Protestant criticism that Catholics do not take the loss of the *Imago* seriously, is as unjustifiable as the opposite, namely, that if the "material" view is meant, the Catholic criticism, that Protestants make the sinner into an animal, over-shoots the mark.

From Irenaeus onwards, down to the present day, patristic theology, and later, scholastic theology, made a distinction between two conceptions of man's likeness to God: the one— related to *Tzelem* exegetically—pointing to man's natural endowment of reason, and the other—related to *Demuth*— that of his relation to God, which had been lost since the Fall. This might pass, at least as a reflection of the Old Testament (structural) and the New Testament (material) conception of the *Imago*. But, further from Irenaeus down to the present day, alongside of this twofold division, another dual distinction has been added, that of the "natural" and the "supernatural". The "structural" conception of the *Imago* is then identified with the "natural", and the "material" conception of Man's relation to God is equated with the "supernatural". The *similitudo—Demuth*—means the likeness to God which is effected by the Holy Ghost in man, in love, whereas the "structural-formal" conception—*Tzelem*—simply means man's natural endowment of reason.

The Reformers protested against this severance of ideas (and rightly), but on their side, they were not able to give a satisfactory explanation of the fact that even the human being who has become sinful still retains, to some extent, a certain likeness to God. In their embarrassment they took refuge in the idea of a "relic" of the *Imago*, thus regarding it as a purely quantitative entity; this fails to do justice to the qualitative distinction of the Old Testament concept, with its emphasis on structure, and to the material concept of the New Testament. Thus on the one hand—the Catholic— there is a clear distinction, which, however, leads to a dualism, and on the other—the Reformers'—side, there is a uniform idea of Man, which ignores the actual dualism of the Biblical concept of the Imago. Thus on the one hand there is the unfortunate distinction between a "natural" and a "supernatural" state of existence, and on the other the highly unsatisfactory idea of a "relic" of the Imago. This confronts us with the problem, which we are now trying to solve in our new formulation of the doctrine of the *Imago*. This is the solution I suggest: first of all, that the formal structural *Imago* does not consist in the possession of reason, or a "rational nature" existing in its own right (as it were), but in man's relation to God as responsibility (a relation which cannot be lost), as responsible personal being; secondly, that the existence of a merely formal responsibility, without its material fulfilment through the love of God, is the result of the Fall and of Sin.

The likeness to God which still remains—namely the structural—is thus, in fact, as the Reformers say, merely a "relic" of the original *Imago* in accordance with Creation, in which the merely structural element and the material element, that is, personal existence as (mere) responsibility, and personal existence as "being-in-the-love-of-God", are not separated, but are one. This original unity, however, is only restored through redemption by Christ. Thirdly, the merely structural likeness to God which now exists is closely connected with "standing under the Law"—that is, with the personality which is controlled by the sense of obligation—which can then be understood as the effect of the Fall.

In the Bible itself, as we have seen, there is no consideration of the fact that this distinction between the two conceptions of the *Imago* does exist, and yet that they are vitally connected. Catholic and Protestant theologians have indeed tried to retrieve this situation, but with little success; in this new formulation of the doctrine, however, both the dualistic development of the Catholic doctrine, and the merely quantitative grading of the two conceptions by the Reformers, have been overcome; the Old Testament and the New Testament conceptions of the *Imago* have been united in the idea of man's relation to God; at the same time, anthropology is related to the doctrine of the Law. The fact that this view has been attacked, and rejected, by both sides, was only to be expected. (For the Catholic side see J. Fehr, *Zweierlei Offenbarung, Offenbarung und Analogie, Offenbarung und Glaube*, all in *Divus Thomos*, 1936–38; for the Protestant side, see Karl Barth, *Nein, Antwort an E.B.*, as well as various observations in the *K.D.*, I and II; also Ed. Schlink, *Der Mensch in der Verkündigung der Kirche*.) But already, there are signs of a more considered view, cf. the Catholic tribute by Lorentz Volken: *Der Glaube bei E.B.*, and above all the appreciative references to my anthropology by Karl Barth, *K.D.*, III, 2, pp. 153 ff. which may be understood in a positive sense, since the question which he leaves open must obviously be answered in the affirmative.

(B) CHRISTIAN ANTHROPOLOGY IN RELATION TO NATURAL SCIENCE

I. Adam and the Theory of Evolution. The most important difference between the Biblical view of the world and the modern view given by the natural sciences is not associated with the names of Copernicus, Galileo, or Newton, but with that of Darwin. For the Bible, and for the whole of ecclesiastical theology down to the beginning of the nineteenth century, man was as old as the universe. Through the theory of Evolution man has become one of the latest forms of organic life, for the history of the earth had already been going on for more than a thousand million years, and the development of living creatures also occupied vast tracts of time. Man is one of the newest phenomena in the earth's history. Yet he too has behind him a history of something between one and ten million years. For the sake of making this vivid to ourselves, we might say that "the life of a man bears the same proportion to the age of the earth as a blink-of-an-eye to a month".

The earliest discoveries go back to the beginning of the Quaternary Epoch, but no further; thus they do not extend into the Tertiary period (cf. Weinert, *Die Entstehung der Menschenrassen,* 1941; Giseler, *Abstammungskunde des Menschen,* 1933). After the exciting discoveries of the Neanderthal, Heidelberg and Piltdown Man, as well as that of the Ape Man of Java, long and heated controversies took place, for or against the acceptance of these discoveries and the dating of these primitive forms of life. Since the discovery of the Peking Man (*Sinanthropus*) the question seems to have been decided, to this extent, at least, that it is agreed that the *Sinanthropus* was actually a human being of the early diluvial period and that the Java Ape Man was an ape-like creature on the verge of being human. This does not mean, of course, that the "descent of man from the ape" has become an established scientific truth. On the contrary, to-day, in the main, people seem to have abandoned this over-simplified view. The genealogy of man is so complicated that many scientists have ceased to try to solve these problems in a direct and simple way.

In whatever way this question will be answered—one thing can no longer be conceived as a mere hypothesis, but must be regarded as a proved scientific truth: that man has evolved out of the more primitive forms of animal life, even though this may not have taken place gradually, but by leaps and bounds. It is against this view that Christian theologians—very naturally—have reacted so violently. "Man cannot have descended" from the animal kingdom, his origin is peculiar to himself. It would have been wiser—before rushing into indignant denials—to have given some careful consideration to the exact meaning of words like "descend", "descended", "independence", etc.

Should it come to pass—and this does not seem so improbable to-day—that Palaeozoology should succeed in drawing up an exact genealogical table of *homo sapiens*, tracing his descent through the Neanderthal man, the Peking Man and the Ape Man of Java, to some mammalian form, whether that of apes or some other animals of the same type, what would this mean for the question: "Is man in principle different from the animals?" In any case, as soon as we are able to make a distinction between the question of the *humanum* and that of the *Zoon homo sapiens*, it cannot be answered in the negative. Whatever theory may be evolved, one thing is clear: the being *homo sapiens* is quite different from the *humanum*. The *humanum* is characterized by something which is entirely lacking in the animal, subjectively speaking by the mind (*Geist*), and objectively, by the creations of culture. The questions, where and how this new element arose, how the *humanum* entered into the evolutionary series (animal-man), is a quite different question from that of the physical relation between *homo sapiens* and the animal.

Whether the Java Ape Man (*Pithecanthropus*) already possessed the rudiments of the *humanum* we do not know. Perhaps we might assume that this was true of the Peking Man, since he was discovered with the remains of stone implements, and traces of fire. At present we have no idea at what point in the development of these beings between "man" and "the ape", the first beginning, however minute, of human mental activity took place, but this is not really very important. The point that matters most must be decided apart from all palaeontological and zoological questions, namely, that the *humanum* is, in itself, something which cannot possibly be derived from the animal kingdom, however modest its origin may have been, and therefore very difficult to distinguish from the animal. The development of the brain—even if we knew it fully—cannot give us an answer to this question. For we do not know—and never will know—what kind of brain is required to achieve the simplest human act, in contrast to the acts of animals. The human act is that which cannot be explained from vitalistic motives alone; a *human* act desires to achieve something mental for its own sake, something beautiful for the sake of its beauty, something good for the sake of its goodness, something true on account of its truth, something holy for the sake of its holiness. No animal reveres its dead. Where there is reverence for the dead, there already the *humanum* is present—whether we find it in the Ape Man of Java, or in the Peking Man. Where men decorate an object, there is the *humanum*—it does not matter what the object is that is thus decorated. There is no point in opening up a wide gulf between the species *homo* and the animal kingdom; but there is every reason to recognize the unfathomable gulf which exists between *animalitas* and *humanitas*: *animalitas* here denotes a form of existence which achieves no personal acts at all, but merely acts of self-preservation and the preservation of the species; *humanitas* means, however, that in which—even if at first in a very rudimentary way—something personal, something which transcends *animalitas*, is achieved. Once this truth has been perceived, we can watch the further development of the theory of physical descent with the utmost indifference, and we shall not be in the least disturbed by any theories or hypotheses which may be put forward. The whole problem is not one of zoology, but simply of logic, and it is quite independent of the results of natural science, whether of the past or of the future. The whole storm raised by "Darwinism" is based upon the confusion of two questions, upon a logical error, namely, the question of the descent of *homo sapiens*, and that of the nature and the origin of the *humanum*. Even if man is descended from the animal world, as *humanus* he is something wholly new, not only in contrast to the ape, but over against the whole of Nature.

But there is still another point to be considered. The *humanum*, in its distinctiveness, is not understood in the light of its primitive origins, but in that of its highest achievements. We learn to understand art not by studying the works of primitive man, but that of the great masters like Pheidias, Mozart, and Titian. Only when we have seen the fully developed forms and acts which betray the presence of mind, are we in a position to enquire into questions of origin. And then, as so frequently happens—if not always—when zoologists touch these questions, mind and the psychical element, instinct and will, are confused with one another. What is wanting is not facts but the *exercitium logicum*. Lotze (*Kosmos*) and Max Scheler (*Der Mensch im Kosmos*) have written excellently on this subject, and they have not been surpassed; only unfortunately zoologists are rarely willing to learn from philosophers.

A good preparation for the distinction between the *humanum* and the animal is the study of animal psychology, since this shows very plainly the impassable gulf which exists between the typical acts of human beings and of animals (cf. Katz, *Die Seele der Tiere*; Uexküll, *Lebenslehre*; and among older writers Wundt, *Menschen und Tierseele*). Only in pursuing these studies we must not forget that they do not solve the problem. In the "human" sense, what is a "human being", and what is a "mere animal", is independent of the question: in which zoological species do we find the one or the other? It is a fact that the studies devoted to the psychology of animals hitherto do not betray the slightest traces of the presence of the specifically "human", even in its most rudimentary form. But this does not prove that possibly among other animals, for instance among the ancestors of man, such traces might not be found. Then human history would date from those animals. Yet the opposite is more probable: that there was a series of human forms, in the zoological sense, in which there was not yet any trace of the *humanum*.

"Adam", however, in the meaning of Christian theology, is the unity of humanity, not in the zoological sense, but in the sense of *humanitas*. Whether it includes the Neanderthal Man we do not know for certain. But that it includes human beings of the late diluvial period is proved by the discoveries of the rudiments of characteristically human civilization. These human beings are "Adam", like every one of us; only, like the infant, they are human in a less developed form. The fact that St. Augustine would ascribe sin to the suckling child, in order to support his doctrine of Original Sin, is based upon a confusion of ideas, upon the same error which led him to the false interpretation of Romans 5: 12. But if we once take up our position on the basis of the story of Adam, then the conception of Irenaeus—that Adam was man in the stage of childhood—is more correct than that of St. Augustine, which even the Reformers adopted as their own. It can also be supported by St. Paul's words in 1 Cor. 15: 45.

II. Personality, the Brain, and Heredity. In modern science two facts constantly raise difficulties for faith: the fact that the mental and psychical powers of man are conditioned by the brain, and the influence of heredity on the individual. How can Christian Personalism be combined with these two elements of exact scientific knowledge?

(i) *The Central Nervous System and the Unity of Personality.* If "that which is called 'soul' is not a being at all but something which merely exhausts itself in flowing processes" (Wundt), if it is only a mass of brain functions and the mechanical work of the ganglion cells (Haeckel), what meaning is left for what the Christian Faith has to say about the "person"?

Here, if anywhere, it is absolutely essential to keep facts and theories separate. Modern study of the central nervous system and of the brain has brought a mass of facts to the light of day which all point to one conclusion: that man's mental powers are conditioned by physiological processes and anatomical conditions. To-day we know precisely how lesions of certain parts of the brain cause definite loss or deficiency of mental functions. We know that certain chemicals introduced into the body cause definite changes in the mental characteristics, or cause unconsciousness. "Recently a medical remedy has been found against examination fever", and "medicines which change the character" (Bavink, *op. cit.*, p. 466). These facts, at least in their main features, have been made available to the layman or non-specialist through works like the large book by Titius (*Gott und Natur*, pp. 562–613), which on this point is far more detailed than Bavink.

But when we turn to the question of the *interpretation* of these facts, we are plunged into an ocean of confusing theories, ranging from the grossest materialism to an animism which sees "spirit" everywhere. In addition to the facts which show how the mind is conditioned by physical changes and states, there is also the opposite: the fact that the body is affected by the mind, from the familiar phenomena of blushing or palpitations, with which everyone is acquainted, to facts which border on the occult—suggestion, auto-suggestion, and hypnosis. Psycho-analysis has called our attention to the fact that there are physical illnesses and disabilities which are due to mental conflicts and repressions, which vanish when these repressive conflicts are brought to the level of consciousness. "Para-psychology", (or the study of the Occult as a science) which is gradually being taken seriously by science, confronts us with relations between mental and physical processes which seem quite inexplicable. A brain specialist with a world reputation like the late Zürich scholar C. von Monakow, has outlined, on the basis of his formidable empirical material, a daring theory: *Syneidesis, das biologische Gewissen* (*Schweiz. Archiv. fur Neurologie u. Psychiatrie*, Bd. XX, 1927).

The great physician K. L. Schleich describes the gradual conquest of the mental sphere by narcotics. "Only with the cessation of all imagination and all logical ideas, perhaps at the tenth remove, does the Self become submerged in the ocean of forgetfulness" (Titius, *loc. cit.*, p. 611). With his scientific discoveries he links daring theories on the relation between body and mind (*Bewusstsein und Unsterblichkeit*). A Zürich brain specialist and psychiatrist, E. Frey, writes about "the human conscience, according to F. M. Dostoevsky and C. von Monakow, and in the light of the study of deep analysis" (*Schweiz. Archiv. fur Neurologie*, Bd. LVII, 2, 1946). On all this I would only say one thing: Research is going on, but it is still in a very fluid condition, and at present there are no established results. All the philosophical theories which have appeared in the course of history, and have dealt with the relation between body and soul, are still represented to-day: e.g. the materialistic view, which holds that the mental and spiritual faculties are derived from the physical; psycho-physical parallelism, which regards the two spheres as independent of one another, but regards both as of equal interest, like two clocks which run the same course without affecting each other at all, the theory of mutual influence, which is at the same time that of "sound common-sense", which everyone follows in practice; the pan-psychical, which conceives all that happens to be ultimately psychical in character, or the theory which conceives everything material as a pure projection of the mind. Each theory thrives on the inadequacy of the others. This is true, most of all, of the materialistic view, which is in itself the most contrary to ordinary common sense, and the most impossible from the point of view of philosophy, but which can point to facts which other theories cannot explain.

One point, however, is quite clear, and cannot be contested: all these ideas are observations and theories which the Self initiates, which the thinking Self shapes and alters, estimates logically, verifies, corrects, accepts or rejects. Apart from the unity of the Self there would be no unity of theory, nor indeed of experiment and observation—apart from the validity of the

laws of logic—which are not causal laws—no scientific statement could claim any validity. Without the freedom with
which the Self examines and ponders, in a critical way, not
only the various observations and hypotheses which it meets,
but also the deductions and theoretical constructions drawn
from them, there would be no progress in Science at all. And
without the strictly scientific ethos, which constrains the man
of science to subordinate all his personal interests to that of
the Truth, there would be no scientific progress.

Whatever the relation between the brain and the mind may
be, one thing is certain: all these relations are established by the
mind, and have a spiritual or intellectual significance, whereas
as processes in the brain they are absolutely unknown and
unintelligible. Brain processes are movements in space—
possibly ultimately electro-magnetic processes, "packets of
waves (or *'quanta'*)", to use Schrödinger's phrase; but whether
they are movements of particles or of waves, a unity, such as
each thought, or theory, presupposes, does not exist in space,
whether true or false. The brain, whatever its relation to the
mind may be, cannot be compared with the mind. The brain
serves the mind, perhaps it even tyrannizes over it; but in no
case is it the mind. We can look calmly forward to the further
developments in scientific research in this mysterious region.
What we now know of the Self, and what man has always
known about himself, and what we as Christians know about
the nature of personality, will never be overthrown by any
physiological theory of the brain.

(*ii*) *Heredity*. The fact of the inheritance of physical and
mental characteristics has long been known to mankind. But
this truth has been greatly extended and deepened by the progress of recent research; above all it has gained a precision and
a reliability which makes it almost impossible to compare it
with our previous popular knowledge. Above all, it was the
discovery of definite laws of inheritance by Father Gregor
Mendel, an Augustinian monk, which raised the scientific study
of heredity almost to the rank of an exact science. It is, of
course, true that in this field of research biologists have had
to confine their efforts to those living creatures which were
available for such experiments. In this connexion the fruit-fly
(*Drosophila melanogaster*) occupies a unique position—almost
a monopoly. For the discovery of the laws of inheritance two
further points were of fundamental importance: the discovery
of the *chromosomes* which pass on the stuff contained in the

original nucleus, and that of the still smaller bodies known as *genes*, which transmit particular characteristics.

Through a highly developed system of experiment the Mendelian laws of inheritance have been confirmed, all along the line, and the research into the nature of the *genes* has enabled us to observe the processes of inheritance still more closely. What does all this mean for man?

For the study of the facts of heredity in man the most important means of research, the experiment, almost entirely disappears. In its place there appear: on the one hand, statistics, the hypothetical application of the results of research in empirical genetics to man; on the other hand, as a kind of substitute for experiment, there is the observation of the phenomenon of twins.[1] Statistics have practically established the validity of the Mendelian laws of inheritance for man first of all in the sphere of the physical constitution, and physical diseases, that is, in tendencies to disease. The exact study of the laws which govern the human "mechanics of development" —the development of the cell which has been fertilized—shows a far-reaching agreement between human and animal development, which seems to admit the possibility of the application of experimental genetics to man. All this suggests that the human individual is largely determined by his physical inheritance.

This applies first of all to the sphere of man's physical constitution. Now, however, on its part, the statistical study of the human constitution has shown that, to a large extent, the mental nature of man is largely determined by his physical constitution. Further, statistics of mental diseases and their heredity point to the possibility of the inheritance of mental qualities. According to the statistical results of research by Rüdin, "in a marriage between two manic-depressives, on the average two-thirds of the children inherit the same tendency", and in "the marriage of two schizophrenics more than half have children of the same kind" (quoted by Bavink, *loc. cit.*, p. 623); this shows—together with the more precise working out of further statistical results—the immense influence of the laws of inheritance, even in the sphere of the human mind. The study of twins from one ovum leads to similar results.

[1] I.e. "Stimulation can sometimes be performed parthenogenetically. If an *ovum* divides by falling into halves, it forms 'identical twins'; if two ova are fertilized simultaneously, 'fraternal twins' result' who are no more alike than other children of the same parents" (cf. Dampier, *A Shorter History of Science*, p. 131 (TR.)

The fact that intellectual endowment, in the broadest sense of the word, rests upon inheritance, and depends very little upon environment, has long been known, but now it has been proved up to the hilt; it is this truth indeed which lies behind the words "gifted", or "talented". More important, and more or less new, and certainly rather depressing, is the truth that emerges from the study of twins, that even criminal tendencies are to a large ex:ent a matter of heredity, and this is the negative aspect of being "gifted" (cf. the conclusions in the book entitled *Verbrechen als Schicksal*, by the Breslau psychiatrist Lange, 1929, quoted by Bavink, *loc. cit.*, p. 631). "Of 13 cases of 'identical twins', in 10 cases both partners were punished, and indeed for the same offences; of the 'fraternal twins' on the other hand, only in two cases did both partners fall into the hands of the Law, and then for dissimilar offences". "Thus in the majority of instances the criminal is born and not made" (Bavink, p. 631).

All these facts must be taken into account, if we aim at the truth about man. But they do not constitute this truth itself. At bottom they do not tell us any more than we have always known. Thus if in spite of this knowledge people do not cease to believe in a certain freedom of self-determination, and if the Christian Faith makes responsibility the heart of human personal existence, all this means that these facts do not touch the ultimate central, secret, heart of human personal existence. Inherited tendencies are firstly, not *qualities*, but, rather, dispositions of a particular kind; and qualities are not the person, but simply an endowment given with the person, an inner sphere of action, but not the actual agent himself. Even the criminal with a heavy burden of heredity does not cease to regard himself as a responsible active personality, and to admit personal guilt, where a superficial view would only see it as Fate or Destiny.

Evidence of the psychiatric objective kind needs to be compared with the testimony of prison chaplains, who show in a most impressive way that Christian personalism is true, and have proved that in the extreme darkness of criminal life, due to a bad inheritance, the light of divine grace does break through, and the miracle of the New Birth does take place. The human person cannot be treated as a *thing*, as an "object". Its secret cannot be attained by statistics or by any scientific descriptions. All that science, statistics, and analysis of all kinds can attain, ultimately only deals with the outer garments of personality, not with its heart—certainly a garment which, like the body, belongs to us, which we rightly describe in our language as "belonging" to us, but not as the Self. The many layers of this outer garment will doubtless be further studied and analysed; but the heart of the personality always eludes observation; this is the Self which cannot be made into an object, and then analysed in the effort to "explain" it. The personality is truly disclosed to God alone.

CHAPTER 3

MAN AS SINNER

(I) THE TASK

As the message of redemption is the centre of the Biblical message so also it contains, as a negative presupposition, the knowledge of sin. In the Bible "sin" does not mean something moral, but it denotes man's need of redemption, the state of the "natural man", seen in the light of his divine destiny. Just as man can only be understood in the light of the divine Creation, so also sin can only be rightly understood in the light of the Christian revelation. Here too we must make a clear distinction between the fact itself and the light in which it is perceived. We can only see what sin is, what man is as sinner, in the light of the Christian revelation, which effects the transition from the state of "being-a-sinner" to that of "being redeemed"; here, however, we are not dealing with *this* change, because we are not thinking (at the moment) of the justified sinner, but of the sinner in need of redemption. Only thus can we go further, and understand that "justification" is both a divine gift and a new creation. We are here concerned with the sinner as he is before the process of justification, even though we can only understand this truth because we have already been "justified", so that in its light we can see what man is without this light.

Here once more we take our stand on the theological principle that we must start from the witness of the New Testament, and not from that of the Old. There is perhaps no part of the Old Testament which impresses us so directly as a divine revelation as the story of the Fall in Gen. 3. We can never brood long enough over this marvellous story, in order to learn what sin is. In spite of this, however, we are not tied to this narrative, and we must not make it our starting-point, any more than when we were considering the Doctrine of Creation we had to start from the idea of the "Six Days" of Creation. In principle we learn what sin is and what the Fall means, from the *New* Testament; not first of all from the Old Testament narrative, which, like the whole story of Adam, implies a view of time and space which has passed away, and therefore cannot be utilized without falsifying the whole of our present view of time and space. If we take our stand on the principle that Christ, the Incarnate Word of God, is the *principium cognoscendi* of the whole work of dogmatics, then in our understanding of Sin and the Fall—regardless of the whole question of the scientific view of the universe—we are quite naturally set free from bondage to the Old Testament narrative, without having to abandon any truth we can learn from it. Two things will then become evident: (*a*) that the narrative contained in the third chapter of Genesis has had very little influence upon the *doctrine* of Sin in the Bible—whether in the Old Testament or the New; (*b*) that so many of the intellectual and theological difficulties connected with this question have been caused—inevitably—by its mistaken relation with the myth-narrative in Genesis.

On the other hand, only when we accept this strictly Christocentric basis of the doctrine of the Fall, do we see what a mistake it is to think that because the concept of the Fall is traditionally connected with this myth, we must therefore renounce this concept itself; we also see that this renunciation has had a most disastrous effect on Christian doctrine as a whole. Apart from the doctrine of the Fall it is impossible to understand Sin as the presupposition of the New Testament message of Redemption. Only a *fallen* humanity needs a Redeemer. The statements of the New Testament only apply to a fallen humanity; for these statements describe the human situation before, and apart from, the redeeming Act of Jesus Christ. Every conception of Sin which tries to establish itself without this mythical idea of a Fall, proves, on closer examination, to be an optimistic re-interpretation of the actual fact of sin, which makes sin either a fact of nature, or merely the moral concern of the individual.

(2) SIN AS REBELLION

Even if we had never heard of the *story* of the Fall of Man, and if we could leave out the few passages in the Bible in which reference is made to this narrative, still the truth would dawn upon us that sin is apostasy, rebellion. The story of the Fall is nowhere else mentioned in the whole of the Old Testament, and in the whole of the New Testament it is only mentioned twice: in Rom. 5: 12 ff. where it is dealt with in detail, and in an impressive theological manner, and in 1 Tim. 2: 14, where it

is only mentioned casually, without any theological explanation. On the other hand, in many passages in the Bible we
come upon the idea that sin is a "falling-away" from God, or
rebellion. At the basis of this conception of sin there is always
the idea of an event which *reversed* something. What this
means comes out most clearly by way of contrast.

The conception of sin in Greek philosophy, which accom-
panies the whole of the development of Western thought, and
to a large extent influences it, is this: that evil is due to the
life of the senses; that is, it is based upon the fact that the
sense instincts of man paralyse the will, or at least hinder or
suppress it. Evil is thus due to the dual nature of man; it
springs, from the outset, from his twofold constitution. It
is indeed the fault of the spirit that it cannot master the
natural instincts, that it cannot bring them under better
control, that the higher element in man proves too weak to
keep the lower element in hand; but evil itself *is* this "lower"
element, the natural "double" of the spirit. If this evil is to be
brought into relation to time it has to be described as that which
is "not yet good", or has "not yet reached the plane of spirit",
or is "not yet" dominated by spirit.

The Biblical view of sin, however, replaces the phrase "not
yet" by "no longer". Sin is not the primary phenomenon, it
is not the beginning, but it is a turning-away from the beginning, the abandonment of the origin, the break with that which
God had given and established. Wherever the Prophets reproach
Israel for its sin, this is the decisive conception: "You have
fallen away, you have strayed, you have been unfaithful.
You have forsaken God; you have broken the Covenant, you
have left Him for other gods. You have turned your backs
upon Him!" Similarly, the Parables of Jesus speak of sin as
rebellion, as leaving God. The Prodigal Son leaves home,
goes away from the Father, turns his back upon him. The
Wicked Husbandmen usurp the master's rights and wrongly
seize the land which they only held on a rental. They are
actually rebels, usurpers. The Lost Sheep has strayed away
from the flock and from the Shepherd; it has gone astray. We
might of course reply that here there is always the presupposition of an historical covenant which had been made between
God and His people, and that the "falling away" really refers
to this historical beginning, and therefore applies to Israel
alone.

This view is so far correct in that the prophetic summons

to repentance does apply to Israel first of all, and even Jesus is primarily appealing to the people of Israel. But behind all this lies the view that the situation is the same for all other peoples, excepting that possibly their guilt is less, because, in point of fact, they have never known God in the way that Israel has known Him. Hence it is not surprising that in the passage where Paul proclaims his own doctrine of the Fall (Rom. 1: 19 ff.) without mentioning the well-known story of the Fall he describes the Fall of all men as a kind of blasphemy, an act in which that which belongs to God is given to others; nor is it surprising that (equally without reference to Gen. 3) he takes an Old Testament statement and intensifies it, in order to express the truth that the "mind" of the flesh is enmity against God.[1] Sin is apostasy, rebellion, because it is not the primary element, but the reversal of the primary element. The primary element is the creation in the Word of God, but the second is the contradiction of this creation. Sin is not a "not yet", but a "no longer". Therefore it is not sensuality, nor weakness, but defiance, rebellion.

(3) SIN AS APOSTASY

Almost all non-Biblical definitions of sin—if not all—are impersonal. Evil is "something". It is a part of our being, of our nature, or it is a negatively moral act—that is, a non-moral act, an injury committed by something or someone. It may be the transgression of a law. But in any case it is not directly, and above all not exclusively, related to God. "Against Thee, Thee only have I sinned"[2]—that is the essential, and the exclusive view of the Bible. It is thus that sin is described in the story of the Fall. Sin is disobedience to God, and is due to distrust. Evil, understood as sin, is a change in man's relation to God: it is the break in communion with God, due to distrust and defiance. The story of the Fall reveals the fundamental cause for this breach in communion: the desire to be "as God". Man wants to be on a level with God, and in so doing to become independent of Him.

Sin is like a fire which is kindled by the divine destiny of man. Actually, man's divine destiny means being "like God", freedom. Man is intended to be free, to be like God; but now man wants to have both apart from dependence upon God.

[1] Rom. 8: 7; Gen. 6: 5   [2] Ps. 51: 4

The deepest root of sin therefore is not the senses—they are, at most, occasions of sin—but the spiritual defiance of one who understands freedom as independence, and thus only regards himself as free when he "feels that he owes his existence to himself alone" (Marx). Sin is emancipation from God, giving up the attitude of dependence, in order to try to win full independence, which makes man equal with God. The nature of sin is shown by Jesus in the son who asks his father for his inheritance in order that he may leave home and become "independent".

Certainly, not everyone who sins is aware of this deepest motive. The ordinary man, and man in general, is not capable of such depths. This does not alter the fact, however, that this is the hidden root of what he does when he sins, although he is not aware of it. His sin is deeper than his awareness of it. The deepest wish that he has is deeper than his consciousness. He needs the revelation of Christ, and the knowledge which this gives of his divine destiny in creation, in order to be able to perceive this falling away from his true destiny; for the real heart of the question lies here: in man's falling away from God. In Jesus' parable the sinner is the rebellious husbandman, who plays the part of the owner, who thus denies his responsibility in order to gain for himself complete, unconditional freedom.[1] Sin is throwing off restraint, denial of responsibility, hence emancipation from that which makes us responsible, in whose Word we have both our freedom and our bondage. Sin is the desire for the autonomy of man, therefore, in the last resort, it is the denial of God and self-deification: it is getting rid of the Lord God, and the proclamation of self-sovereignty. The Θεὸς παντοκράτωρ is replaced by Ἐγώ αὐτοκράτωρ. Hence it is "enmity against God".[2]

(4) SIN AS A "TOTAL ACT"

When we regard sin—in the light of the divine destiny shown us in Christ—as the effort to achieve absolute freedom, this implies that we are here concerned with a decisive act, which determines the whole of existence. Sin then means the creation of a whole new conception of life, a new "state" of life. It means that man declares his whole existence to be "free"; the whole man shakes off all the bonds which tie him to God. The son severs his relation with his father, and "stands upon

[1] Matt. 21: 33 ff.   [2] Rom. 8: 7

his own feet"![1] The meaning of sin, by its very nature, affects the whole, because it aims at making the whole man "free". Once more we must make a distinction between the psychological and the concrete aspects. This totality, which is of the essence of sin, is rarely conscious, just as in a political revolution most of the revolutionaries are not altogether clear about what is going on. But the fact remains: it is with this total aspect that we are concerned; this is the meaning of sin.

That is one point: the *Telos* of sin is totality. But the other point is this: the *Origin* of sin. Sin is the total act of the person. This again we can see most plainly when we look at the opposite. The non-Christian understanding of sin is characterized by its partial nature. The "lower part" of man: the senses, the instincts—that is, not the whole man, the person, is made responsible for evil. This is particularly true where individual manifestations of evil are concerned. They are regarded as derived from some partial tendency or another, from some "qualities" or tendencies, from certain instincts. Evil has been disintegrated; it is no longer a whole.

We do not deny that this conception contains some elements of truth; we shall be returning later on to this aspect of individual, localized sin. First of all, however, we must establish the fact that just because we are here concerned with the *telos* of the whole person, the whole person must take responsibility. It is as a whole that the person *commits* sin; this is not due to some part of the personality. *I* am a sinner, not this or that aspect of my nature. Sin is falling away from God, therefore it is the act of the whole man. Again, this totality can only be perceived in the light of the revealed destiny of man through the divine Creation. Only from that point of view can man understand himself as a whole person, only from that standpoint does he see himself as a whole, as a unity of body, mind and spirit. The organ of the whole personality (seen as body-mind) is, as we have already seen, the heart. Hence sin comes from the heart. The *heart* of man is evil. Sin has its seat in the heart of man.[2] It is the Headquarters of the General Staff, not the office of some lesser official, it is the summit of the personality, the Self, which rebels against the Lord. The psychological, partial aspects of sin have a right to be considered separately, but this is only justified after the

[1] Cf. the work of André Gide entitled *L'enfant prodigue*, in which he re-tells the Parable of the Prodigal Son in the opposite sense: The son was quite right to sever his relation with his father, in order to become independent
[2] Matt. 5: 18 ff.; Rom. 1: 21; Acts 5: 3; Eph. 4: 18

whole has been recognized. The whole is before the parts. The whole man rebels against God, *ego totus*, and in this rebellion all the individual powers of his body-mind economy are mobilized.

At this point it is instructive to look at Kant's theory of Radical Evil,[1] not because it is in complete agreement with the Christian view, but because it shows how an exact and unprejudiced analysis of evil comes very near to the Christian truth. Here—as elsewhere—Kant rejects the explanation of evil as due to man's nature as a ᷓense-determined being. Evil does not consist in the fact that sense impulses are present but in the fact that man makes these into "maxims of his conduct", by absorbing them into his will. The sense impulses as such are not evil. They only become evil when man allows himself to come under their control, when he surrenders to temptation, or rather, when he goes over to the Tempter. Hence, according to Kant, evil is the act of the whole man, that is, it is an act of the person. This is why Kant speaks of the "evil heart". "This evil is radical because it destroys the basis of all maxims".[2] Kant is able to conceive evil in its personal unity, because he understands man as a unified personality. He is able to do so, without starting from the Christian revelation, because, and in so far as, he starts from the idea of the divine Law; as soon as the idea of the divine Law gives place to the law of Reason, as soon as he once more regards the person as autonomous, as a self-legislator, then he also loses the view of radical evil.[3] This oscillation in Kant's thought is due to the fact that he connects the person and the freedom of man with the divine Law and not with the divine Revelation. The law is ambiguous, for it can be interpreted sometimes from the aspect of theonomy, and sometimes from that of autonomy, and for this reason the depths of evil cannot be perceived. The ultimate depth of radical evil has remained hidden from Kant. It is true that he comes as far as the statement: *ego totus*. It is true that he recognizes empirically a *nos toti*, but the unity of both has remained hidden from him. It can only be perceived from the standpoint of Christ.

(5) SIN AS UNIVERSAL

It is not very difficult to admit that "all men are sinners". We find statements of this kind everywhere, even in pre-Christian

---

[1] *Die Religion innerhalb der Grenzen der blossen Vernunft*, Pt. I
[2] *Ibid.*, p. 37 (Reclam.)   [3] *Ibid.*, pp. 47 ff.

paganism. The phrase of Horace *vitiis nemo sine nascitur* has several parallels. The universality of sin as a numerical totality, as *nos toti*, is far more acceptable than a theory of Radical Evil, in the sense just outlined. Yes, we can even go a step further, without meeting very serious opposition: Evil which individuals commit, forms a whole, a "kingdom of evil" (Ritschl). Even a complete Pelagian like Ritschl made this statement and commented on it with much seriousness and acuteness. Indeed experience shows us daily how evil "infects" society, spreading from one person to another, and perhaps involving them in it against their will. The power of the "infection" is as great in the moral sphere as it is in physical epidemics. We ought to be aware of the fact—and to remind others of it—that evil spreads to institutions and conditions, "infects" them, and then breeds further evil, which, in turn "re-infects" the lives of human beings as individuals. Further, it is evident that the evil which is incorporated in social institutions, and the evil which becomes a mass phenomenon, waxes great and assumes demonic forms, which, as a rule, are not found in any individual evil. Evil which takes the shape of social wrong, or is incorporated in institutions, or as a mass phenomenon, is worse than evil in any individual form, in isolation. All this may be summed up in the idea of a "kingdom of evil"; in saying this we acknowledge our debt to Ritschl's contribution to our thought. But all this does not yet lead us into the mystery of the Biblical idea of the *solidarity* of sin. This conception is strictly connected with the truth of the Christian revelation.[1]

It is only through the Christian revelation that, as we have seen, the individual can be perceived, in the full sense, as an individual *person*. "I", the individual, stand before God, "I", the individual, must believe. "I", the individual, am summoned by God to decision. But this is only one aspect of the truth. The other is this: that before God we men are all one in Christ: "Adam", Man. Sin is not only something which affects us all in the same way, but it is something which concerns us all as a whole. The one divine revelation in Jesus Christ, in which we become aware of our divine destiny in the Creation, reveals our human sin to each of us in the very same way; we are each aware of the sin of humanity, as a whole. In the Presence of Christ we cease to particularize sin and to

[1] It is accordingly only hinted at in the Old Testament. Cf. Eichrodt: *Theol. d. A.T*, I, pp. 200 ff., III, pp. 90 ff.

apportion to each his share in the blame for sin. In Jesus Christ we see that this individualizing calculation of sin is Pharisaism, and therefore a lie.

It is *I* who brought Christ to the Cross. He died for me.

> "Thy grief and bitter Passion
> Were all for sinners' gain;
> Mine, mine was the transgression,
> But Thine the deadly pain."

This is what "I" know when I stand before Christ. And since I know it about "myself", I know that it is true of everyone else who stands before Christ. It was in order to show this, or rather in order to show how Jesus Christ is the Redeemer of the whole of mankind that Paul went back to the story of the Fall[1]—once, and not again. He did so in order to say this one thing, in the language which enabled him to say it most plainly. As in Jesus Christ all have been redeemed, so in Adam all have sinned. Adam is the τύπος τοῦ μέλλοντος. The same universality, which in the one Christ includes all men, includes all men in the one Adam. Before Christ we are one indivisible humanity. The act of rebellion which I see in Christ as my sin, I see there as the identical act of all. All particularization and calculation is impossible. This act *is* the same; it is not only similar, but identical. Here we stand before a mystery we cannot fully understand—at least not intellectually; a mystery, however, which is a mystery of *faith* for every one who stands before Jesus Christ as his Lord and Saviour. It is thus and not otherwise, in this solidarity in sin, that we men stand before Him.

We are allowed, and indeed commanded, to do what we can to throw light upon this mystery; but we cannot penetrate to its heart. Thus with Kierkegaard we may say, it is part of the nature of man, that each of us is both "the individual" and humanity.[2] We can relate this thought of Kierkegaard still more clearly (as he does himself) to the divine destiny in Creation, which is the same for all men, in spite of the fact that God creates each individual as a distinct person. Our true *humanitas* is based on the Word of God—the same for all. Hence we can say that whatever concerns one human being, concerns all, that in one human being the whole of humanity is disgraced. We can go further, and say that the destiny for which each of us was created includes as its τέλος

[1] Rom. 5: 12   [2] *Der Begriff der Angst* § (1)

the fellowship of all—each of us is destined for the Kingdom of God, not only for an individual divine *Telos*—and, therefore, the fact that I am a sinner concerns everyone else. Hence it is true of man not only in the positive sense, but also in the negative, that *unum noris omnes*, so that our knowledge of the fact that all men are sinners is not primarily the result of a comprehensive enquiry, but is an *a priori* truth. All this, however, does not constitute a complete explanation of the statement of faith about the unity of "Adam" in sin.

We can go further and consider the notion of the collective unconscious of modern psychology, and thus make it clear that the individual person is not merely an individual person but is connected in the depths of personality with the soul of every other person; moreover each person is like a solitary lake with an outlet to a common ocean, so that both our divine destiny and our sin are both personal and universal, both our responsible act, and our common destiny. This idea of the "collective unconscious" helps us to explain a great many elements in the mental life of the individual, from the psychological point of view, which would otherwise remain unintelligible; and we can also apply this to the sphere of sin. But this is only *one* aspect of the mysterious whole. The most inexplicable point of all, however, is retrospective unity.

(6) THE UNIVERSALITY OF SIN IN TIME

In the doctrine of Creation we have already pointed out that Creation "once for all", "in the beginning", and the *creatio continua* are parallel conceptions. The Bible includes both ways of looking at the subject, namely: that Adam was created by God, and that all men are descended from him in the course of nature; and that "I", this individual, have been directly created by God, even though this creation may be mediated to me through my natural parents.

Hence "I", this individual human being, am both "Adam", who has been created by God, *and* the *descendant* of Adam. Now it is extremely significant that, when the Bible speaks of sin, it never reminds us of the story of the Fall, either in the Old or in the New Testament. Thus the ecclesiastical doctrine, which is based entirely upon the idea of the Fall of Adam, and the transference of his sin to the succeeding generations, is following a method which is in no sense Biblical. Even that passage, Rom. 5: 12 ff. which seems to be an exception, and has been regarded as the *locus classicus* of Christian theology from the time of Augustine, cannot be regarded as supporting this Augustinian view, which was followed by succeeding generations. For here Paul is not trying to explain what sin is; indeed, there is really nothing in Rom. 5 which describes the nature of sin. Paul's theme is rather that Christ has conquered death, that He is the bringer of life for all. In order to explain *this* truth Paul refers to the story of the Fall, in order to interpret *one* point in its light: in "Adam" all are sinners; in Christ, all are redeemed. The phrase, *in quo omnes peccaverunt*, which Augustine took to be the heart of the matter, has proved to be a mis-translation; rightly translated, these words mean the exact opposite: namely, that each of us becomes a sinner by his own act. Paul's intention is to expound the unity of the human race, within the framework of the view of history then at his disposal, and indeed—we may thus explain his intention—as a unity which can only be rightly understood in Christ. In Christ two things happen: humanity is seen to be one in sin, and *this* unity of mankind is replaced by the unity of the redeemed. "The reference to Adam, therefore, is not intended to *explain* the origin of sin, nor to excuse man for his sinning; all that is meant is that the reference to the historical origin of sin emphasizes the universality of sin, which is confirmed by faith."[1]

This is the thought, which we take from Paul, without adopting his view of time. From the standpoint of Christ as we look backwards we see Humanity as a "unity" of sinners; when we look forward, from Christ, it is a unity of the redeemed—that is, in so far as they really are in Christ. Only *in Christ*, that is, as believers, do we see the solidarity of sin to which we belong; only in Christ do we know that we are united in His redemption. This means: the knowledge of Christ creates unity both in the past and in the future. Looking back, in Christ, we see ourselves as a closely-knit sinful body of mankind which is under sentence of death; when we look forward in Christ, we see ourselves as a redeemed humanity, which shares in the life of Christ. Thus our solidarity in sin also refers to past generations. It refers to our individual past as well as to that of humanity. We are not aware of any moment in our existence when we were not sinners. So far as our consciousness is concerned, the state of "being a sinner" began with our first sin. But this first sin cannot be

[1] Kümmel, *op. cit.*, p. 38

reconstructed by us in psychological fashion; it is lost in the mists of infancy or childhood. So far as our recollection as persons is concerned we are aware of ourselves as sinners. The same is true of humanity as a whole. So far as it can be perceived in history, it is seen to be sinful.

(7) THE LIMIT OF ENQUIRY INTO THE FALL

We cannot speak of sin without speaking of the Fall, that is, without understanding sin as apostasy and rebellion. It is of the essence of sin, as we know it in Christ, that it is a defiant act of apostasy; it means that man deliberately turns away from his Creator; it is the total act of the human person, thus it is radical evil, and it is universal, with a universality which includes us all—even those who have preceded us—in a unity. We are aware of sin as our constitution, as something which is indissolubly connected with our present existence. But the question of *When* and *How* of the Fall is one which cannot be answered from the standpoint of human history, either by the individual or by humanity as a whole. The first sinful movement in the heart of a *homo primigenius* has certainly no more to do with the Fall than the first sinful movement in the tiny child, who stands on the borderline of personal existence, and possibly has never yet said "I". If we were forced to say at what point the Fall takes place in the life of the individual person, then I suppose we might say this: it is the moment when the little child first becomes conscious of himself as an "I", and when he actually expresses it, the very moment which Fichte extolled as the birth of man.

Kant calls evil, in the sense of radical evil, an "intelligible act", which lies beyond empirical knowledge. It is scarcely allowable to introduce this concept of philosophy (which indeed has other than Christian presuppositions) into Christian dogmatics. But it may serve to remind us that here too we have reached the limits of human knowledge. Even the New Testament does not give us a comprehensive doctrine of Sin, and does not allow us to fill this gap with that doctrine which has become the standard one in the tradition of the Church, and indeed was believed to be that of the New Testament. To-day, however, every expositor of the New Testament knows very well that this is not the case; but he also knows that the New Testament does not possess another theory of

Sin which is equally compact. We have got to resign ourselves to the fact that here our knowledge is limited. Are we not also aware of the fact that man is both subject and object, person and part of the world, and we do not know how this can be?

(8) THE GNOSTIC-DUALISTIC THEORY OF THE FALL

The fact that the "historical" doctrine of the Fall can no longer be accepted and since we dare not, at any price, give up this doctrine (or we would be pouring away the indispensable content from a vessel which we can no longer use) has led many thinkers, in recent times—or has led them astray—into a meta-historical doctrine of the Fall, like that contained in Plato's *Phaedrus*, in the Gnostic writings, and in the works of Origen. This theory has the great advantage of making us independent of limitations of time and space. The Fall is then on the borderline of this historical world of ours. Moreover, through sin, humanity has "fallen" into this concrete historical world. Thus it is not necessary to ask the question "When?" since this already belongs to the temporal sphere, any more than it is necessary to ask the question "How?" Thus an intelligible meta-historical metaphysical "Fall" would correspond to the intelligible concept of the person.

For a time some of us may indeed have sought to solve the problem in this direction. Only gradually did we become aware of the danger of this tendency, indeed of the fact that it could not by any stretch of imagination be combined with Biblical thought. Belief in the Creator of heaven and earth cannot be combined with this view. This world, this concrete historical world, with its forms, and figures and structural laws, with its plants and animals, with the actual human being of flesh and blood, who reproduces himself through sexual procreation, is not the world which has been created by God, but a "fallen" world. This is simply what the Gnostics, and above all, Marcion maintained: the contrast between God the Creator and God the Redeemer.[1]

Equally questionable is a second conclusion, drawn from this view: the equation of the original Creation with Redemption. The world out of which man has fallen is so perfect, so heavenly, that redemption cannot but consist in its restoration.

[1] Berdyaev has been the modern thinker who has taken this Gnostic line most seriously

The formula *"Urzeit gleich Endzeit"* (the end is like the beginning) is, however, the formula of pagan mythology in contrast to the Biblical view. For this formula necessarily leads to the idea of the eternal cycle of events. If the Fall was derived from this beginning, then also it could be derived from a world which has again returned to this beginning. This whole way of thinking is not only foreign to Biblical thought, but it cannot possibly be reconciled with it. The Bible does speak, it is true, of a "renewal" of man according to the original Image of God.[1] But this restoration never expresses the whole content of redemption. What will be at the end of Time will also be something new, compared with the beginning of creation. The beginning and the end are to be distinguished from one another as earthly and heavenly.[2] Hence, because the End will be different from the Beginning, because history proceeds from the beginning to the end, and the restoration of the original element is only one element in this movement, there is no eternal recurrence, but an End, which cannot become the beginning of a new similar process and so on *ad infinitum*. The idea of a meta-historical, transcendental Fall, leads to the view that this whole earthly world, since it is temporal and earthly, and man as a body-mind entity, and above all a creature determined by sex, does not belong to the original world but to the fallen world. This, however, means nothing less than the abandonment of the Biblical idea of Creation; then the characteristic elements in its anthropology, the "body-mind" totality and the God-willed fact of sexual reproduction, are replaced by a "spiritual religion" which is absolutely foreign to the thought of the Bible. The fact that in this connexion the ancient myth of the androgynes and the glorification of virginity once more re-appears, is only logical.[3] All this belongs rather to the sphere of Platonist thought whence it is derived, than to that of the Bible. Anyone who carries this line of thought further in a logical way must finally replace the central Biblical idea of personality and community with the impersonal abstract idea of unity. From the standpoint of Jesus Christ, and in the light of the Bible, we cannot be too decided and vigorous in our rejection of this plausible, but erroneous line of thought.

[1] Col. 3: 10; Eph. 4: 24   [2] I Cor. 15: 45 ff.   [3] Berdyaev, *op. cit.*

(9) THE PROBLEM OF ORIGINAL SIN

The theory of Original Sin which has been the standard one for the Christian doctrine of man, from the time of St. Augustine, is completely foreign to the thought of the Bible. It has, however, the great advantage that it combines both elements in the Biblical understanding of sin, that is: sin as a dominant force, and the fact that all men are connected in the solidarity of sin; the doctrine of Original Sin manages to combine these two elements in a vivid way. The sin of Adam has been transferred to the whole human race through the fact of procreation, that is, to humanity as a whole. This idea of "inheritance" combines, with the two main elements which have just been mentioned, two further ideas which connect the idea of Original Sin with daily life, firstly, by the connexion between sin and the sexual act of procreation, and secondly, through the inheritance of qualities. Everyone knows that sin is very often confused with sexuality; and everyone knows that we inherit qualities from our parents. These two ideas, derived from our everyday experience, have contributed essentially to the victory and dominance, for centuries, of the Augustinian doctrine of Original Sin. Thus when I maintain (as I am about to do) that this idea is a perversion of the Biblical doctrine of Sin, and of the genuine Christian truth about sin, I want to make it clear from the outset that I am in complete agreement with the twofold aim of Augustine: to represent sin as a dominant force, and humanity as bound together in a solidarity of guilt. What we have to combat is not this anti-Pelagian *motif*, but its *formulation* in a doctrine of Original Sin.

The doctrine of Original Sin is supported by two passages in the Bible: Ps. 51: 5 and Rom. 5: 12 ff.; from the time of Augustine onwards they have been regarded as *loci classici*: yet when these passages are rightly interpreted, nothing of the traditional meaning, which has been read into them for centuries, remains. Psalm 51, with its Hebrew form of expression, simply means that "I" am the sinful son of a sinful mother; that is, that a common experience of sin binds the generations together; but it does not mean that conception as such is peculiarly tainted with sin. Romans 5: 12 ff. could only be used by Augustine in support of his doctrine of Original Sin because he mistranslated the phrase ἐφ' ᾧ πάντες ἥμαρτον *in quo omnes peccaverunt*; and he took the *in quo* to mean *in lumbis Adami*. To-day all expositors agree that this is a mistranslation. As we have already seen, the passage in Romans certainly expresses the solidarity of the human race in sin, from "Adam" to the present day; but it says nothing about the way in which this unity in "Adam" came into existence. It does not refer to the transgression of Adam in which all his descendants share; but it states the fact that "Adam's" descendants are involved in death, because they themselves commit sin. Through "Adam" death came into the world, and each human being comes under this ban, due to his sin. This passage, however, does not say a word about an "inherited" sin through natural descent, nor about a special connexion between sin and conception.

This view is completely foreign to the thought of the Bible, and especially to that of Paul; indeed it is irreconcilable with it—in spite of the fact (to repeat what I have already said) that the deepest *motif* of this doctrine is in agreement with the Biblical view of Sin. Through the doctrine of Original (inherited) Sin[1] sin becomes a biological, natural fact. But this is never the view of the Bible. Where sin is mentioned, the human being is seen as the "person before God"; there he stands within the dimension of responsibility, of responsible personal existence. The fact that this responsible personality "before God" is one of human solidarity does not alter its personal character. In Jesus Christ we stand *before God* as *one* "Adam", as a humanity which is totally infected with an indissoluble identical burden of guilt. The secret of this unity must not be cheapened by being removed to the region of visible biological facts, into the realm of heredity. Here— to use modern terms—we are not dealing with *chromosomes* and *genes*. Here we are dealing with an actual situation which lies at the very opposite end of the scale of existence—where the "I", which is called by God, stands before the divine "Thou". We are here concerned with the mystery that every human being has been made responsible by God for the death of Christ. And it is because every man *is* this Self, this sinner, that sin is not something accidental, something momentary, or which could be avoided, but it is inseparable from our present existence as persons—until Christ breaks these bonds.

These two obvious elements in our daily experience which have so often made the doctrine of Original Sin popular—the elements of sex and heredity—are actually grave distortions of the Biblical idea of Sin. In his idea of Sin Augustine includes

---

[1] Lit. *Erb-sündenlehre*: doctrine of *inherited* sin (TR.)

the Hellenistic depreciation of sex, characteristic of his time. His idea of *concupiscentia* is strongly coloured by the sexual element. But this depreciation of sex is foreign to Biblical thought. It is opposed to the Biblical view of the creation of man as "man-woman"; it belongs (like the whole glorification of virginity) to the myth of the androgynes, to the theory of unity. Sex is a glorious creation of God closely connected with the great mystery that man has been created in the Image of God. To make it the source of sinful infection is therefore contrary to the spirit of the Bible, to the Divine Creation. Similarly, the close connexion between *concupiscentia* and sexual desire distorts the idea of Sin, brings it close to the Hellenistic conception which understands sin essentially as the life of the senses, and removes it from the Biblical view which regards Sin, essentially, as defiance and arrogance.

The second element, the fact that we inherit certain qualities, is certainly an empirical fact. But we ought to look at this fact from two angles: we inherit from our parents both good and bad qualities; from the biological point of view we inherit a "blessing" as well as a "curse". But when we speak of "qualities" we are still dealing with something which is *there*, something which can be seen and handled, the sphere of the impersonal. Qualities can be ascribed to *things*, as well as to human beings; to possess certain "qualities" is not a personal definition. But "Sin" is not a "quality", it is that which *determines* a person. Man is a sinner; this means that man as a whole is going in a wrong direction, that he is altogether in the wrong dimension. Bad qualities are inherited as well as good ones; but sin, godlessness, alienation from God can never be inherited.

In any case, what the Reformers were trying to express in their theory of Original Sin was the fact that sin involves the whole personality. Above all, it was Luther, who, like many others, had adopted the doctrine of Original Sin—just as it was—who also laid great stress on the fact that to be a sinner involves the whole *person*. He saw that it is possible to be a "person" both positively and negatively—"faith" and "sin" are the religious terms for this truth. In both cases the whole personality is involved. Thus only faith—faith in Jesus Christ— can transfer "the person" from the sinful sphere of existence into the rightful sphere where we can please God.[1] Outside

[1] For illustrative passages from Luther, see *Der Mensch im Widerspruch*, p. 144

the Christian Faith man is so entangled in his sin that he is one with it. When we speak of Sin we must insist on the truth that sin is not merely "something in man", but that it is the very *existence* of man apart from God—that it means being opposed to God, living in the wrong, perverted relation to God. Sin ought not to be confused with vice; it is possible to be a virtuous or a vicious sinner. Sin belongs to a quite different category from that of vice and virtue. Vice and virtue belong to the empirical sphere, to that of the "qualities". But sin, like faith, lies beyond the empirical sphere, in the sphere of man's relation to God. Indeed they *are* his relation to God; the one is negative and the other positive. The idea of *inherited* sin is therefore a most inadequate expression of this existence. Over and over again it leads to the mistaken view of Sin as something which can be described in naturalistic, deterministic terms, and therefore as something which cannot be avoided.

In the statement, man "is " a sinner, the "is" has a quite different meaning from the "is" in the sentence, the elephant "is" a mammal. This second "is" is used in a determinist sense. The elephant is part of the established order of the existence of mammals. He "can't do anything about it". Man also *is* a mammal. He too can do nothing about it. In theological terms this means: man has been created by God in the form of a mammal. Mammalian existence is the zoological form of human existence, from the standpoint of the Divine Creation. Man cannot help it, and he has nothing to be ashamed of in the fact. God has made him so. But when we say "man *is* a sinner" then we say the exact opposite: God did not make man so; man *can* help it, indeed this is his great, and his only guilt. Sin and guilt are inseparable. Where the one begins the other begins; where the one ends, the other ends too. Sin and guilt are co-extensive. Now this is the paradox of sin, that man can, it is true, "do something about it"[1] and thus he is guilty, but he cannot alter the fact that he is a sinner. Man is imprisoned in his own sin. He has become entangled in sin, so that he cannot get out. By the very fact of sinning he has become the slave of sin.[2] By the fact of sinning he has put himself under the dominion of sin, which he now cannot shake off.[3] He was able to close the door, but he cannot open it again. Sin is therefore responsible action, which closes the door to freedom—not to all freedom, but to the freedom of being

[1] This is precisely the meaning of Rom. 5: 12, "*because* all sinned"
[2] John 8: 34　　[3] Rom. 6: 16

no longer a sinner but a human being who is well-pleasing to God.

We understand this better from the point of view of guilt. When man became a sinner, he lost his power of being in communion with God. He cannot restore this by his own efforts, for he cannot forgive his own sin. Between himself and God there is now a great gulf, which he cannot cross, however hard he tries. The Gate of Paradise is now guarded by the angel with the flaming sword. Once man has lost his true relation to God he cannot get back into the right relation because he has no right to do so. He has gambled away his rights. Between him and God stands his guilt, and he cannot get rid of his guilt.

This, however, is only one aspect of the situation. The other side is this: that man, who has lost communion with God, has also lost a way of existence which he cannot re-discover. He is no longer "in the love of God"; he no longer possesses that freedom which is identical with "being in the love of God". Since he stands outside the love of God, he stands also outside that freedom which is based only upon the love of God, the freedom which is identical with "being in the love of God". This freedom he no longer possesses. He cannot get back to the previous way of existence as God meant it to be, in His purpose in Creation. This return to God cannot be made by a human act, but—like the forgiveness of sins—only by an act of God.

This is what the doctrine of Original Sin really means, although it expresses it in a very awkward and perverse way: that the *peccatum* involves the *non posse non peccare*. We must now turn to the relation between Sin and the "demonic" element.

(10) SIN AND THE DEMONIC ELEMENT

In the story of the Fall the force of temptation plays a significant part in the form of the Serpent. It is possibly quite as untrue to say that the Serpent "is" the Devil, as it is to say that the serpent "is only a serpent". To change colour rapidly is not only a quality of the serpent, but also of the evil powers, and even describes them, as we shall see later on. What is evident is this: that in this classic description of the Fall, there is already a force of temptation outside man, which suggests evil to man. This means, that man did not himself invent evil. This predicate is reserved absolutely for the Devil. Man is too small, too weak, too closely connected with his senses to be the inventor of evil. He is tempted to evil. Hence human sin is never identical with demonic sin. Demonic sin— understood first of all purely in a phenomenological sense— has no sensual element; it is pure defiance, pure arrogance, purely intellectual and spiritual sin. Human sin always contains an element of frailty, of the non-spiritual, of the sense element. In the story of the Fall this is marvellously described in the combination of the desire to be "like God", with the attraction of the fruit which was lovely to the sight. The sin of man is, it is true, arrogance, defiance, the presumption of alienation from God; but it is also at the same time a deception of the senses, the power of being tempted, weakness. Man is not sufficiently astute to have invented evil. Thus it has to be "suggested" to him. But the more genius a man has, the closer his sin approaches the demonic.

Thus human sin presupposes a force of temptation, or sin would be demonic. Hence, especially in the New Testament, what is said about sin is very often, though by no means always, connected with a statement about the "powers" which tempt man to sin, which stand behind the dominion of sin over man. Since man is dominated by sin he stands under demonic influences. But this order is never reversed. The dominion of demonic forces is never the reason for sin. We can never shelve our responsibility for sin by saying it is due to these demonic forces. Through sin man is drawn into these uncanny realms, but not the other way round. It is true that temptation is present before sin is committed. This was true even for the Lord Himself.[1] But as a pure force of temptation it is outside man. Through sin, however, it is no longer outside of, but within man. Now it shares in the dominion of sin over man.[2] The more that man gives way to sin, the more he falls under the dominion—not only of sin, but also of the demonic forces. More will be said about this later on.

(II) THE SINFULNESS OF THE SINFUL ACT

The Bible speaks both of "sin", and of "sins". This means that it makes a distinction between "being a sinner" and "committing sin". Now it is extremely significant that only at the very end of the story of revelation does the concept of sin

[1] Matt. 4: 1 ff.; Heb. 4: 15   [2] Col. 1: 13; Eph. 2: 2

in the singular, that is, the state of "being a sinner", appear. This suggests that the nature of sin can only be understood in the light of the sinful act. If we start from the fact of "being a sinner", it is very easy to misunderstand this in a naturalistic sense. Sin is first of all to be understood as an act, namely as a "fall", as an active break with the divine beginning, as an active departure from the divine order, as the abandonment of the position given to man by God. Sin is an *act*—that is the first thing to say about sin. Only as a second point can we say: this act is always, at the same time, a *state*, an existence in action, a state in which one cannot do otherwise, a state of slavery. But we ought not to speak about sin in this formal way. We only speak of sin aright when we speak about God. Because sin is always concerned with God, it is an act—the personal act of apostasy, of disobedience, of alienation from God. But at the same time, because it concerns God, the fact that this act takes place means that it has already become "fate", something which we "can do nothing about". Man cannot turn away from God without becoming different; and when we have become different, we cannot be what we were before. Because our existence, on account of our creation, is existence-in-God, therefore, as severance from God, it is an alteration of existence which cannot be reversed. When we look at the origin of sin, we see that it is this inevitable combination of an "act" and a "state" which constitutes the depth of sin.

But the relation of this "primal" sin (*Ur-Sünde*) to the many particular sins is not—as is so often taught on the basis of the doctrine of Original Sin—that of a cause to its effects, or of a law to its manifestations, but a relation *sui generis*, which has absolutely no analogies at all. Certainly, we can say that sins arise out of our sinful state as the fruit is produced by the tree. The Bible itself often uses this metaphor. But this is not the whole truth. Sins do not grow as a natural necessity, out of "primal sin", as crab apples grow on a crab apple tree. It is true, of course, that once man has become a sinner all that he does is infected by sin, and in everything he does the constant factor, Sin, reappears. But a particular sin does not of necessity follow from the state of sin. The fact that "I am a sinner" does not mean that I must tell lies, steal, commit adultery, or murder. Here a mistaken theological zeal has done a great deal of harm to tender consciences. Here we ought to make important distinctions, so that in avoiding the Scylla of Pelagianism we do not fall into the Charybdis of a mistaken moral determinism.

Let us start first of all from the opposite end. There is an absolute difference between virtuous and vicious human beings. It is a mistaken formula of Augustine—even though he means something quite right by it—when he says that the virtues of the pagans are brilliant vices. This is wrong, because the contrast between virtue and vice has no relation to the fact of being either a pagan or a Christian. To be a pagan or a Christian is not related to the contrast between vice and virtue, but to that between sin and faith. The distinction between the "virtuous" and the "vicious" exists within paganism. There are honest and dishonest, truthful and untruthful, faithful and unfaithful, reliable and unreliable people, those who care for the common good and those who are pure egoists. There are people like Socrates and others like Nero; there are people like Antigone and others like Messalina. When we say: "all men, without exception, are sinners", it is very foolish to deny these differences between "good" and "bad" people. The Bible itself does not do so. Paul, for instance, who has spoken more forcefully than anyone about the dominion of sin over the will, also teaches that the State has been established by God in order to reward "the good" and to punish "the bad".[1] The difference between the "good" and the "bad" lies on this side of the difference between sinners and non-sinners. In a word, there are two kinds of sinners, virtuous and vicious, good and bad. How can this be possible? and how are we to understand this?

First of all we must make a distinction between the Good which only consists in the One, and that which consists in the Many. The Good which consists in the One is the same as being in God. This Good is in harmony with faith, and is opposed to sin. But the Good which consists not in the One but in the Many belongs to the moral category. It is a sum-total of ways of behaviour, related to a variety of laws or commandments. These laws or commandments, taken separately, can also be observed by a man who is a sinner. As a sinner, it is absolutely possible to renounce lying and stealing and adultery, if by this we mean actual actions which can be described in legal terms. This is that "keeping of the commandments", to which Paul himself bears testimony, in which—before his conversion to Christ—he was blameless.[2] He really did keep all the

<hr>

[1] Rom. 13: 3   [2] Phil. 3: 6

commandments. He was extremely virtuous; he led an heroic-
ally moral life, he was impeccable—measured by the standard
of the Moral Law. And what Paul was able to do was also
possible for a pagan like Aristides, Socrates, or Camillus.
Here we are in the sphere which the Reformers used to call the
justitia civilis· that is, the "virtue" or righteousness of the
citizen—a conception which is not tainted with philistine,
capitalistic, or "bourgeois" ideas. Its positive meaning is:
that which is right or wrong in the common life of man. When
we speak of a "situation which can be described in legal
terms" we necessarily turn away from the "inmost disposition",
otherwise the "situation" could not be described in legal terms.
This does not mean that the whole disposition is ignored, but
only its heart. Thus when we say that a man is "honest" or
"honourable" we mean a man who has an honourable disposition; if we describe a person as "truthful" or "genuine", we
mean one who has a truthful disposition. All this we find among
sinful people, among persons who do not know Christ. There
are pagan virtues which are certainly not "brilliant vices",
although they may be the *virtues* of *sinful* people.

What then is the limit of the *justitia civilis*, that "inmost
disposition"? Speaking precisely, it is identical with perfect
love to God and man, as required by God, and as intended in
the original creation. Thus it is identical with not being a
sinner, with being-in-God. This can neither be formulated in
legal terms, nor is it possible for the sinner. A sinner in particular
cannot have this kind of disposition. But where this "inmost
disposition" is ignored, the difference between good and evil
can be regarded as lying within the dimension of the sinful
human being. We must, however, leave this abstract speculation and come to the real and actual situation. The more
that the inmost disposition is meant, the less possible is it to
make a distinction between "good" and "bad", the more all
men are "not-good". The less that this inmost disposition is
meant, but only certain particular facts which can be formulated in legal terms, the more possible it is to make a distinction
between "good" and "bad" people. Hence, as we have already
said, it is a mistake to regard any particular sin as the necessary
result of primal sin (*Ur-Sünde*). On the contrary we must say:
the sinner is in principle capable of avoiding every particular
sin. But what he cannot do is this: he cannot *not* be a sinner.
To be a sinner does not necessarily bring with it the particular
sins; every particular sin in itself can be avoided. If it is

committed, this increases the compulsion to sin. If it be avoided, moral freedom is increased. But the sinful tendency never becomes absolute un-freedom, and moral freedom never becomes the freedom of not being a sinner. Even in the Bible the sphere of the *justitia civilis* is left explicitly to sinful man. This freedom does exist; on account of the *non posse non peccare* it must not be denied. Sin has not destroyed all freedom, but the central freedom, the freedom to answer God as He wills it. Therefore *before God* everyone is a sinner, and all that one does, says, or thinks is sinful.

APPENDIX TO CHAPTER 3

ON THE HISTORY OF THE DOCTRINE OF SIN

THE doctrine of sin in Biblical Theology, in the Old and the New Testament, must be presupposed as familiar to the reader. (Cf. the monographs of J. Köberle, Staerk, Hempel, as well as the studies in Old Testament theology by Eichrodt and Köhler. On the New Testament, in addition to the works of well-known New Testament scholars—the latest and most important is that of Bultmann—see the monographs (dealing with anthropology) of Lüdemann, Gutbrod, Schlier; the latest and the most comprehensive is that by Kümmel: *Das Bild vom Menschen im NT*, 1948. See also the article in Kittel's *Wörterbuch zum NT*. on ἁμαρτάνω and ἁμαρτωλός.)

In the early days of the Church, until the time of St. Augustine, the doctrine of sin was comparatively little developed. The interests of theologians were absorbed in the conflict against Gnosticism, against Monarchianism, Subordinationism, and Arianism, and later on, almost entirely, by the problem of Christology. At the same time, the universality of sin was already affirmed by Justin Martyr (in the *Dialogue with Trypho the Jew, c.* A.D. 95). Justin Martyr, however, only glances at the doctrine of the Fall in the above work; but Tatian develops a detailed theory of the Fall and its consequences (*Oratio contra Graecos*) according to which, through the Fall of Adam, man lost that "capacity for goodness" (later described as the *dona supernaturalia*); this weakened his moral nature, though not to the extent of losing moral freedom. The latter point is emphasized still more strongly by Theophilus.

Irenaeus regards "Adam" rather as an infantile, undeveloped being than as an adult; thus he conceives the *justitia originalis* as a goal to be attained rather than a lost reality. He has little to say about the effects of the Fall, in the later historical Augustinian sense; on the other hand, he makes an effort to interpret sin and its origin in theological terms which are independent of historical descent; to some extent this attempt is similar to that expressed above in the text (*Adv. Haer.*, III: 21; 9; XVI: 2, etc.). Tertullian, on the other hand, takes the opposite line, and has a literal historical conception. Here we find already the ideas which, through Augustine, have become classical: *vitium originis, naturae corruptio*, the *tradux peccati* through procreation, and the terrible statement that man's origin is *vitium*, because *et unae nuptiae ex eo constant quod est stuprum*. This is the necessary presupposition of his glorification of virginity. The Alexandrines, Clement and Origen, emphasize the sensual character of the first sin, and its connexion with the "first stirrings of lustful appetite"— Origen, however, develops his Platonist theory of a "Transcendental Fall" (*De princip.*, II, 9, 6; 8, 3): that is, God created a fixed number of "intellectual essences" or "rational beings" who were good, and possessed free-will. Some persevered; others gave way "to idleness, and weariness of the labour of preserving goodness"; they fell from the super-sensible world and became enmeshed in matter—a theory strikingly similar to that of Plato in the *Phaedrus*. Later, Origen, like Augustine, based the doctrine of the Fall upon the fact of Infant Baptism (*Lev. hom.*, VIII, 3). At the same time his view came nearer to the Pauline doctrine of Sin. (Cf. *The Ideas of the Fall and of Original Sin*, by N. P. Williams, 2nd edition, 1929.)

The real founder of the classical doctrine of Sin is St. Augustine. We need waste no time in dwelling on his greatness as a Christian thinker in general, and on his immense importance for the understanding of the Gospel of the free Grace of God in Jesus Christ. His doctrine of sin, with all its faults, is a great achievement, without which the understanding of saving grace was in danger of being perverted into a moralism based on common sense. It is significant that again and again, whenever the Biblical Gospel is re-discovered—as, above all, at the Reformation—this is due to the influence of Augustine. His main achievement in the sphere of the doctrine of Sin may be summed up in the following points:

(i) The Universality and the Totality of Sin.

(ii) The *non posse non peccare* as the state of unredeemed man.

(iii) The incapacity of man to acquire merit in God's sight or even the grace of God.

(iv) The perception of the truth that in the redeeming grace of Jesus Christ we are concerned first of all with the removal of guilt.

Before Augustine, all these points had—very largely—been left uncertain, or they had even been contested. This comes out in the emergence of Pelagianism, not so much perhaps in Pelagius himself, as in the teaching of his followers, Caelestius and Julian. The truth of this statement is confirmed by the widespread sympathy accorded to Pelagianism within certain sections of the Church. If, however, Augustine did not win all along the line—the East never really accepted him—this was due not only to the Pelagian leaven which he could never entirely eliminate, but also to the questionable character of many of his doctrines in which he defended those four great points which I have just mentioned. The most important of these points, which seem to be open to question, are:

(i) His doctrine of Original Sin, which made sin a fatality due to natural causes, and thus transferred the idea of sin from the sphere of responsible existence into that of natural existence.

(ii) His doctrine of Original Sin was directly connected with his doctrine of sexual concupiscence as the "primal" sin and of sexual procreation as the source of sin in every human being, above all in that of the new-born child.

(iii) His theory of *inherited* sin (*Erb-sünde*) has obscured the truth of the nature of sin as disobedience to God.

(iv) His argument for Infant Baptism has eliminated the Biblical, personal, view of sin by the introduction of alien ideas.

The semi-Pelagianism of the following period, which more or less determined the thought of medieval theology, was certainly no improvement; indeed it was a weak compromise, in which the most dangerous elements in the Augustinian doctrine and in Pelagianism were not eliminated, but, rather, were combined with one another. Its historical justification consists solely in that of a protest, both against Pelagianism and against Augustinianism; it merely states a problem which remains unsolved.

The medieval doctrine contained another element which was not only foreign to Biblical thought, but was even opposed to it; for it was derived from Neoplatonism pure and simple, and had already appeared now and then in Augustine: in this theory sin is described as "non-being" or "non-existent", as *absentia* or *defectus boni*, which for its part, is equated with the *esse*.

In contrast with all these theories the Reformation doctrine has the great merit of placing the doctrine of Sin once more upon a genuinely Biblical foundation. In this view sin is essentially disobedience, unbelief, arrogant rebellion against God. The first point which the Reformers stress is the fact that sin is the exact opposite of man's true relation to God. Man is either in a state of faith or in a state of sin. This means the restoration of the personalism of the Biblical understanding of sin. Sin is the wrong kind of personal existence; what matters is the *persona*, not the life of the senses, nor any "element" in man,—a truth which Luther re-discovered in connexion with his understanding of Justification by Faith. The Reformers take over from Augustine those four important elements which I have just enumerated: the universality and the totality of sin; the *non posse non peccare*; the impossibility of acquiring merit; and the central significance of guilt; although they emphasize the last point more strongly than Augustine. But they also adopted the whole Augustinian doctrine of the Fall and of Original Sin; although in so doing the personalist and theocentric elements continually break through the traditional forms of the doctrine. The Biblical emphasis on the impossibility of acquiring merit is transferred, in their teaching—still more evidently than in the thought of Augustine— into the sphere of a metaphysical determinism. Misunderstanding the Divine action in Grace they teach that "fallen man, as such, possesses no more power of loving God or turning towards Him than a stone, a tree-trunk, or a piece of mud". The true statement, that man's relation to God's grace consists in receiving only, and not in co-operating, is turned into the false statement, that man must be merely passive.

Protestant orthodoxy has contributed no original element to the doctrine of Sin; rather at some points it has lost some of the best insights of the Reformers. Thus in the definition of sin it has given up the theocentricism of the Reformation doctrine —sin as unbelief—in favour of an orientation towards the Law: Sin is *aberratio a lege divina* (Hollaz) or *malum quod legi Dei repugnat* (Polan). The Lutheran idea of sin as a personal act, the act of the sinful person, was soon lost; the interest in inherited sin (*Erb-sünde*) and the sinful nature dominated theological thought. Hence the reaction of Socinianism and of the Enlightenment was intelligible. Then, of course, the pendulum swung in the other direction. The whole period of the Enlightenment was Pelagian in outlook, and indeed, Pelagianism, the purely rational and moralistic view of responsibility and of freedom is one of its fundamental *motifs*. The Kantian principle: "you ought—therefore you can!" is an expression of the universal conviction. In the course of development towards speculative Idealism moral common sense is replaced by the Neoplatonist idea that Sin is non-existence; in Fichte this is said to be due to spiritual indolence; in

Schleiermacher, to the fact that the sense element is stronger than the spiritual forces, or to weakness of the consciousness of God, to the fact that the existence of the spiritual has "not yet" taken place, or that the animal element "is still" present. The Kantian doctrine of Radical Evil, which has already been discussed in the text, stands out like a "foreign body", a witness to another spiritual world, in the midst of rationalistic Moralism or Idealistic "evolutionism".

In the thought of Julius Müller—his book on Sin is one of the most valuable books of the whole of the nineteenth century—with the aid of Kantian ideas, Origen's idea of a Transcendental Fall is once more adopted. Ritschl. has the merit of having combined the conception of Sin with the social problem. His "Kingdom of Sin" (*Rechtfertigung und Versöhnung*, III, para. 41) points to a significant state of affairs, without being able to give an adequate re-formulation of the notion of Original Sin. Further, Ritschl is a full-blown Pelagian. Far more significant than the work of the official theologians was that of the unofficial thinker, Kierkegaard. In two important works he has wrestled with the problem of sin, in the *Concept of Dread*, and in *Sickness unto Death*. His aim is, to bring the truth of the *peccatum originale* to the fore once more, without using the "historicizing" form of the Augustinian doctrine of the Fall. His statement that man is always both the individual as well as the species (*Concept of Dread*, para. I) suggests an important direction in which the problem might be rightly solved: his contrast between sin and faith, and his acute observation "that sin is not a *negation* but a *position*" (*Sickness unto Death*, third chapter of the second section) takes up once more the central theme of the Reformation doctrine of Sin.

The development of Natural Science and of the Theory of Evolution has not contributed anything to the understanding of sin, but has rather led people astray: leading them to regard sin as atavism—that is, going back to a pre-human stage of development; on the other hand, the later development of the study of Psychology with its emphasis upon "deep analysis" may be expected to produce valuable results.

CHAPTER 4

THE CONSEQUENCES OF SIN

(1) EXISTENCE UNDER THE WRATH OF GOD

THE fact that man has been created by God means that his whole existence is determined by his relation to God. His existence, as we have seen, is that of a "subject-in-relation", or, responsible existence. In two directions, this relation of man to God is based on freedom: first of all, the freedom of the generous love of God, which calls man to love Him in return, and in so doing calls him to communion with Himself; secondly, the freedom of man, who has to respond to this call. But this freedom does not exist in a neutral sphere, far above the world in which man has to make this response; it is not an indestructible freedom, or a freedom which is entirely independent of the kind of answer man has to give. On the contrary, if a person gives the wrong answer to the call of God, if he turns his back on the generous grace of God, by this act he loses his original freedom. "Everyone that committeth sin is the bond-servant of sin."[1] From the standpoint of man, the breach with God is irreparable; man cannot get back, unless God does something about it. His communion with God has now been destroyed, and this means that he has also lost his original freedom. It does not mean that *all* freedom has been lost; man does not cease to be a subject, and his existence does not cease to be one which is based on decision. Man is, and remains a moral personality; but he has lost the possibility of ordering his life in accordance with his divine destiny.

But this lost possibility is not something purely negative, that is, something which is no longer there, but it is something which may be described as "negatively positive", or "positively negative". Man's sin does not shut God out of human existence. The man who has "distorted" his relation with God finds God's presence in a different way.[2] To the sinful man God is present as the Holy God, who allows the disobedient man to feel His resistance.[3] The Bible calls this "resistance" the Wrath of God. Instead of God attracting man, He now repels him; this is the negative form of the original love of God.

[1] John 8: 34   [2] Ps. 18: 26   [3] 1 Pet. 5: 5

As sinner—and this is his "theological existence"—man stands under the Wrath of God.

Subjectively, this objective situation is reflected in the bad conscience, in the state of "anxiety" before God. The first consequence of the Fall, in the story of the Fall, is this: that man tries to hide from God.[1] All human religion outside the particular revelation is characterized by this effort to hide from God; indeed, not only all religion, but the whole life of the sinner bears this mark. There is no expression of human cultural activity which does not bear this stamp. It is also an effect of sin that man cannot decipher this characteristic of his existence; indeed that he does not even notice it. Blindness is due to sin. The sinful man does not know how great a sinner he is, in spite of the fact that he is constantly tormented by his bad conscience, even when he does not want to admit the reality of sin at all. The consciousness of guilt is suppressed and driven below consciousness; there it assumes the strangest forms, which the psychoanalyst or the psychiatrist describes for us.[2] In the mythical consciousness this sense of the Wrath of God is expressed in the figures of the Furies and of the avenging deities.

(2) THE LAW

The idea of "Law" in the New Testament, and especially in the writings of St. Paul, is foreign to man's original relation with God. "The law came in beside . . .".[3] In the original relation of man with God nothing "came in between" the generous will of God and the childlike trust of man—no abstract, impersonal "law". Man stands directly over against the generous God who claims him for His Love. The only duty is this: Let yourself be loved, live in My Love! But this obligation, just because it is the summons to receive love, is not a "law". Man may eat "of all the trees of the garden", or, as St. Paul says later: "All things are yours".[4] The only tree whose fruit man may not eat is that which grows on the "tree which is in the midst of the garden". Man is not to trespass on God's preserve; he is to be wholly dependent upon God; thus he is wholly unlike God, since his freedom consists in dependence,

[1] Gen. 3: 8

[2] Cf. C. G. Jung: *Psychologie und Religion*; A. Maeder: *Selbst steuerung und Selbstheiligung*, especially the analysis of Cellini

[3] Rom. 5: 20   [4] I Cor. 3: 21

not in independence. The eating of the tree of knowledge and of life, the infringement of the divine preserve, is the effort to achieve autonomy, to be entirely self-centred; it means exchanging the *a Deo esse* for an impossible *a se esse*. If man had not yielded to this temptation, he would have lived in communion with God; he would have received life as a gift; daily he would have received it as a gift at the hands of God.

This would be the right way to live as a human being; it would be life in the love of God. But now, through man's breach with God, this direct relation has been lost. Its place is taken by the law. There is now a neutral or abstract authority between God and man. God no longer confronts man personally, but He is represented by an impersonal authority, by the Law. Instead of the living Presence of God there is this "representative presence" through the law. Henceforth man cannot help misunderstanding his existence in a legalistic manner. He has now fallen into the moralistic error of feeling compelled to do the Good, by his own efforts, believing that because he *must* do so, he *can*. All natural religion, and all natural morality is legalistic. It is as though the Father had said to the son, who wants his share of his inheritance, "Well, you want to be independent! *Be* independent!" "Work out your own salvation! Do good in your own strength!" The wrath of God consists in the fact that when man asserts his independence God takes him at his word. Legalistic existence, and self-righteous morality and religion are the same thing.

The Law is the will of God, it is true, but it is no longer the fatherly, personal will, which touches man directly, but it is impersonal, concrete, and fixed. The law is the concrete form of the will of God. Hence it is the will of God, and yet it is not, it is ambiguous. The more legalistic it is, the more it takes statutory form, the less is it identical with the real will of God. It always requires "something", whereas God does not ask for "something" but always wants "me" for myself. Even where the law is summed up in the commandment of love, and the statutory element has been removed, still, as law, it is not the essential will of God. For the real will of God is not first of all a demand, an abstract demand, but it is first of all the offer of love, and the claim on man to respond to this offered love which is the gift of God. The will of God cannot truly be expressed in the form of the law, of the law in an established or fixed form.

In the Old Testament the Law certainly appears as an element in the revelation of the Covenant. Thus it is not primary but secondary. "I am the Lord thy God who brought thee out of the land of Egypt, out of the house of bondage, therefore thou shalt have none other gods before Me." The Law is embedded in the Gospel; only so is it the true will of God. But this is still not the whole truth. The whole truth is only seen fully where God first of all and without conditions, reveals Himself as the loving generous God in Jesus Christ, who is therefore the "end of the Law".[1] But this revelation at the same time breaks through wrath and legalism, and removes guilt by vicarious suffering. This sinister legalism and the reality of wrath can only be removed when its nature is fully recognized.

The Law is therefore, on the one hand, the wrathful answer of God to the sin of man; on the other side it is the means through which God brings the sinful apostasy of man to a head.[2] Man has to be shattered by the Law, if he is to understand and receive the grace of God. Only through the fact that God binds man wholly to the Law, and confronts him wholly with the law and its radical demands, can man learn that he is a sinner, that his way of living is perverted, that if there is no other way for him, he is lost. Through the radical Law man must learn what the "curse of the Law" means, in which the curse of his sin is seen in God's sight.[3]

(3) UNFREEDOM, THE *SERVUM ARBITRIUM*

The decisive point for the understanding of man is the understanding of human freedom. It is no accident that it is at this point that conflicts break out, which have never yet come to an end; some, indeed, are still going on at the present time. Those who do not understand human freedom, do not understand man. Those who do not understand the "unfreedom" of man do not understand sin. The earliest Christian theology, that of the Greek Fathers, entered the lists primarily in defence of man's freedom; for it was the concern of these early theologians to break through the barrier of ancient determinism, and to understand man in the dignity of his person, given him by God, and in his God-given responsibility. But this interest in freedom prevented them from gaining a right understanding of sin and guilt. It is with Augustine that

[1] Rom. 10: 4   [2] Rom. 7: 7 ff.   [3] Gal. 3: 12 + 3: 22 ff.

the reaction sets in. Even he had first of all to free himself
from the determinism of the Stoics and the Manichees before
he could take up the cudgels on behalf of freedom. Then,
however, he saw the nature of sin as "un-freedom", and
stressed the truth of the *non posse non peccare* against Pelagius.
His doctrine of Original Sin was an attempt to express this
non posse, but this, for its part, led once more to a dangerous
determinism. In the Middle Ages there was a set-back in the
emphasis on the *liberum arbitrium*; the profound understanding
of sin which Augustine had revealed was lost. The Reformers
were needed, in order to remind men that the sinner is
characterized precisely by the *servum arbitrium*. Once more,
however, the stress on the *servum arbitrium*, combined with
the Augustinian doctrine of Original Sin, made an opening
for a wrong kind of determinism, which to-day—in the era
of naturalism or pantheism—cannot fail to have a devastating
effect. It is therefore an urgent necessity to re-formulate the
doctrine of freedom and of unfreedom.

Through sin man has lost his original freedom. He is no
longer free to realize his divine destiny, and to be good, as God
would like him to be. Evil has taken possession of us; it is
radical evil, from which we cannot be freed by any mere
"revolution in the disposition" (Kant). If we could do so, we
would not need redemption. To see the necessity for redemption,
and the impossibility of achieving it, comes to the same thing.
Augustine's formula, *non posse non peccare*, hits the nail on
the head. This *is* our condition. Thus we are incapable of
realizing the fact that we have been made in the Image of
God in its material sense, that is, to be truly loving towards
God and man. No moral or religious effort will enable us to
break through this barrier of the *non posse non peccare*. This
is the true meaning of the *servum arbitrium*.

We must, however, be on our guard against the error of
combining this *servum arbitrium* with any kind of determinist
metaphysic, or against regarding it as part of a doctrine of
predestination, understood in a determinist sense. Rather we
should always start from the fact that man never ceases to
be subject. Thus even as sinner, man is not an animal but a
responsible person. He still always possesses that quality which
in the Old Testament—in contradistinction from the New—
distinguishes him as "person" from the animal: namely, all
that is meant by "being made in the Image of God", the
quality which makes him, as person, like the divine Person. It

is then quite irrelevant to ask whether man has lost the *Imago Dei*, either wholly or partially. He has lost it wholly—through sin. He is not a truly human, truly loving being. His nature does not reflect the nature of God, who is Holy Love. We are not taking sin seriously if we speak of a "relic" of the *Imago*, which man still possesses—presupposing that by the *Imago* we mean the New Testament conception. If, however, we mean what we see in the Old Testament—that which distinguishes man as man from the animal, or from the other creatures—that is, to put it more exactly, existence in responsibility, then we cannot speak of the "loss" of the *Imago Dei*. Sin itself is a sign and an expression of the fact of our humanity; the more we understand man as sinner, the more we understand him as a responsible being. The depth of human sin does not diminish man's responsibility; on the contrary, the greater the sin, the more responsible and therefore the more guilty does man become. Thus we would be minimizing the gravity of sin, were we to deny that man possesses the *Imago Dei* in this sense, or even were we to minimize its reality. This means, however, that the two forms of the *Imago Dei*, the formal and the material, are not in competition with one another; to describe the one as permanent, as untouched by sin, does not deny the fact that the other kind has been completely lost. Even the sinner is a personal being, and in this fact, even as a sinner, he resembles the personal God; but this similarity does not alter the fact that through sin, in another sense, he has *completely* lost his "likeness" to God.

Now although, in itself, it is quite easy to perceive this distinction, there is one point which raises a difficulty: namely, the fact that human existence, in the formal sense, is combined with all that we call capacity for culture and creative freedom. Man has not lost his capacity for culture by being a sinner. Even as a sinful human being he can be an artist, a scientist, a legislator, or a statesman. Now in all this cultural thought and activity sin is evident, so that, in point of fact, there is no culture which is not sinful—art, science, law, politics. But the fact of sin does not make itself felt everywhere in the same way, or to the same extent. The more we are concerned with the relation between man and man, and still more with the relation between man and God, the more does sin become evident; but the further a sphere is from these personal relations, the less evident does sin become. In the sphere of mathematics for instance, the sinful man is no worse off than the less sinful person, but his sin does affect his personal relationships; moreover, the State with its power of legal compulsion cannot be conceived apart from sin, while marriage is never actually without sin, although it can well be conceived without sin.

Thus, even as sinner, man possesses freedom, namely, freedom which forms part of his capacity to create culture; but he has not the freedom to create a truly *human* culture, one which is really pleasing to God. He is free to be a virtuous sinner, but he is not free not to be a sinner at all. He possesses freedom in the sense of a *libertas civilis*—not only freedom from compulsion, but creative and moral freedom, in so far as we eliminate from this freedom the element of true goodness, in the sense of real love to God and man. When we look at the subject more closely, however, we see that the abstract formula "man has . . . man has not . . ." is not adequate. All that we can say with complete confidence about human existence as a whole are two extreme statements. There is no man who is not a sinner; "we are all sinners".[1] On the other hand, no man is without responsibility, and thus without a certain degree of freedom, namely, that degree apart from which he would not be a human being at all. But between these two ultimate points there are endless gradations of freedom and unfreedom, both of the cultural creative capacity, as well as of moral freedom, which man can increase through discipline, and can diminish through lack of it. Hence the degree of freedom for each individual varies greatly. But what does not vary, and is true for every human being, is the truth that everyone is a sinner, and everyone is a responsible being.

(4) MAN IN REVOLT

It is not simply characteristic of a certain type of human being—the divided self, the sick soul (William James)—to be man in revolt. To be "in revolt" *is* to be a sinner. For through sin man is in rebellion against his destiny; therefore he is fighting against his nature as God created it. The sinner is in revolt within himself—that is his chronic disease, whether he knows it or not, whether he is conscious of the "contradiction" or not. Sin is being divided not merely from God, but also— since human existence is always a relation to God—within himself. This situation has been expressed with devastating effect in the Epistle to the Romans: "The good that I would

[1] Rom. 3: 23

I do not, but the evil that I would not that I do."[1] But what Paul says of himself is true of every man, whether he knows it or not. The man who is there described is the sinner, essentially. All that varies is the degree in which man realizes this situation.

The most direct consequence of sin is the fact that the whole direction of man's life has been distorted. Instead of thankfully accepting his life from the Hands of God, and loving Him who has first loved us, man is now, in his inmost nature, a *cor incurvatum in se ipsum* (Luther); that is, his very heart has been deformed and perverted. His perversity is of two kinds: self-deification and deification of the world, egoism and love of the world, the craving for the pleasure which the world offers. Since, however, even as sinner man does not cease to be destined for God, sin manifests itself as a perpetual state of conflict, in which man oscillates between the desire to escape from God, and the longing for Him; between an atheistic denial of God's existence, and a superstitious fear of God; between impiety, and pseudo-piety, between secularism and religiosity.

This fundamental conflict recurs in a great number of particular variations. For instance, one result, and one symptom of this conflict is the false relation between morality and religion, which leads partly to a mistaken autonomy on both sides, and partly to a mistaken combination of both. There is a morality without religion—to the extreme of mere utilitarianism and conventionality—and there is an a-moral religion, which goes to the other extreme of immorality and cruelty practised in the name of "religion". In the sphere of human relations this conflict is expressed on the one hand as an intense individualism (which has no use for the community), and on the other hand, as a collectivism which is hostile to persons; thus here both individual freedom and true community are misunderstood. Human history is the story of these conflicts within human nature, in which the changes are rung now on one aspect and then on the other, sometimes the one and sometimes the other getting the upper hand. Hence a dialectical view of human history has in fact a good deal to be said for it; such a view can throw a good deal of light on many points, while, on the other hand, owing to its connexion with a monistic-evolutionary *schema* it does violence to the facts (Hegel).

[1] Rom. 7: 19

The real "dialectic" of man, however, always consists in the dualism of the *grandeur et misère de l'homme*. There is nothing human which does not bear some traces of the original glory derived from the Creation; again, there is nothing human which does not bear traces of the Fall! But it is due to the sinful blindness of man that he always misinterprets the traces of this "greatness" and this "misery"; sometimes his view of human nature is pessimistic and cynical; sometimes it is idealistic and optimistic. The conflict between materialism and idealism, between cynicism and utopianism is one of the most characteristic symptoms of this conflict; another symptom is the fact that this conflict never ends, because it is fostered by the interaction of the untruth in both views.

The conflict comes out most plainly, however, in the sphere of subjective psychological phenomena. In his masterly work *Sickness unto Death*, Kierkegaard has examined the psychological signs of the conflict, and has created a Christian psychology of incomparable depth and wonderful richness. The only thinker with whom he may be compared is Pascal, whose *Pensées* are to a large extent a Christian psychology, that is, the disclosure of the psychological elements in the conflict between the "greatness" and the "misery" of man. As these phenomena can only be understood by means of the contrast between the *grandeur* and the *misère*, this Christian psychology is a kind of "proof of the truth of Christianity", and therefore it is a most important method of Christian apologetics; this is what Pascal intended it to be, and it was further developed by Kierkegaard. The development of this Christian psychology is not the task of dogmatics, but we must at least mention the main "signs" of this conflict.

The most important of these symptoms is that self-knowledge which drives man to despair,[1] as represented in the seventh chapter of Romans. Here the conflict itself is disclosed as the "rent" which goes right through human nature. Paul sees it in closest connexion with the "Law"; the deepest effect of sin in the inner life of man is this, that it drives him, inevitably, to the legalistic understanding of himself. He cannot help misunderstanding himself and his relation to God in a legalistic manner. Hence, conversely, the deepest, most central, effect of Christian redemption is the liberation of man from the curse of the Law, the new creation of human existence χωρίς νόμου. The

[1] Lit. *Ver-zwei-felt*: divided into two (Tr.)

legalistic existence as such contains that conflict between desire and inability to achieve one's desire, which is most movingly and truly expressed in that heartfelt cry: "O wretched man that I am, who shall deliver me out of the body of this death?"[1] It is of course obvious that this means something much deeper than the obvious conflict between instinct and the higher will, than the bondage of the spiritual man entangled in the senses, which even pre-Christian thinkers and poets had already observed and described in their writings.

A second phenomenon, which also lies in the depths of the human heart, is that unrest of which Augustine speaks in his famous words: *Cor meum inquietum donec requiescat in Te, Domine.* It is true that in Augustine the phrase does not refer so much to the phenomenon of conflict, but it is rather an expression of the *anima naturaliter christiana.* The fact that the human heart seeks so *restlessly* for rest in God can only be understood if the human heart is not at the "place" where it ought to be "by rights", that is, by right of the divine Creation. The longing of the heart is also a sense of being "out of place", the inner tension which arises from being so far from its origin. Certainly, here the Christian and the Idealistic interpretation come very close to one another. Since the Platonist doctrine of Eros was formulated, idealistic thinkers have understood this "unrest of heart" as the sense of distance, and of great longing, but they have not understood it, as in the Christian Faith, as "homesickness", as the pain of banishment, as the result of *alienation* from God. This truth only emerges in the light of a third phenomenon: the fact of the "bad conscience", or the sense of guilt.

The "bad conscience" is the passive aspect of the legalistic existence. The more sincerely and seriously a man accepts the divine command, "Thou shalt", the more inevitably arises the sense of total, and not merely partial guilt, of total, and not merely partial failure. The human heart, it is true, is sufficiently inventive to manage to keep the whole truth of this situation from becoming conscious. Man invents all kinds of modifications of the truth, which tend to obscure it; he is very good at making excuses, and even at shutting his eyes completely. Above all, man is a past master at silencing the voice of the "bad conscience", to the point at which it can no longer be heard; he does this mainly by filling his life with "distractions"

[1] Rom. 7: 24

—whether coarse or refined—or by evasions and "escapes" of all kinds, idealistic or materialistic. In spite of all his efforts, however, the "bad conscience" still persists, often clothing itself in strange forms; and it accuses us not of this or that sin, but as a whole. It makes us aware of the contrast between what we are and what we ought to be. It fills the whole of life with a certain pervading melancholy.

Finally, we must think of "anxiety". "In the world ye have tribulation", says Jesus.[1] The "anxiety" here meant is that which infects the whole of life, and seems to be due to no special cause. The more intellectual a man is, the greater is his "anxiety"; it cannot be banished by any system of life insurance. It is a sign of the wrong relation between what we actually are, and that for which we have been made, between the actuality and the possibility of our human nature. This is the deepest reason for the fact that we cannot bear to be alone, that we shrink from solitude; it produces that profound *ennui* which Pascal describes so wonderfully with all its effects. It is not fear but "*Angst*" which produces those terrible "divinities", those myths which show us, in symbolic form, that we live under the wrath of God, until the reconciling love of God is revealed to us.

(5) EVIL AND DEATH

The Bible knows nothing of a "fallen world".[2] Once anyone begins to think on these lines he should be on his guard, and see whether he can then preserve his faith in God, the Creator of Heaven and Earth, and whether he can be prevented from falling into a dualistic world-view which regards the whole concrete world we know, with all that lives upon it, as the work of the Evil One. According to the Biblical view, as we have already seen, this concrete earthly existence, with its time and space, its growth and its decay, the incomprehensible variety and rarity of its forms of life, from the fly to the whale and the elephant, is God's Creation. We have no right to turn the divine promise[3] that things will one day be different from what they are now, into the conclusion that "once they were not".

[1] John 16: 33. The German text has "*Angst*" for "tribulation" (TR.)

[2] The only passage which might prove an exception is Rom. 8: 20 ff. It is, however, obscure, and there is much controversy about its meaning. In any case, it does not allude to a "fallen world"

[3] Isa. 11: 6 ff.

For the equation of the "end with the beginning" is the
formula of the mythical view, not of the Biblical understanding
of the world. It is the formula, which, as the necessary consequence of the everlasting cycle of events, includes within
itself the possibility of continually beginning afresh. For
believers in the Biblical revelation, the fact that this creaturely
existence is not only transient but also contains suffering, is
no reason to deny that it has been created by God. Those who
recorded this revelation had the strength to believe that God
had created a world, in which "the young lions roar after their
prey and seek their meat from God".[1] There is a form of
suffering which is necessarily connected with the temporal,
and with corporeality, as such. To eliminate this from
the picture of all that has been created by God, simply
means denying the corporeal temporal character of man as
created by God—as is the case in Gnosticism of a Platonist
kind.

On the contrary, the Biblical revelation posits a clear
relation between sin and death. "The wages of sin is death."[2]
"Through one man sin entered into the world, and death through
sin".[3] This is not the view of the Old Testament, it is true.
The interpretation of that threat of death to Adam in the
sense of the Pauline phrase "the wages of sin is death", which
has become customary from the time of Augustine, will not
bear the test of critical examination. Here is a threat, not of
death in general, but of immediate death. Death, mortality,
however, for the whole of the Old Testament, is a divine order.
Man, as a corporeal being, is mortal, and life upon this earth
as such is not eternal life. Paul's thought was almost the same.
For Paul, therefore, the kind of death which is the "wages of
sin", is not physical mortality, which is simply the result of
age, of the organic physical existence. Θάνατος, in Paul's
thought, is something far more complex than the facts of
physical death.[4]

It is not the fact that men die, that is the "wages of sin",
but that they die as they do, in fear and agony, with the
anxious uncertainty about that which lies on the other side
of death, with a bad conscience, and the fear of possible punishment, in short, *human* death. We know no other death than
this; we do not know the purely natural death of one who is
sinless, and so sure of the divine promise that he sleeps away

[1] Ps. 104: 21   [2] Rom. 6: 23   [3] Rom. 5: 12
[4] Cf. the article Θάνατος in Kittel's *Wörterbuch z. N.T.*

into eternal life. We know only the death of the sinner. We only know something of the other kind of death as the death of the true believer, who is eager to "depart and be with Christ". The θάνατος of which Paul speaks also includes another element, namely, the fact that sin is a destructive force, an element of disintegration, in the whole of human life.

The effect of sin extends far into the unconscious, and into the organic sphere, and manifests itself in phenomena which the medical science of the present day is beginning to understand. It knows the connexion between bodily suffering and the sense of guilt, between lack of inward peace and nervous disorder. The physiognomist knows how sin sets its mark on the features, and on the expression of the face, and he also knows how joy, through the communion with God which Christ brings, can alter a face entirely. Both in the individual and in the community, sin is a source of corruption, an element of social disintegration, of conflict, of destruction. "The body of death", from which one who has discovered the "contradiction" that runs right through his nature wishes to be set free, is both an individual and a social, a personal and a suprapersonal fact. As there is a "Body of Christ", which binds all believers with Christ as members with their Head, so there is a "body of death" which binds all men together as "children of wrath", a universal force which covers the whole historical life of men as a negative force, from which the individual tries in vain to set himself free, a struggle which is all the more useless, because its seat is in "his members". It is deeply and indelibly interwoven with our existence itself; it extends to the most profound depths of the unconscious, especially of the collective unconscious. It is, moreover, a poison which infects the bloodstream of humanity—in body, mind, and spirit; it is a constant factor in all historical epochs and events, a negative inheritance which never ceases to be transmitted. This "death" comes nearest to the meaning of the ecclesiastical doctrine of Original Sin.

It is the same with evil as it is with death. While, to a certain extent, some kinds of suffering are inherent in the physico-temporal existence of man, yet neither the whole mass of suffering, nor its character, nor its effect on man, is independent of the fact of sin. The worst sufferings of human life are those which men bring upon themselves. Indeed, all that has just been said of the Pauline conception of θάνατος could just as well be applied to human suffering. The destructive force in human life, due to evil, is the greatest source of suffering. We do not know what the suffering, which, as such, belongs to physical and temporal existence, would mean for man, were he without sin and absolutely united with God. We only know the suffering that affects sinful man, and sinful humanity, the experience with which humanity has to deal, that is, the suffering which cannot be separated from sin. One final daring idea may be suggested, for which, however, there is no directly Scriptural basis, and we only venture to mention it here with great reserve. The idea of a "fallen creation" has no place in our view of the world in which man, and human sin, is a latecomer, preceded by hundreds or thousands of millions of years. And yet there *is* a relation—even though an indirect one—between the cosmos as a whole and human existence, through the fact that God, before all creation, knows what man will do with the freedom which is granted to him. Even Augustine saw that the view that divine fore-knowledge and human freedom are incompatible was mistaken. It is equally mistaken to hold the view that man was able to regard himself as the centre and aim of the divine creation, so long as he had a geocentric view of the world. The quantitative greatness of the universe does not militate in any way against the Biblical doctrine that man, whom God has created alone in His image, qualitatively is the centre and the real meaning of the history of the cosmos. He is indeed the only creature who is aware of the cosmos and its infinite greatness, for whom indeed there is a cosmos at all. The world of the astronomers is the human cosmos; we know no other.

If then God knew beforehand that the Fall of man would take place, should not His creation of the world have taken *this* sort of man into account ? Is it unallowable to think that the Creator has created the world in such a way that it corresponds with sinful man? Is not a world in which, from the very beginning, from the first emergence of living creatures, there has been the struggle for existence, with all its suffering and its "cruelty", an arena suitable for sinful man? We cannot assert that this is so; still less have we any reason to say that this is not the case.

This speculation is certainly nothing which could be regarded as the doctrine of the Church; is it then something we have no right to think? It forces itself upon our attention particularly in view of the next theme of our dogmatic consideration. If there is a supra-human and a pre-human power of evil in the world, which is at the same time not a god, but a fallen creature, of whose origin we know nothing—might not this idea be in line with that which several theologians have been trying to say, with the impossible conception of a "fallen creation"?

CHAPTER 5

ANGELS, SPIRITS AND THE DEVIL

WITH the doctrine of angels and devils we enter a theological sphere which bristles with controversial questions. For the Fundamentalist, of course, this subject presents no particular problems. The Bible speaks of angels and of devils; in accordance with the Scriptures therefore, we can do so too. But for us *this* way is impossible. Here we must follow the dogmatic rule that we have already accepted as final: our final authority is not what Scripture says, but its relation to the centre of the Christian Faith as a whole, that is, to the will of God made known to us in Jesus Christ. Those who take their stand, in this question, upon the doctrine of Verbal Inspiration, find themselves confronted by the greatest difficulties. It is true that the Bible speaks of angels, of spirits, both good and evil, but it really tells us very little; what it does say is not at all instructive, and it presents no uniform view. It is impossible to formulate a doctrine of angels and spirits, understood in this sense, without arbitrary unification and expansion of the text of the Bible. Further, angels—good angels at least, and particular ones—are only mentioned as it were on the outskirts of Biblical truth, e.g. in apocalyptic passages, or in those which are evidently legendary in character. At this point, too, as in no other sphere of Biblical theology, we can see clear traces of the influence of ideas originating outside the Biblical revelation, especially in the world of Persian religion.

From the other angle, the influence of the doctrine of angels on the Church, it is evident that the doctrine of angels and devils has provided much food for the myth-forming imagination, and that where the Christian message has been concerned with this subject it has been obscured rather than illuminated. A third point, possibly the most important of all, comes under consideration in a negative sense. Every believing Christian, on the basis of the testimony of the Bible, has a personal experience of, and a real and permanent "meeting" with Jesus Christ, and thus with the God who deals with us in Him. But which of all these believers could testify that he is personally convinced of the reality of angels? Which of those who "believe in angels" would be able to base this belief on anything else than the fact that the Bible teaches that they exist? We do not maintain that the answer to this question must be: "No one"; but possibly those who could give a positive answer are so rare as to be exceptional.

It is, of course, true that the argument for such a belief is supported by theological ideas which cannot be brushed aside without further consideration. It would be strange, people say, if God, who is so deeply concerned with personal existence, that is, with the creation of beings who can respond freely to His love, should not have created purely spiritual beings, in addition to man with his physical limitations.[1] This idea of a higher creaturely existence—an idea which is quite possible to conceive—cannot then be a *mere* idea. It is human arrogance to believe that man is the climax of creation. This argument is supported by ideas derived from a certain conception of God. The argument runs like this: the glory of God is enhanced if we believe that not only through the perfecting of man at the end of time but also from the very beginning God should have around Him created spirits who praise His power and glory, and moreover reflect his glory.[2] It is further argued that the service of eternal adoration is mentioned in the New Testament as the primary and real task of the angelic beings. The heavenly Lord implies the "heavenly host".

All this can quite well be argued, and it is scarcely possible to produce any cogent objections to it, save one; namely, that these are theological hypotheses and nothing more. We would not venture to build an ecclesiastical doctrine upon them unless there were some other urgent reason for such a doctrine, namely, that the truth of Christ, the Victor, implies negatively, the presupposition that there is a supra-human power of darkness.

This alone would constitute the sure theological foundation upon which a responsible ecclesiastical doctrine of angels and spirits could be constructed. In the New Testament this dark background—the existence of a power of darkness (however this may be conceived)—is integral to the story of Jesus Christ. *Nullus diabolus nullus redemptor*—this thesis can scarcely be denied. Thus it is no accident that in the main canonical writings of the New Testament—in contrast to the legendary features of the narrative and to elements on the "fringe" of the New Testament—where the significance of Jesus Christ is

[1] Cf. e.g. Schlatter, *Das Christliche Dogma*, p. 92.
[2] Beck, *Christliche Lehrwissenschaft*, p. 178

taught as canonical truth, these dark supra-mundane forces are mentioned, but not "angels", or even particular angels (with names); on the other hand, although "angels" seem to play an almost negligible part in genuine Christian life, many Christians (though by no means all) and particularly those of mature experience and deep conviction, testify to encounters with the "powers of darkness".

People will say, of course, that to believe this is to revert to the darkness of the Middle Ages; but we need not take this objection too seriously. Those who live in glass houses should not throw stones! A generation which has produced two World Wars, and a totalitarian State with all its horrors, has very little cause to designate the Middle Ages as "dark" (the whole of the Christian period up to the Enlightenment must be included with the Middle Ages). On the contrary, it is just because our generation has experienced such diabolical wickedness that many people have abandoned their former "enlightened" objection to the existence of a "power of darkness", and are now prepared to believe in Satan as represented in the Bible.

At the same time, we must never forget that at this particular point, the myth-forming imagination is apt to run riot. The whole sorry story of witch-hunting and of a supposed diabolic influence of earlier centuries—post-Reformation, as well as of the Middle Ages—was doubtless derived, in part, from the ecclesiastical doctrine of Satan: any such doctrine, unless kept within the strictest bounds, could produce equally disastrous results to-day. On the other hand, modern psychology with its discovery of the effects of "deep analysis" has taught us that realities are not abolished, nor even rendered innocent and innocuous, if we simply declare on rationalistic grounds that they do not exist. Possibly this is not the only service which, in this matter, such psychology is able to render. The connexion between the "power of darkness" and the unconscious processes of the mind, can scarcely be denied, whatever they may be.

On the other hand, from the very outset there is one idea, closely related to this whole sphere of thought, which must at all costs be resisted. Even to-day, and even among highly educated modern people, there are not a few to whom it seems "perfectly natural" to assert that the existence of a good God implies or includes the existence of a "corresponding" evil principle. Metaphysical dualism seems to be a logical necessity once we admit that there *is* this irreconcilable conflict between good and evil.

We shall not be far out if we regard this way of thinking, or one which is very similar to it, as the fundamental *motif* of the classical example of a dualistic religion, Zoroastrianism. This dualistic religion is characterized by a streak of ethical rationalism. It reduces the pantheon of the "gods" to two, to the two moral principles of Good and Evil. Although the Good finally overcomes the Evil force, and thus proves to be the stronger, yet there is no doubt that the evil force is regarded as a real divinity. This metaphysical dualism of two opposed "gods" cannot be combined with the Christian Faith in the One God who has created the world out of nothing, and thus has no uncreated reality alongside of Himself. Whatever the power of darkness may be, it cannot be a "god"—it cannot be an uncreated, supra-human, being.

Apart from the doctrine of angels in general, however, what the Bible has to say about Satan has a direct connexion with the heart of the Biblical revelation—with the redemptive work of Christ. Here, then, we must be ready to listen to the Voice of Scripture. What does the Bible say about the Devil? The first point that emerges is a negative one—in line with our previous rejection of a metaphysical dualism—namely, that the Devil is not God's "opposite number"! He is powerful, it is true; he is stronger than man; but he is not "almighty" like God. He is a "ruler"—Paul goes so far as to call him the "god of this world", or "of this age",[1] but he is subject to the will and the power of God. Indeed, the great event of Good Friday and Easter has already despoiled him of his powers.[2] Jesus Christ came "to destroy the works of the devil".[3] Even though in the New Testament the dark power seems far more uncanny than, for instance, in the Book of Job, where Satan belongs to the court of the Lord of Heaven, and has a kind of footing there, yet in the New Testament Satan is nowhere regarded as on a level with God. Here it is true, as Luther says, that "he can't do anything! he is already judged", the decisive battle against him has already been won; he is already regarded as a dethroned prince, who is led as a captive in Christ's triumphal procession; although from the empirical point of view he is still very powerful, and is still raging.

On the other hand, however, the Bible says nothing about his beginning, about his origin. On the contrary, we are told

[1] 2 Cor. 4: 4   [2] Col. 2: 15   [3] 1 John 3: 8

that he is a liar and a "murderer from the beginning".[1] He is simply "there", no one knows whence, or how this has come to pass. The ancient doctrine of the Church, namely, that he is a fallen angel of light, has no directly Scriptural basis. The passage in Isa. 14 which is often quoted in this connexion, where the fallen "morning star", Lucifer, is mentioned, does not refer to Satan but to Babylon and its fall; the second passage, 2 Pet. 2: 4, does not refer to the fall of Satan but to those mythical beings in Gen. 6, to a narrative which is not only on the "fringe" of the Biblical revelation but is really outside it. The Bible tells us equally little about the nature of Satan and the diabolical forces. Is it one? or are there many? Paul speaks of a whole army of forces which are hostile to Christ: but he does not make it clear how these "powers" differ from one another, and how—if this expression may be permitted—they are organized. Paul, like Jesus Himself, speaks of the power of darkness—not only in the plural but also in the singular—and of the "devil", or Satan, and Jesus speaks of the "devil and his angels".[2] Paul also lays stress upon the fact that the kingdom of the devil is—if one may say so—well organized, an orderly, unified, hierarchy.[3] There is a hint of a devilish "plan" of action, a kind of diabolical strategy, characteristic of the effective activity of the diabolical power. But all this tells us very little; at any rate it is not enough to give us any right to build upon it a clear "doctrine of the devil". Here, evidently, we shall not get very far without a good deal of our own reflection. On the basis of all that we can glean from the Bible, what can we teach about this sinister power?

Rationalism has always made short work of the devil—at least in theory! For this must be Goethe's meaning, when he says of Mephistopheles: "People don't know the Devil is there! Even when he has them by the throat!" The Enlightenment simply declared "There is no Devil", and explained belief in the devil as the product of the "myth-forming imagination". Of course, it is obvious that the "power of darkness" does not fit into the optimistic world-view of the Enlightenment. Reflection upon stories about the devil, and the horrors of witch-hunting belonging to earlier ages, and a not wholly unjustified pride in the fact that these unhappy phenomena had disappeared with the spirit of the Enlightenment, helped to justify and support this view.

[1] John 8: 44   [2] Matt. 25: 41   [3] Matt. 12: 25; Eph. 6: 11; Rev. 3: 10

But this rationalistic attitude does not do justice either to the teaching of the Bible, in which the power of darkness forms the necessary dark background to the message of redemption, nor to the more mature Christian experience. In any case we cannot remain at this point. One of the rationalistic arguments of those who deny the existence of a "dark power" must be regarded as particularly weak, that is, the view that, if we accept the existence of the devil, human responsibility is either eliminated, or at least greatly weakened. This is, of course, out of the question. Even in the Bible, the power of the devil, or the power of darkness, is never described as irresistible. It is not of such a kind that it could in any way influence human responsibility. The devil leads men astray, he suggests evil; but the man who allows himself to be led astray, and to be incited to evil, is wholly responsible for his action.

But as soon as this first point has been established, another theory arises—one which may seem to be less rationalistic, but comes to the same thing in the end: the devil is partly a psychological and partly a sociological reality. According to Ritschl, as we have already seen, there is a "kingdom of Evil", which simply means the sum-total of the sociological facts and factors which can lead men into temptation. Evil which is incorporated and objectified in institutions, becomes, for the individual, an incitement to evil. We have already admitted the element of truth which this idea contains; but it is not sufficient to explain the very phenomena which imply the existence of the devil. The psychological explanation goes rather deeper, especially where the results of "deep analysis" are used to support this view. Of course, the usual rationalistic psychology, which has no other category at its disposal than that of "emotional fantasy", is scarcely any use for the solution of this riddle. On the other hand, the psychology of the Unconscious, especially since the Jungian discovery of the Collective Unconscious, has certainly something essential to say on this point. Through the Collective Unconscious the mind enters into not merely super-individual but irrational and "occult" spheres, which are wholly unknown and unintelligible to the rational man, which therefore he is ready to declare to be non-existent. We have already referred to this kind of psychology in connexion with the doctrine of Original Sin. Here levels of reality are reached, and glimpsed, whose reality is unshaken by psychological interpretation. Along this path we may look for important contributions to the solution of this enigma, among others. We shall point out later on the connexion between the Diabolical and the phenomena of the psychology of the Collective Unconscious.

First of all, however, we must try to follow another path, that of hypothetical phenomenology. First let us ask: Is the sphere of sinful *possibility* exhausted with the phenomenon of human sin? This question, first of all purely as a possibility of thought, is to be answered in the negative. Human sin, thanks to the fact that we are not pure spirits, but body-mind creatures, is never "complete". Its negative "perfection" would be pure defiance, pure arrogance, that is, purely spiritual sin. But our sin, thanks to the fact of our human constitution as "body-mind", is always a mixture of defiance and weakness, of tendency to temptation both on the side of the mind and of the senses. We have already pointed this out.

In contrast to the Greek conception of sin, namely, that sin is due to man's sense-nature and thus the body is regarded as the source of evil, the Christian Faith regards sin mainly as pride and rebellion. Hence the statement: the more intellectual a man is, the greater—not perhaps the sin—but the possibility, or the extent, of his sin. It is not the primitive, mentally undeveloped man who sins most deeply, but the intellectually gifted and talented human being, or the genius. The nature of sin, in the Christian sense, is best represented not by the semi-psychopathic criminal type, but by the cynical defiant person who denies God, and is a genuine anti-Christ; he manifests sin in its purest form. But even he does not reach the height which can be reached in theory, because he too is infected with the weakness of the physical sense-constitution. Pure sin, sin which is only rebellion, would be without weakness; such sin could only be produced by a pure spirit, a being who was not hemmed in by the weakness of the body. This sin would then be irreversible, unforgivable, and incurable. In the Bible such sin is never ascribed to man; he never sins quite so spontaneously, so independently, so proudly, as we would have to conceive the sin of a purely spiritual being.

Satanic sin, conceived as a possibility, as a phenomenon is quite different from human sin, by the very fact that it is not due to temptation, but is purely spontaneous sin, that is, self-generated. It would not be the sin of the tempted but of the Tempter. It would be sin that is self-suggested, not due to suggestion from without. But man has too little ability to invent sin. He has too little genius to be the first to conceive this possibility. The more genius he has the nearer he approaches this possibility; but his degree of genius, even at its extreme point, does not extend to this possibility. At this point we perceive the reason for the deep dislike of the rational man for the belief in the existence of the devil. He is always inclined to look for evil in the sphere of the senses, and therefore to regard his mind, his autonomous human personality, as free from this hindrance. On the other hand, his pride of independence is such that he cannot bear to admit to himself that he could not have invented sin for himself if he had so desired. He believes that he can and ought to be able to bear sole responsibility for evil; he regards temptation as a quite secondary matter. But to admit that in order to sin at all man needs temptation, which does not proceed from himself, is intolerable for his pride.

We have, however, not yet put the question: what is the *reality* of such "pure" sin, as described in intellectual and phenomenological terms? But we have already touched it. For if man, as a psycho-physical being, is really capable of "inventing" sin—sin that is spontaneous, self-generated— then, certainly, the fact that he does actually commit sin, and thus that sin which he has not invented, is still *there*, would suggest the presupposition which has been postulated, namely, that there is a power of temptation which leads him astray, and that this power of temptation can only be a being who is able to sin spontaneously, that is, a being who sins "satanically". This line of thought would be an absolute proof of the existence of a diabolical power, that is, if the premises which lead to this conclusion are accepted. In point of fact, this is correct for Christian thought, but not for any non-Christian school of thought.

The Christian Faith is bound to admit the existence of a sinful supernatural power, and indeed of a purely spiritual sinful being, to which we can ascribe what we may call "Satanic" sin, in contrast to human sin. Now this result of our process of reflection coincides exactly with the result of our consideration of human solidarity in sin, from our re-interpretation of what is called "Original" (or inherited) sin. Man, as sinner, is under the power of sin, in a way which cannot be explained merely from the standpoint of psychology, as "habit", or as "vice", which increases with practice. When man gives way to sin, he wanders further and further away

from God, till at last he falls under a wicked spell from which
he cannot extricate himself. This does not affect the essence
of man's responsibility for his acts, but it does show the
contradiction between self-responsibility and the incapacity
to do justice to it—the tension between the "sense of ought",
and the sense of helpless impotence to achieve what one
"ought" to do and be.

The Christian Gospel describes the deliverance from this
conflict as the effect of the act of Jesus Christ, understood in
faith. Jesus Christ is described as the only One who was able
to resist the power of temptation, which assaulted Him from
without, not from within. This power proves that Jesus is
more than Man, that He was not, like other men, held captive
by this spell, which no human being can overcome. As the
God-Man He conquers this evil enchantment, which emanates
from the being who weaves the spell, that is, the Satanic power
itself. Hence He came to "destroy the works of the devil".
It was He who "delivered us from the power of darkness, and
placed us in the realm of the Son of His Love." If sin be what
the Christian Faith believes it to be, and if this be man's
situation, namely, that he is in bondage to the power of sin,
and is thus under a spell which he cannot break, then it is
clear that man's redemption by Jesus Christ can only take
place if He breaks this fatal spell; thus redemption through
Jesus Christ cannot be imagined without that dark background
of Satanic power.

But before we take the final step, we must once more deal
with a difficulty which arises out of this line of thought.
People raise the objection that it is quite unnecessary to admit
the existence of such a power: that all actual forms of human
sin, all kinds of evil, can be, and therefore ought to be, explained
apart from this view. The element of truth in this objection
is that of himself, apart from the knowledge of Jesus Christ,
man is not forced to relate the evil which he knows from
experience to the existence of a dark power. We would add,
that if he does try to do so—as for instance in the metaphysical
dualism of Zoroastrianism and in the Manichaean systems—he
immediately goes further than he should, and gives this evil
power the dignity of a "rival God".

Further, we must add, that even the particular experiences
which a Christian may have of the power of darkness in his
own personal life, do not lead, of necessity, to such an interpretation, but that this interpretation only becomes convincing

and powerful on the basis of the witness in the Gospel to Satan as the Enemy of Christ. In point of fact, why should not man have invented sin spontaneously? Why should what man experiences as the compulsion of sin be anything more than the compulsion of his own nature? Why should there be any need to explain the emergence of individual evil as due to another "temptation", in addition to that evil which is already present in an objective form, and is derived from human society, which is already evil ?

And yet, the rationalist may be brought to a halt by the fact that one of the greatest of his kind, Immanuel Kant, threw up the sponge when confronted by the problem of the Origin of Evil, after he had examined and proved all the usual explanations to be useless, because they all came to the same thing in the end, namely, that evil comes from the senses. He simply says: evil comes from a tendency towards evil, which cannot be explained. Now, however, not only is there this inexplicable "evil" of the "ordinary" kind, but there are also extraordinary phenomena, which, even for those who do not believe in Christ, do suggest the notion of the Diabolic, the Satanic, or at least of the Demonic. The ideas of pathology: sadism, hysteria, paranoia, etc., are of little use here, since they all reduce evil to the biological level and thus eliminate the sinister element from the phenomenon. Certainly, those who cannot see the distinction between that which is sinister, and that which is dangerous or unusual, cannot discuss these matters until their eyes have been opened. But anyone who has had his eyes opened to the phenomenon of evil, in its most sinister form, will not allow himself to be led astray so easily by these biological pathological classifications.

But the rationalist thinker may take another, line which is to some extent reasonable, a way which does not need the help of the Transcendent. He will say that these phenomena can only be explained in terms of the psychology of the Unconscious. Thus he will point to the Unconscious, and will explain certain uncanny evil phenomena, especially those which are of an "epidemic" kind, with the aid of mass psychology, and that means with the aid of the psychology of the Collective Unconscious. Yes, but what does this explanation explain? Does it not simply replace X by Y? That is, by an idea which is just as unintelligible as that of the Collective-Unconscious? At least recent research has shown us that there are phenomena in the sphere of the Collective Unconscious which go beyond the limits of normal psychology. Research into the Collective Unconscious seems to lead, of necessity, into the sphere of the occult, and thus at least to the very limits of that which the Bible means by the "powers of darkness".

On the other hand, even we who approach the subject from the theological point of view, upon the basis of the Bible, will only venture with the greatest caution to say, in doctrinal terms, what the devil "is". For on this question the Bible is—more or less—silent. It hints at more than it says, and its hints are so indefinite that, as we have already said, we cannot weave them into a "doctrine of the Devil". What the Bible says plainly is this: that there is a power of darkness, and that it is of great significance. As a force of a super-human kind it stands over against man. It is an "objective reality", that is, it is a reality which is objectively encountered, not merely a reality within the mind. It is a purely spiritual force, which works directly upon the spirit, without the mediations which are normally necessary for contact between human minds in order to communicate with each other, and to have an influence upon one another. Its method of influence is "occult"; in saying this we do not know whether there is a closer relation between this power and that other which is usually called "occult". The diabolical power is both one and many. But we do not know how it can be both one and many. It is of the essence of the power of darkness that it does not reveal itself, although it manifests itself. It is of its nature to will to remain hidden, and to refuse to reveal itself. This characteristic is the objective reason why there cannot be a clear doctrine of Satan. It defies all definition because it refuses to come out into the open, and be made manifest. It can only develop its power in darkness. It loves and understands the art of dissimulation, of camouflage. It even dissimulates its nature by pretending to be an "angel of light",[1] in order that it may carry out its dark designs all the more undisturbed. It works in an impersonal manner, and indeed, so impersonally that it destroys the personal element; for this very reason it makes it impossible to grasp its own personal character. It loves to reduce man to a mass phenomenon, that is, to place him in such a situation that his personal consciousness, and thus his personal responsibility, ceases to exist, where man is no longer "I", but only a psychic "it". It loves men's careless, unthinking ways, and hates men to begin to think. It loves dumbness, and

[1] 2 Cor. 11: 14

it hates speech, for speech is the favourite means of personal communication. All the phenomena of the Demonic and Satanic are characterized by secrecy and reserve.

These considerations have brought us into that sphere where the testimony of the Bible and of Christian experience meet. We have already said, that only a few Christians have a personal experience of good angels, while there are many who can testify that they have experienced the reality of the Satanic—as a superhuman reality. They point to the incomprehensible, direct suddenness with which, like a flash of lightning out of a clear sky, the temptation is there; they speak of the *mysterium fascinosum* by which things in themselves insignificant are as it were illuminated by a magical radiance, and may assume an incomprehensible force of attraction: they speak of the sinister element—in the strict and profound sense of the word—connected with temptation; they point to the strategy, the "planning" with which the power of darkness goes into action where its chances are the best, and where its help is most needed; especially they point out the connexion between magic and the diabolical. In itself the sphere of occult magic—whose reality only an extreme rationalism can deny—may be neutral, and an interest in the subject, if it be of a purely scientific character, certainly has nothing to do with diabolical enchantments. But where the magical is clothed with a numinous garment, and a person dabbles in it almost as if it were a religion, the spell-binding effects are so strong that they defeat all the efforts of the spiritual adviser until he dares to make a frontal attack. For the Satanic element in human experience is *not* the instinctive animal instinct, greatly intensified, but it is evil with a numinous halo: not evil which repels, but evil which fascinates and allures by the magic of its attraction. We should therefore seek for traces of real devilry rather in the sphere of literature and art than in the criminal world. The devil does not care very much for what is low and insignificant, he prefers what is high and exalted. It is evident that he knows how to assume the form of the "perfect gentleman", as well as that of literary and artistic greatness. He certainly prefers to fly high rather than low! But these are matters about which our own generation, and probably the theologians of this generation, know much less than was known centuries ago.[1] To a great extent, all this is a *terra incognita*, waiting to be explored. In all probability this research will take place

[1] Cf. Obendick, *Der Teufel bei Luther*

under the aegis of a combination of theology and the psychology of the Unconscious.

The most important truth about the Devil is this: Jesus Christ has conquered him. The Cross is the exact opposite of, and therefore the reaction against the "fall of Lucifer": the rebellion against God of that being who could not endure not to be equal with God. The Cross is the Sign of the Devil's defeat, and a continual reminder of Him who conquered him; it is also the Sign of Him who "emptied Himself" of His Divine power, in order to express in His own person the Divine self-giving to the uttermost. Therefore it is also true that all genuine dynamic proclamation of the Name of Christ is a challenge to the devil, and "corners" him. Just as a magnet will draw iron out of wood, so the word of Christ draws the devil out of his hiding-place. He must stand at bay, and make a desperate effort to defend himself. That is why Christ came not "to bring peace but a sword". The power of darkness does not abandon its position without a struggle.

To believe that wherever the true Gospel is proclaimed with power, men will open their hearts without further difficulty, is a mistaken optimism. Rather, a living proclamation of the Gospel often sifts the hearts of men, and the more powerful the message the more violent is the hostility of the powers of darkness. Hence it is precisely those Christians who have the deepest Christian experience, who have the greatest personal experience of the reality of the power of Darkness. C. F. Meyer's words about Luther:

"His soul is the battle-field of two worlds
I marvel not that he sees demons",

may be contrasted with the rationalist Hutten whose experience was very different from that of Luther.

Hence, because Satan is a supra-human reality, the work of redemption of Jesus Christ is a real conflict, and redemption is a real victory. The crucifixion of the Son of God, who came into this world in order to bring man back to his lost communion with God, is the supreme point at which the abysmal hatred of the devil for God achieved its supreme and most direct manifestation; at the same time it was the Event which secured his defeat. The devil, as Luther puts it, "fell into God's trap". His highest triumph is only a sham; actually he has been truly conquered. Satan himself had to be used to effect that which the unfathomable love of God manifested to the highest

degree. Hence it is not wrong to speak of the "stupid devil"—
as people do sometimes—in spite of Luther's lines about "the
ancient prince of Hell" with his "strong mail of craft and
power". That picture by Michael Pacher, in which the devil
is obliged to hold a real Christian's prayer-book for him,
expresses a real truth. God's wisdom and power is manifested
in the Cross in the fact that even Satan is made the instrument
of His redeeming will. The external victory of Satan over the
Son of God, when seen from the inside, is the decisive victory
of Christ. "After He had despoiled the powers and principalities
He led them openly in triumph and triumphed over them".
This is how the Cross of Christ looks "from behind the scenes";
externally we see the triumph of evil and blindness. But on the
inward side we see both that "evil" is the Evil One, that the
blindness of diabolical hatred against God is a hatred of which
man alone would be incapable—and that this Evil One is
already deprived of his power, in spite of the fact that, externally, he still wins one victory after another.

From this standpoint too we see the possibility of a doctrine
of angels in a new light. Because the testimony to Jesus the
Redeemer is connected with this truth of a hostile world of
supra-human, unearthly spirits, for faith the reality of a world
of angels becomes a certainty. This truth is in accordance with
the teaching of the New Testament, at least to this extent—
that apart from some obviously legendary passages in the
New Testament the Apostles speak more frequently and
more vigorously about hostile "powers and principalities"
than about good angels. "The dear angels" of the tradition of
the Church, which also play a part in her hymnology, as well
as the winged angels, and those who are known by special
names, must be regarded as products of a "myth-forming"
imagination. On the other hand, we have no reason to doubt
that there really is a great host of good angels, who serve God
and are always at His disposal.

Central significance is not ascribed to them, but they remind
us that our senses which perceive the external world and this
earth do not constitute the whole of the cosmos which God
has created, and that the worship of God never ceases even
apart from the worship of human beings. Worship of angels
of course, does not come into the question at all, and it is
explicitly forbidden.[1] Not only so; although the fact that they
are not bound to this earthly existence and to the corporeal

[1] Rev. 19: 10

nature of human beings, and—as we know from the truth about Satan—although their powers are greater than ours, yet according to the witness of the Apostles they are in many ways subordinate to man. Are not mysteries revealed to men in Jesus Christ, "into which the angels desire to look"?[1] and are not the elect promised that they shall "judge angels"?[2]

If, however, we are not to relapse into a literalistic interpretation of the Bible which has already, in principle, been overcome, a literalism which would force us to try to harmonize contradictory views and statements with one another in a thoroughly dishonest way, then if these meagre statements are to have their justification we must be ready to admit that even the Biblical writers were children of their own day and that the world from which they derived their ideas has no authority for our faith.

[1] 1 Pet. 1: 12   [2] 1 Cor. 6: 3

CHAPTER 6

OF PROVIDENCE, PRESERVATION, AND GOD'S GOVERNMENT OF THE WORLD

(1) THE THEME AND ITS IMPORTANCE

UNDER the heading of the idea of Providence, classical works of dogmatic theology deal with the relation of God to the created world, which we expand in the ideas of the preservation of the world and the divine government of the world; that is, that action, and that present activity of God in the world, which is only indirectly, not directly, related to the redemption of the world. Here then we have to discuss the relation between God and Nature, between the divine action and the course of History, between divine and human action, between human freedom and divine over-ruling, between events which are determined by human aims, and those controlled by the Divine Purpose.

The particular subject of this chapter is God in His relation to "the world as it is"; or, to put it more exactly, this world, as it is, as the result of God's activity. It is at this point that questions are raised which are a problem even for the simplest and most un-intellectual Christian, theological problems which are everybody's concern, above all, the two most popular theological problems of all: the question of theodicy, and that of miracles, as well as the most important philosophical problem, that of determinism and freedom.

In both instances, we might describe these problems as "lay" problems, in contrast to the typical problems of theologians. Here we are evidently dealing with questions which everyone has to meet, which are of burning interest for everyone, whereas there are many theological problems which the layman leaves confidently in the hands of the theologians without caring much what kind of answer they will give. Is God responsible for the things that happen in this world? If He is—how can He be a God of Love? if He is not—how can He be Almighty God? No one can ignore this question, even if otherwise he may be little given to reflection.

(2) PRESERVATION AND CREATION

If, as we have already said, the world was not merely created once for all, but there is a continuous creation, that is, if God has not merely created, but goes on creating, then should we not give up the distinction between the creation of the world and its preservation? There are theologians who emphasize the divine causality so strongly, and give so little attention to the independent reality and effect of that which has been created, that in their thought, it is true, the distinction between creation and preservation almost disappears. If all that is, and all that happens, is simply the activity of God, that is, if the doctrine of the Omnipotence of God becomes the doctrine of His *sole* power, and the doctrine of His total activity becomes that of His *sole* activity, then, in fact, the difference between creation and preservation becomes very indistinct. But if we reach this point it means that we have lost the distinction between God and the world, and have virtually adopted Pantheism. In an earlier volume[1] in the chapter on the divine omnipotence, we pointed out the serious consequences which result from this idea of God's sole activity; in the light of the fundamental Biblical conception of God as Creator and Lord of the world, we firmly rejected this dangerous view.

Since we take the idea of the Creation of the World seriously, we say: There is an existence which is not that of God, but is a creaturely existence, one therefore which is distinguished from the existence of God. Without a certain independent existence the creature cannot stand over against God, and if it does not do so, then it is not a creature as contrasted with the Creator. Even if we do not speak of a *creatio continua* we imply that even now God does not cease to create an existence distinct from His own, and a manner of existence which is different from His. If this be so, then there is also an activity of God in and on this existence which is distinct from himself, in and on the world He has created, which is not the activity of the Creator, but of the Preserver, the Ruler, or even the Redeemer (although for the moment we do not consider the latter point). Then preservation and creation are not the same.

But Pantheism is not the only danger; there is also Deism. This consists in laying so much stress on the independence of the created existence that the world is regarded as so independent

[1] Vol. I, pp. 265 ff. (G.), pp. 248 ff. (E.T.) (TR.)

of the divine activity that it is self-sufficient. This means that God's influence is reduced to that of a Prime Mover, a spectator, who looks at the world from the outside, who may possibly, occasionally, and as an exception, intervene in its course, whereas normally the world goes on its own way by itself. This is the attitude expressed in the words:

"What kind of God were this, who only from without
Would move the world,
Letting the universe flow in circles round His finger?"

against which Goethe rightly claims:[1]

"For Him 'twere meet, to move the world from within,
To enclose Nature within Himself, and Himself in Nature."

However difficult it may be for philosophical thought to avoid the "Either-Or" of Pantheism and Deism, both these rational possibilities are ruled out by the Christian doctrine of Creation. When we say that God is Creator, and the world is His Creation, we are not using the language either of Pantheism or of Deism.

Here, however, it is not our task to present a third speculative possibility; we simply have to state—both negatively and positively—the Christian position, derived from the centre of the Christian faith. God the Lord creates a creature, in whom He wills to be glorified, and with whom He wills to have communion. But He can only have communion with that which is not Himself. Communion pre-supposes differentiation. Further: God wills to have communion with His creatures in such a way that they freely return Him love for love, and in so doing give glory to Him. The whole of creation has been made for this maximum of creaturely independence, for the free creature, capable of loving God in freedom. On the other hand, if God wills to be glorified in His creation, then the freedom of the creature cannot be inherent in man's nature, it can only be derived from Himself. It is not independence which constitutes the freedom based on God the Creator, but on the contrary, it is that freedom which is identical with complete dependence.

It is from this standpoint, from the very heart of revelation, not from any kind of neutral metaphysical principle, that we have to define the relation between the independence and the dependence of the creature. It is not for us first of all to

[1] A Deism of this kind has been presented by William James, *A Pluralist Universe*, and by C. S. Brightman, *The Finding of God*

philosophize on metaphysical lines about the independence and the dependence of the created universe, and then to try to see how the relation between God and man, given to us in revelation, fits into this argument: on the contrary, we must begin here, and our "metaphysic", in so far as we need one at all, must be determined by it. It is true, of course, that the correctness of these statements of faith will have to be guaranteed by the fact that they do not contradict facts which everyone can see.

(3) GOD'S ACTION AND THE ESTABLISHED ORDER OF NATURE

There is an order in "Nature" which we can naturally perceive. There are regular happenings, laws of nature and the like. There are more or less constant forms of nature which are so arranged that they reproduce their kind with unfailing regularity. There are kinds and species in the animal and the plant world which are regarded as "fixed". There are constant qualities among chemical elements, the weight of metals, the mobility of water, and the like, of which everyone—even the most careless observer—is aware.

Science has studied these constants, formulated them in terms of the laws of mathematics and physics, classified them and also to some extent "relativized" them. Modern technics is built upon detailed research into these constants, as our daily behaviour is based upon our daily experience of the same constants in our contact with things, plants and animals. There would be no human activity at all without a knowledge of these constants, and without confidence in their constancy. All our human plans, calculations, and actions, presuppose this constancy. Apart from the laws of nature there would be no human freedom, no significant action. All our action in the external world consists in using things on the basis of, and in agreement with, their known constancy. Where this ceases, our activity ceases. Thus it is not only the scientist who is interested in this element of constancy, but it is a matter of vital concern for the ordinary person in his daily business.

What is the relation of this constancy of Nature—even though it is only relative in character—to the divine action? Here we are not yet raising the question of what are called "miracles", we are asking rather whether this constancy—so far as it goes—has anything to do with the divine action? The Bible gives a clear answer to this question, an answer which it is bound to give from the standpoint of the revelation of the Living God. God has given the world its "orders", and it is precisely in these orders that He constantly reveals His Creator-Spirit, and His Power as Creator.[1] Order and regularity are characteristic of His arrangements.[2] The very order which can be mathematically conceived is the expression of a mathematical Creator Spirit. Plato's words, ὁ θεὸς γεωμετρεῖ, have often been repeated with approval by Christian theologians. But the Bible lays more stress upon another aspect of this constancy. This constancy of the order of Nature, and of the forms of Nature, is the expression of the divine will, of the limitations imposed by God, and of the divine faithfulness.[3] With His Law God also gives to everything its limits and its barriers: "So far and no farther"; and in the reliability of things God reveals something of His faithfulness, even if not its deepest mystery. The fact that we can rely on the stability of this order means that, whether we are aware of it or not, we are relying on God's faithfulness. This constancy of natural laws, and also of natural forms, is also the pre-supposition of the divine revelation in Jesus Christ. Jesus Christ is "true Man"; He appears in human form, as "a man of flesh and blood", a man "born of a woman". And His whole way of living and acting is that of a man within our familiar ordered world. For Jesus, too, stones are stones and not bread; for Him too the Cross is hard, so hard and so heavy indeed that another man had to carry it for Him. He, the Crucified, suffered in mind and body what every human being must suffer who hangs upon a cross. Only thus can He be the Christ.

But when we say that something of God's faithfulness is revealed in the constancy of natural things and the order of Nature, we have already eliminated the deistic error which suggests that the causality of Nature exists on its own account, as if it were wholly independent of God's presence and God's action.[4] God reveals Himself and His Presence in this constancy which He grants to things. It is thus that *God* acts—not Nature, independent of God. We must certainly ask: is that expression Luther used so frequently, that Nature and natural events are only "masks of God", really tenable on the basis of Scripture?[5] Of course, we understand Luther's intention: Nature does not stand between us and God like a "foreign body". Even in the encounter with Nature God encounters

---

[1] Job 38: 33; Jer. 33: 25 [2] Rom. 1: 20; Ps. 104: 24 [3] Jer. 33: 25; Ps. 148: 6
[4] Cf. particularly Gen. 8: 22 and Jer. 33: 20–25 [5] *WA*, 23, 8; 40, I, 174

us: even the limits which it makes, the resistance which makes us feel its reality, are limits and resistances which God has established. Everywhere we have to do with God. And yet Luther's idea of the "masks" and the disguise of God seems to us to go beyond the limits of Biblical sobriety, and to be sliding into Pantheism. Nowhere does the Bible question the reality of the world as an independent reality which has been established by God.

Certainly, the world is real, and it is ordered, because God "preserves" it. Without the preserving will of God the world would fall into nothingness in a flash. The world is not so "solid" and indestructible as it looks. In this age of Atomic Energy perhaps it is easier for us to understand how it is that the world is not, as a matter of course, able to go on its way, or to prevent itself from being destroyed. At every moment God "upholds" the world above an abyss of nothingness, into which it could fall at any moment, and into which it would fall, if God were not holding it.[1] In any case this Biblical view seems to be in greater harmony with the present aspect of scientific knowledge (in the sphere of Natural Science) than with that view put forward a hundred years ago, following in the steps of the physicist Laplace, of the causal world, in its independence, understood in a fully deistic sense as an Absolute. Nowhere in the world do we find an absolute—neither the laws of Nature, nor matter, nor the atoms, nor space are absolute. It would be worth while to deduce from the Christian belief in Creation the cosmological and ontological consequences; but this problem must be solved outside the realm of dogmatics.

Scholastic theology tried to formulate the relation between the causality of Nature and the divine work of preservation in the doctrine of the *Concursus Divinus*. God, it is said, is the *causa prima*; natural causes are the *causae secundae*. Now there is a constant *influxus* of the *causa prima* upon the *causae secundae*. This doctrine (which was also adopted by orthodox Protestant theologians) seems to us to be valueless and extremely doubtful. First of all, even the application of the causal idea to God is more than questionable. There is causality between created objects, but there is none between the Creator and the Creation. Particularly in the question of human freedom[2] do we see how questionable it is to attempt to transfer the

[1] Augustine, "ita mundus vel ictu oculi stare poterit, si ei deus regimen sui subtraxerit" (*de Gen. ad Litt.*, 54, 12, 22)

[2] Cf. Vol. I, pp. 339 ff. (G.), pp. 321 ff. (E.T.)

principle of causality to the relation between God and the world. Secondly, however, this doctrine is dangerous because it severs that which ought not to be divided: the independence of the Creation and the Divine work of Preservation. The mystery consists in the fact that God carries on His work of preservation within—and not outside of—the real independence of His creatures. We human beings cannot even understand—with our minds—how the human spirit and brain can exist in and alongside of one another; if this is impossible, still more must we renounce all attempts to understand *how* the independence granted to us as created beings and God's preserving activity can be interwoven. Here we come to a full stop. We are not meant to probe any further.

To some extent the scholastic doctrine of the *concursus divinus* reduces the harm caused by the application of the idea of causality to the Divine activity, by defining causality as varying greatly in degree: God influences free creatures, and those who are not free, in different ways. This removes the danger of determinism, but at the same time it obscures the clarity of the idea of causality. Influence freely exercised is not what we mean by causality. A personal relation simply cannot be rendered by the causal idea which belongs to the sphere of "things". Therefore it is better not even to suggest a causal explanation, and to renounce the causal idea altogether in relation to the Divine activity.

This question may be more concerned with the intellectual methods which must be used in our study of the activity of Divine preservation, but there is another question which is of direct practical religious interest: the relation between preservation and grace. The preservation of that which has been created, and of the Creation itself, is seen to be an act of divine grace when it is viewed from the heart of revelation, from God's self-giving to His world. Hence just as there is a "natural revelation" so there is a "natural grace": that is, a grace which is given to all existence, which must be distinguished from the grace of redemption. It is true, of course, that we can *know* nothing of the divine activity in preservation apart from the redeeming revelation and the grace of God which is manifested therein; but we do know that preserving grace is different from the grace of redemption. It is, quite simply, "the grace of preservation".[1] God spares our life—to which we have no claim—whether a life finally ends in Eternal Life or not. But

[1] Matt. 10: 30, 5: 45, 6: 26

the idea that God spares our life because He wills to redeem us, and thus that the grace of preservation is only an element in the grace of redemption, can only be held by those who believe in universalism, in an ἀποκατάστασις πάντων, a view which we have already firmly rejected.[1] God also "preserves" "unto the day of wrath"; He preserves even those destined for the Final Judgment.[2] This "preserving grace" is not the same as "redeeming grace", just as the revelation of Creation is not the same as the revelation of Redemption.

(4) DIVINE PROVIDENCE

The idea of Divine Providence is also the absolute denial of the idea that the universe has no meaning, that things only happen "by accident". All that is, and all that happens, takes place within the knowledge and the will of God. Thus there is nothing "casual" about life, nothing that happens "anyhow". Everything that happens has its final ground in God. All that happens is connected with the divine Purpose; all is ordered in accordance with, and in subordination to, the divine plan and the final divine purpose. Here we go beyond the statement of the Hegelian philosophy of history that "all that is real is rational", all reality is a means to the final divine Purpose.

The Biblical idea of Providence has certain non-Christian parallels. Even Platonism, but above all the Stoics, knew the idea of an all-inclusive and all-determining divine Providence (πρόνοια). Hence from the outset we must take into account the fact that in the history of Christian theology these two streams flow into one another, and indeed that this is one of the most important points for the synthesis between Christianity and the ancient world. From the standpoint of the revelation in Jesus Christ what are we to make of this possibility? What is the relation between these two views of Providence?

Firstly, the Stoic idea of Providence—like that of Platonism and of Modern Idealism—is impersonal. It is an impersonal world-reason which lies behind all that happens in the world. The divine πρόνοια is identical with the εἱμαρμένη, and the latter is the absolute power of Destiny, the all-penetrating, all inclusive causal connexion, the absolute necessity of all that happens, or absolute determinism.

Of course, this is only one aspect of providence, the impersonal; the other approaches a personalist idea of God, as we see in

[1] Vol. I, p. 363 (G.), p. 353 (E.T.)   [2] Rom. 9: 22

the celebrated hymn to Zeus, by Cleanthes.[1] So that what looks like absolute causality from one point of view, from another, is the fatherly providence and care of God. Man may fearlessly put his trust in this divine providential necessity; but whether he does so or not he is bound to obey it, like a dog which is tied to a cart and has no choice but to follow its course.[2]

When we read Zwingli's *De Providentia*, or Calvin's remarks in the closing chapters of the first book of the *Institutio* we often seem to catch echoes of the very language of Chrysippus or Zeno. And yet there is a great gulf between the Biblical and the Stoic idea of Providence. For the God who is revealed in Jesus Christ, in His Word, is not the same as the "Father-God" who is identical with the εἱμαρμένη. He is the God who addresses us personally, and therefore also the God whom we are to address as "Thou". If His Providence excludes the accidental character of any event, His providential over-ruling of the world is never the same as causality. For we do not, like the Stoics, invent a necessity out of the permanent causal nexus (*perpetuus nexus causarum*) and a kind of immanent series which is supposed to be included in Nature.[3] This does not mean, as Schleiermacher argues, that the divine providence is identical with natural causality. The fact that this is not so becomes clear to us above all in the fact that the Christian idea of Providence includes the divine power to work miracles, the divine sovereignty over nature. The personal idea of God which is real, and not imagined, implies the divine freedom over all causality, over all necessity. Here there is no room for the idea of Fate or Destiny (εἱμαρμένη). The identification of Providence with εἱμαρμένη is an indication that we cannot take Stoic personalism very seriously, in spite of all the impressive religious language of the Hymn to Zeus. The Christian, however, knows that he, and all that happens, are in the hands of Him who speaks to him as "thou", to whom he may and must respond in the same personal terms.

The second difference, which is indissolubly connected with the first, is this: explicitly the Stoic is only aware of a general, but not of a special or personal Providence. In faith in the God revealed in Christ I know that God not only "calls me by my name," but that also, quite personally, He has included me in His plan for the world. I am not like the dog which is bound to the chariot of Zeus; I am one whom God has called to Himself,

---

[1] *Stoic. vet. fragm.*, I, No. 527   [2] *Ibid.*, No. 975   [3] *Institutio*, I, 16, 8

and this personal election is never to be severed from His Providence. He who says to me "I have called thee by thy name, thou art mine",[1] says also "All things work together for good to them that love God—to those who have been called according to His purpose".[2] Even for God I myself am never a means to an impersonal and unknown end, but because I am thus in relation to God I remain, for God, an end in myself. For this is what Election means; and it is only from the standpoint of Election that we can think of Providence at all. For here we are not thinking of the providence of a deity known to us through metaphysics, but of the providence of God the Father, made known to us in Jesus Christ, who, as my Father, loves me, His son, from all eternity, and therefore will never treat me like a dog bound to the chariot of Fate. The Christian doctrine of Providence is not a system of metaphysics, but it is the truth given to us in Him in whom God has unveiled the mystery of His will and His nature. For the Stoic deterministic conception of Providence, in spite of the idea of πρόνοια—at least so far as we are concerned—is blind. But for the Christian, "Providence" is only another name for the fact that the God who looks at me, and who never ceases to look at me, at the same time with His glance embraces the whole, and unites His will for me with His will for the world.

There is a third difference between the Christian and the Stoic idea of Providence: the Christian view, but not the Stoic, is wholly teleological, related to the End, determined by the End. The God of revelation does not only "fore"-see, but He sees right down the course of events to the End of all things, to the final End. The will and the thought which is revealed in Jesus Christ as the will and thought of God is His thought and will expressing His purpose for the whole world; the Providence which is the origin and the basis of all that happens is the Logos, who, as the Son, is at the same time the final End of all that happens, the chief corner-stone, the κεφλή, in whom all is knit together,[3] towards whom everything is moving, or to put it more exactly: towards whom God has ordered everything, and in whom therefore everything must finally end and reach its goal. Pagan philosophy knows nothing of this world-teleology. Indeed it knows no real history, and no final goal of history. It only knows the cycle of events in the cosmos.

The Biblical Idea of Providence—even if we have to express

---

[1] Isa. 43: 1   [2] Rom. 8: 28   [3] Eph. 1: 10

it in a very philosophical way—is the absolute unity of causality
and finality, although we must hasten to add that here both
causality and finality are completely transformed, since they
have lost their neutral abstract character, and their lack of
historical meaning, and have entered the dimension of the
personal and the historical.[1]

We are here thinking of Providence, Election, and the
Purpose of the world together. This eliminates that dangerous
popular misunderstanding of Providence, nourished by certain
phrases in the Psalms, which seem to suggest that those who
trust in God "will always escape disaster". Certainly *ultimately*
this is what is intended and real trust in God is based upon
this conviction. But this does not mean that penultimately,
within this world of space and time, even the most Christian
people will not have to face the worst disasters! The disciple
is not above his Lord. If Jesus the Son of God was crucified,
owing to the most terrible miscarriage of justice and judicial
murder in the history of the world, as a sacrifice to the most
incredible blindness and malice, can any of His disciples expect
to receive a guarantee that nothing of that kind will happen
to him? A certain pietistic exposition of Providence, in the
sense of direct "guidance" which removes all difficulties, and
constantly turns everything to good, has done a great deal to
discredit the idea of Providence; indeed, it has led some people
into a state of complete bewilderment and loss of faith. The
Good Shepherd does permit His sheep to go through the Dark
Valley.[2] The just man must suffer much.[3] Indeed is there not
a secret proportion between the measure of Christ's presence
and a share in His sufferings?[4]

If the Cross of Christ be the great stumbling-block of the
world, then the visible fate of so many Christians in the world,
measured by the standards of the world, is also a stumbling-
block. Things do not happen as they do in little pious tracts;
they do *not* "always turn out for the best". God does not take
sides with His own, in the sense of the secular idea of good
fortune or happiness. Rather, we may say that Luther's
words, in his famous hymn, express the right point of view:

"And though they take our life, goods, honour, children,
        wife, . . .
    These things shall vanish all: The city of God remaineth."

[1] The magnificent witness for this is the book of the anonymous Prophet
of the Exile, Isa. 40 ff.
[2] Ps. 23: 4   [3] Ps. 34: 19   [4] 2 Cor. 4: 8 ff.

The "good" lies in the invisible world, where "to those that love God" all things must "work together for good".

But this does not mean that there are no visible signs of divine help and guidance. A purely ascetic and heroic conception of Divine Providence is just as untrue as an exaggerated eudaemonistic idea of the experience of faith or of the divine promise on the other hand. The undercurrent of divine co-operation comes to the surface now and again. To try to eliminate this feature from the life of the saints—of those that is who are "saints" in the Biblical sense—would be to act in a very arbitrary manner. God constantly gives His own "signs" of His fatherly guidance; clear witness to this truth is given by those apostles who had such a full share in the sufferings of Christ that they have a valid claim to the title of "martyrs".[1] But these "signs" cannot be foreseen; they are free gifts of God; there is no certainty that they will be repeated in each case. We shall have more to say about this in connexion with the doctrine of the divine government of the world.

For one who lives in the knowledge and certainty of the Providence of God, what we were obliged to deny as a general truth comes true in his own life: for him the grace of preservation and the grace of redemption are one.[2] For him this temporal life is part of the way to the eternal goal, therefore the preservation of the temporal life is by permission of God who arranges that he shall follow this path. He knows that he is preserved by God for redemption; he knows no other meaning of his existence than this, which is the whole meaning and the final meaning, *the* Telos, not *a* Telos. For this very reason, however, the fact of "non-preservation", death, even what is called "premature" death, cannot alter this meaning. "Whether we live or die we are the Lord's." For such a man nothing that happens to him personally can make him doubt God. But what about the things that happen to others? And how can we combine the thought of the love and the righteousness of God in face of the mass of innocent and unjust suffering with that of an all-inclusive Divine Providence? This problem, that of the theodicy, cannot be separated from that of Providence; we must put it to ourselves. But before we do so there are two other burning questions to answer.

---

[1] E.g. 2 Cor. 1: 10; Acts 18: 10, 27: 24 ff.

[2] This distinction, 2 Cor. 4: 3; 1 Cor. 1, 18

(5) MIRACLES

"Miracle is the dearest child of faith": Goethe puts these words into the mouth of Faust. This phrase suggests that Faust's theological studies cannot have progressed very far! Miracle is rather the essence of faith. Faith and the miraculous are indissolubly connected. If miracle is eliminated the dimension of faith also disappears. Miracle is the correlate of the supernatural, of the Living God. When we speak of God we also speak of miracle; that is, if by "God" we mean the true God, the God of revelation, not the God of human speculation. To deny the reality of miracle would be to deny the freedom of God, of the God who is the Lord of the whole world. To see this God at work, who is the free Lord of the world which He has created, means encountering miracle, whether this miracle of the divine action works through the laws of nature or outside them. We do not say this in order to evade the actual "problem of miracles"—this will be clear in a moment—but in order to set the whole problem in its right perspective. The freedom of God is a vital concern for faith, but it is no more and no less concerned with what is called "miracle", or the so-called "miracles", than with the working of God through the constancy of nature and its laws. As against the Deistic view we would say that God is actively at work even where no "miracles" occur; as against the Pantheistic view we would say, that God's working is not confined to the sphere of natural causality. Both the "ordinary", and the "extra-ordinary" action of God, is equally wonderful; for everything that God does is wonderful, for those who see that it is *God* who does it.

Philosophical criticism of the Christian idea of Miracle[1] often appears in the guise of the "religious" argument that it is unworthy of God to have to intervene in the natural order which He has Himself created; for this would imply that this order is imperfect, that it needs to be expanded, or even repaired. This criticism is derived from the familiar idea of God as abstract and impersonal, which is not the idea of the "Lord God". It is either the God of Deism, who must allow the world to run along the lines for which He has created it once for all; or it is the God of Pantheism, whose action is identical with that of natural causality, as the Stoic πρόνοια is identical with the εἱμαρμένη. But if we say that God is the Lord of the

---

[1] Strauss, *Chr. Glaubenslehre*, I, para. 17; Biedermann, *Chr. Dogmatik*, II, pp. 478 ff.

world, we are really saying that God is not tied to the laws (or the orders) which it has pleased Him to give to the world. The laws of Nature are relative; God alone is absolute. God's freedom is not limited by any "laws", whether of nature or of reason. God—and God alone—is the Lord—*extra legem*—or as the Scholastics put it, He is *ex lex*. This is precisely what is meant by the idea of the sovereignty or the freedom of God.

The contrast between the Biblical Idea of God and that pseudo-religious argument of the abstract idea of God, comes out particularly clearly where we are dealing with God's relation to His sinful creatures. Sin consists in the fact that the order of God has been broken; even if this does not destroy the natural order, yet *quoad hominem* it has become different. The man who has become perverted sees the order of nature quite differently from the man who sees it as the divine creation. To use picture-language—if God only wanted to restore the balance of the cosmos then He would have to work *extra ordinem*. The intervention of God in the events of the world cannot be separated from the idea of a God who reveals Himself in History as the Redeemer.

It is precisely the God who does not change His purpose who must meet His creature *extra ordinem*, because the creature (i.e. man) has changed its order and purpose: this is because He wills to restore its original relation to His creatures. Thus the God of the Bible, both of the Old and of the New Testament, is the living God, who intervenes in the course of history. He is the God who works miracles, in contrast to both the Absolute of speculative philosophy, and the deity of Mysticism, who, as original Truth, stands above or behind all that happens, but takes no part in the events themselves.

(a) *The Orders of God.* God, the Lord of Creation, has power over His creation. He is not bound by it. But this does not mean that He is only present and working in it when he works *extra ordinem*, as the God of Miracles. Even the laws of Nature are the expression of His will and manifestations of His Presence. God is a God of order, not of disorder, even if order is not the supreme principle of the divine reality. Order is always neutral, not personal. Order is therefore the principle of the divine presence in the sphere of Nature; in the personal sphere order is always the neutral representative of the personal; hence it is something subordinate, temporary and— measured by the standard of the truly personal—secondary in character. In the sphere of nature, on the contrary, order is the sign of spirit in contrast to chaos, to disorder as a whole. Hence in the laws of Nature the Bible sees God's wisdom, power and faithfulness. Above all the Bible regards the regularity of the stars in their courses, of the seasons, and—to-day we would say the relative—constancy of the different species as a sign of the all-wise and all-mighty Creator God and His royal dominion. Order is the opposite of caprice, of moods and whims. As law in the State establishes the security of justice, and in so doing manifests a spiritual and moral power, so order in nature—whether it be in the sphere of astro-physics or of biology—is the sign that in Nature we are not dealing with a plurality of blind elemental forces, totally unconnected, but with a unity which transcends and controls all variety, which gives us the impression of reliability, a feeling of cosmic security, which is the very antithesis of all that is un-homely, sinister, or terrifying.

Even though this world is not suited to be our true home— since it has no room for our eternal destiny—yet through this law-abiding order it is to some extent homely, not un-homely and weird. Its laws point to Him in whose Hands it is good to rest, under whose mighty control we can live quietly, and in confidence. This does not mean that these laws can themselves reveal to us the inner mystery of God; since these laws are always impersonal they cannot show us His inmost meaning. But they *do* reveal "His everlasting power and divinity".[1] If we cannot hear this witness of the cosmos and of the created world—if we cannot perceive that it points to an all-mighty and all-wise Creator,[2] it is due to sin, it is the result of the blindness derived from original sin.

(b) *Law and the Freedom of God: the Cross.* God's will is incorporated in the orders of creation. They are the basis of all material moral precepts. This order is—not eternal, it is true, any more than creation is eternal—but constant and abiding, so long as the created world endures. It is explicitly emphasized in the Law of God, in order that it should not be overlooked. It is inviolable. It is provided with the sanctions of divine wrath and divine punishment in order that man may realize that it must be taken seriously. "God is not mocked; for whatsoever a man soweth, that shall he also reap".[3] God stands by His Law because He stands by His creation, because He stands by Himself. He cannot allow the

[1] Rom. 1: 20   [2] Rom. 1: 20   [3] Gal. 6 : 7.

transgression of the Law to go unpunished; were He to do so He would not be taking Himself seriously.

In the final revelation of God, however, at the point where His innermost mystery is disclosed, we see that He, the God of order and of law, stands above His order and His law. Thus He is able to forgive the sin which has incurred the penalty of the Law. There is a revelation of His Righteousness, that is, of His inmost attitude towards us, "apart from the Law",[1] in the revelation of His generous love to us in Jesus Christ. Here we are no longer concerned with the Creation, but solely with the rescuing love of God; by God's act man is lifted into this Divine Love, and in so doing he achieves his destiny; he finds the fulfilment of the end for which he has been made. But God takes His own Law so seriously that even this free revelation of His love is not achieved without confirming His law and its gravity in the fact that He in whom His own love is revealed, the Son of His Love, bears the punishment for us, which should be ours by right, as transgressors of the Law, in order "to show His Righteousness". Thus without love there is no fulfilling of the law.

Thus both the legal order, and the supra-legal freedom of sovereign love are deeply rooted in the nature of God. Thus even the God who transcends the natural order, in the fact that He works miracles, is not a God of disorder. The miracles of God are very different from the "wonders" worked by pagan gods or miracle-workers.

(c) *Higher Causes.* Now can we, who belong to an era dominated by the natural sciences, still "believe in miracles"? Is it not evident that, from the standpoint of our knowledge of Nature, we must postulate a world without miracle, with the further implication that the very conception of "miracle" belongs to a magical view of the world which we can no longer accept? Indeed, were we to admit the possibility of miracle, would this not destroy the harmony of our present view of the world? since actually, in our own experience, we know that "miracles do not happen"?[2] These are some of the objections raised against the use of the idea of miracle within the sphere of Christian doctrine which feels constrained to be in strict accordance with scientific thought. These objections, however, presuppose a remarkably "monistic" view of the world, which

[1] Rom. 3 : 21.
[2] Cf. Kant's ironical observation, that wise governments declare, it is true, "that miracles may have occurred of old, but that new miracles" are not permitted: *Die Religion*, p. 90

is in sharp contrast with the reality of experience. The first task laid upon us, then, is to destroy this fictitious "pan-causalism" by showing that there are levels on which "higher causes" operate.

Actually there is only one sphere in which the strictly mechanical and causal idea can be carried through—or should we say it *seemed* to be possible to carry it through?—the sphere of so-called "dead nature", in the phenomena of astro-physics and chemistry. It was indeed from this point that in Newton's mechanism of the heavens, and above all in the statements of Laplace, the pan-causal view was proclaimed as the inevitable result of the new knowledge in the sphere of Natural Science. This view was confirmed by the conviction that in the sphere of astro-physics, from the time of Kepler, Galileo, and Newton, the strictly causal view had become dominant. Here, it was claimed, everything could be calculated.[1] The past state of the world contains the future. To-morrow can be calculated in strict accordance with yesterday or to-day. The past absolutely determines the future.

This absolute causal determinism which—as we shall see in a moment—at the best, applies to the sphere of astro-physics, has never been applied to the historical world, nor have historians ever really believed it; in any case, even the most thorough-going determinists have always lived as though they were not determinists. Further, within the sphere of physics itself there has been a reaction: to-day this *absolute* determinism is no longer held, owing to essential changes within its own dimension. It is true, of course, that the well-known laws of physics still hold good; but their validity is no longer absolute but limited, and the limits are exactly defined. The destruction of pan-causalism in the sphere of "dead nature" is the revolutionary achievement of that most modern, and most exact science, the physics of the twentieth century.[2]

Pan-causalism, however, has never been applied to the sphere of life-processes. Without the idea of spontaneity, organic totality, an organism in contrast to a mechanism, no

---

[1] "Laplace conceived a mind able to foretell the progress of nature for all eternity if but the masses and their velocities were given": Dampier, *Shorter History of Science*, p. 80 (TR.)

[2] At the same time we who are theologians should not rush to far-reaching conclusions based on this change of outlook, so long as the physicists themselves are not agreed about the consequences of the quantum theory, as affecting the principle of causality. See the warnings uttered by so devout a physicist as Planck (*Die Physik im Kampf um die Weltanschauung*, 1935; *Determinismus oder Indeterminismus*, 1938)

vital process has been either described or understood. All that man has learned and presupposed in his daily contact with plants and animals may, it is true, have been denied by materialistic scientists in their abstract theories, but never in concrete descriptions and explanations of Nature. As we move from the sphere of "dead nature" into that of living nature, the phenomenon of the organic, which controls everything, is a "miracle". We cannot explain it in terms of the categories of physics and chemistry alone. So the student of "living nature" has to use other ways of thought, above all, the idea of a whole, which is more than the sum of its parts. For a time those who held "pan-causal" ideas attacked those who championed organic life-processes—and all that this implied of spontaneity and freedom; to-day, however, the shoe is on the other foot: the champions of the organic theory are attacking the upholders of the mechanistic view.

However, for us, both these questions are of secondary interest. Our central and immediate interest only begins with Man. That Man is a mechanism has often been asserted in theory, it is true, but in practice it has never really been believed. Never has a champion of pan-mechanism really regarded his fellow-men as mechanisms, nor has he treated them so. No one can evade the idea of responsibility and therefore of freedom. Indeed, every thought which claims validity, and even simply to be understood, is not a mechanism, but a living symbol, and thus something which is fundamentally different from the mere termination of a process of thought.

There are, of course, no traces of the mechanistic type of thought in the Bible, for it can only be the result of a profound spiritual blindness. The Bible takes for granted the obvious distinction between the sphere of things, the organic, and of man; it always reckons with the responsibility of man, and the freedom this implies. The "un-freedom" involved in the slavery of sin, the *servum arbitrium* in the religious sense, has nothing to do with mechanistic determinism; the "bondage" of sin implies a mode of existence which is both responsible and free, not an impersonal, deterministic view of life.

Each higher stage, however, when seen from below, seems "miraculous", that is, it cannot be explained in the specific categories which apply on the lower plane. Of course, man is also a mechanism, who moves according to the law discovered by Galileo, and similar mechanical laws of motion. Only from *this* point of view, he is not man, but merely a body. Man is, of course, also an organism, like the plant or the animal, determined by the same biological laws which hold in that sphere. Here, however, as such, he is not *humanus*, but merely a mammal. From the biological point of view his human existence, his *Humanitas*, is marvellous, incomprehensible. It possesses a "dimension" which is lacking in biology, the law of norms, the faculty of grasping meaning, freedom, responsibility. Just as the organism is "marvellous" to the mechanical scientist, so humanity is a marvel to the biologist: the marvel (or the miracle) of freedom, related to a norm, which we simply call "mind" (*Geist*).

These limitations of causality belong to our normal experience of the world. The following question also belongs to our normal human experience of the world: must we simply accept these limitations of human freedom? or can there be another, real, freedom which is higher than human freedom—that of a divine reality? No human being lives without asking this question: it is part and parcel of his humanity. A human being who does not ask himself this question at some time or another is not fully human. He may answer this question in the negative, or perhaps of himself he will never answer it in the affirmative with any certainty, but he cannot help asking it, even if he only does so "in passing"—as it were—as is the way of the secularized human beings of the present day. Sometimes such people think that they can establish a relation between their existence in responsibility and this higher existence. They may even speak of "conscience" as the "Voice of God". But by their own efforts they do not attain clarity or certainty.

The divine revelation, however, is the answer to this question. This is the answer: Human freedom is based on the freedom of the Creator; hence man's freedom is also his responsibility. But the meaning of responsibility is life in the love of God, given to us freely in Jesus Christ. In this love man has his true freedom, namely, the freedom through which alone he becomes true man, and by which he is set free from the compulsion of sin. But the Divine freedom cannot be known from the human standpoint; it is only revealed in the freedom of revelation, the miracle of the "supernatural" revelation, in its perfection: the miracle of the Incarnation and Redemption. And this miracle of the divine revelation is the real "miracle" of which the Bible speaks. All the so-called "miracles", those of the Old Testament and those of the New, are only the "accompaniment" of this one miracle of revelation, the miracle

of the Coming of God to man. They are events which point
to this one supreme Miracle, which give it an expression like
the "instrumentation" of a melody in music; they exist for
its sake alone; in themselves they are not important. The
difference between the Biblical miracles and the miracle
stories of paganism is this:—that, apart from a few insignificant
exceptions on the fringe of the Old Testament, they are all
intended to serve this one end alone, the miracle of the
revelation of the free God. They are all seen in the light of
"Saving History" (*Heilsgeschichte*); they are miracles of revelation and salvation, not miracles which draw attention to
themselves; they are not done simply to startle or amaze.
This is the meaning of the New Testament word σημεῖα
"signs". All σημεῖα "point" to God, and to Him in whom
He is present and acting, the Son, the Messiah: messianic
deeds, messianic signs. That is what they were in the time
of the Apostles.[1] They took place "in the name of Jesus";
they glorified His Name, and bore witness to His power and
His love.

(*d*) *Miracle and the Miracles.* What, however, is the relation
of these miracles, whether the essential miracle of the saving
revelation, or the accompanying "miracles", to the natural
order? Once again we go back to what has already been said
about the order of stages. The organism presupposes the world
of mechanism. The spontaneity of the life-processes does not
do away with the causality of the material, concrete world,
but "uses" it. The life-processes would be impossible to conceive without the natural laws of chemistry and physics. The
same is true for man as *humanus*. Genuine human action does
not put mechanics or the laws of biology or of the organism
out of action. A spectator in a sculptor's studio could fully
describe what he sees (*a*) as a mechanic (*b*) as a biologist
(*c*) as a humanist. Carving is a thoroughly mechanical process,
and presupposes the whole of physics. Working is a physiological process and presupposes the whole of biology. Artistic
creation is a wholly human activity of mind and spirit, an
act of freedom which is related to the law of norms and the
significance of Beauty. All three are interwoven with one
another, and are at the same time above or under each other.
The muscle controls the hammer, the mind moves the arm.
The "miracle" of the organism presupposes the mechanism;
the miracle of creative activity presupposes the mechanism

[1] Acts 3: 1 ff.

and the organism. What then is the position of the miracle of the Divine freedom?

Jesus Christ, the God-man, is "born of woman and subject to law". The miracle of Divine revelation takes place without the removal of the natural human presuppositions, in a truly human life. In the Passion all three are interwoven: the mechanical, the organic, and the human—and the miracle of the revelation of the glory of God in the suffering and death of a human being, and indeed, in such a way that it is precisely this divine revelation which brings out completely both sides of the divine nature: the constancy of His holy will, expressed in law, and the freedom of His merciful will of love. But the fact that the Cross becomes revelation is only possible through the Miracle of the Resurrection. By itself, the Cross *can* be understood from a purely human point of view, just as the death of Socrates is regarded as the martyrdom of a man who sacrifices himself for the truth. The fact that it is more than this, that it is the reconciling act of God, that Jesus is the Son of God, has been "declared with power . . . by the resurrection of the dead" (Rom. 1: 4). Believers alone are eye-witnesses of the Resurrection. Only to faith is it given to see this new dimension above the *Humanum*—the freedom of God— "miracle" in the truest sense of the word. Just as a dog does not know Michelangelo as a Master, but only sees him as a man who strikes a stone with wood and iron, so for the un-believer there is no Christ, no Risen Lord, but only a man, Jesus of Nazareth, who died on the Cross. The miracle of revelation can only be seen by faith. But this miracle of the God-Man is achieved without eliminating the natural order. The Son of God lived a natural human life, so that to many He seemed to be an ordinary man, and only the eye of faith was able to see the Son of God in His human "form of a servant". This central miracle is, as we have already said, surrounded by accompanying miracles whose significance is to point to the supreme central miracle; they are, if we may say so, miracles of a lower category. They too transcend what we usually call "normal" experience. They break through the enclosure within which our "ordinary" world is confined. We cannot say that in themselves they are more wonderful or "miraculous" than the wonders of the living organism, or than the wonder of human freedom; but they are more wonder-ful than these things because "usually" they do not happen. They are exceptional events whose purpose is to point to the central miracle in the Person of Him who works them.

From the standpoint of faith it would be remarkable if the God-Man did *not* do such unusual things, if He who is wholly New, in all that He is, and in all that He says, were not accompanied by an action which points to His uniqueness. So, as we contemplate His life, we see the two aspects existing side by side: the quite natural, completely human—truly man, as we are, *vere homo*—and the wholly marvellous, which had never before been seen or heard, in word or deed, which proves Him to be Unique, not only as One who is *primus inter pares*, yet He does not force this conviction on any one. It is both true and untrue to say that He breaks through the framework of our world view. It is untrue—for what He does, does not alter the normal processes of things—and why should not this world have room for what has not yet happened? It is true—for the Resurrection from the dead is really the beginning of the end of *this* world, the beginning of the new world, which is to come. So too His miraculous deeds are messengers which foretell what is to come, breaches in the walls of this natural world of ours.

The fact however that they are not *the* supreme miracle is shown in the fact that they are not without analogies. Jesus is not the only person who has worked miracles; His apostles also did so, and indeed according to what Jesus Himself has said, some Pharisees did so too.[1] These "accompanying" miracles are not in the strict sense of the word "unique", though they are exceptional.[2] They are not even without analogies in our own day. It is impossible to make a distinction in principle between the miracles of healing which took place during Blumhardt's life-time in Möttlingen and Bad Boll, and those which were worked by Jesus and His disciples. And the kind of thing which happened in Blumhardt's circle still goes on in secret, far more than anyone knows. It does not matter how many miracles, as they are recorded in the New Testament, actually took place. There is no doubt that legend has intruded even into the Gospel narrative—to see this plainly we need only look at the Apocryphal Gospels— and that now and again elements of this legendary material have penetrated into the canonical Gospels. But these legendary stories of miracles do not follow the law of miracle narrative

[1] Matt. 12: 27

[2] Hence it is a fundamental mistake to desire to support our belief in the Divinity of Christ by an appeal to His miracles (on this cf. Strauss, *op. cit.*)

peculiar to legend, but are wholly subordinate to the law of the divine revelation. Even the New Testament *legends* do not record miracles meant only to impress or to startle, but with marvellous delicacy they bear witness to the wonder and mystery of the Person of Jesus Christ.

There are no absolute, fool-proof criteria at our disposal by which we can distinguish a legend from a credible miracle story. Here the subjectivity of the judgment of faith is given a great deal of play. This, however, does no harm; no one becomes a Christian by believing in all the recorded miracles. And no one ceases to be a Christian because he does not believe in all the recorded miracles. But we may well assume that no one can be a Christian who does not believe in the one great miracle, which is Jesus Christ Himself.

(6) DIVINE PROVIDENCE AND HUMAN FREEDOM

If all that happens is determined by the will of God, how can human freedom be possible? If all that happens is determined by the will of God, then, confronted by the actual course of this world, how can we possibly call God a God of Justice and of Love? These are the two questions which inevitably arise, whenever we try to teach the truth of Divine Providence. Now let us turn to the first of these two questions.

As there is a "determinism from below" so also there is a "determinism from above". The former view denies human freedom from the point of view of the assertion of a causal natural order of all that happens. If this conception of causality be strictly conceived, i.e. as the power to calculate the future on the basis of the past, then, this determinism amounts to a mechanistic view of the universe. In our discussion of the question of miracles we saw that this "pan-causalism" distorts the view of reality, since it forcibly imposes an artificial theory of unity upon the graduated qualitative variety of reality. Its champions believe that this category can cover all that happens. They do not perceive that in so doing this view destroys itself. The distinction between "true" and "false" presupposes two equally possible conceptions of causal possibility, one of which is "true", and the other "false". Within a purely causal system of thought there is no room for this distinction; "true" and "false" presuppose the law of norms, not the law of causality; this means, however, that causalism ceases to be a system of thought which can claim to be true,

and can set itself up over against another which is "false".
It is a self-contradiction. It also shows itself to be a contradiction in the fact that no human being, not even the determinist, actually holds this causalism in actual life. "In practical
life" nobody believes in absolute determinism; practically
everyone presupposes an element of freedom which contradicts
the theory of determinism. Finally, pan-causalism, or determinism, is opposed to our moral knowledge of responsibility;
if everything happens because it *must*, then there is no room
for responsibility; responsibility can only be maintained by
the aid of intolerable sophisms. It is, of course, obvious that
this determinism is opposed to the truth of revelation, given
to faith.

But there is also a "determinism from above", which
declares that human freedom is an illusion, because all that
happens, even human action, is due to divine Providence.
Only a few Christian thinkers, like Zwingli, for instance, have
dared to draw this conclusion from their view of Providence.
Where this takes place, God also becomes the cause of Sin,
as Zwingli openly admits. "One and the same crime, for instance, murder or adultery, in so far as God has caused, moved,
and urged to it, is no crime at all; in so far, however, as it is
due to man it is a crime; for the former is not bound by the
Law but the latter is judged by the law". But if God incites
the robber to commit robbery, "is he not then forced to do it?
I admit he is forced, but in order that he may be executed"
(*De Providentia*, Ch. 2).

Calvin is less logical; although like Zwingli he conceives
Providence as the absolute determination of all that happens,
he tries to escape from the final conclusions, that even sin is
inevitable and God becomes the Origin of Sin and Evil. Such
an assertion seems to him—very naturally—to be blasphemy.
Only we cannot see how he can avoid drawing this conclusion,
save by a forcible act of will which refuses to admit a logical
conclusion. Of course, Calvin cannot be aided by the notion
that here we are speaking of a necessary or inevitable paradox.
A genuine paradox only exists where there is a real contradiction between two necessary ideas. But in Calvin's thought
this is not the case. For him the only thought that is necessary
is that of the truth that all that happens is determined by
God; he is not concerned with the thought of human freedom
and responsibility. At least, where Calvin develops the idea
of Providence he does not treat this second conception as one

which has final and equal necessity. Calvin denies human freedom, but he also maintains full human responsibility, while at the same time he asserts that God alone determines all that happens, without, however, ascribing to Him the origin of evil. This is the element in Calvin's thought which is so unsatisfactory, not to say painful and dishonest. He does not admit for a moment that there is an insoluble dilemma here, a paradoxical statement which cannot be regarded as free from contradictions, a statement which includes within itself two opposed assertions, but he proceeds as though everything were in order, while actually he is flying in the face of logic.

This raises the question: ought we perhaps to conceive the idea of Providence in another way? or must we come to terms, somehow or other, with this paradox, to be clearly formulated as such? The first answer is given by those—and in the long history of the controversy on this question in theology these are by far the most numerous—who make a distinction between divine determination and divine foreknowledge. God does not *do* everything that happens, but He *knows* it all beforehand. But does not such foreknowledge of an action in which God has no share seriously menace the idea of the Omnipotence of God? in order to avoid this a third idea has to be brought into play: that of divine *permission*. God does not will, nor does He cause the "Fall of Adam"; the rebellion of man, and all that flows from this; but, on the other hand, not merely does He foresee without being able to alter the course of events, but the very fact that He foresees it means that He leaves room for it to happen.

Our first question cannot be: which of these intellectual solutions is logically or metaphysically the most satisfactory? Rather, in accordance with our dogmatic canon we can only ask: What does revelation teach us more exactly about Providence? Here, first of all, we must remind ourselves of what was said earlier about the Omnipotence and the Omniscience of God. The God of revelation is indeed not the *potestas absoluta* of speculation, but the God who limits Himself, in order to create room for the creature. God wills to have a real "counterpart". God creates a creature, since He limits His absoluteness. The two ideas, Creation and self-limitation, are correlative. Anyone who has taken the first idea seriously has already conceived the second. It is not that the second is a result of the first, but the second is the same as the first, only it is seen from the opposite end. The idea of the divine self-limitation is included in that of the creation of a world which is not God, and in so doing the idea of *potestas absoluta* or of omni-causality has been given up.

This whole question of the independence of the creature, has, however, real religious significance only in view of human freedom. God wills and creates free creatures because He desires communion, not unity. He wills to be worshipped in freedom. This is the only sense in which Omnipotence, Omniscience, and Providence are conceived within the sphere of the Christian Faith. This is the primal *datum* of revelation, namely the revelation in which God addresses and calls man as person. The personalism of man's relation with God, which is based upon revelation, and is indeed identical with it, is not open to question at any point in further developments of religious thought. Whatever may be said about Providence, one thing is certain—that this original relation of the revelation which contains God's "call" to man, and responsibility, may not and cannot be questioned. This is the firm framework which is established from the outset, the original structure of truth-as-encounter, which cannot be broken by any further development in knowledge. All other interests, logical, metaphysical, religious, and ethical—are secondary, all have to fit into this framework.

From this standpoint, then, we must also consider the question of Providence. We have already seen, in the comparison between the Christian and the Stoic conception of Providence, that the former is personal and the latter impersonal. The Christian revelation not only allows us, but strictly commands us to begin by thinking of Providence in personal terms: "*Thou* art known beforehand, thought out beforehand, and willed . . . Thou, as one who is loved by God, determined by Him in order to respond to His love". We have to begin at this personal centre, not with the conception of Providence "in itself". This is what we know first of all, and all the rest we only know in the light of this truth. This is the way to teach the doctrine of Providence in accordance with revelation, instead of in accordance with philosophy and metaphysics. Only thus can we make a statement which is really Christian, instead of being a "foreign body" of natural theology in the midst of Christian belief. And in point of fact this is why we must object to the Idea of Providence not only of Zwingli, but also of Calvin, as well, of course, as of the younger Luther.

This view is deeply infected with natural theology and metaphysical speculation; it is not a purely Christian statement. Hence both views, the first admittedly, the second in spite of asserting the opposite, are connected with the Stoic conception of Providence—not all along the line, but so far as the problem of Determinism is concerned. Zwingli accepts the Stoic *necessitas*, Calvin rejects it in theory, but introduces it again without calling it by its right name. And he does so in the name of a conception of Omnipotence which is not that of the Bible, but of speculation.[1]

But if we start from the point where Election and Providence are identical, in the further development of the idea of Providence we come to the following conclusion: as those who have been called by God into responsible existence, we know that God's action gives us existence in freedom. We do not know how this happens; no amount of thinking will help us to get either "behind" or "above" this mystery. Secondly, we know that God does not will our sin, but that He does not allow our sin to drive Him out of our lives. Even as sinners we remain under God's Hand. God knows our sin beforehand, but He does not will it; nor does He commit it; and yet it does not happen apart from His will. He does not look at it helplessly, as though it could frustrate His plan. Even when we sin, He remains the Lord of our existence, in every part of it. What we have done against His will has already been, from the very beginning, part of His plan. How this can be we do not know; this interplay of "not-willing" and "not-doing" on the one hand, with the will that plans and rules on the other, is something far beyond our understanding. It has no analogies with the world with which we are familiar. To wish to operate here with such an absolutely concrete category as that of causality is contrary to sense; is it not true that we no longer understand anything about "persons" or "responsibility" when we try to think in causal terms? On the other hand, here we are not dealing with a "dilemma" or a paradox; that could only be the case if we wished to comprehend the divine omnipotence by means of the causal idea, and would then have to contrast it with freedom.

If in our definition of Divine Providence we remain within the sphere of revelation, the question does not arise: How can causality or determination, and freedom, co-exist? This

[1] Calvin's line of argument, e.g. in *Institutio*, I, 17, 5, is exactly in line with that of Zwingli

problem only arises when we leave the sphere of revelation and try to deal with it in the sphere of metaphysics. Here we are not faced by an intellectual problem, nor by a paradox, but by the impenetrable mystery of the divine working of Omnipotence, the working of Almighty God, who limits Himself, in order that He may make room for His creatures, and yet, because He *limits Himself*, does not cease to be Lord of all that happens. We know that both these statements are true, and indeed that the one is only true because the other is true. But we certainly have no idea *how* this can be so. To see through this mystery is the prerogative of the Creator, the mystery of His Nature and of His action. From the standpoint of revelation we must accept both statements; that God rules and directs all things; and that we alone, and not He, are responsible for the evil that we do.

The idea of "permission" in contrast to that of "effective causation", is no real solution of the problem. At bottom, it simply represents a kind of popular metaphysic, placed at the disposal of religious truth. Strictly speaking, it is no more admissible than the idea of "causation". It appears to provide a solution, which is no solution. But at least it does leave room for man's responsibility and, although somewhat inadequately, it does suggest that self-limitation which lies in the Divine Creation as such. The other line is that which is taken in the Bible as a whole: Human responsibility and freedom are placed alongside of the divine sovereignty over all that happens; the unconditional, clear, sole, responsibility of man for evil, and the divine power and wisdom which turns this evil into one of the threads used in the divine web—both without reflection on the logical possibility of combining the two statements. Our reflection just outlined is simply a justification of this Biblical way of expression, by going back to that which is given to us in the revelation itself.

(7) THE DIVINE GOVERNMENT OF THE WORLD AND THE ACTUAL STATE OF THE WORLD; THE PROBLEM OF THEODICY

The divine government of the world is to be distinguished from the divine preservation of the world. The former is related to natural existence as such, the latter to history. The "Divine preservation" of the world means that the actual existence of a natural order and of humanity cannot be self-derived, but that it can only be explained as derived from a continuous divine activity, and a divine presence in all that has been created. The doctrine of the "Divine government" of the world means that the natural course of history—of course, in its connexion with the natural order—cannot be understood in itself, but only in the light of a continual activity and presence of God, who, in this historical course, orders the whole of History towards the final divine goal. As the statement of the preservation of the world establishes the relation between natural existence and divine action, so the statement of the divine government establishes the relation between the natural historical course of events and the divine action.

It is obvious that these two questions cannot be entirely kept apart. The fact that natural existence is what it is, as something which has come to be thus through nature; the fact that it "is", is itself only intelligible in the light of history; it is itself an historical fact. Even Nature is not static; it has gradually reached its present stage by a process of development, and this development is still going on. For us to-day Nature has become far more historical than it was for the men of the ancient world and for the writers of the Bible. Not only have the forms of life gradually become what they now are but even the arrangement of masses in space, and indeed, according to the latest scientific cosmology the masses themselves, possibly even astronomic space has also developed gradually. Nature is thus far more historical than is generally supposed.[1]

And yet the theological problem of the government of the world by God is seen to be different from that of the preservation of the world only where man comes upon the scene. Once more, we are confronted by the problem: how can divine and human action coincide? but this time not from the point of view of human freedom, but from that of the divine love and righteousness. Here we are confronted by a problem of experience. It is the *quality* of the content of our historical experience, it is the character of the process of human history which forces us to consider this problem.

This problem is one which causes pain and difficulty both to the thinker and to the simple man or woman; has the theologian, then, the right to evade it, by stating that it is a question which ought not to be raised? The theologian can support this view by two facts: first, the human arrogance implied in the very idea of a theodicy—the attempt to "justify

[1] Cf. C. F. V. Weizsäcker, *Geschichte der Natur*

the ways of God to man"—and secondly, the fact that the question is never explicitly raised in the New Testament. These objections, as we shall see, have a solid religious basis. For in the long run, for those who really believe in Jesus Christ, this question of theodicy cannot be raised. Nevertheless, we have no right to skate over the surface of this question as though it did not concern us. In any case, it actually *is* the most burning problem in the realm of faith. Why this is so, and why, in spite of this, the question is wrongly posed is, in any case, a problem which we must face at all costs; we have no right to evade it.

It is, of course, possible to eliminate the problem at the outset, simply by abandoning the idea of the divine government of the world; this transfers the sole responsibility for history to man, and leaves God out of account. This is the easiest way of escape. Ought we, indeed, to make *God* responsible for something which *men* do? But this is tantamount to saying that God has nothing to do with history. Such a view might be possible for those who hold a certain Platonist Idea of God, but within the Biblical doctrine of God it is absolutely impossible. For the living God is the "God of History". Hence it is not strange that the question of Theodicy should arise within the *Christian* world, and be scarcely mentioned outside the world of Biblical religion. The more firmly God is regarded as the God of History, the more urgent does the problem of theodicy become.

This problem is presented in its most acute form at the centre of the Christian revelation, at the Cross of Christ. The Crucifixion of Jesus is an event in history; from the standpoint of the Christian Faith it is the central fact of history. But the Crucifixion is on the one hand the act of God, indeed *the* act of God absolutely, the Act upon which the whole Christian Faith rests; at the same time it is the most incredible, the most terrible scandal in the whole history of the human race. Thus we can only evade this problem if we evade the Cross, that is, if we renounce the Christian Faith altogether. Thus the view that seeks to release God from responsibility for historical events is incompatible with the Christian Faith. Here we are confronted by a clear choice: Either-Or.

Thus we can neither deny that History is full of injustice, shameful acts and sufferings, nor can we deny that God is the Lord of this History. The question is: how, in face of this twofold fact, faith in the God of love and righteousness can still be maintained. The awareness of injustice, suffering and cruelty within the sphere of human life is so pressing, and the contrast between this actual human situation and the idea of the divine love and righteousness is so sharp, and so urgent, that we are justified in saying that no one can preserve his Christian faith in God without having found an answer to this question. To find no answer here is to have to confess to loss of faith.

It is, of course, possible to give the following answer: I do not understand, and I do not need to understand: that is God's secret. That is Job's answer. Job pleaded with God. He never doubted God's almighty power, but he did doubt His righteousness and His love; he did not only doubt; he had been reduced to despair. All the smooth "solutions" of the problem which his friends suggested seemed to him to be simply futile excuses. Job felt that he was like a man who had been stricken to the dust, powerless to defend himself, who could at least still make a protest. The weak and fainting soul, who in spite of his weakness feels himself to be in the right, protests against the Almighty, who allows him to suffer unjustly—until, through a special revelation, God makes it clear that he, puny man, is not in a position to judge God's action, God's government of the world. And when he perceives this truth he becomes quiet. The problem has not been solved—far from it!—but Job, as man, acknowledges that he is utterly unable to judge, and thus that it is simply impious arrogance to try to bring God to account. This truth is sufficient for Job, and the profound unrest of his heart is stilled; through faith he enters into peace. Humbly he bows before the mysterious Almighty God.

This "solution" of the problem of theodicy belongs to the Wisdom literature of the Old Testament, which lies on the fringe of the Old Testament, because it bears little trace of the historical revelation of God which is the basis and content of the message of the Prophets. But what makes the book of Job, in contrast to the rest of the Wisdom literature, a precursor of the New Testament conception of the divine government of the world, is the suggestion of the rôle of Satan. The immediate cause of all the sufferings which fall upon Job is Satan, whose aim all through is to destroy Job's faith. Although here Satan still belongs to the court of Heaven, there is here a hint of the mighty conflict between God and the power of darkness, which forms part of the New Testament message. The problem of theodicy comes to a head in the

question; how can there be a diabolical power alongside of the
almighty and good will of God? but this question is certainly
not raised in the Book of Job.

At the other end of the scale are all the "solutions" of the
problem of theodicy which seek to divest the evil in the world
of all its problems—from the time of Origen, and indeed of
Irenaeus—and in some way or another try to explain it away;
this line of thought reaches its culmination in the "theodicy"
of Leibnitz. The arguments which are used are very varied in
character. The conflict between good and evil in the world
only causes the good to shine forth more clearly (Irenaeus);[1]
the evil in the world serves to intensify human intelligence
(Origen);[2] evil is non-existent, it is *privatio boni*; in the total
economy of the world it is good to have something like poison
for instance, which, rightly used, may be good (Augustine);[3]
evil is necessary, and is therefore a difference of degree (Thomas
Aquinas);[4] this world with all its imperfection is still "the best
of all possible worlds", since the very imperfections necessarily
belong to the nature of the finite; only God Himself can be
perfect but not the world (Leibnitz).

In all these "solutions" the tension which exists between
the will of a God of righteousness and love, and the actual
state of the world, is eliminated in thought, and the problem
thus becomes innocuous. It is not only intelligible, but it was
a good thing, that the Lisbon earthquake shattered this far
too easy optimistic solution. For our own generation, which
has experienced the first and the second World War, which
has seen the massacre of millions of Jews, the hell of Buchen-
wald and Maidanek, and also the devastation caused by bombs
at Wuppertal and Dresden, and by the Atom Bomb at Hiro-
shima, the revival of such rational solutions of this terrible,
and truly existential problem is unthinkable. They all seem to
us—with all respect for the seriousness of the thought which
lies behind them—to be playing the fool, and their efforts to
"explain" inevitably cause deep resentment and indignation
to hearts torn by the terrible wounds of this suffering world.

The "evolutionist" "solution" which for a time pushed all
other explanations into the background, is equally unsatisfy-
ing; here it was suggested that the suffering of the world and
the injustice in the world is inevitable in a world which is

[1] *Adv. Haer.*, IV, 39   [2] *De principiis*, II, 9
[3] *De Civ. Dei*, XI, 22 (cf. Origen and Athanasius)
[4] *S. Theol.*, I, qu. 48 and 49

only gradually becoming human, or to put it more exactly, the result of the imperfection which is essential to the nature of a humanity which is only gradually coming into being. This reply only pushes the question further back: Why did God create a world, in which all this injustice and suffering is the law of its growth? And, secondly, the injustice, the evil, which creates so much suffering, is not the result of a development which is either slow, or not yet finished; it is not a "not yet" but a "no more". It is not imperfection, but contradiction.

Far closer to Biblical religion than all these attempts to smooth things out, is the dualistic solution. Behind the suffering, behind the evil of the world, there stands not the will of God, but the power of evil. We cannot make God responsible for what the devil does, any more than we can hold man responsible when he is vanquished by diabolical temptation. Even in the Christian Church this view has been held; in ancient times by the Gnostic sects and in movements influenced by Manichaean dualism,[1] in modern days by Christian thinkers, who could only see that the idea of the divine Omnipotence had to be abandoned if we were to save the moral Idea of God from distortion. We have already called attention to the fact that the message of the Cross makes this solution impossible. A God who looks on impotently while the devil, or the evil in man, devastates His Creation, who is indeed innocent of all this evil and suffering, but also unable to do anything to prevent it, is certainly not the God of the Biblical revelation, of the Christian Faith.

The thought of Luther is quite different; he suggests that we must distinguish a twofold work of God, namely His *opus proprium*, the "real" work of God, in His saving revelation in Jesus Christ, in the revelation of His perfect love and righteousness in His Word, and, on the other hand, His *opus alienum*, His "strange" work, the work of His "left hand", the work of God which is "foreign" to Him, which we see when we try to look at God from the point of view of the world itself, when we only know Him as the hidden God, and not as He really is. This distinction is indeed correct, and it is inevitable for everyone who sees both sides of truth in God's light: the Cross of Christ as our salvation, and the crucifixion of Christ as the result of human malice and blindness. God does not will both in the same way, although it is certain that for the sake of the one, which He really wills, He wills the other

[1] Lactantius inclines to this idea; cf. *Inst. div.*, L, II, c. 8

which He does not really will. This distinction may be said to create a necessary intellectual clarification, but it does not solve the problem of theodicy. We may, however, say that it brings us to the right standpoint, from which we can look at the question as a whole.

It may be said, that the Message of the New Testament *as a whole* is an answer to the question of theodicy. It shows us the rift, which goes right through the world which God has created. God did not create either the evil in man, or the devil as the power of darkness. At this point the New Testament shows the element of truth in dualism. Evil, and the suffering which it causes, is the result of the contradiction, which has arisen in the creation created by God to be free, but which has turned against His will and His order in rebellion. God has not only created the creatures who are not free, who cannot do anything other than obey His will; but He has also created creatures who have a free will, who *can* become disobedient, who can decide against His will. The fact that this has happened, is evident to all; *why* it happened—that is the irrational element, to which there is no answer. The doctrine of twofold predestination, which also derives this evil in the same way as good from God's original free will, is, as we have already seen, incompatible both with the Biblical idea of God and with the testimony of the Bible. The reality of this contradiction is plainly stated in the New Testament in all that it tells us about Christ's struggle with and victory over all the forces ranged against God. The realm of darkness and the Kingdom of God are at war.

Thus Evil, and all the harm which comes from it, is opposed to the will of God, and God is opposed to it. It is the product of apostasy from God, of the perversion of the divine order of Creation. It is the product of the misused gift of human freedom. But this does not mean that God has nothing to do with the historical course of this world, which is so full of evil and suffering; that, if we may put it so, He simply looks on and can do nothing. The God of the Bible is not like that "God" who in Borcherdt's drama *Draussen vor der Tür* (Outside the Door) is represented as a pitiful old man who is always weeping and wailing and saying "I can't help it!" The whole question looks entirely different when we contemplate it from the centre of the Christian Faith. If there ever were an event in which evil, innocent suffering, malice and human pain reaches its climax, it is in the Cross of Christ. From the human point of view, from that of freedom, it is the maximum of that freedom which men have sinfully abused, which is fighting against God, and to which God Himself is opposed. At the same time, the Cross is God's sovereign act of redemption. Judas, Caiaphas and Pilate are the enemies of Christ and God is therefore their enemy. At the same time they are instruments of God, through which, more than in any other event, He reveals His righteousness and His love. Thus, here, at the Cross, it becomes evident that evil is that which God does not will and does not do, and at the same time, that God has such power over this evil, which He does not will, that He is able to make it an instrument of His saving work. At this point we perceive the unity of the mercy, the righteousness and the omnipotence and omniscience of God. At this point it is granted to us to have a glimpse into the mystery of the divine government of the world; the impenetrable darkness which otherwise lies upon it, is lifted like a curtain before our eyes. As soon as we look away from the Cross and try to explain world history ourselves in theological terms, the curtain falls once more, and we are left gazing into impenetrable darkness.

Thus here, in the centre of the revelation, the problem of theodicy is solved, but not in theory (as in those theories of the philosophers and the theologians), but "existentially", and practically. We stand before the Cross it is true, not as innocent or neutral spectators, who gaze with horror into an abyss outside themselves which appears within the world, with all its injustice and pain, but we ourselves stand in the midst of the abyss. The rift which cuts through the world passes through us. It is for us that He hangs upon the Cross. Since we know this, we also know that there is no suffering in the whole world which could be too "great" or too "unjust" for us to bear. The only "innocent" suffering is that which He has endured who Himself bore it for us.

In the presence of the Cross we cease to talk about "unjust" suffering. On the contrary, as we look at the Crucified all our suffering gains a positive significance. "To those who love God all things work together for good"[1]—we know this as those who have perceived that the sufferings of Christ were for the good of the world. Now we may unite our sufferings with the sufferings of the Crucified; as those who are united with Him in faith we may conceive them as suffering with Christ, even when from the moral point of view our sufferings are well

[1] Rom. 8: 28

deserved. For us suffering loses its negative character; it becomes fruitful, as God's means of discipline, by means of which, in paternal severity, He draws us to Himself. This is the greatest transformation possible in the sphere of human experience. Without taking away the sting of suffering, without fostering a desire for suffering, suffering becomes a positive instead of a negative principle.

Finally, there is yet another result: "I reckon that the sufferings of this present time are not worthy to be compared with the glory which shall be revealed to us-ward".[1] The believer looks beyond his suffering to the final goal which it must serve; compared with that promised glory, his suffering does not count. Suffering becomes the way to eternal life. Here, then, the theodicy problem is not solved *intellectually*, but, by a real redemption, it is overcome. This does not mean that what is terrible becomes less terrible; terrible as it is, it is conquered by Him who permits us to bear this suffering, in order to purify us, and thus to prepare us for that life which no longer contains suffering. The real solution of the problem of theodicy is redemption.

But how does this problem look to those who do not believe, to those who cannot understand it from the standpoint of the Cross? They too suffer, and feel sure that they, or others, are "innocent," and that such suffering is undeserved. We must answer, there is no second solution, outside the true solution of faith. It belongs to the unredeemed sinful state of man, it forms part of the punishment of sin, that man cannot solve the theodicy problem—unless he repents and believes. Indeed, the theodicy problem finally proves to be a form of unbelief, in so far as man allows himself to adopt the rôle of an objective neutral spectator, in so far, that is, as the question is raised from a point outside one's own responsibility, according to the connexion between the will of God and the evil in the world, and in so far as, in so doing, man takes his seat on the accuser's bench alongside of God, and pretends that he is the judge (theodicy), where man really stands in the dock, before the heavenly Judge. It is not for God to justify Himself, but it is He who judges and justifies us through Jesus Christ the Crucified, through whom He reveals to us both our guilt and His almighty mercy.

This is why we no longer hear Job's question in the New Testament. In faith man is disarmed from the outset, not

[1] Rom. 8: 18

merely like Job, by the thought of God's impenetrable wisdom and power, but by the disclosure of a guilt for which no suffering would be too great a punishment, and by the revelation of love which takes from us the real punishment and pronounces us sinners free from guilt by grace. Only the man who yields to the temptation to abandon this attitude of faith, and to usurp the place of the judge, is confronted by the theodicy problem; and then it is insoluble. To this extent those theologians who call it a question which is wrongly posed, and therefore turn it down altogether, are right. But we ought not to refuse to answer this question of the natural man; only we must not look for an answer at the wrong point. The right answer is certainly one in which the problem is not *solved*, but it disappears, because we see that the real solution lies in the acknowledgement of guilt and in the hope of redemption.

Only now does it become clear why all these theoretical speculative "solutions" of the question of theodicy are false solutions. They all come to this: that they try to solve the problem by way of thought, instead of recognizing the contradiction as a reality which can only be eliminated by another reality. In the problem of theodicy the contradiction, in which the creature is engaged against the Creator, is theoretically objectified and thus already falsified in the posing of the question. Hence too all attempts to answer this question on the plane of theoretical objectification are sham answers, sham solutions. The Gospel of the Cross forces us to abandon this attitude of the spectator in which alone the problem of theodicy can be posed, and in so doing to renounce all theoretical solutions. Thus the message of the Cross completes that which had been begun with Job; only that the believer in Christ no longer, like Job, reverently and with resignation is dumb before God, but he regards the true solution as an act of God.

One particular point, however, should still be mentioned explicitly: the arrogance of the human opinion that God "ought" to allow Himself to be measured by *our* standard of justice. Our conception of justice (as a duty) implies the norm of equal treatment. If we want to be just, then we must—in some way or another—treat others in the same way. But God is not under any obligation to deal with us as equals. This demand only applies to our relation to those who are on a level with ourselves. Because we are—and in so far as we are—equals, the demand for equal treatment between us holds good, as the content of the idea of justice. As equals, we owe equal treatment to others. But God owes His creatures nothing. He can create as He will, great and small, strong and weak, higher and lower living beings, human and sub-human life. It is only the arrogance of man who sets himself up alongside of God as His equal who thinks that he has a standard of justice. God does not live with us in a democracy as *primus inter pares*. As Creator He is absolute Lord, who is not bound to give any account of Himself to His Creation. He owes no one anything. What He gives, He gives in complete freedom. He is not tied to our standards of justice. He proves His justice in the constancy with which He provides validity and effectiveness to His Law which He has given to us. The element of equality which is decisive in all human justice has no validity in the divine justice. But the divine justice is completed, it is true, in the free and generous gift of His Mercy. That is the content of the message of the "righteousness of God revealed apart from the Law", which is the great stumbling block for all thought about justice which desires to restrict God's freedom.

APPENDIX TO CHAPTER 6

THE QUESTION OF MIRACLES AND THE POSTULATE OF "DE-MYTHOLOGIZING"

DURING the nineteenth century the question of miracles was a prominent subject of discussion; in the theology of our own generation however, on the whole, the interest in it has died down. But it has recently been revived, quite unexpectedly, by Bultmann's theory of the *"Entmythologisierung"* (or de-mythologizing) of the Christian Faith. On the basis of this hypothesis Bultmann rejects a whole series of ideas contained in the message of the New Testament, which have been hitherto regarded as central elements of the Christian Faith. Bultmann, however, condemns them as "mythology", since they are in accordance with a view of the world which we no longer hold and can therefore no longer combine with our present view of the world; thus we cannot retain them in our faith and doctrine without an inner conflict. The two irreconcilable pictures of the world may be described by the formulae "mythical" and "scientific". "Our thinking is irrevocably moulded by science" (*Offenbarung und Heilsgeschehen*, 1941, pp. 27 ff.). By a world "moulded by science" Bultmann means a causal view, that is, an understanding of objective events which is determined clearly and on all sides by causality.

This antithesis has suddenly placed the problem of miracle in the centre of theological debate. Here it is not the credibility or non-credibility of this or that miraculous incident recorded in the Bible which matters, but our understanding of the Biblical message as a whole. Possibly in this debate it may not be very wise to contrast the "mythical" view of the world with the "scientific", because the idea of Myth is itself many-sided. Apart from that, however, we are here dealing with a problem which neither the exegete nor the systematic theologian can evade. (On the exegetical problem in Biblical Theology the following is excellent: Kümmel: *Mythische Rede und Heilsgeschehen im Neuen Testament*, in *Coniectanea neotestamentica in honorem Antonii Friedrichsen*, Lund, 1947.) Here what is at stake is nothing less than the central theological question of revelation, of "Saving History", and the knowledge of God as a "Living God", who is the Lord of Nature and of History.

Now, however—quite apart from the discussion raised by

Bultmann—we must admit that the witnesses of revelation who speak to us in the Old and in the New Testament have a view of the world which is foreign to us, and that an important task of theology is to distinguish, and even to separate this from their actual witness to revelation itself. We have already dealt with this point (above) in the doctrine of Creation, as well as in the doctrine of Man, and that in some detail. It must also be granted that modern man, including us all, lives in a different world from that of the Middle Ages, to whom the most extraordinary miraculous narratives seemed credible, incidents which none of us nowadays would accept. Further, we would not deny that the difference between that world and our own is determined, not solely, but to a large extent by the development of the Natural Sciences, especially since the time of Galileo. In the world in which we live, "miracles", in that ancient medieval sense, "do not happen". But it is not so easy as it looks at first sight to define the difference between these two worlds.

This might seem easy to anyone who follows the line of thought which—like that of Spinoza—identifies Nature and God; to whom, therefore, everything and nothing is miraculous. Spinoza indeed was the first radical critic of the Christian belief in miracles—whether of the Bible or of the Middle Ages (*Tractatus theologico politicus*, Part X). With the Enlightenment the belief in miracles began to decrease visibly— (though one cannot say that it disappeared altogether) including the unusual events recorded in the Bible which everyone calls "miracles".

Idealism may, it is true, have ridiculed the rationalist explanations of miracles of that epoch, but only in the sense that, like Spinoza, it emphasized the miraculous character of *all* events. This was particularly true of Schleiermacher, who in the interest of genuine piety rejected miracle outright, because he believed that "absolute dependence" upon God was better based on the uniform interrelatedness of nature than on a partial suspension of this relation (*Glaubenslehre*, I, para. 47). Since then, this phrase—"the uniform interrelatedness of nature"—has very largely, even among theologians, gained the force of a modern axiom. This has been taken for granted, to such an extent that any attempt to question this "axiom" would be regarded as the act of a reactionary and superstitious person. Moreover, this axiom was reinforced by the powerful authority of Kant.

This axiom, however, is far from being infallible. It was criticized first of all by theology, then later by philosophy, and finally by science itself. The theology which has not been infected by the Pantheism of Spinoza, the rationalism of Kant, or the Monism of Idealism, but which believed in the God of the Bible, emphasized the truth that the God of the Christian Faith is certainly not the God postulated in the theology of Schleiermacher, whose action is identical with the processes of nature, but that He is the Living God, who, as the Creator of the natural order, is also its Lord. *Either*, there is revelation, there is "Saving History", in the sense of the fundamental message of the Bible, and then God influences the course of nature, a process which cannot be explained in naturalistic terms; all the theologians of the nineteenth century who held to this belief were agreed about this. *Or*, there is only that revelation, which can be perceived by the religious mind in the natural course of events, as such; but this is not "Saving History", and there is no Living God. Of course, a theologian like D. F. Strauss could only make fun of such a faith: "The most modern view to-day is to be seen in the abandonment of the strict idea of miracle, of the *miraculum* and still more of the *mirabile*, the influence of forces of a higher order—as it is called—in the life of Jesus and in the Biblical narrative as a whole" (*Glaubenslehre*, I, 252). Of course, such a view does not escape the reproach of being a "weakening of the interrelatedness of nature" (*ibid.*, p. 276). In spite of such condemnation, a large number of theologians who cannot be accused of lack of scientific education or of reaction, continued to hold this notion of miracle—namely, of the miracle which is posited by the recognition of God's sovereignty over Nature, including particular revelation and saving history. The theoretical justification for this retention of the view of miracle over against that of the claim for a "uniform interrelatedness" of nature is not always expressed in the same way; but this intellectual explication is secondary as compared with the fundamental attitude, and this fundamental attitude was and is for all these theologians identical with the Christian Faith.

Criticism of the axiom of a "uniform interrelatedness of Nature" followed, however, not only from the theological, but also from the philosophical, and finally from the scientific side. As soon as, and wherever, the difference between Nature and History, between natural and spiritual events was grasped, the idea of a "uniform interrelatedness of nature" ceased to carry conviction. If there is a real free activity of man, how then can this form part of the "uniform interrelatedness of Nature"? From the point of view of such considerations Lotze—one of the few German Theistic philosophers—began to question this axiom; above all, however, it was Bergson, with his idea of *Évolution Créatrice*, who made a breach in this wall. Finally, the scientists themselves came upon the scene, and partly on the basis of the presuppositions of Historical Science, and partly on those of Biology, and finally on those of Physics itself, they subjected this axiom of a "uniform natural order" to sharp criticism. This idea was indeed not a scientific postulate but a metaphysical hypothesis, the hypothesis of the uniformity of all that happens. Above all it was Laplace who gave it logical mechanistic expression by his theory that it would be possible to foretell the progress of nature for all eternity, if only "the masses and their velocities were given".

Thus instead of Galileo's scientific working hypothesis that first of all we must seek for a causal explanation of all physical happenings, Laplace formulated the metaphysical axiom that everything must be explained in this way, that nothing happens that cannot be explained in mechanistic terms. The severely determinist mechanistic formula has been proved untenable, not only in the sphere of Historical Science, but also in that of Biology, and finally even in Physics. To-day, not even the physicist believes in the "closed universe" of a thinker like Laplace. But this means that the idea of a uniform inter-relatedness of nature becomes not only suspect but meaning-less. All that happens every day constantly "weakens the interrelatedness of nature". Every meaningful idea which is thought, every artistic idea which takes shape constitutes such a "weakening". The idea of the "uniform interrelatedness of nature" has ceased to be taken seriously in theological discussion of Miracle. Apart from theology, it has long been proved to be impossible.

Unfortunately, this truth is not generally recognized in the usual treatment of the idea of miracle, or at least it is not made clear. The idea of miracle is held, it is true, in the sense of the miracle of revelation, in the sense of belief in the Living God, the Lord of Nature, but the effort is made to support this belief with inadequate intellectual methods, most of which have been derived from Thomist or Augustinian theology. Thus Augustine had already formulated the idea that Miracle does not happen against Nature, but "against the nature of

anything from what it was before unto Man's knowledge"
(*de Civ. Dei*, XXI, 8, 2). Certainly, there is some truth in this
idea. The free action of man not only breaks through mechanical
causality, but also uses it. But both St. Augustine and St.
Thomas are working with a conception of Nature which may
have received a theological interpretation or expansion, but
which was never the idea of the Living God, of the Lord of
Nature. It is theologically questionable; it "naturalizes" God
Himself. It is, however, not only theologically, but scientifically
untenable, for it makes the sphere of daily happenings uniform.
It does not recognize the plurality of spheres of existence, and
of varied relations to causality, which this implies. We can
therefore agree with theologians like Ihmels (*Die christliche
Wahrheitsgewissheit*, 3, pp. 225 ff.), Stange (*Naturgesetz und
Wunderglaube* in *Christentum und moderne Weltanschauung*),
Seeberg (*Christliche Dogmatik*, I, 252 ff.) in their effort to
justify the central miracle from faith in the Living God of
revelation, but we must at the same time maintain that the
intellectual methods by which they do this are inadequate,
both from the point of view of theology, and from that of
scientific method.

This brings us back to our starting-point, to Bultmann's
postulate of "de-mythologizing". Doubtless there does exist
a legitimate task of this kind, because the world-view of the
Bible actually helps to determine the witness of revelation.
But when Bultmann claims that our faith must eliminate
everything that suspends the "interrelatedness of Nature" and
is consequently mythical, we must seriously remind him that
in so doing he is using, as a criterion, a concept which has
become wholly untenable. This unity is broken by the first
appearance of an organism which cannot be explained, as a
mechanism can be, from its parts; with the first meaningful
word spoken by a man, which makes havoc of all causal
explanations. We do not even need Biblical miracles to get rid
of this dead stock of a mechanistic eighteenth-century natural
philosophy.

The question of miracle is the question, whether outside
the non-mechanical happenings in the organic sphere, and
outside the free action in the human sphere, there is a still
higher freedom, namely, that kind of happening which cannot
be grasped even with genuinely human categories, namely
happenings due to the freedom of God. It is the failure to
recognize this situation which causes Bultmann's thought to

oscillate between, on the one hand, the desire to admit the miracle of revelation, and even of special revelation, and the rejection of the Biblical concept of miracle, which he regards as derived from a world-view based on myth. The fruitful discussion of the task of "de-mythologizing" only begins once this bugbear of the idea *uniformity of nature* has been eliminated.

There is still one final question, which is perhaps not of central importance, but is still not unimportant. We have hitherto only taken into account the facts of everyday life as they occur in the mechanical, organic, and human spheres. But there are also happenings which are, it is true, well attested, and to a certain extent even established from the point of view of science, but which certainly do not belong to everyday life. We usually refer to these happenings as "the Occult".

This whole sphere of happenings, like the central belief in miracle, has fallen a prey to the Enlightenment. These things cannot be explained, therefore they ought not to exist. Of late years a different outlook has prevailed (see notes on literature in Bavink, *op. cit.*, p. 778). Scientists of proved integrity and objectivity in their methods and tests have examined these "alleged" facts, and to-day there is a whole complex of ideas from this sphere, which used to be regarded as ridiculous, which has been absorbed into the scientific vocabulary, and plays a part in medical practice. I am thinking about "suggestion" with its astonishing effects and its inexplicable physical results, and also of hypnosis. Other phenomena, like telepathy, are already accepted in science, although they have not won general acceptance. Recently, above all, there is "depth psychology" which is forced to take into account the reality of these inexplicable phenomena; indeed the whole sphere of "the Unconscious" was not at first accepted by science, whereas to-day not only the theory, but above all the practice based upon it, has become established everywhere. All these phenomena are, more or less, outside the sphere of that which can be explained. They do not fall into either organic or human categories. They remain, and perhaps always will be, "occult".

Now a great deal of that which is described as "miraculous" in the Bible belongs to this sphere—at least it seems to do so. Many of the events which are there recorded have certainly a relation with the "occult". We ought not to exclude the possibility that where God, in His freedom, intervenes in human history, such things do happen; that is, they accompany, and throw light upon His action. In any case they are important testimonies which help us to understand such inexplicable, rare, and unusual events as "signs" of the divine activity.

In itself the Occult may be neutral, and may have no special relation to the Divine. But this does not exclude the fact that God may and can make use of it as a sign of His special presence in revelation. We should not in any case overlook its connexion with the Power of the Holy Spirit, both in the Old and in the New Testament. The fact that modern man does not care for such ideas, and finds them foreign to his way of thinking does not matter. "There are more things in heaven and earth, Horatio, than are dreamt of in your philosophy." Certainly this does not alter what has already been said: that we cannot and indeed ought not to believe in many miracles, both inside and outside of the Bible; that the world-view of the early Middle Ages was too uncritical, while the thought of the Enlightenment was too sceptical. The idea of the "uniformity of Nature" does not explain away the reality of these strange and unusual happenings.

On the other hand, it is certain that for us the belief in the miracle of Divine revelation is not tied to belief in these "miracles"; that for us, as for our predecessors, they do not lead to faith in the true miracle. When Luther says, that God allowed the external miracles to happen at the beginning of Christianity "in order that Christendom might begin to believe", but that after such beginnings these miracles were no longer needed, this is probably what he meant. The "proof from miracles" of Catholic theology, that is, the basis of faith in Christ on the fact that Jesus worked miracles, has to-day for most people become entirely unconvincing. We believe in the miracles of Jesus when we already believe in Him, but not before. And even then we do not give up the right to criticize this or that recorded miracle, this or that marvel as due rather to the "myth-forming imagination" than to the historical fact. But a modern theologian ought to be open to the possibility that the great miracle (of revelation) may produce most unusual results.

CHAPTER 7

HISTORY AND SAVING HISTORY

HISTORY is not a theme usually included in treatises on dogmatics; for the idea of history is foreign to the thought of the Bible. Yet Biblical theology differs from all other religious doctrine in the very fact that it is historical through and through. All that the Bible has to teach us is based on the historical revelation. It is in that light that we have considered God's Nature and His Will, His Creation and His government of the world, the doctrine of Man as created by God, and man as sinner. In the light of Jesus Christ, in the light of the revelation of the Old and the New Testament alone, have we been able to see what we have seen. Now we turn to the source of our knowledge, the historical revelation itself. What we believe as Christians, we believe because something particular has taken place in history. This "particular thing" that has happened in history we call "saving history" (*Heilsgeschichte*), or the history of salvation, or the history of revelation, or the historical revelation.

Before, however, we begin to consider this revelation—the divine revelation in the Old and New Testament—from the theological point of view, we must let our gaze range over the wider field of human history in general, within which this particular "revelation" history—or "saving history" plays its part. In the light of the historical revelation, in the light of Jesus Christ—what ought we to think about history as a whole? the history of mankind and of nations? What is the Biblical, the Christian understanding of History?

1. Although the Bible may lack the idea of history, yet it has the perspective of world history. Though it may possess no explicit doctrine of history, yet it has an implicit understanding of history. The historical, the universal historical horizon, is already present in the fact that the Bible begins with the narrative of the Creation, and the story of the beginnings of humanity. Even if we have to admit that the divine Creation of the world lies on the further side of all that we can conceive as happening within history—and this not merely accidentally, due to the absence of historical material, but necessarily, because the Creation is the "other-worldly"

mystery which lies beyond all that it is possible to know—on this side—as development and as history,—yet this historical presentation of the mystery of Creation does suggest that the world created by God has been created as an historical world.

We speak to-day of a "history" of Nature, and we are right. Here there is something to tell. The world as we know it to-day was not always what we see now. In the long process of transformation it has become what it is to-day. Nature is far more historical than the ancients used to think. Scarcely anything we see to-day was there from the very beginning. Not only are the present forms of plant and animal life "comparatively new", the descendants of earlier flora and fauna which have now died out; not only has our earth assumed its present form in the course of millions of years; not only has the earth itself, and the Solar system developed—some thousands of millions of years ago—out of something which was neither sun nor planets, but even the original material constituent "elements" of this world, which seem impervious to change, the atoms, have developed through unimaginably revolutionary processes out of conditions which were not the elements or the atoms as we now know them.[1] Indeed, if certain modern theories of astro-physics are correct, even the universe itself has only become what it is as the result of a process of transmutation of energy in a highly paradoxical process of expansion, a process which is still going on. Nature is far more historical than we knew even a few decades ago. Naturally, the Bible knows nothing of all this; but in contrast to most of the religions and philosophies of the ancient world it knows that the Creation of the world has been achieved empirically, that is, on the side which is accessible to our perception, as Creation-*History*. This is, however, not its main interest. The history which the Bible relates, is the history of man.

The world-historical outlook, or as we would say to-day, the horizon of world history, of the Old Testament (which is also that of the New Testament), comes out very clearly in the fact that the history which it narrates is that of man, of mankind as a whole. We often forget that "Adam" and his early descendants were not Hebrews. Before the Bible tells the particular story of Abraham's descendants, it deals with the origin and the early history of all the races of mankind.

Thus the Bible sets the particular history, presented to us

[1] According to a lecture by the Zürich astronomer, Professor M. Waldmeier. Cf. the writings of the Berlin physicist Jordan in *Nationalwissenschaften*

as the history of the self-revelation of God in Israel, within the comprehensive framework of world-history. Even though this historical narrative may have no particular historical value—no historical scholar to-day would use the early chapters of Genesis for a history of human origins (though this was done as a matter of course till well on into the eighteenth century)[1]—yet these early chapters are of great importance for the historical understanding of the Bible, and thus for our own view of the meaning of history.

First of all, this means that the history of mankind is a unity. This is certainly not something we can take for granted; indeed, from the purely empirical point of view, it is a very doubtful, not to say improbable assertion; for according to the present position in the study of Palaeontology it seems far from likely that mankind is derived from one common origin. This, however, is not the point of the Biblical narrative. The history of mankind is a unity in the Bible because it understands man—whether Jew or pagan—as man "before God". There is a unity of mankind which is wholly independent of the question of the biological origins or beginnings of humanity. As *"Humanus"* man is "Man" *tout court*. This is what we were discussing when we were speaking of his creation in the Image of God, and of the Fall. Man is always and everywhere the responsible person, whose constitution always and everywhere points to this relation with God, and with other men, in community. Man, absolutely, of whatever race or whatever biological origin he may be, is always, everywhere, and at all times, wherever we may meet him, the same, with the same fundamental constant factors of his nature, as *Humanus*, always everywhere the being capable of humanity, civilization and culture, the being who can speak, and who has a conscience. Man is always and everywhere "Adam", the being of whom (on the evidence of the Bible) we have been speaking in the previous chapters. Through this destiny as *Humanitas*, given by God to every human being, the unity of the human race and of human history is guaranteed, even if the biological unity, which the Old Testament narrative implies, is merely the temporary garment of a deeper truth.

The second point is this: that from the very outset man is regarded as an historical being. Man has been created for community. He has been created to make the earth subject

---

[1] Cf. W. Kaegi, *Voltaire und der Zerfall des Christlichen Geschichtsbildes*, in *Historische Meditationen*, 1942

to himself. He has been created to name the rest of the creation and thus to know it.[1] The feature of *universalitas* is also imprinted on his *humanitas*. Although the whole of the historical life of man stands under the shadow of the expulsion from the Garden of Eden, yet the fact of being historical is not regarded as a result of the Fall. The Bible makes none of those suggestions which later on became the subject of theological speculation, which were secretly inspired by the Platonic myth of the Fall. Historicity belongs to the nature of the *Humanus*, for it is part of his nature that he must make his own decisions, and that he can do so, that he shapes his own life and does not vegetate.

Above all, however, the historicity of man is unmistakably expressed in the fact that he, man, that all nations, not merely Israel, move towards a goal which God has set for them, and towards which He leads them. This theological character of history does not come out so plainly in the narratives of Genesis, it is true, as it does in the Prophets. All nations are figures in God's universal plan.[2] All nations therefore should in some way have a share in the Messianic goal for which Israel is destined.[3] Whereas this universal historical teleology is only foreshadowed in the Old Testament, and is secondary to the special vocation of Israel, in the New Testament the universal purpose for the whole of humanity is the content of the message of the Kingdom of God, and of the proclamation of Parousia and Resurrection, the Final Judgment and the End of the World. That which was at first only known in Israel, and at first too was only understood as meant for Israel, is in the New Testament freed from all national limitations. Jesus Christ is the Saviour of the whole world. His salvation is God's Purpose for *all nations*; all the currents of history must merge in the one goal of the Kingdom of God. The history of humanity is the correlate of the message of Christ; where Christ is proclaimed humanity and world-history are seen to be one.

We may indeed say that the conception of world history is derived from the Bible, even though it does not use this word.[4] There is no conception of the history of humanity in any other religion, or in any philosophy of the Ancient World.[5]

---

[1] Gen. 2: 19   [2] See for this, chiefly, the Second Isaiah
[3] Isa. 2: 3 ff., 49: 6, 60: 3
[4] Cf. Eichrodt, *Theol. d. A.T.*, I, pp. 266 ff.; J. Hempel, *A.T. und Geschichte*, 1929.
[5] In a purely empirical sense Polybius already had "The conception of universal history" (Schrenk, *op. cit.*, p. 71, *Jahrbuch der theol. Schule Bethel*, III)

Polytheism is not capable of such a unified view, and the non-historical religion of the East has no conception of the goal of history. Those religions which have freed themselves from their local or national limitations—such as Buddhism and the higher forms of Hinduism—show no interest in history. Judaism is the one exception; it derives its view from the same Bible as Christianity, although it only uses the first half of the book. Islam also comes under the same heading; but its teleology of History is derived from Jewish and Christian sources.

On the other hand, it is an extremely characteristic and significant fact that the whole of Greek philosophy, which contains the germ of almost all the other elements of later thought, and has developed most of them to a large extent, has no conception of history, any more than the great religions of the East.[1] The theme of world history, and thought controlled by the outlook of universal history, which has become natural among Western nations—and through them to a large extent also among other nations—is due to the Bible. On the other hand, the form which this world-historical thought has assumed in modern times, is a mixture of Biblical teleology and an Idealistic or Naturalistic theory of the evolutionary process in History. The belief in progress which, especially in the last century, was the hope of the nations, cannot, indeed, be conceived apart from the teleology of the Bible; but here it is in a secularized form. Four elements combine to create this belief: the Biblical Hope, the Idealistic idea of development, the causal theory of Evolution of Natural Science, and the experience of the progressive technical domination of Nature. The two World Wars, the menace to humanity of the Totalitarian State, and the development of technics, which has outstripped man's power of dealing with it, have cut away the ground from under the feet of those who believed in Progress. Humanity oscillates uncertainly between absolute despair and an optimistic view that still believes in "progress".

The Christian belief in the goal of human history[2] is solely based on God's purpose for the world revealed in Jesus Christ. "Having made known unto us the mystery of His will according to His good pleasure, which He purposed in Him unto a dispensation of the fulness of the times, to sum up all things

[1] Windelband, *Lehrbuch der Geschichte der Philosophie*, pp. 212 ff.
[2] Cullmann, *Christus und die Zeit.*; Delling, *Das Zeitverständnis des N.T.*; Wendland, *Geschichtsanschauung und Geschichtsbewusstsein im N.T.*; Schrenk, *Die Geschichtsanschauung des Paulus*; Kümmel, *Kirchenbegriff und Geschichtsbewusstsein in der Urgemeinde und bei Jesus*

in Christ, the things in the heavens, and the things upon the earth."[1]

The unity of world history, not only as the history of humanity, but as the history of the cosmos, is based upon the eternal divine decree, as it has been revealed to us in Jesus Christ, the Crucified. This goal of history, whose inmost meaning is the kingdom of God, the perfect dominion and perfect self-communication of God, is destined for the whole universe.[2] God is the God of all nations; He has created them all; He guides them all; He leads them all, in a way which we cannot see, towards the eternal Goal.

2. This historical outlook, the greatest that could ever be imagined or thought, includes the particular history of the people of Israel, and of the Church of Jesus Christ. Outside this particular history, the specific history of revelation and salvation, we do not know the living God. It is true that God has not left Himself altogether without a witness, even in this wide sphere; He has made known "His everlasting power and wisdom" in the works of His Creation. Hence no nation, no group of mankind is without some consciousness of God, without religion, without that *"sensus numinis"* (Calvin). For, whether they know it or not, they are all "Adam", Man, who has been created by God. But also—whether they know it or not—they are the "Adam" which has fallen away from God, to whose Fall it is due that the divine revelation in Creation is misunderstood—as polytheism, pantheism, deism, atheism, idealism, materialism and the like. Without a new beginning, which is the work of God alone, and can never be understood as having "developed" out of pagan precedents, we human beings would know nothing of the unity of humanity and its history, which is implicit in the Divine Purpose.

The fact that at first this new beginning does not stand out very clearly from the general course of history, that the first beginnings of the divine revelation in Israel are still difficult to distinguish from the heathenism of the surrounding nations, does not mean that this is *not* a new beginning. The situation is similar to that of the divine new creation, man. Man as *Humanus* is never to be understood from his animal origin. But this specifically *human* element in man begins, almost imperceptibly, as a new thing, so that an unthinking believer in the theory of evolution is convinced that this element is derived from the animal creation. The first beginnings of the

1 Eph. 1: 9   2 Eph. 1: 9-11

particular revelation of God in Israel are embedded in the mythology and religion of the Semitic religions of the Near East. The divine revelation which we connect with the names of the patriarchs, Moses and the Prophets, takes place in a series of acts of revelation, which, when we look back later on, we are bound to understand from the goal in Jesus Christ as a progressive revelation. God's historical revelation is added, so to speak, to the natural process of human development, and above all to that of the people of Israel. The picture of "revelation-history" which is given to us in the Old Testament can no longer be ours. Historical research has shown it to be a later Priestly theological construction, which probably contains historical elements, but at the same time conceals as much as it reveals of the real course of events. Thus the origin of the bearer of this history, of the people of Israel itself, is far more complex than the presentation in the Old Testament shows us which, in the form which we now possess, is the theological view of history of the priesthood of the post-exilic period.[1] The actual course of the divine history in revelation is essentially different from what it seems to the simple reader of the Old Testament.

If we wish to be honest we cannot help speaking of a history of "progressive revelation". God did not reveal Himself in the time of the Judges, or even in the time of Moses, as He did to Isaiah, Jeremiah and the great unknown Prophet of the Exile. In His revelation God took into account the stage of development man had reached; He did not disclose everything at once, but gradually, through a history of some fifteen hundred years, whose first beginnings are dimly seen through the mists of antiquity. So much, however, is quite clear—through the more exact work of research into the sources of this revelation, as they lie before us in the Old Testament, namely, that the beginnings so far as we can know them, and the peaks of this history which lie in the full light of historical knowledge, are far from one another, not only in time, but also in concreteness and actuality. God has acted like a wise educator who imparts to His pupils according to their power to receive. What He gave to the primitive people of the time of the Judges is not the same as that which He gave through His prophets in the later years of the Monarchy.

This point of view, of an educative, gradual revelation, had already been worked out very clearly by the first great

[1] Kittel, *Gesch. d. Volkes Israel*

theologian of the Early Church—whose close dependence on the Bible we have often mentioned—Irenaeus, who developed this idea in his conception of the economy of revelation. "It is one and the same house-father, Oikonomos, who rules the whole household, giving to the slaves and the undeveloped a suitable law, but to the free men and to those who through faith are justified, imparting corresponding rules and opening up to the children the riches of their inheritance . . . namely, the Word of God, our Lord Jesus Christ."[1]

This idea of the economy of divine revelation was taken up again by Calvin. *"Si pater familias* aliter *suos liberos in pueritia,* aliter *in adolescentia,* aliter *in juventute erudiat regat et tractet, non propterea dicemus ipsum levem esse aut a sua sententia discedere."*[2] What these two great theologians say about the difference between the Old and the New Testament is also true of the differences within the Old Testament story of revelation itself. There is nothing "evolutionary" about this point of view; the divine revelation cannot "evolve". But the divine revelation can be so ordered as to be adapted to the natural development of man, and actually this is what has been done. This does not menace the unity of the divine revelation at all. All that matters is always the self-revelation of the One God; but this self-revelation of God has taken place gradually, through a long process of history. It has simply pleased God to give first the imperfect, then the more perfect, and finally the perfect. In so doing God gives us both the justification for, and at the same time the pattern of educational adjustment from stage to stage.

The fact that the particular divine revelation in the Old Covenant only gradually and slowly began to be differentiated from the religious life and practice of the surrounding world, does not alter the fact that in contrast to it, it is something wholly new and incomparable. The new element in it is to be seen, above all, in the fact that the God of the Old Testament, from the very beginning, makes Himself known as the God of History. Not in Nature, but in historical events and persons, in the Exodus from Egypt, in the wonderful deliverance at the Red Sea, and during the years of wandering in the wilderness, through the creation of an elect people for Himself, through a covenant, through mighty helpers and heralds of His will, who intervene in the History of Israel and at the same time make known that its history is from God both in Judgment

[1] *Adv. Haer.,* 4, 14, 2   [2] *Institutio,* II, 11, 13

and in Mercy, God reveals Himself in Israel—and in Israel alone. The fact that the Old Testament stands "between" the New Testament and the common religious world of paganism makes no difference. Certainly in the Old Testament we still find much of what is found in the other religions of the Near and Middle East: Myths, rites, polytheistic features, various blends of religious and moral elements with the magical element and the like. But in spite of all this there is something in the Old Testament which does not exist outside it, and that is what binds the Old Testament plainly and exclusively with the New Testament: the revelation of the Living God of History, of the Holy and Merciful God, of the God who marches towards a goal with His people. The God who has perfectly revealed Himself in Jesus Christ, is the same as the One who reveals Himself in Israel in a provisional and preparatory way.

3. This duality of identity and non-identity, of the *unitas* and the *diversitas testamentorum*, has already been clearly expressed in the New Testament. At first the impression given by New Testament doctrine as to the relation between the Old and the New Testament is confusing. It seems to contain contradictory statements which suggest that they are due to some persistent confusion or uncertainty of thought. Actually, this variety of statement is not due to uncertainty, but to the variety of the points of view from which this relation may be contemplated. We can group these statements under three headings: (a) that there is a fundamental difference between the Old and the New Testament which almost amounts to a contradiction; (b) that they are so closely united that they are almost the same; and (c) the interpretation of this very dualism by the all-inclusive conception of Promise and Fulfil-ment. In each instance, however, one point is unmistakable. Where revelation is concerned, it is not the *Book* that matters, first of all, the writings of the Old Testament as such, but always the revelation of God in history, to which the Scripture bears witness. For all the witnesses, whether of the Old or of the New Testament, the God of the Old Testament is always the God of History, who reveals Himself through His "mighty acts", and not through the dictation of an Infallible Book. It is, of course, true that His Prophetic Word is also part of His "mighty acts" in so far as this is due to His command, it is also "the Book". But the Book is never the canonical form of His revelation, but the Living Word, expressed as His acts in History, as His intervention in the history of men. To hold

that the revelation of God, the "Word of God", is an inspired
Book, taken down by infallible dictation, is an "intellectualistic"
misunderstanding. For this view turns the divine revelation
through history into a timeless doctrine.

The difference, indeed the contrast between the Old and
the New Testament is emphasized most decidedly in St. John
and St. Paul. "The law was given through Moses but grace
and truth came through Jesus Christ."[1] In the Fourth Gospel
those who oppose Jesus are simply called "the Jews". Paul
calls the service of Moses "the ministration of death", the
"letter that killeth" and "the ministration of condemnation",
while the Gospel of Jesus is Spirit, Life and Freedom.[2] We
find this antithesis, however, even in Jesus Himself. "Ye have
heard that it was said to them of old time—*but I say unto
you*":[3] John is the greatest of the prophets, but "he that is
least in the Kingdom of heaven is greater than he".[4] Similarly,
Paul contrasts the whole period of revelation before Jesus
as the period of the Law, with that which is now revealed
"apart from the Law".[5] The words "now however", this sense
of something *wholly new*, is the keynote of the whole message
of the New Testament.

Over against this series of statements there is another,
which, on the contrary, emphasizes the identity of the Old
and the New Covenant. Jesus Christ was already at work in
the "revelation-History" of the Old Covenant before He came
in historical form as the son of the carpenter. It was in His
Name that the fathers who wandered through the desert were
baptized; His body is the manna which sustained them; He
was the spiritual rock from which they drank, for "that rock
was Christ".[6] Alongside of the "Jerusalem which now is"
described as Hagar, Mount Sinai and the synagogue, there is
the other—the "Jerusalem which is above", which is characterized by the names of Abraham, Isaac, and Jacob, and by the
Promise which is given to faith alone.[7] Abraham is the Father
of the faithful, and he represents the contrast to the righteousness of the Law.[8] The whole of the Scripture of the Old
Testament bears witness to Christ.[9]

The passages which contain the twofold idea of Promise and
Fulfilment show us how these two series of statements, which
seem to be contradictory, are to be reconciled. The whole of
the Old Testament is Messianic promise. The Prophets looked

[1] John 1: 17   [2] 2 Cor. 3   [3] Matt. 5: 21, 27 ff.   [4] Matt. 11: 11
[5] Rom. 3: 21   [6] 1 Cor. 10: 1 ff.   [7] Gal. 4: 24 ff.   [8] Rom. 4   [9] John 5: 39

forward to the time of the revelation of Christ, they foresaw
and foretold His sufferings and His glory, and in so doing they
showed that what they said was not meant for their own day
but for the future.[1] Abraham saw the Day of Christ and he
rejoiced.[2] The Prophets are the precursors of the witnesses
and heralds of the coming Anointed King. Thus the identity
(of the two Testaments) only exists in retrospect, when seen
from the standpoint of Christ. The content of the Prophetic
message was Christ; but the *way* in which they proclaimed it,
as the fore-shadowing of something which would happen in
the future, is different from the witness of those who look back
on something they have really seen, who can tell it as the story
of a real man of flesh and blood.

Even the idea of Irenaeus and Calvin, of "educational
preparation", is not foreign to the Bible. Even if the *paidagogos*[3]
of whom Paul speaks is not an educationalist in our sense of
the word, but a "superior" slave, "entrusted with the moral
supervision of the child" until he came of age, yet a "tutor"
of this kind is used by God to prepare the way for that which
Christ alone can do in reality; before Jesus Christ came, the
People of Israel were in a state of minority and slavery; they
served God as though He were a stranger, but now they have
become children and sons who serve their Father.[4]

It is therefore a mistake to say (a) that there is a great
difference between the Old and the New Testament; (b) to
urge that the relation between the two is that of likeness or
identity. Those who see only the difference do not see the
necessary connexion, the unity of all that is most important in
all divine revelation; those who see only the unity do not see
the real history, and do not notice that it has pleased God to
prepare the way for the perfect by the imperfect, to prepare
the way for His coming by ways and means which are merely
temporary. The truly Biblical Christian view sees both
together: the difference and the unity. If we only see the
difference we lose the sense of the value of the Old Testament
as God's revelation; if we only emphasize the unity, we turn
revelation into a timeless doctrine. The same tendency towards
timelessness also occurs where the temporal terms "afterwards"
and "beforehand", are changed into the spatial terms "behind"
and "before". Because the Prophets *foresaw*, they did not yet
see the fullness of that which the Apostles were able to say

[1] 1 Peter 1: 11   [2] John 8: 56
[3] Gal. 3: 24 (cf. Lightfoot, *Galatians*, p. 147 ff.) (Tr.)   [4] Gal. 4: 2 ff.

after it had actually happened. Those who place the Old and the New Testament on the same level deny the significance of the Event, and turn revelation into an idea; then it does not matter *when* the idea is perceived. The community which has experienced the Incarnation of the Word in Jesus Christ, His Cross and His Resurrection, does not possess the same, but infinitely more than the community of the Old Covenant, which had to live on the mere Promise of something which would happen one day. The Apostles, and indeed the Lord Himself, always stressed the fact that here is something "more", something "wholly new", in spite of the bond which unites the Old Testament with the New.

4. From the standpoint of the New Testament the Old Testament must be regarded from the twofold aspect of pre-interpretation, and preparation. The New Testament regards the Prophets as those whom God appointed to proclaim Jesus Christ and His significance beforehand. The prophetic revelation of God was indeed the revelation of the Nature and the Will of the true God; but all this was on the understanding of its temporary character, its imperfection, and its limited character. For the revelation of the personal God could only be completed in the Person of the God-Man. No prophetic Word could reveal God as He reveals Himself, present in person, in Jesus Christ. This temporary character of the Old Testament comes out equally at all points of doctrine, but especially in the truth about sin, reconciliation, and the culmination of God's eternal Purpose. The Old Testament teaches practically nothing about Eternal Life; yet from A to Z it is eschatological, directed towards a goal which God gives to His people.

At the same time, however, the Old Testament is preparatory; the Old Testament revelation itself creates the presuppositions for the reception of the revelation of the New Testament. As we cannot imagine the prophecy of the Second Isaiah taking place in the period of the Judges, so also we cannot think of the life of the Son of God as taking place in the days of Isaiah. The preparatory revelation of God alone created the conditions in which one "born of the Seed of David", "under the Law",[1] could live as the Son of God.

The idea, moreover, that Jesus Christ "might just as well have been born in the Athens of Pericles, or in the Nanking of the ancient Emperors of China", is absurd; Jesus Christ

[1] Gal. 4: 4

had been long foretold; and the coming of Christ as an Event had long been prepared. The phrase which is so often repeated "that it might be fulfilled which was written" is not only "proof from Scripture", but at the same time it points to the unity of the history of revelation. The Christ, in order to be true Man, had to take up into Himself, in His own Person, the history of His people, and incorporate it. He had to be a true Israelite, both in body and mind. We understand the unity and the difference of the preparatory and the fulfilling history more clearly when we hold firmly before our eyes the three standard forms of the revelation of the Old Testament: the Chosen People and its King; the Temple with its sacrifices and priests; the Prophet and the Word of God.

(a) Israel is the only nation in world history whose existence and distinctiveness is based upon historical divine revelation. Israel is what it is in virtue of the Covenant. Its historical existence is not a natural one, nor is it a simple political fact, but it is the product of the Mosaic revelation, of the divine Election as this particular people, with which God from the very beginning works out His purposes, to which, as to no other people, He makes known His Will, and in which, through this, His proclaimed will, He rules and shapes His people. Therefore from the beginning Israel is not merely a national political entity, but it is at the same time a "Church", which, through faith in the historical revelation, is also established and held together.

Although its origins are partially hidden in obscurity, and although certainly they are not identical with the picture which is given in the Old Testament itself, yet this one point cannot be refuted, that at the outset of the history of Israel there is the Event of Moses and the Exodus from Egypt, in the remembrance of which Israel continually renews its unity and its distinctive character.

Israel is a "prophetic Theocracy". Therefore its Royal House is in a kind of twilight.[1] On the one hand it had lost something of its special character, when compared with other nations; on the other hand, its Davidic Dynasty is the preliminary basis of its Messianic Hope. "Personified Divine Sovereignty", the unity of a nation under one head, in which the will of God is achieved—this is the idea of Israel. And yet it is precisely in the fact that the national element and religious

[1] Cf. Procksch, *König und Prophet in Israel*; Eichrodt, *op. cit.*, pp. 237 ff.; *"Die zwiespältige Beurteilung des Königtums"*

unity, divine revelation and the Law of the State, are inseparably, and even indistinguishably interwoven, that the temporary
nature of Israel consists. This national element defines and
delimits the Hebrew "People" of God. The moment will come
—connected above all with the name of the Apostle Paul—
when this unity had to be broken, when the wall of partition
which separated Jews and pagans had to be torn down. The
way for this severance was already prepared in the political
weakening of Israel by the foreign occupation of the post-
exilic period. It is difficult to imagine that Jesus Christ could
have done His work in a politically independent Israel—for
instance, in the brilliant period of the Davidic monarchy. It
was only the personal piety of the Psalms, which was the result
of the political weakening of Israel in post-exilic Judaism,
which prepared the way for the message and the work of Jesus.

(b) From the standpoint of the Epistle to the Hebrews we
understand the revelation which was both foreshadowing and
preparatory, and at the same time merely temporary, reflected
in the Hebrew system of worship. The great doctors of the
Church, and Calvin above all, have continually drawn our
attention to the educative value of the Jewish system of
worship. It made plain to the people of Israel that God in
their midst is Holy, that He desires from them service, the
service of worship, that sin requires sacrifice, that the people
need atonement. But the prophetic protest against a mistaken
confidence in the Temple and the offering of sacrifice drew
attention to the ambiguity of this ritual manifestation of
revelation. Only through the sacrifice of Christ, however,
could the sacrifices brought by man, but accomplished through
animals, be fulfilled. For here at last it becomes clear that the
sacrifice which is adequate for sin is that of the whole man,
and that we human beings cannot offer this sacrifice. It is not
that the prophetic protest denied the value of the cultus, or,
when it did mean this, that it was right. For the sacrificial
system, even in its very questionable form, always implied
that there must be sacrifice. On the other hand, we cannot deny
that the sacrificial system in the Old Testament is its most
temporary element.

The most immediate, direct and clearest prefiguration of
revelation is the Prophetic movement. For it was through
this movement above all that the truth of the Holy and
Merciful God, who is the Lord of the whole world, was revealed.
The divine revelation in *History* first became truth through the

Word of the Prophets. In the prophetic Word, as nowhere else, God made His Name known to His people. So it is also the Prophetic Word in which there was a suggestion of a future revelation, through which alone the full Presence of God with His People, and the complete sovereignty of God over His People, was to be effected, by which not only was Israel at last to become the true People of God, but in which other nations were to have their part. Modern scientific study of the Old Testament has shown us, in a way which would have been impossible before, that the Prophets were not primarily "foretellers" of the future, but men who proclaimed the present claim of God to sovereignty. And yet the older conception, which indeed can be traced to the New Testament, was right to this extent, that the most wonderful thing about this prophecy of the Old Testament is the fact that it points beyond itself. The Prophets know themselves to be the forerunners of the Coming One, as the last of the Prophets, John the Baptist, is the divine Herald who points to the Christ who is coming and is already present. Old Testament prophecy is nullified if it is conceived only as "prophesying"; we empty it of meaning no less if we suppress this feature which points to the End, to that which is not yet, but is to come.

Thus too that prophecy, which, from the standpoint of the New Testament, is the real witness to Christ of the Old Testament, the vision of the Suffering Servant, is not accidental, but is necessarily an enigma which cannot be understood in its own light. No "sober historical" exegesis of this most mysterious and marvellous chapter in the Old Testament, could really do it justice. The Servant of the Lord of the Second Isaiah is sometimes Cyrus the King of the Persians who frees Israel from exile, sometimes the people of Israel, which suffers for the other nations, sometimes a solitary prophetic figure, which stands over against the rest of the nation as a vicarious sufferer, whose description, however, fits no historical personality. It is impossible for us to say plainly "whom the Prophet meant". What he says, is most intelligible when we look at it from the standpoint of the historical Jesus, who was crucified upon Golgotha. So the early Christian interpretation hits the nail on the head, although certainly we cannot assert that the Prophet who wrote this chapter "meant Jesus". Here we are confronted by an exegetical enigma, which cannot be satisfactorily solved by the methods of scientific exegesis. The foreshadowing of the real Servant of the Lord, who came six hundred years later, is quite obvious, and yet, how much was needed before the disciples were able to see their Lord in this light!

The unity, and the real meaning of the historical revelation of the Old Testament cannot be understood from the Old Testament itself, but only from the standpoint of Jesus Christ, just as, conversely, Jesus cannot be known as Christ where He is not understood as the One who fulfils the Old Testament revelation through history. But this only becomes completely clear when we grasp the unity and differences of the two Testaments from the standpoint of the contrast between the Law and the Gospel.

APPENDIX TO CHAPTER 7

THE orthodox intellectualistic conception of the Bible which crystallized later on in the theory of Verbal Inspiration, very early forced the Church to reinterpret the Old Testament, in order to make the crude meaning of certain sections, if too literally understood, tolerable, and to bring them into harmony with the New Testament. Thus an "allegorical" method of exposition was developed in which the text was claimed to possess secret hidden meaning, which lay behind the text itself. This alone made it possible, to some extent, to retain the theory of the doctrinal unity of the Old and the New Testament, in the orthodox sense. It is obvious that in so doing the door was thrown open to a very arbitrary method of exegesis. A student of the Bible could read into a given passage anything he liked, simply by referring to a secret, deeper meaning. The Reformers wanted to get rid of this allegorical system of exposition. They urged that the Bible should be expounded according to the simple and obvious sense of the actual words, and in so doing they helped to prepare the way for understanding the Scriptures in the light of historical criticism. Otherwise, how could they dare to give the Bible into the hands of simple readers who were not in a position to produce such brilliant allegories, or, if they were to try to do so, would only end in falling into a morass of arbitrary interpretation of the Biblical text?

The Reformers[1] held that this method of allegorical interpretation was not wholly mistaken. This is intelligible, because the New Testament itself, and Paul in particular, used this method a great deal. This use of "types" does not mean that anyone can read any meaning they like into the Old Testament; it refers only to witness to Christ, prophecy concerning Christ. Not only did the example of the New Testament point in this direction, but also the fundamental Christian truth of the relation of the Old Testament to the New: prophecy and fulfilment. The Gospel of John, indeed, which does not say much about "types" contains the words: "Ye search the Scriptures [i.e. the Old Testament] . . . and these are they

---

[1] Zwingli was more in favour of this method than Calvin

which bear witness of me"[1] Typological interpretation chiefly differs from that of ordinary allegory in the fact that it sees in the event itself, in the history of the Old Testament, the "type" of the history of the New Testament, the "foreshadowing" of the story of Christ. Anyone who accepts the fundamental Christian principle that the Old Testament, the ancient dispensation as a whole, is the Promise of the New, must admit that there is a certain justification for typology. Ultimately, the one thing it wants to say is this: that the true significance of the Old Testament can only be understood in the light of the New Testament.

In spite of this, however, this method of typological *exegesis* arouses deep misgiving. The aim of "exposition" is to bring out what the text actually says, what the writer intended to say. This is the unchanging rule for all exposition which is concerned with truth. Any method of exposition which ignores this rule leads to arbitrary interpretation. The critical historical theology of the past hundred years or so has quickened our consciences on this point, and has helped us to try to listen more attentively to the actual language of the text. How then can we combine this regard for truth, which throws light on the relation between the Old and the New Testament, and should therefore be preserved, with the concern of typological exposition? The answer to this question lies in a distinction which has not been sufficiently emphasized in the past, that is, the distinction between exposition and arrangement (or classification). The primary task of the expositor of the Old Testament is simply to work out clearly what the text itself says. He remains true to the Reformation-principle of the historical or "natural" explanation of the Scriptures.

But when he has done this part of his work, if he is a believing Christian, he will certainly want (and be able) to relate the text which he has thus expounded to all that which he knows as a believing Christian. He will see both the event, and the record of the event, in the context of New Testament history and teaching. He will admit that—actually in the critical historical exposition of the Old Testament Scriptures—a revelation is given which points to the New Testament as promise to fulfilment. This comes out most clearly in the genuine Messianic prophecies (not in those which have been created artificially by an arbitrary method of interpretation). As Christian believers we cannot help understanding Jeremiah's

[1] John 5: 39 (TR.)

prophecy of a New Covenant in the light of the New Covenant which, the New Testament says, has taken place in Jesus Christ. But this does not mean that we can then say Jeremiah "intended" to say what is said in the New Testament. What Jeremiah said, however, is integrated by faith into the context of the New Testament. Here we are not thinking of "exposition"—exposition must always be natural and historical—but of believing integration (or arrangement).

This is really what the witnesses to Jesus Christ intended, who "searched the Scriptures" in order to "see if these things were so". But they did not know how to make this distinction between exposition and arrangement. Their uncritical method of exposition cannot be our example or our norm any more than their view of the world. To some extent they were not afraid of the wildest methods of allegorical exposition because they knew as little about a critical method as about a scientific view of the world. When Paul expounds Deut. 25: 4[1] by saying that these are not real "oxen" but "apostles", then we must have the courage to say: at this point Paul is wrong. It is *oxen* and only oxen, and not apostles, that are meant. This is arbitrary "allegorizing", customary in the Rabbinical schools. Here we must not follow Paul, any more than we can follow him in his idea of the vault of heaven, which is that of the ancient world as a whole. But when he speaks of the rock from which Moses drew living water, and then of that "spiritual Rock", and then adds "the Rock was Christ", and then speaks of the manna in the wilderness, and relates both to the Sacraments of Baptism and Holy Communion,[2] this is certainly not an "exposition" of the text, but it is a way of relating the revealed truth of Old Testament history to the revealed truth of the New Testament, which brings out the inner significance of both.

Hence a work like that of W. Vischer, *Christuszeugnis des Alten Testamentes*, is both a valuable gift, and a book with a dangerous tendency to arbitrary exposition. It is a valuable gift, because the writer accepts, fully, the fundamental truth that the Old Testament, as a whole, witnesses to Christ, points towards Him, and is a precursory revelation of Him. The exposition of the Old Testament from the "evolutionary" point of view of last century retained little of this fundamental truth, and was therefore unable to show the connexion between the precursory and the final revelation. Hence Vischer's

[1] 1 Cor. 9: 9   [2] 1 Cor. 10: 1 ff.

reaction was necessary. But this reaction has gone too far in one direction, just as "purely" historical criticism went too far in another. The method of historical criticism failed to relate the text to its main significance: but Vischer's treatment confuses exposition and significance;[1] in so doing it has opened the door to arbitrary methods of exegesis. Thus when anything "red" is mentioned, this must be a reference to the "Blood" of Christ. Wherever "wood" or "gallows" is mentioned, the writer sees a secret allusion to the Cross of Christ.

Over against this well-meant, but devastating and arbitrary method, it does one good to read Calvin's commentaries, with the sobriety of their historical critical exposition. In the eighth Psalm, the writer really means "man"—in spite of the Epistle to the Hebrews—and this is the sense in which Calvin expounds this Psalm. The greatness of Calvin—we may indeed say his unparalleled greatness as an expositor—consists in the very fact that he, who knew more about the actual connexion (in revelation) of the two Testaments than perhaps anyone else, in his exposition of the Old Testament kept so close to the historical "natural" sense, and resisted the temptation to allegory, even in its typological form.

The typological method of exposition is to-day a great temptation, especially for the preacher. The preacher's task differs from that of the expositor, although he must base what he has to say upon the labours of the exegete. His task is to preach God's word, on the basis of the actual text. Thus his work includes both a thorough exegesis and a sense of the main significance of the passage. But the exegete who offers him his Biblical material already arranged, calling it typological "exposition", takes away from him a great deal of the work which he ought to do for himself; and ought not the overworked parson to accept this gratefully? The mistake is not in the actual presentation of typology, but in the fact that typology is misrepresented as "exposition". The effect on the members of the Church is disastrous; they have no clue to the interpretation of the Bible. They will say: "We cannot explain the Bible like our Minister, he . . . is so clever, and so ingenious—he can 'find Christ' in every part of the Bible!" This means that such people will probably do one thing or the other: *either* they will give up their own private Bible reading altogether: *or* they will try to imitate their Minister; then they will indeed fall into a pit, and indulge in flights of the wildest allegory! They

---

[1] Lit. *Einordnung* = arrangement—classification (TR.)

too will see a reference to the "Blood" of Christ every time anything "red" is mentioned, and they will feel highly edified! But they will have lost *one* blessing: they will have ceased to *read* the Old Testament; for they will be reading into the Old Testament either the views of their Minister, or their own fantasies.

To argue that it is right to use typology as exposition because it was used by the Apostles is an argument that would only enter the head of a Fundamentalist. For him the whole Bible is God's infallible oracle, and all that the Apostles say has equal divine authority. This unfortunate confusion of thought which we can already see to be the influence of the school of Wilhelm Vischer, and the so-called "methods" of Biblical exposition which they breed, can only be described by the word "terrible". We can only warn people most urgently against this confusion of thought, which inevitably leads us back to a religious position which the Reformers had overcome; indeed, this victory constituted the Reformation.

CHAPTER 8

THE LAW

THE idea of Law in the Bible—both in the Old and the New Testament—is a very comprehensive idea, not at all easy to grasp. *Torah*, for instance, is the description of the Pentateuch, in contrast to the Prophetic writings and the *Kethūbīm*; thus it is here a method of Biblical classification. *Torah* also means the whole Covenant-revelation of the Old Testament, the sum-total of all that God has revealed to His People. Thirdly, *Torah*, according to its original, linguistic meaning (from a root meaning "to direct") signifies God's explicit *claim*—His "direction" for man's life. This "direction" is laid down in three ways; to us their importance varies considerably; we must therefore distinguish them clearly from one another.

First, there is the legal code itself, especially that which we would to-day call the Penal Code; secondly, there is the ceremonial law, or the directions for the cultus; this deals chiefly with the sacrificial system and the directions for ceremonial purification, both in connexion with, and apart from, the Temple; thirdly, there is the ethical or Moral Law, containing the rules and principles governing the life of society, and right behaviour towards one's fellow-men—including the right inner attitude towards them—rules which are not found in either the ceremonial or the civil law.

On the other hand, the Old Testament itself does not contain that idea of "law" which has become the standard one in the teaching and theology of the Church: the law of the Ten Commandments, the Decalogue. In the New Testament, especially in the thought of Paul, in addition to these four to seven meanings of the word "Law", there is another, namely, that which contrasts Law and Promise, or the Law and the Gospel; and finally, there is the idea of law which identifies the Law with the Old Covenant or the Old Testament, contrasted with the New Covenant and the New Testament. It is obvious that the use of such a complex idea, capable of bearing so many different meanings, can lead to terrible confusion of thought, unless it is drastically clarified; indeed, this confusion still exists, and influences the most vital social and political problems of the Church. So we must look at this subject again,

in its relation to the heart of revelation, and then try to clear
a path through these confused ideas out into the open.

We are following a specifically Reformed tradition—and
indeed a tradition which may be particularly described as a
Zürich tradition—when, in order to clarify our thought, we
return to the idea (which the work of modern Old Testament
scholars has emphasized afresh, as the centre of the understanding of the revelation in the Old Testament) of the
Covenant.[1] The God of the Old Testament revelation is the God
of the Covenant, and His revelation is the revelation of a
Covenant.[2] From the standpoint of this central conception
that complexity of the idea of Law which at first sight seems
so confusing and accidental, becomes intelligible, and is seen
to be "in order", and not "accidental" at all. First of all,
however, we must get rid of all those definitions coming from
the later Reformed tradition, gathered up under the term
"Federal or Covenant Theology", since their juridical, rationalistic terminology, combined with a rather dangerous *theologia
naturalis*, would create further confusion rather than clarification.

1. The God of revelation, the true and living God who is
revealed in Jesus Christ, is a *God of the Covenant*. This is not
only the explicit testimony of the Old Testament, but also
of the New Testament. God's revelation is a covenant revelation. God's fundamental act in History is the establishment of a
Covenant. His will is a will to community, and His will to
community relates not only to isolated individuals but also
to "His People". The prophetic word (Jer. 7: 23) "I will be
your God, and ye shall be My People", is not only Old Testament but New Testament, if we give the term "people" its
New Testament, supra-national breadth. In mysticism, and
in the speculative philosophy of religion, the main concern is
with "union", but in the Bible the central concern is "community". God's Nature is *Agape*, and *Agape* is the will to
community.

But this will to community is at the same time the will to
sovereignty. Because God's nature and will is Holy Love, the
realization of communion with God is at the same time the
realization of the sovereignty of God. Since God communicates
Himself perfectly, His will to proclaim His sovereignty is fully

[1] Cf. Schrenk: *Gottesreich und Bund im älteren Protestantismus*

[2] Eichrodt rightly develops all his theology of the Old Testament from
the point of view of the "Covenant relation"

achieved. We have treated this subject in detail in the volume on the Doctrine of God.[1]

Equally important, however, is the other aspect, namely the fact that because God's will is a will to community, and not to unity, the realization of this will presupposes someone "over against" Himself, who is willed as a genuine "counterpart" and is not overwhelmed and crushed by the will of God. The "I and Thou" of the divine relation to the world and to Man is certainly not a *schema*, introduced into Christian doctrine by the "I-Thou philosophy", but it is the true, fundamental relation between God and Man. God takes fellowship seriously; hence He is not only concerned to assert His claim as "I"— the Lord—but He also cares for the human "Thou". He wills to "rule" in such a way that His sovereignty is freely accepted by man; His love desires to awaken responsive love in man, the "obedience of faith"—ὑπακοὴ πίστεως. True communion between God and man can only be expressed in the words: "Let us love Him, for He has first loved us".[2] The love which God gives awakens in us an answering love through faith. It awakens us, however, in such a way that the fact that we are called means that we know we have to answer.

This is the heart of the Biblical idea of the Covenant: the realization of the divine self-communication and sovereignty in communion with and amongst men, which comes into being as a free answer to God's generous grace. God wills to rule, but He does not wish to overwhelm; He wills to rule in the freedom of obedience. God wills to create community, but He wants to have a genuine community, in which the voice of the partner, the human "Thou", is also heard. Man is not an equal partner, for he can only say "Yes" because he has already received the "Yes" of God as a gift; and yet he is to be a real partner, who may, and indeed should, say "Yes".

The unity of the Old and the New Testament consists in the fact that in both instances what matters is the revelation of the God of the Covenant, and thus the establishment of a covenant.[3] God takes the initiative. He establishes the Covenant. The covenant comes into being through the Grace of God who has "come down",[4] who has mercy on His People, indeed, who has only created the nation as His People through this merciful gracious revelation of Himself. It is thus that the Prophets understood the event at Sinai. It was thus—

---

[1] See Chapters 14 and 15   [2] 1 John 4: 19
[3] This is the *motif* of the Epistle to the Hebrews   [4] Exod. 3: 8

although with all kinds of foreign additions—that the Priestly tradition regarded it as History, and this primitive constituent of the Old Testament view of History has held its ground against all assaults of historical criticism, although many details of the narrative have had to be eliminated. Thus we have to understand the Law in the light of this establishment of the Covenant. Zwingli and his friends rendered a great service by their emphasis upon this connexion between the Covenant and the Law, over against a one-sided, polemical severance of the Law from the Gospel. Rightly understood, the "Law" of the Old Testament is not the "*Nomos*" of Paul, which is a Jewish misunderstanding of the true *Torah*.[1] But this true *Torah* can only be rightly understood from the standpoint of Jesus Christ. Without Jesus Christ the *Torah* of the Covenant becomes the *Nomos* of a "righteousness of works". We now have to go further, and examine the particular elements combined in the idea of the *Torah*, in their true context, and also in view of the misunderstanding developed within Judaism.

2. *The Literary Idea, connected with Biblical Study, of the Torah as the Pentateuch.* Although this section of the Old Testament revelation is a comparatively late scholastic doctrine of Judaism, yet it does express an essential element of the idea of the Covenant. The establishment of the Covenant, connected with the person of Moses and the events at Sinai, is primary; the work and the teaching of the Prophets, and still more the wisdom of the *Kethūbīm*, are secondary. At the same time, however, the connexion with the book of "beginnings" (Genesis) implies that the historical establishment of the Covenant, the historical revelation, while it is certainly primary for truth, is not the first thing that *happened*. The Creation of the world and the Creation of Man is an act of the Covenant-God.[2] Responsibility is the nature of *all* men, from the very beginning, and the meaning of responsibility, as well as the basis of man's existence in responsibility, is the gracious will of God the Creator, and the community which is rooted in Him. From the standpoint of God certainly the Covenant which stands at the beginning is a "natural covenant" in so far as it constitutes the God-created nature, the true being of man.

3. *The Unity of the Civil, Ceremonial and Moral Law.* The relation of man to God which is based on the Covenant is

---

[1] Cf. K. Barth, *Evangelium und Gesetz*   [2] Barth (rightly), *K.D.*, III

a total and social community. The *cultus* expresses the truth that man belongs to God, that God is "his nearest relation" (Pestalozzi). On the other hand, communion between the Holy God and sinful man cannot be taken for granted, and so it is connected with certain conditions laid down by God. In spite of the "accidental" nature, historically speaking, of some of the ceremonial laws, and in spite of the irrational, primitive character of the Idea of the "Holy" preserved in the *cultus*, yet we could not imagine—nor would it have actually been possible—that Israel was "the People of God," without this *cultus*, in which the primacy of the fact that the "People" *belongs* to God, is explicitly stated. The life of the People (or the nation) is to be "Divine service"—the whole *cultus* is a reminder of this fact.

The same is true of civil law. The will of God is to be the principle and the norm of human life in everything. Legal laws and penalties are only necessary because men no longer live, as a matter of course, in the love of God, so it must be made plain, particularly to the man who has sinned, that the will of God is also a social law, and a legal system, and indeed a political law as well. For in all these relations man stands under the will of God. The will of God is always directed towards human life as a whole, and the whole body corporate. Hence everywhere, even in legal and political relations, the will of God is to be the norm, the principle of order, and of the development of institutions.

Above all, however, the will of God is addressed to the individual as person. God does not will only, and not in the first place, action, as such, but the heart, out of which all action springs. "Give Me thine heart."[1] Even if the Old Testament does not yet know a formulated dual commandment of love to God and love to man, yet this is the actual meaning of all the Commandments. The expression, the "Moral Law", is therefore misleading. An isolated Moral Law, existing for itself, is an idea foreign to the Bible, both in the Old and in the New Testament. The "right disposition" can never be other than that which flows from the obedience of faith in God, from love of God. The exposition of the Commandment in Luther's Catechism: "Thus thou shalt fear and love God in order that thou . . ." is therefore wholly in line with the idea of the Covenant of the Old Testament. But the other point is equally important, namely, that it is not this or that that is

[1] Prov. 23: 26

required, that what God wills first of all is not even our relation to Nature, or to things, but simply "community", namely, the fellowship of human beings, which is rooted in communion with God. Hence the first actual expression of the love of God in the sphere of human life is the love of our neighbour.

4. *The Decalogue.* The law of the Ten Commandments does not play the part in the Old or the New Testament which it plays in the teaching and theology of the Church. It is indeed only a part of the whole legislation; certainly it is a very important exemplary part, but it is never "the Law". This habit of isolating the Decalogue is not justified, either in view of the Old Testament or of the New; it is the product of a certain interpretation of the Law which is only partly in harmony with the meaning of the Biblical revelation. It owes its existence mainly to the needs of catechetical instruction, and from that angle it is continually re-emphasized. In point of fact, indeed, the Decalogue is a wonderful summary of the Law as a whole, or—from the point of view of the twofold Commandment—it is a classical exposition of the One Commandment in reference to the essential aspects of human life. But it has always caused considerable difficulties to catechumens, and the differences in the reckoning of the Commandments shows that this *summa legis* in *Ten Commandments* should not claim absolute validity. The Sabbath commandment, in any case, is difficult to harmonize with the Pauline New Testament statement that for the Christian Church no day is more "holy" than another.

The way in which the Reformers, and Luther in particular, have expounded the Ten Commandments, is simply an expansion of the one twofold Commandment; inevitably this introduces a certain artificial element into the exposition. The ecclesiastical theological exposition ought not to have skated quite so lightly over the fact that in the Sermon on the Mount Jesus also included the Decalogue, when He said: "Ye have heard that it was said to them of old time . . . *but I say unto you.* . . ." Nor should they have overlooked the fact that in the New Testament the Decalogue scarcely appears to be the norm for the Christian Church. Taken literally, apart from the exposition "read into it" by the Church, the Decalogue is a blend of "religious", legal, and moral precepts, which can only become valid norms for the Christian Church by artificial means.

No one was more aware of this, and said it more plainly, than Luther, who, in spite of his own catechetical application and exposition of the Decalogue, was of the opinion that the Christian Church could create, under the guidance of the Holy Spirit, *novos decalogos et clariores*.[1]

5. The greatest difference between the Old and the New Testament comes out in the fact that the Old Testament knows nothing of that contrast between Law and Grace, between the righteousness of the law and the righteousness of faith which constitutes the central point of Pauline doctrine, of which John also is aware.[2] This is the point at which the temporary character of the revelation in the Old Testament comes out most plainly. Or are we to believe, as has been maintained recently,[3] that this Pauline contrast between Law and Grace, and his problematic and even polemical idea of the Law, is merely due to a Jewish misunderstanding, which does not really affect us at all? Then was Luther mistaken when he said that to make the right distinction between the Law and the Gospel was the most important, and at the same time the most difficult, theological task? Indeed, have we any right to suggest that Paul, in his struggle against "the righteousness of the Law", was only dealing with a misunderstanding of the Law? so that the sharp antithesis between Law and Promise, or Law and the Grace of Christ, is not really the centre, but merely a secondary element in his doctrine? Anyone who teaches this must realize that this means that the significance of the Reformation at the decisive point was based on a misunderstanding; to do this therefore means that the struggle of the Apostle Paul against the "righteousness of the Law" was a matter of no particular theological importance. This is a very serious step to take.

We will try to give, at least, a provisional answer to this decisive question, as we consider once more the central Biblical idea of the Covenant.

The Biblical idea of the Covenant implies two truths: that God is free generous love, and that He claims man for this love of His. Thus the first is God's gift, which man receives "without any merit or effort", towards which his only attitude can be that of receptiveness. The second point is God's claim on man. Man cannot receive the love of God save through

[1] *Thesen de fide, WA.*, XXXIX, I, p. 47
[2] John I: 17
[3] K. Barth, *Evangelium und Gesetz*

being commanded to accept it, and in being *claimed* by God. Thus the right relation between God and sinful man is not restored by man's own effort, but simply by receiving something which *God* does. It is precisely this truth which is not made absolutely clear in the Old Testament understanding of the Covenant with God. In the Old Testament, particularly in the message of the Prophets, the obedient action of man is placed in the foreground, so that it continually creates a disposition which the New Testament is forced to call the "righteousness of works". It is this misunderstanding which clings particularly to the idea of the Law.

Even in the writings of the Prophets, the impression may be given that through the fulfilling of the divine law, man could become "righteous", and there are many passages in the Old Testament[1] where it does not only *seem* to be so, but where this is actually said. In spite of this we would maintain: it *seems* to be so, because the fundamental idea of the Covenant, the idea of the divine Election of Israel, excludes legal thinking or "righteousness of works" in the Pauline sense. But the legalistic misunderstanding continually re-appears because the claim of God, contained in His grace in revelation, is understood as Law, and indeed as a law which in essentials can be fulfilled.

The idea of Law makes the will of God concrete. "Something" is demanded, and because "something" is demanded, it must be something that can be fulfilled. No distinction is made between the Law which can be fulfilled, which stands in the civil code, and the radical personal commandment of love. The *justitia civilis*, which even a sinful human being can observe, and the unconditional commandment of love, before which even the best and the most religious of men become sinners, are not sufficiently clearly distinguished from each other. That is why it seems possible to divide mankind into "righteous" and "unrighteous", pious and godless. The same imperfect, temporary and provisional character which infects the Old Testament idea of Sin, and is expressed in the fact that it speaks of *sins* and not of *sin*, shows itself in the understanding of the will of God which makes demands. The will of God, as a "law", can be fulfilled. The righteous man, therefore, is one who does the will of God. The "righteousness of works" and the "righteousness of faith" have not yet been differentiated, just as a political or civil community is not yet distinguished from a religious community.

[1] Cf., for instance, Pss. 15, 17, 26, 131; Ps. 18: 21–25

This view of the Old Testament is confirmed by the fact that the New Testament avoids describing that demand of God contained in the gift of grace by the idea of Law. Christians no longer stand under the Law[1] but under Jesus Christ as ἔννομοι χριστοῦ.[2] For them the Law, as a concrete impersonal court of appeal, has been done away. "Standing under the Law" is the very sign of the fact that one has not yet grasped and appropriated the grace of Christ. The will of God revealed in Christ can no longer be summed up in a law. Christ is the end of the law, even as He is its fulfilment. That claim of God which is still contained in the summons of Grace is not described by the idea of "Law".

Law involves "works", or *doing* something definite; but the grace of Christ involves an existence, "a way of being", being "in Christ", being "in the love of God", being "in the Holy Spirit" or being "filled with the Holy Spirit", which issues in the doing of God's will. The effect of "law" is to make God's will impersonal, and this corresponds to the process of breaking up "the law" into several laws, into many "works of the law". Being "under the Law"—in contrast to being "in Christ"— means that man stands upon his own feet; it appeals to that which man can do for himself. All this is what Paul means when he contrasts the "righteousness of law" with "the righteousness of faith".

6. Thus in the Old Testament (as understood by Paul and John) two lines of thought run alongside of each other. The one is the legalistic one, designated by the words, Hagar, Sinai, Moses, the "Jerusalem which is from below"; the other is the line of Promise and Grace, which is designated by the words, Sara, Abraham, the "Jerusalem which is from above"— the Promise and Grace which is fulfilled in Jesus Christ, and is represented by those devout Advent figures who were waiting for the Christ, Anna, Simeon, and John the Baptist, who constituted—so to speak—the Christian Church before Christ. After Jesus Christ had come in the flesh, the one criterion is this: do you receive or reject Him as the true Messiah?

But in principle there is no difference between the Jews who reject Jesus, and the heathen who in their own way do observe the Law—as the second Chapter of Romans shows us—save possibly that the former ought to be judged more sternly because they could know the Christ. Those sharp contrasts

[1] Gal. 5: 18   [2] 1 Cor. 9: 21

which the New Testament makes between "Moses" and the "Law" on the one hand, and the Gospel of Grace in Jesus Christ on the other hand, between the letter and the spirit, apply to them. The service of Moses was a "ministration of death"—that is, for the unbelieving Jews, who reject Jesus, and trust in the "righteousness of works", until their eyes are opened, and the veil which lies over the Old Testament is done away, and they accept Jesus, and in Him the generous Grace of God.

7. Paul, however, has still another historical category for "the Law". It has "slipped in between".[1] It belongs neither to the original, nor to the final understanding of God. The man of the Creation, of the Primitive State, does not know the Law. He lives without this impersonal interim court, he lives directly in the presence of God. He is simply told to do one thing: he is not to eat of the tree in the midst of the garden; that is, the recognition of the divine privilege, or, and it amounts to the same thing, the recognition that he lives on the generous giving of God, thus that he only possesses freedom as dependence, and that only so should he possess or desire it. The Fall consists in the fact that he has freed himself from this dependence, that he wants to feel independent, and to "know" for himself "what is good and evil".[2] But in becoming a sinner he comes under the Law. The Law therefore belongs, as law, to sin, so that to be "under sin" and "under the law" is the same. The Law itself may indeed be good and holy,[3] so far as its content is concerned. For what it demands is God's demand. But the fact that man possesses this demand in the form of the Law, is the result of sin; it has "slipped in between". The revelation of the Law—in spite of Sinai—is not real revelation. The law is given "through angels",[4] "with the aid of a mediator", with the help of a "go-between".

The law is not an original divine entity; as law it makes the will of God neutral; yet, in itself, the will of God is not neutral, but it is wholly personal. God does not will "something"; He wants "me for Himself". It is not the will of God that I should "do" something, but He wills that I should love Him with my whole heart, and in so doing also love my neighbour as myself. Hence the idea of a *lex aeterna*, taken over from scholastic theology (which had formulated it), and adopted by Reformed and Orthodox Protestant theology is a very doubtful idea. It is the product of a platonizing re-interpretation of the will

[1] Rom. 5: 20   [2] Gen. 3: 5   [3] Rom. 7: 12   [4] Gal. 3: 19

of God revealed in the Bible. Certainly, God's will is eternal, but the will of God is not primarily law. The conception of the *lex aeterna* contains two ideas which are very dissimilar, namely, that of the will of God directed toward the person, which is no law, and the divine order established by the Creation, that is, the law immanent in the creation, of concrete right order. The will of God which is directed to the person, who wills to possess the "heart" of man, is no law; and the order established with the Creation and thus willed by God is not eternal, any more than the creation itself is eternal. These two aspects of the divine will cannot be subsumed under *one* conception, that of a *lex aeterna*. For the will of God, in the first sense, is not "law" at all, and the law of the divine creation is not eternal.

The will of God which is directed towards the person, is God's will of love. This implies the paradox that it is the sum of all law, that it is the actual intention of the law, and that for this very reason it cannot ultimately be law at all. The commandment of Love is not only the heart of the law, it is also its end. Christ is the end of the Law, not only its fulfilment. He who is in Christ is "no longer under the law".

One who is filled with the love of God does not need to be *commanded* to love God; we cannot "order" such a person to do this or that, as the law does. Love—and this is the paradox—is the one thing signified in all these commandments, but by that very fact it cannot be commanded, and does not come into existence through the Command. The Commandment of Love, since it emphasizes the whole meaning of all the commandments, eliminates itself as commandment. Love can only be present where it is given, not where it is commanded.

On the other hand, the concrete order that God wills, which He establishes with the Creation, and requires man to respect, does not refer, like the commandment of love, to the motive, the heart, the disposition—but to definite ways of human behaviour, necessary actions which are given in the order of Creation. The classic example of this is marriage. *Agape* does not produce strict monogamy. Love in the sense of *Agape* means that I am to love *all*; love in the sense of marriage means that I have to love *one* human being. Why is this? Because God has so created man and woman, that one belongs to one, and not one to many. The specific demand for exclusiveness which is involved in the sex-relationship alone, cannot be understood in the light of the meaning of *Agape*, but only in the light of the order of creation. What the husband owes to the wife, and the wife to the husband, what the father and the mother owe to the children and the children to the parents, is not derived from *Agape* as such, but solely from the special character of being husband, wife, father, mother, or child, that is, from the order of Creation. Hence Jesus Himself, when He is speaking about the indissolubility of marriage, that is, of the exclusive nature of the bond between one human being and another, refers to the order of Creation,[1] and contrasts it with the Mosaic law as the original norm. At the same time, however, He points out that this order has only temporal, but not eternal, validity.[2]

What matters here is not the motive, but right behaviour. It is not a requirement of *Agape*, but a material demand. It does not deal with *me*, with *my heart*, but with *marriage*, and with the rightly ordered matter of sex-relationship. Hence when we are dealing with the subject of marriage it is not right to refer to that passage in the Epistle to the Ephesians where the relation of Christ to the Church is shown as a parable, and at the same time the norm of the true marriage relationship. This is not an argument for monogamy as an institution, but an attempt to show how the relation to Christ ought to influence the *inner* relation of husband and wife to one another. *Here* what matters is the motive, *Agape*, but the other passages refer to the actual order of marriage, as an institution. So far as *motive* is concerned, love, the love which is revealed to us in Christ, is all that matters. But where the material requirement is concerned—which must also be met with love—the norm is the order of creation. It is because this fundamental distinction has not been preserved that infinite confusion has arisen in theological social ethics, and this confusion, in the last resort, goes back to the unfortunate idea of the *lex aeterna*, which combines widely different notions in one conception.

The Commandment of Love never says *what* we are to do; it does not tell the Good Samaritan what he ought to do for the poor man who fell among robbers. All it says to him is this: Here and now do everything you can for him! *What* he has to do, he knows from observing the order of creation, and the sound human body. This he must observe if he is to do the right thing for the wounded man. Thus even *Agape* does not

[1] Mark 10: 6 ff.   [2] Matt. 22: 30

tell us what is the right relation between the sexes; *that* is given to us in the order of the Creator, who has created man and woman in this way, and in no other: that the one must belong to the other. Likewise *Agape* does not tell us what should be the distinction between the relation of children to parents and the relation of parents to children; that is given to us in the Order of Creation. The material order is derived from the order of Creation, but the motive from which conduct should spring is always and everywhere *Agape*, which, however, is only present where it is not merely commanded but given.

So far as motive is concerned, our motto is: "all from Christ", but where the concrete demand is formulated, the only rule is: loyalty to the order of Creation. But these two things are so very different from one another that they cannot be summed up in one conception, in that of the *lex aeterna*, without causing the greatest confusion. But where Paul speaks of Law, he is not thinking of the order of creation, but of the demand of love which affects the person. And through union with Christ this is not essentially any longer a demand but a gift. "If ye be under the Spirit, then are ye no longer under the law." But of course Paul regards the order of Creation as the basis of all material demands, and speaks of it in connexion with all that concerns the relation of the sexes to one another, and the relation between parents and children. This law has *not* "slipped in between", but is given in the Creation. But this law, like the Creation itself, is not eternal but temporal.

8. What is the relation of the Biblical Law to the law which God has written in the hearts of all men in creating them? to the Categorical Imperative? to the law of conscience? to the so-called *lex naturae*? The sense of responsibility belongs to the *Humanum*, to the nature of man absolutely. Anyone who denies this law—which is independent of the Biblical revelation —should see to it how he can continue to speak of a *Humanum* and make man responsible for sin! Even the Bible itself presupposes this awareness as universal. And all Christian teachers do the same, from the very earliest times down to the Reformation, and then on to the present day. The words *"habent cognitionem legalem"* which Luther applies to the heathen, has been the logical consensus of opinion in the Church right down to the present day, as also it is an explicit Pauline doctrine.

The Reformers, however, emphasized more strongly than

earlier theologians, especially those of the Middle Ages, that the content of this "law written in the heart" of man is not clear, and therefore cannot be interpreted in one way only. The law in man's heart has been obscured by sin; hence it must be illuminated by revelation, and thus clarified. This, however, does not alter the fact that it must be presupposed of all human beings, if the Gospel of the Grace of God and especially of the forgiveness of sins, is to be preached to them. It belongs absolutely to the nature of man apart from which a being cannot be called "man". It belongs to the nature of man who must be called a sinner. A man who had no conscience could not be addressed as a sinner.

And yet, apart from the Christian revelation, man does not know the real meaning and content of this law. It is true, of course, that here there are many degrees of perception, from the primitive sense of taboo up to the high ethical perception of a thinker like Plato or Aristotle, and the command to love one's enemies which one finds in certain Eastern faiths. Here it is doctrinaire nonsense to want to treat the whole alike, as theologians often do. But there is one element which is always and everywhere absent from non-Christian moral perception: the knowledge that love is not only the fulfilling of the law, but its end. True, final, moral knowledge is identical with the true knowledge of God. Only he who knows the generous grace of God knows also the true nature of the God of Love. And where this is really known, we also know that this love is the end of the law, because it cannot be anything other than a sharer in the generous grace of God. This is one thing which has to be said about the *lex naturae*.

The other point is this: that where we are not concerned with this innermost and final meaning, but rather with that which is penultimate and external, with "this and that" commanded by ethics, with those things which are called the "second Table of the Decalogue", the "blindness" caused by sin is not necessarily perceived. The commandments: "Do not kill, do not commit adultery, do not steal, do not lie", are familiar to many peoples, and have been expressed with great clarity and explicitness by many individual sages who knew nothing of the Bible. The same is true of the material demands of the order of Creation. The ancients therefore called this law which is "written in the heart" a *lex naturae*, because in it they saw the relation to "Nature"—to the created order of things—and of man, even where they were not aware of the Creator.

The command of the Stoics, "to live according to nature", simply means that man should not live against nature, but naturally, according to the law immanent in Creation. Even the Apostle Paul uses this idea on occasion, for instance, where he is condemning unnatural sex-relations, or the failure to observe the rules of behaviour which apply to the female sex in particular. Hence the *lex naturae* is regarded as very important in social ethics; that is, in the realm which is not concerned with personal relations but with external behaviour and the right ordering of human life: in the family, in the economic order, and in the State. Much of the legislation in the Old Testament for civil, political and economic life, is simply the *lex naturae*, though it certainly is the *lex naturae* illuminated by the Covenant-revelation. Here the historical revelation brings out very clearly what is inherent in the revelation in creation, and therefore *ought* to be known by all men; and indeed, what all men actually do know, even though in very different ways.

Just as the historical revelation should not be pitted against the revelation in Creation, so the Biblical Law ought not to be pitted against the law "written in men's hearts". But it is precisely in the light of the historical revelation, through Jesus Christ, that we see that the law, even the *lex naturae*, just because it is "law", is not in a position to apprehend the depth of the divine will. The phrase *habent cognitionem legalem* must be qualified by the word "only": it is *only* legal knowledge that they possess, not the true knowledge. Therefore they are living under the law. Thus the doctrine of the Natural Law belongs to the Biblical doctrine of law, and throws light upon the significance of, and the limitations inherent in, that complex entity which we call "law".

9. Finally, however, we have to consider the Law—and especially that of the Old Testament—in the light of the New Testament from one more angle: that of a divine method of education. Like the Old Testament in general, so the law in particular, is something which God gives first of all, in order to educate men for the reception of the Ultimate, and to make them ready for it. The Law is compared with a "tutor",[1] who prepares the growing youth for something better, or acts as a kind of "guardian"[2] who preserves the "ward" for a later experience of grace; or it is compared with the relation of

---

[1] Gal. 3: 25. A "tutor", a guide, a trainer of boys, often a trusty slave (Tr.)
[2] Gal. 3: 23

a servant which precedes that of a son.[1] Our reaction against a naturalistic or Idealistic theory of "development" should not blind us to the fact of this graded view, which is inherent in the Bible itself. The relation of the law to the revelation of the generous Grace of God is not only negative, but positive—in this sense of "education" or "preparation". Man, as he has become through sin, the "natural man", must first of all learn the law, before he can understand grace. Above all, through the law, he must learn that he is a sinner, before the message of the forgiveness of sins can mean anything to him. Even if this perception of sin—through the law—is not yet the right one (which indeed only comes through the knowledge of Jesus Christ) yet it is the presupposition for this true sense of sin. It is this which the older theology expressed in the phrase *usus elenchticus legis*, the accusing function of the Law, a doctrine which both Luther and Calvin regarded as important, and is indeed behind the truth that the Law precedes the Gospel.

10. Thus we see that in the concept of law there is a very complex relation between the Old and the New Testament. It is part of the incompleteness of the Old Testament, of the temporary character of this revelation, that in it both Law and Gospel—in the sense of the "righteousness of works" and the "righteousness of faith"—are not clearly distinguished. We *can* conceive the Old Testament as a "religion of Law"; there are sufficient statements to confirm what Paul describes as the "righteousness of the Law". And there are many others which at least can be misunderstood in this sense, if we take them literally, apart from the whole context of the Covenant-revelation, in which they stand. Just as the Old Testament does not make a clear distinction between Israel as a political and as a religious community, or as we would say: between the State and the Church, so also it does not make a clear distinction between the "righteousness of the Law" and the "righteousness of faith", between Law and Grace, between particular, avoidable sins, and the state of "being a sinner".

And yet, when we look at the whole, we must say this: the legalistic view of the Old Testament is a misunderstanding, because the controlling conception of the Old Testament revelation is that of Divine Grace, freely choosing whom He will. Israel is what it is through Election, not by its own act.

[1] Gal. 4: 1 ff.

The Law is not the real meaning of the Old Testament; it is its outer garment which conceals its inner meaning: the revelation of the generous grace and free election of God, the witness to Christ of the Old Testament. But this veil could not be removed by man himself; it could only be removed by the new Act of revelation in Jesus Christ, the Incarnate Word.

CHAPTER 9

THE FULLNESS OF TIME

"WHEN the fullness of the time came, God sent forth His Son." We are right—and indeed we are obliged—to consider the problem of the Law and the temporary character of the Old Testament revelation in the closest connexion with one another, because the Apostle does the same.[1] "Once more Paul surveys the great movement of God in building up His Kingdom in a single comprehensive glance, in order that we may see how God's purpose moves steadily forward. The Law is the beginning. Then comes the Son and the Spirit, in fullness of time." This is Adolf Schlatter's comment on the beginning of the fourth chapter of the Epistle to the Galatians, in which this phrase, the "fullness of time"[2] occurs. The divine revelation, which is so deeply influenced by the figure of the legislator Moses and his Law, that it obscures the divine generosity of grace, keeps humanity in a condition which, in comparison with the freedom of the children of God which has been brought to us by Christ, seems to be that of a minor, and even of a slave. This is the "covenant which I made with their fathers" (as Jeremiah puts it), which the prophet contrasts with the "new covenant", when "they shall teach no more every man his brother", "for they shall all know me, saith the Lord";[3] thus they will have attained their majority, in direct communion with God, without the Law which had "slipped in between".

The period before the coming of Jesus Christ is a period of minority, of immaturity, and its characteristic principle is precisely: the Law, which has been "our tutor to bring us to Christ", by which men are held as in a kind of "protective custody" because they are not yet ready for freedom. Other expressions also point to this passage which suggest the educative aspect of the divine economy of salvation: the "elements of the world" to which they were enslaved, the "guardians" under whose discipline they had to wait until the time had come to attain their majority and their freedom.

[1] Gal. 4: 4 ff.
[2] Schlatter, *Erläuterungen zum Neuen Testament*, II, p. 72
[3] Jer. 31: 31 ff.

At the same time, the idea of the "elements" points to the religious principles of paganism. In so far as the community of Israel, in its relation to God, was bound by enactments, by the statutory law, it was in a state rather like that of the adherents of a pagan religion. We have already said: The Law, as the principle of man's relation to God, does not connect the Old and the New Testament, but does connect the Old Testament with paganism. The *Lex*, severed from the Covenant, is a principle common to all religions, it belongs to the natural man as such.

This connexion is in entire harmony with the arrangement of the Epistle to the Romans, where pagans and Jews are connected with one another through the idea of the Law, and are contrasted with the man who, apart from the Law, starts his new life from the revelation of the righteousness of faith, in Jesus Christ. Therefore, in view of the "fullness of time" which began in Jesus Christ, we are justified in regarding the period before His Coming as a time of waiting and preparation both for Jews and pagans. But I hasten to add that, of course, I do not mean that I support the view that the Old Testament and pagan religion are, in principle, on the same plane. So far as the Old Testament is characterized by the Covenant with God, by the election of Israel from among the other nations, there is a very marked contrast between Old Testament religion and all others; only in so far as it is regarded from the standpoint of the Law may we assert that in principle it is on the same plane.

Thus we are right, and indeed we are obliged, to speak of a divine preparation for the revelation of Christ, not only in Israel but also in the world of nations as a whole. Although the Incarnation of the Word, of the Logos, is a new divine thing, the great decisive miracle of history, yet this miracle itself is not miraculous, but is a fulfilment of something which God had been preparing for ages. God is indeed not only the God of Israel but also the God of all nations. Saving History is not the whole of His work, but He is also the Ruler of world history. This is the message of the Old Testament itself. As God chose Israel out of the nations and made it the Chosen People of God, so also He used the other nations, in order to realize His plan for Israel. From the standpoint of the "secular" historian, the fact that the history of Israel is interwoven with the general history of the nations of the Near East seems to be a "fact" and no more; but in the light of revelation we see it as the realization of a divine purpose, in which the destiny of Israel is indissolubly connected with that of the great neighbouring nations.

It is God who executes judgment on Israel and Judah through Assyria and Babylon. It is He who "whistles" for them, as a bee-keeper entices the bees.[1] He it is, too, who frees the exiles of the Babylonian Captivity, by means of the Persian King, Cyrus, whom the great Prophet of the Exile calls the "Servant of the Lord". The history of the ancient People of the Covenant is thus not to be isolated either from the point of view of profane history nor from that of theological and religious history, but in a thousand ways it is connected with world history, whose God is the Lord. Since the Jewish people, by the very fact that it was no longer a sovereign state, but only a national religious community, was specially prepared for the coming of the Redeemer, in this preparation the nations themselves took a direct part, which destroyed the Davidic kingdom and deprived the Jewish legal authority of power. Looking back from the history of the expansion of the Christian Church in the world we may stress the following facts as elements in this preparation.

1. The expansion of the Christian Church throughout the whole world could scarcely be imagined in those days when national religions were separated from one another in national states, as was the case before Alexander the Great and the Roman Empire. The campaigns of Alexander and the Roman Empire broke down the barriers of nationalism and religion which had previously separated the nations from one another, and would have erected insuperable barriers to any mission from the outside world. Not only the Jewish and the Christian religion, but other religions too in those days had their mission-aries, and tried, either deliberately, or unconsciously, to carry on the business of the infiltration of the Mediterranean world with foreign religions. Thus the messengers of the Christian Church found the doors already wide open for them, in an era of world-wide religious movement.

2. Through Greek philosophy and Roman civilization an inner uncertainty had crept into all the previously closed religious systems. Everywhere we can detect a questioning and a seeking, a dissatisfaction with their own tradition. The

[1] Isa. 7: 18, "For then it shall be that the Eternal whistles for fly and bee, for foes that swarm and settle all in the steep ravines and crevices of cliffs..." (M) (TR.)

old national religions had had their day: they were no longer adequate for this universal striving and questioning of the nations. Men had become more exacting in their religious and intellectual demands. Greek science had worked out a conception of truth, and critical standards, which showed that polytheistic mythologies are merely superstition. Greek philosophy discovered "Man". What happened in Athens, and then spread into the world, cannot simply be set in contrast to that which took place in Palestine. The Logos, who was there discovered as the principle of a universal Humanism, and who at the same time is understood as a rational order which pervades the whole world, which makes it a cosmos, is indeed not that Logos proclaimed in the Prologue to the Fourth Gospel, but it has some relation to it.

From the autobiographical passages in the writings of Justin Martyr and Augustine, we know how greatly for the former the Platonist-Stoic-Idealism, and for the latter the Hortensius of Cicero, which was inspired by the Stoics and by Plato, influenced them as a preparation for the Christian Faith. For those who believe in the Lord of world history it can be no accident that, at the time when Paul was preaching the Gospel in Rome, a slave named Epictetus taught an ethical Theism, whose practical conclusion was the demand for trust in God and universal love to all men. Above all, however, that epoch was a time when almost all the nations of the Mediterranean world were full of the longing for and expectation of a Coming Deliverer,[1] a time when the conceptions of sin and guilt and the need for redemption were realities in human life, to an extent hitherto unknown.

3. One of the most important facts in the book of the *Acts of the Apostles* is the immense extent of the Judaism of the Dispersion. They were everywhere, these Jews with their synagogues, with their preaching of the God of the revelation of the Prophets. We may think what we like in dogmatic terms about " the point of contact "—but the fact remains that the great missionary Apostle on his travels through Asia Minor and Greece everywhere first of all sought out these synagogues, and there won his first disciples. It was especially the "God-fearers"—that is, the non-Jewish attenders at the Hebrew services of worship—from whom the first Christian Church recruited those who constituted the nucleus, or cell, for further growth. We cannot rightly understand the swift

[1] Jeremias, *Die ausserbiblische Erlöserenwartung*

extension of Christianity apart from the vigorous preparatory work of the Jewish mission.

4. But facts of a purely secular nature must also be taken into account, from this point of view, to which the New Testament in particular bears clear witness. One is that the world of that day had been opened up, in a marvellous way, by Roman civilization and by Roman Law. What is said about our own day, and rightly, in view of the whole extent of the globe, applies also to the more limited *orbis* of the world of the Mediterranean, dominated by the Roman Empire: the world had become a unity, and it was comparatively a small world. There were people who travelled from Jerusalem to Rome dozens of times—and yet it was only a thousand years since the Wanderings of Ulysses, since the time when the Mediterranean Sea was full of monsters and other mythical dangers. Now everywhere the ubiquitous Roman police saw to it that there was order and comparative security. Now everywhere there were roads which the Roman soldier had made, and "colonies" where, under the protection of a Roman garrison, Roman officials made Roman Law a reality in practice.

Still more important, however, is the second factor: the use of Greek as the world language. Though it may have been to some extent a "basic Greek", which Christians of the Hebrew tongue (like the author of the Gospel of John) spoke, and was also the Greek of the other Christian missionaries, and far from correct from a literary point of view, yet it was understood everywhere; and again, it is no accident that the whole of the New Testament has come down to us only in this language, the language of Athens and of Alexander the Great, and not in that of Palestine which Jesus spoke. Rome provided the external communications, Greece the intellectual means of communication. Just as we can hardly imagine the extension of the Gospel at a time when a "foreigner" would be described by the same word as an "enemy", and where especially the fact of not belonging to a national religious community was a matter of life or death, so we can scarcely imagine such an expansion at a time when men were separated by language barriers. Certainly, with God all things are possible, but this truth does not allow us to overlook what God Himself has done in the world of nations for the preparation for the Gospel, which was to be proclaimed to the whole world, and is the salvation of the whole world.

5. There is still one final, and most important, thing to say—

which brings us to the doctrine of Jesus the Christ—the doctrine we are about to consider. "But when the fullness of the time came, God sent forth His Son, born of a woman, born under the law." Jesus Himself, the Son of God, the content of the Christian message, was also, according to the flesh, a Jew of His own time. By this very fact He is something "quite special", and the fact of His Saviourhood cannot be separated from this special characteristic of His person according to the flesh. We cannot imagine Him without this special character of the Jewish people, and indeed of the Jewish people of his period of history, and not of an earlier day.

It is only recently that we have begun to understand how much of the "ecclesiastical discipline" and religious knowledge of later Judaism has entered into the life of Jesus, into His message, and that of His Apostles. Previously we had over-estimated the influence of Hellenism; now we see how much the influence of Judaism has been under-estimated. Not only the Old Testament but also Judaism is the soil upon which Jesus stands, and out of which, spiritually, He grew up. He was "subject to the Law" in a way which was not perceived in earlier generations. In this sense, He was a child of His own day and of His own people. This is what Paul is always trying to say. In His own Person He had to fulfil that Law (this is the meaning of the phrase in its context) in which Judaism saw the whole content of the revelation of the Old Testament, which on the one hand is one with the New, and on the other is the principle of that which is merely temporary, of the minor and the slave. In the maturity of the Old Testament God creates the New; in the fulfilment of the Law Jesus becomes the one who brings in the Gospel, of righteousness "apart from the law". So historically, and—if this dangerous word may be allowed for once—so "organically", does God carry out His purpose in His own self-revelation.

In spite of all these traces of the fulfilment of "the time" we must never forget that the decision *when* the "time" was to be fulfilled lay wholly in God's secret purpose. If the Apostle's phrase means undoubtedly those visible traces which permit us to look a little way into the workings of God, yet above all he means the mystery which is known to God alone. The Redeemer came when it pleased God. God stands above all time; He is Lord of Time. He Himself is not in time, but He creates and gives time. For this reason alone, because God stands above Time, and releases Time from Himself, as He

wills, is there a "fullness of time". The idea of the "fullness of
the time" confronts us with the eternal supra-temporal decree
of God, and the historical reality of time. There is a "fullness
of the times" because the historical event in its wholeness is
based in God's decree, and is decreed by Him. Just as the
Creation of a material world is based upon God's immaterial
existence and will, so also the historical reality of time is pre-
formed and posited as a reality in God's supra-temporal nature
and will.

"The fullness of time": the historical process which is based
in the will of God, has now reached the point where God can
create that through which He wills to reveal the meaning of
all history. All historical time, regarded from the standpoint
of Jesus Christ, tends towards Him; all historical development,
from God's standpoint, is preparation for that which He will
give in Jesus Christ as something wholly new. In this sense
not only the Old Testament, but the whole of world history
is to be understood as "Messianic". All that God had allowed
to develop before Jesus Christ came, is now fulfilled in Him.
This does not alter the particular and peculiar relation of the
Old and the New Testament to each other. But in the light of
this special fulfilment we may, and ought, to see how the whole
of world history is directed towards Jesus Christ as its Fulfiller.
Thus it is precisely from the relation between the Old and the
New Testament alone that this universal-historical view is
right; namely, it means looking backwards, not forwards; from
above, not from below. The New Testament cannot be understood from the Old, but conversely the Old must be understood
in the light of the New. Jesus Christ cannot be understood
from the point of view of world history, but world history is
to be understood in the light of Jesus Christ.

But if world history is to be understood in the light of
Jesus Christ, then it is understood as the time of promise and
preparation. This does not mean that we are in a position to
trace out in detail this preparation and this promise in every
event in history, or in the course of world history as a whole—
as the philosophy of history of Hegel does—nor that we are
in a position to expound every passage in the Old Testament
in a Christological sense.

Here and there, however, and especially in the history which
is close to the Coming of Jesus in space and time, we can
perceive something of this preparatory character, as we have
tried to do. Not only the Pharaoh of the time of Moses and

the Cyrus of the time of the Second Isaiah, but also Plato and Alexander, Cicero and Julius Caesar must serve God, in order to prepare the way for Christ. It is significant that the Gospel of Luke begins with the incident of the census taken by order of Augustus, and the Gospel of Matthew begins with the story of the Magi from the East who prepare to leave their homes to follow the Star which leads to Palestine and the Court of Herod. These two legendary stories reflect the theological truth that "the nations have waited for Thee until the time was fulfilled". Long ago, from the very earliest beginnings, God had prepared that which He then willed to give as the salvation of the world "in the fullness of the times", as something which on the one hand—according to its human nature—grows out of this history, as well as something which came into history, as something which could not be explained from itself. Henceforth we shall be dealing with this "new thing", with the salvation given to us in Jesus Christ.

CHAPTER 10

THE FOUNDATION OF THE CHRISTIAN FAITH

THE Christian Faith is simply faith in Jesus Christ. Therefore the whole of Christian theology is simply the explication of faith in Christ. Hence faith in Jesus Christ is not simply part of this faith, and Jesus Christ is not one "subject" among other subjects in the Christian Creed. The doctrine of God, of His Nature and of His Will, of the Creation and the Divine government of the world, of man as created in the Image of God and as sinner, of the Old Covenant and the preparation for the New—all these doctrines are elements in the one faith in Jesus Christ. All that has hitherto been presented (in this book) as the content of the Christian Faith has only been possible because all this truth is derived from Jesus Christ alone.

Now, however, in that section of dogmatics which bears the traditional name of "Christology" we are not only standing in the light which proceeds from the Christian revelation, but we are now approaching the Source of Light, the historical Revealer Himself. Hitherto all that we have considered has been regarded from this point of view; now, however, we look at the Source itself. Jesus Christ is the *ratio cognoscendi*, the foundation of all Christian truth. But Jesus Christ, the *Incarnate* Word, is not the *ratio essendi*, the basis of all existence. To maintain this would be to turn the Incarnation into an eternal truth, and this would destroy its historicity. The fact that the Son of God became *Man* does not stand at the beginning of all things; but Christ is the centre of history; He is the One who divides history into two parts: *ante* and *post Christum natum*. The Incarnation and the Incarnate Son of God was, it is true, determined by God from all eternity, but it only became a reality in the fullness of *time*. If, from the point of view of *knowledge*, Jesus Christ comes first, and all that we can say about God is secondary, yet actually God, the Three in One, comes first, and the Incarnate Son, Jesus Christ, comes second. When this distinction between the *ratio cognoscendi* and the *ratio essendi* is misunderstood, it necessarily leads to speculation and fantasy.

Thus now that we are approaching the Source of Light

itself, we must take a different line from that which we have followed hitherto, when we have been considering certain truths in its light. In the last resort, of course, we shall have to say: We know Jesus Christ through Jesus Christ; we believe *that* Jesus is the Christ, *because* He is the Christ. But if this statement is to be more than mere tautology, it must be placed at the end, and not at the beginning of our Christological enquiry.

The question with which we have to begin is of supreme and vital importance for every Christian; it is indeed a very *actual* one, that is, it is a question which could not be answered at the outset. This is the question: How does a person come to the point of knowing and confessing this Man, Jesus of Nazareth, as the Son of God, and the Redeemer of the human race?

I. This brings us to the fundamental question of the Christian Faith: How does one become a Christian? Why is the Christian Faith the true Faith? What is it that impels a human being to believe in Jesus as the Christ? To ask this question implies that we have already made a twofold decision: on the Right hand and on the Left. On the one hand we have rejected the "liberal" view of Christ, and on the other the "orthodox" view; for the "liberal" never asks this question at all, and the "orthodox" always assumes that it has already been answered. Liberal theology represents the view that Jesus is not the Christ, the Son of God, nor is He the Saviour of the world; He is merely one outstanding religious personality among many others, a *primus inter pares*. In orthodox theology, however, the question we have just stated is never raised, because it already presupposes a positive answer, on the basis of the testimony of the New Testament. We believe in Jesus as the Christ because the Bible teaches that He is the Christ, and "thus we must believe it".

Owing to its clerical or Fundamentalist *a priori* outlook, for centuries orthodox theology has refused to face the problem: Why do we believe in Jesus, the Christ? This is all part of the absence of a genuine missionary consciousness at a time when people were all "Christians" as a matter of course. It was then taken for granted that from the moment of one's baptism one is a Christian. Hence the question: "How does anyone become a Christian?" is never raised. Children are simply instructed in the faith of the Church, which is the true faith. Theologically, this means that from the outset it is assumed that the Christian Faith is the true Faith, because this faith is taught either in the Bible or by the Church. But the fact that the doctrine of the Church, or of the Bible, is "the truth", must be accepted as axiomatic. We believe in Jesus Christ, because we believe first of all either in the doctrinal authority of the Church, or in that of the Bible.

In the first volume of this series we pointed out at some length why this axiomatic belief in the Church, or in the Bible, which precedes faith in Jesus Christ, is not the Biblical understanding of faith, but one which is entirely opposed to the thought of the Bible. This, however, faces us with the task of expounding the basis of our faith at the decisive point. *Why do we believe that Jesus is the Christ?* How did a former unbeliever, whether an atheist or an Idealist, a Mohammedan or a Jew, come to believe in Jesus Christ? what was it that moved him to do this? and what is it that moves a non-Christian to become a Christian? We are not enquiring into the accidental and therefore very varied motives which may have helped to bring a person to the faith, but we are trying to penetrate to *the* reason which, in every case, when a person becomes a real Christian, is the decisive, and the only valid one. If we put the question like this, at first the answer sounds bafflingly simple: the answer lies wholly in Jesus Christ Himself. Because He IS the Christ, it is possible for a person whose eyes are open to the truth to recognize Him as the Christ. Whatever may be the more exact exposition of this curiously simple answer, it does express the one fundamental truth, namely, that the only true, concrete, valid ground for faith in Jesus Christ consists in what Jesus Christ Himself *is*. Faith in Jesus Christ is living contact with reality, pure and simple; but it is certainly contact with reality of a special kind, and therefore it is also a way of coming into contact with reality which is itself of a peculiar character. In order to make this easier to understand let us take an analogy—certainly only an analogy— and consider the different ways in which reality is grasped in a sphere not connected with religion. We can grasp the reality of Rembrandt's picture the *Night Watch* in very different ways, and each time we see a different aspect of reality. Even a dog who stands before this masterpiece of art will grasp something of this. We do not know exactly what he sees, but we know for certain that he does *not* see the "Night Watch" of Rembrandt. An intelligent man with no understanding of art will understand what is portrayed in this picture, the "subject of the picture", but he will not understand Rembrandt's picture as a "work of art"; all he will see will be something which could just as well have been painted by any "tuppenny-ha'penny painter" without talent, but with a certain facility for "representing" a subject. The work of Rembrandt is only understood by one whose "eyes are open" for what is beautiful in art. He understands—in a particular way—a particular reality, the beauty of the work of art. This beauty confronts him; it is inherent in the work itself; it is not something derived from the spectator. But although it is a reality, it will only be understood under particular subjective conditions, that is, in a particular act of receptive understanding.

There is a sense in which everyone who is in a position to understand a personality in history can understand the Man, Jesus Christ, but this is not faith in Christ. He understands it, so to speak, as the man who does not understand art, but is otherwise intelligent enough, "understands" Rembrandt's picture. But when, quite suddenly, the "inward eye" is opened, and the "real truth" of Jesus, namely, that He is the Christ, is understood, something quite new has taken place. We must now proceed to examine the nature of this "reality" and of the act by which it is grasped.

2. There are two objective facts of a complex nature, differing from one another, which are inseparable from the Christian Faith, but which can be understood without grasping the reality of "Jesus the Christ": firstly, the fact of the "records concerning Jesus", His life, His teaching, all that He did and did not do, His sufferings and His Death; secondly, the fact of the "witness of the Apostles", or the Apostles' teaching concerning Jesus the Christ.

So far as the first of these objective facts is concerned: the Biblical records about Jesus, the very fact that they disagree with one another at several points, inevitably raises the question: what is their objective historical value? This is the question of the "Jesus of History". The point of this question is this: when the Gospel records have been subjected to the most searching historical and literary criticism, what is the picture of Jesus which emerges? How do we regard His life, His acts and His words, His personality, and the fate which befell Him? To-day, however, this formulation of the question is not accepted by all schools of thought; it is actually rejected outright by two different groups. One extremely radical group maintains that we cannot penetrate behind the sources themselves, that is, behind the view of the life of Jesus formed by the Early Church, to the real "Jesus of History". This real, historical Jesus, it maintains, is an X, about whom nothing certain can be said. The final truth that can be reached is that which the first generation of Christians recorded concerning Him; and we know just enough to know that these records are extremely unreliable, full of legend, and of a theology created by the Church. But who "Jesus Himself" was, that we cannot possibly discover.[1]

On the other side there is a certain "Christo-centric" school of thought which holds that to go back to the "Jesus of History" is irrelevant for the Christian Faith, since it is based upon the witness of the Apostles—which includes both doctrine and record—concerning Jesus the Christ. The "Jesus of History" is an abstraction, in which the Christian Church has no interest.

Now so far as the radical critics are concerned, we must admit that it is not easy to discern an objective core of actual fact in the traditional material, that is, of the genuine traditions concerning Jesus—a substratum of the genuine words of Jesus, and dates of which we can be sure. But just as the earlier conservatism regarded the Biblical presentation as absolutely reliable, so this modern scepticism has proved to be untenable.[2] In spite of all sceptical suggestions, there is a hard core of tradition, which cannot be eliminated, which emerges intact from every critical examination, however searching and meticulous it may be. No serious historian doubts the existence of Jesus of Nazareth as an historical fact, nor the main features of the course of His life as recorded by the Evangelists,[3] namely, that He appeared in Galilee, gathered a body of twelve disciples, proclaimed the Kingdom of God, healed all kinds of sick people, was hated by the Jewish religious leaders, and finally, after His entry into Jerusalem, was crucified by them, and by the Roman Procurator Pontius Pilate. Nor is there any doubt about the fact that a number of the parables, and other sayings ascribed to Him, are part of His actual teaching. To try and shake the veracity of these facts would be as exaggerated as it would be to throw doubt upon the historicity

[1] E.g. Bultmann, *Jesus*, pp. 15 ff.

[2] Cf. Windisch, *Das Problem der Geschichtlichkeit Jesu*, Theol. Rundschau N.F., Heft 4

[3] The controversy between Albert Schweitzer and the representatives of the school of "Form-Criticism" does not touch these facts themselves, but only the extent to which the Gospel records have been shaken by the work of the critics

of Julius Caesar. On the other hand, the view that the Christian Faith has no interest in disentangling the truth from an historical picture of this kind is theologically untenable. For this would simply mean that the Christian Church had no interest in the historical existence of Jesus, nor in the fact whether Jesus really was what the Evangelists describe Him to be, whether He actually taught what the evangelists say He did, and what they record as His words. The phrase, the "Word made flesh" in the Gospel of John, would then have to be expounded thus: God has revealed Himself in the fact that at a certain time apostles maintained the following facts concerning a man called Jesus: that He lived, that He was crucified, and that He was the Son of God; but it would not be worth while to prove whether this man, whom they claimed to be Jesus the Christ, really lived, or what He was like. Such a view should be rejected, most vigorously, as extreme docetism in a new form.

It is, of course, true that the Church has less interest in this process of disentangling the objective historical core from the tradition than secular history, for which this is the only thing that matters. It is also true that, to the Christian Church, the apostolic testimony to Jesus the Christ is just as important as the historical record, and therefore that it is not primarily concerned to make this distinction. But this is only true because the Church is certain that both in the gospel record and in the apostolic testimony to Jesus, the Christ, she possesses the real historical Jesus who is the Christ. From the standpoint of faith the distinction between the apostles' testimony to Jesus the Christ, and the historical picture of Jesus, is actually an abstraction; the ordinary Christian believer is only interested in this question in so far as it helps him to know why he believes that "the Jesus of History"—whom he knows as "Christ"—actually existed within history.

Then if we are bound to reject both the radical views of historical scepticism, and a mistaken indifference (on the part of the Church) to the Jesus of History, many questions still remain open which cannot be decided once for all, questions which are constantly being examined by historical critics. Indeed, we must go a step further, and we must say: It is part of the Christian's belief in the Incarnation of the Word, that he believes in a "Jesus of History" who is such that His historical existence is always being subjected to critical research. This, indeed, is involved in the "flesh" in which the

Word of God, the Son of God, came to us. Among many other things, "Incarnation" also means an historical existence, the detail of which will always remain a subject of historical criticism. But the Incarnation of the Word also means that Jesus Christ—His historical existence, the main features of His life, and its chronology—is continually able to withstand the assaults of historical criticism. Correspondingly, too, the Christian Church has always had an absolutely central interest in the Jesus of History; the only difference being that in the pre-critical period this historical Jesus was equated, without further ado, with the Gospel tradition as a whole. Without the Passion *story* there would be no message of the Cross!

3. But once the process of criticism has begun, once we have seen that we cannot accept everything that has been reported about Jesus, just as it is, as historical, and after theological liberalism had made the contrast between the "Jesus of History" and the apostolic doctrine about Jesus, the Christ, we cannot evade the duty of trying to see whether there really is a contradiction between what criticism calls the "Jesus of History" and the apostolic witness to Jesus the Christ; that is, whether the "historical Jesus" is really the One whom faith knows as "the Christ". We would preface this study with the statement: that, in point of fact, the Jesus of whom, after the process of critical examination has been achieved, it can be said: this is the historical Jesus, is the same as the One whom the Apostles call the Christ, the *Kyrios*, the Son of God, the Incarnate Word of God. The aim of our present enquiry, therefore, is to explain this statement more fully, and to prove its truth.

The reconstruction of the historical picture of the life, the personality, the deeds and words, the sufferings and the death of Jesus, cannot here be made in detail. We must regard this task as having been achieved, in essentials, by the work of historical criticism, although opinions differ widely on many points of detail. Here then we will only summarize some of the main features.

We anticipate the literary question, by expressing the opinion that one of the results of historical criticism is that in this reconstruction of the historical picture the Synoptic Gospels are to be preferred to the Gospel of John, although we must never forget that John's aim is entirely different. Certainly, both the Synoptists and John aim at proclaiming Jesus as the Christ. But criticism shows that in so doing the Synoptists have kept far closer than John to the actual "historical" events, which everyone can know in time and space. It is true that their "pictures" also differ from one another at many points, and also that much that they narrate is not historical. They too put words in the mouth of Jesus which He did not say, and they, too, record things which did not happen. On the other hand, the Gospel of John provides more reliable historical detail than was thought to be possible half a century ago. But this does not alter the fact of this fundamental distinction.

When we ask: what has been the result of all this historical criticism? we have to admit with astonishment that the result is remarkably "conservative". The picture of Jesus—of His life and work, His suffering and His death—after all the testing of this prolonged examination, is not very different from that of the Synoptic Gospels.

Even after we have eliminated all the merely "peripheral" narratives, which do not record actual events, but are to be regarded as a literary framework, after the elimination of the words which are not genuine "sayings of Jesus" but later constructions of the Early Church (*Gemeinde-theologie*), and a few legendary stories here and there, the picture which emerges from this process of criticism is, in essentials, very like that of the Synoptic Tradition. The most important difference between this picture given by historical criticism and that of the traditional view of the Church is this: that, as a whole, Jesus seems to have spoken rather in the style of the Synoptic record and not in that of the Johannine discourses. The Synoptists are much nearer to the actual picture of the life of Jesus than the Gospel of John, in spite of the fact that their glimpses are very meagre, occasionally rather dim, and have often been strongly "touched up". But this does not mean that there is any contradiction between the Synoptic Gospels and the Gospel of John. Critical reflection has produced another result: The Synoptic Gospels make it possible to reconstruct, with some certainty, a picture of Jesus which everyone— whether a Christian believer or not—can recognize; but John has no intention of telling us what happened, and how; his aim is to teach us who Jesus was, and what His life means.

4. This statement needs to be confirmed more exactly at certain points. Jesus spoke about Himself more rarely, and more indirectly, in the Synoptic Gospels than in the Gospel of John. But this does not hinder us from believing that in all His

teaching He was really pointing to Himself. Even an extreme critic like Albert Schweitzer says that *all* the acts of Jesus were "acts of the Messianic consciousness".[1] Harnack's view[2] that the Gospel, as Jesus proclaimed it, did not include the Son, but only the Father, is not the result of strictly historical research, but is the product of a rationalistic prejudice which cannot stand the test of historical criticism.

It may be true, of course, that at first historical criticism, influenced by the discovery and development of the differences between the Gospel of John and the Synoptics, may have misinterpreted or overlooked the more indirect and suggestive way in which Jesus spoke of Himself and His significance for faith according to the Synoptic testimony. It has expounded the *incognito* in which Jesus clothed Himself, in a wrong way, as if He never spoke of Himself or of His significance at all. Criticism of this kind evolved this erroneous view: if Jesus really claimed to be the Christ, in the sense in which the Apostles spoke of Him, then He would have had to use the terminology of the Johannine Christ. In any case, earlier historical criticism overlooked the fact that if Jesus really was the Christ, during His earthly existence He could not teach that which the Apostles, after His death and Resurrection, were able to do. We ought not to reproach the earlier school of New Testament critics too violently for this error, since the Church itself thought the same, and was not in a position to make a distinction between the Johannine intention and the historical narrative of events.

The error is not all on the side of the rationalistic critics, who forgot the historic Christ in the Jesus of History, but equally on the side of the Church, which never took the real Humanity of Christ quite seriously, because it believed that to do so was to lose or to obscure the truth of the divinity of Christ. The Church taught "Docetic" views, and historical criticism "Adoptionist" errors—who is to judge which was worse? We can see that the true "Jesus of History" is One who was, it is true, aware of His saving significance, and was continually throwing out hints about it, but who neither could nor would preach it, because this was not His task, but that of His Apostles. Jesus had to *be* the Christ, not to proclaim Him. In what He proclaimed, however, there was enough Messianic self-testimony to show that He was the Christ, or,

---

[1] Cf. E. G. Kümmel, *Jesus und Paulus*, Theol. Blätter, September 1940
[2] A. V. Harnack, *Das Wesen des Christentums*, p. 91

to put it more exactly, there was enough similarity to enable us to identify the Christ to whom the Apostles bore witness with the Jesus of History.

It is strange that that rationalistic school of critics, which believed it necessary to make a great gulf between the "Jesus of History" and the faith in Christ of the Apostles, overlooked the fact that it was the very same disciples who knew the Jesus of History best—much better than we can ever hope to know Him through the process of meticulous examination of the tradition—who believed in Him as "Christ", and who addressed Him in prayer, in their Aramaic language, as "Lord" (*Maran*). For them there was no gulf between the "Jesus of History" and the "Christ of Faith"; on the contrary, because they knew Him, the Man, Jesus of Nazareth, through daily contact, as no one else did, they came to perceive that He was the Messiah, the "Son of the Living God". When they were asked: "Why do you believe that Jesus is the Christ?" they could only reply: "because we have learned to know Him as the Christ".

The testimony of those through whom alone we know the "Jesus of History", the eye-witnesses, who from the first to the last day of His activity upon earth were with Him: who heard all His sayings, and saw each of His mighty acts, who were with Him through the days of His Passion and saw Him hanging on the Cross—that is, the witness of those who, more than anyone else, could say who the Jesus of History was—give their clear and unhesitating testimony: "He is the Christ, the Son of God, our Lord." The historical criticism which has undertaken to outline the picture of the "Jesus of History" on the basis of their records, has not produced anything that is in conflict with this verdict of the Apostles.

5. What, however, is the position of the Apostles' doctrine about Jesus the Christ? Is it unified? Are there not great and important differences between the conception of Christ of the Primitive Church, of the Apostle Paul, of the Gospel of John, and of the later writings of the New Testament? Are there not striking differences, each of which represents a particular brand of Christology? Above all, is not the teaching of Jesus Himself, and particularly His own views of Himself, which can be deduced from His own words, different from that of His apostles?

Only those who hold an obstinately doctrinaire view can answer this question with a blunt "No". We cannot deny that there are these different doctrinal circles, with their differences in Christology. There is a difference between what the Apostles say about Jesus, and what He says about Himself. The only question is: Does this difference amount to a contradiction? We can only reiterate that the first persons to perceive this contradictory evidence would have been the first disciples. How could they have called Him "Jesus the Christ", the "Son of God", the "Lord", if they had heard Him say things about Himself which were in opposition to this belief that He was the Christ? But if we ourselves examine, without prejudice, the tradition of the Gospels, as it has been sifted and examined by historical critics, and their testimony on this point, the answer is plain: there is no contradiction. It is true, Jesus may not have said the same things about Himself as the Apostles did; but it would have been very strange if He *had* done so. The task with which God had entrusted Him was not to *proclaim* the Christ, but to *be* the Christ. Actually, however, within the limits set Him by His calling within history, He said quite enough about Himself for anyone who had ears to hear, who had eyes to see—who could look at His life as a whole, with a mind open to truth, to be impelled to confess: "Truly, Thou art the Christ."

Jesus described Himself as the One in whom the prophetic promise of the Kingdom is fulfilled, because this Kingdom, the new age, has arrived in and through Himself.[1] He described Himself as the One who is "more than a prophet", who is the "Son", in contrast to the "servants"[2]—the prophets who were sent before Him. When He speaks of the Good Shepherd who seeks for the lost sheep He means Himself;[3] explicitly He describes Himself as One in whom the prophetic Hope is fulfilled, as One who alone knows the secret of the Father,[4] as the One who can forgive as God alone can forgive. He confronts the whole Mosaic Law with the absolute authority of His words "But I say unto you". He accepts Peter's Confession, which calls Him "the Christ, the Son of the Living God" as the effect of divine revelation.[5] He is the "bridegroom" whose presence is a festival for the disciples,[6] He is the One who gives His life as ransom for many,[7] whose death is the basis of the New Covenant.[8] It is in harmony with His historical mission that only at the last does He come forth as the Christ, the Messiah, at the moment when, through His imminent death

[1] Matt. 12: 18   [2] Mark 12: 1–12   [3] Luke 15: 1 ff.   [4] Matt. 11: 27
[5] Matt. 16: 17 ff.   [6] Mark 2: 19   [7] Mark 10: 45   [8] Mark 14: 24

on the Cross, the popular view of this title is already shown to be a complete misunderstanding.

But if the disciples speak more directly, more fully, and more openly about Him as the Christ, than He Himself has done, they themselves say why this is so: It was only after His Resurrection that they could understand the significance of His death, and the new meaning which Jesus had given to the Name of "Christ".[1] We know little of the Christology of the Primitive Church; but what we do know with complete certainty is enough. The first disciples know and testify that Jesus is the Christ, the Risen Lord, whom they invoke in prayer, in the same way as a Jew would call upon God alone, using the Aramaic name, which is only applied to God: *Maran*, Lord. In the Lord's Supper they celebrate the Presence of the Living Lord. His death is for them no longer an "offence" or a cause of doubt, but a saving fact, even if they have not yet worked out any doctrine about the two saving facts, the Crucifixion and the Resurrection. Thus the "Christology" of the Primitive Church—if we may be permitted this expression—is in unbroken and unquestioned continuity in two directions: with all that the disciples have handed down to us from His own mouth, and from His Life, on the one hand; and, on the other, with all that the new Apostle, Paul, taught, who was the first to interpret all that they believed in theological terms. There are great differences, it is true, between certain representatives of the Primitive Church and Paul; but there is not the faintest trace in the New Testament of any idea that these differences were related to Christology, to the Person of Jesus. The Primitive Church confesses its own faith in the Pauline doctrine of Jesus, the Christ, the Son of God.[2]

The Pauline doctrine, too, is connected with Christology on both sides: with its earlier conception in the Primitive Church, and with the more developed doctrine of the Person of Jesus in the Johannine writings. John uses other concepts than Paul, but in essentials he says the same thing. Whereas Paul integrates and subordinates the statements about the Person of the Son of God entirely to his interest in the work of the Redeemer, in the thought of John, the theme: the mystery of the Person of the Son and His relation to the Father has its own peculiar significance. The two kinds of Christology cannot be simply equated with one another, but their differences are never contradictory. The mystery of Jesus, the Son of God,

[1] Luke 24: 26   [2] Acts 15: 11; Phil. 1: 18

and of His work of redemption, is deeper than human words can express. No New Testament witness, neither Paul nor John, could ever exhaust it. Rather, the one complements the other, each formulating what he sees in his own way. Their testimony is the same, even if their intellectual and theological formulation is different. Paul may speak more of the Work, and John more of the Person of Jesus, but for both, ultimately both Work and Person are one. Jesus saves him who believes in Him, by what He is; and what He is can only be expressed by pointing to what God gives and does through Him.

As we look back on the whole course of the doctrine, from the beginning, in the testimony of Jesus to Himself, down to the developed Christological doctrine of the New Testament, we can see no break anywhere. The whole Johannine teaching of Jesus the Son of God is simply a further development of that confession of Peter, which first became possible on the basis of the death of Jesus on the Cross, and the Resurrection. Everywhere Jesus is True Man, a man among men, and yet, in the very earliest records, He stands over against all other men with an authority which only God possesses. Rationalist historical criticism which maintained that there was a contradiction between the historical picture of Jesus and the Christ of apostolic theology cannot appeal to historical testimony for its statements. It was those who knew the "Jesus of History" best, His companions, who proclaimed Him as the Son of God, and as their Risen and Heavenly Lord.

6. This then is the objective situation with which we are confronted: a picture of the life of Jesus, uncertain in some particulars, clear in the main points, and a number of doctrines about Jesus the Christ, beginning with Jesus Himself, down to the full Christology of the New Testament, and its further interpretation in the Church.

This twofold testimony is the objective basis of faith. Apart from this testimony, and indeed, not without this *twofold* testimony, no one becomes a Christian. It is a mistake to wish to cling to one element only: whether it be the so-called "Jesus of History", the historical picture, or the apostolic doctrine of "Christ". It is in the providence of God that both have been given to us: the picture of the life of Jesus, drawn by those who knew Him in His life on earth, and the doctrine about Jesus, proclaimed by the same disciples, after they had become witnesses of His death and Resurrection. It is a mistake to contrast "Jesus Himself" with the witness of the Apostles; for the doctrine of the Apostles does not aim at saying anything other than who "Jesus Himself" is, and what "Jesus Himself" means for us. The primary element, it is true, is the picture of the life of Jesus, the Gospels. The doctrine of the Apostles about Jesus is a commentary on the Gospels. For "He Himself," Jesus in His own Person, is the revelation of God. This is exactly what the Prologue to St. John's Gospel means: He Himself, Jesus, is the Word of God who "became flesh". The second element, however, the doctrine about Jesus, is not something which has been added to the first; it is simply the true view of "Jesus Himself"—it explains Who He is.

Theological liberalism is an arrogant attempt to see "Jesus Himself", without being led to this view by the Apostles. Theological orthodoxy, on the other hand, disclaims the right to try to "see" Him for oneself at all; it simply accepts the authority of the Church, or of the Bible, and on the strength of that accepts the Apostolic doctrine, apart from personal conviction altogether. Liberalism is a mistaken autonomy; it consists in the failure to grasp the fact that apart from the witnesses to the Resurrection we cannot see Jesus at all, as He really is. Orthodoxy is a mistaken heteronomy, which substitutes faith in the witness of the Apostles, and thus faith in the authority of Scripture, for personal faith in Jesus Himself. But God wills that we ourselves should be witnesses to Christ, that we should see Him Himself, and to this end He gives us both the historical picture and the testimony of the Apostles, in order that through both we may come to see Him for ourselves.

If the record of His life and the witness of the Apostles were to contradict one another, then faith in Christ would be impossible. There would only be this alternative: either we see the actual Jesus who is not the Christ, or we do not see Jesus Himself, but we "simply believe" that Jesus is the Christ, because others, because the Apostles say so. This alternative does not exist. The wonder of the New Testament is precisely the unity of record and doctrine. The Evangelists do not show us a so-called "Jesus of History" who is merely a man amongst men, but they see, and they help us to see, the real historical Jesus who is the Christ.[1] And the Epistles, with their doctrine of Christ, do not give us an authoritative doctrine which they have evolved, but a doctrine whose one aim is to help us to

[1] Kähler, *Der sogenannte historische Jesus und der biblische geschichtliche Christus* (1928)

see aright the Son of Man and the Son of God, whose Figure is shown to us in the Gospels. The "Jesus of History" of historical criticism is an abstraction, due to the process of subtracting the "Christ" from the "real Jesus". The relation of this "Jesus of History" to the real Jesus who is the Christ is like a view taken from a photographic plate which has only registered certain rays of light, and not others, of the reality which it reflects. The so-called "Jesus of History" is the picture of Jesus seen by those who are blind to the Christ.

7. Thus the view developed in the course of the nineteenth century by a school of thought which was not merely critical, but deeply rationalistic, which contrasted the "historical Jesus" with the Apostolic testimony to the "Christ", does not really present the actual Jesus of History at all; it simply gives us the "Jesus of History" minus all that a Christian believer alone can see. It is the picture of the actual Jesus of the Gospels, from which everything has been eliminated which does not fit into the world-view of a rationalist. It is not, as is constantly asserted, the "Synoptic Jesus" contrasted with the "Johannine" Jesus, and the Jesus of the Church, but it is the Jesus of the Synoptic Gospels from whose portrait all the features of the Christ have been eliminated. The Synoptic Gospels tell the story, and record the teaching of Jesus of Nazareth who is the Christ; this indeed is the aim of all three Gospels: to show Jesus as Christ. To reduce this picture of the Messiah-Jesus to the plane of a mere man—even if an extraordinary one—is not a work of scientific theology, but of unbelief, which shelters under the name of "science". Exact examination proves that there are no intellectual foundations for this depreciation of the Person of Christ; so-called "reasons" are prejudices, arguments derived from a way of thought in which the category of revelation, in the sense of the New Testament, has no place.

This category of revelation, however, is the decisive factor for the whole witness of the New Testament to Jesus, even for the testimony of Jesus concerning Himself. The whole of the New Testament presupposes the revelation of the Old Testament, the Word of revelation given to the Prophets. God gives the prophet something to say which no human being can say; He gives him the "Word" out of His Transcendence. The prophet has the "Word" which "has come" to him. Jesus, too, presupposes this prophetic Word; but at the same time He makes it plain that with and in His Person this stage of revelation has been left behind, and that a higher stage, namely the final one—as against the earlier provisional one—has been reached;[1] Jesus makes it clearly understood that He is "more than a prophet". But the only category which fits His claim to be "more than a prophet" is that of the One in whom Word and Person, that which is revealed and the Revealer, are one, whereas in the prophetic "Word" they are still separate.

We see the same thing from the point of view of "Saving History": the prophet proclaims a presence of God which is not yet present, which will only be realized in the future, a "new covenant", which is distinguished from the present imperfect one by its perfection. The prophet proclaims the Messiah and the Messianic Day as future. But Jesus proclaims the Messianic covenant and the personal Messianic presence of God as present, as having dawned in His own Person.[2] Hence for Him the prophetic revelation belongs to the past, and even *the* Prophet who is greater than all his predecessors, John, still belongs to the old dispensation, which is now over, since He Himself, Jesus, is here. Jesus is "more than a prophet" because He is the One and Only, who can be more than a prophet: Emmanuel, the personal presence of God, divine authority, which is inherent not in the Word but in the Person, which therefore does not appeal to a given word of God which "has come"—as to the prophet—but which is present in and with the Person who says of Himself, "I am come".

As in the prophetic period the Word came—out of the sphere of Transcendence—out of the Mystery of God—so now He Himself, Jesus, is He "who has come". Whether we identify this new and final stage of revelation with the Messianic title of the prophetic message, or whether, owing to the misunderstandings this raises, we leave it out, does not matter. It is not important. It is not the title but the category which is decisive, the category of "more than a prophet", the "new age", the presence of the Kingdom, which had previously only been promised. This is the clear witness of the New Testament, and of Jesus Himself, which cannot be overturned by any theories of the historical critics. A scholar who does not admit this claim, does not do so as an historical critic, but because his own philosophy of life has no room for this category of revelation. As a conscientious historian he can only do so—as for instance Albert Schweitzer does—by admitting that this claim

---

[1] Matt. 12: 41   [2] Matt. 12: 28

is present, but by regarding it as an illusion: "Jesus was mistaken", Jesus was led astray by the Messianic beliefs of His own day, Jesus was an apocalyptic fanatic. At this point specific research ends; here the decision of faith begins. There is no scientific reason to doubt the statements about Christ in the New Testament; there are only reasons which belong to the sphere of faith or unbelief.

8. Thus when a believer is asked: Why do you believe that Jesus is the Christ? he can only answer: Why should I not believe, since Jesus confronts me as the Christ, when He meets me in the story and the witness of the Apostles as the Christ? It is not the believer who needs to give reasons, but the unbeliever; for the believer appeals quite simply to the historical reality which the New Testament reveals. The Jesus of the New Testament is no other than the Christ of faith. The historical picture of Jesus agrees with the apostolic witness to Christ. It is not the one who accepts this claim of Jesus, and obeys it, who has to give "reasons" for his faith; on the contrary, those who do not accept this claim ought to state the "reasons" for their decision; as a rule, these "reasons" are never purely intellectual, but are due to the unbeliever's general outlook on life. Further consideration, therefore, is only necessary in order that we may see clearly why it is that the Christian believer does not stress "reasons" for his faith, while the unbeliever produces "reasons" for his unbelief. All these reasons, as we have said, do not belong to the sphere of academic knowledge, but to the sphere of one's philosophy of life, of self-knowledge, of faith. Again, the believer and the unbeliever speak completely differently about these reasons. The believer says, more or less, what is said in the Parable of the Wicked Husbandmen: they are not willing to accept the total claim of God—through His Son—on their hearts and lives. They want to remain masters, they want to preserve their independence. We could also put it thus: they do not acknowledge Christ because they have no use for Him. Or again: they do not acknowledge Him because their immanent rational self-understanding and their understanding of existence has no room for the category of revelation; and they remain in this immanent self-understanding because they think that they already know the divine truth, because in the last resort it resides within them; and they are able to think so because they do not know that they are sinners who need forgiveness. This is the point at which faith in Christ is decided. Ultimately

there is only one thing that decides whether we believe in Christ or not: either we know that we are sinners, who need the forgiveness of sins, or we believe that we can deal with our sins quite well by ourselves. A person who does not believe in Jesus Christ does so because, in the last resort, he feels he can do without a Saviour, because he is sufficient for himself. But one who admits that he is a sinner, who needs a Saviour, admits the claim of Jesus to be this Saviour.

This is how the Christian believer regards the situation. The unbeliever, of course, looks at it quite differently; he would, indeed, not be an unbeliever unless he saw it quite differently. The unbeliever regards the claim of Jesus, in the whole revelation-category of the New Testament, as a "Myth", which is in opposition to our rational view of the world. He regards Jesus (in spite of all that he may say about His exemplary moral character), as a fanatic, or as a man deluded by ancient apocalyptic ideas, or as a "child of his own day",[1] as one who, entangled in the supernatural categories of his own period, could only explain his extraordinary religious powers to Himself by means of an inherited dogma of the Messiah. Again there is another view, which is not really "critical", but claims to be so, which says: "The real Jesus is not the one of whom we read in the Gospels; in order to recognize the real Jesus of History we must first of all purify His portrait in the Gospels, by criticism, from all the additions of a later theology of the Church, of all the legendary material, of Pauline theology, which have distorted the original picture". Certainly, it is very difficult to take this line nowadays, owing to the work done by historical critics. Hence the main argument of unbelievers to-day is this: Jesus was a visionary, for He believed in the imminent End of the world. The fact that we now see the connexion between Jewish dogmas about the Messiah and Apocalyptic speculations about the End of the world "explains" both the Messianic claim of Jesus Himself as well as Pauline theology—or the theology of the Primitive Church, which is very similar. It also "explains" the witness of the New Testament to Jesus the Christ, and it also means that everyone who is able to see this connexion need not believe in the claim that Jesus makes for Himself. Thus unbelief interprets itself as "scientific love of truth", and in so doing makes itself immune against that quite different interpretation which is given by faith. But this can only happen so long as a man thinks he has no need of a

[1] Cf. Schmiedel, *Die Person Jesu im Streite der Meinungen der Gegenwart*, 1906

Saviour. The moment that a man really sees himself as he is, this whole edifice of self-justification breaks down, and he knows that what he covers with the cloak of "science" and "love of truth" is in reality simply the self-sufficiency of the unrepentant human being, who wants to preserve his independence.

9. There is one more point necessary for the understanding of faith that Jesus is the Christ. As the personal revelation of God, Jesus can only be known, with full certainty, because He unveils not only God's true Being, but also the reality and truth of human existence. Knowledge of Christ is at the same time self-knowledge. Jesus not only reveals what God is, and what He wills, but He reveals at the same time that we are sinners, that we are opposed to our origin and our divinely created nature. In His Person Jesus reveals true God and true Man; and since He reveals true Man He unveils the falsity of our actual state, our existence-in-untruth, our sinful condition. Jesus reveals true human existence as existence in the love of God. Hence we know Him as true Man, as the Man who is what we would all like to be, and ought to be. The love of God, which always manifests itself as love to man, actually constitutes the life of Jesus. But this Love of God, which is the principle and the force which constitutes and determines His human life, He *gives to us* with His divine power. Herein He reveals Himself as the One who comes to us out of the mystery of God and discloses to us the divine mystery. He reveals the love of God as God's generous love, as unconditioned, undemanding love, as *Agape*. The heart of the revelation of God which takes place in the Person of Jesus is that God is this love—a truth which is utterly unknown outside the Bible, and would have seemed absolute nonsense to a thinker like Plato or Aristotle.

Therefore, because Jesus, in revealing God to us, reveals us to ourselves, allows us to know ourselves, in a way that we could never have attained by our own efforts, He makes His revelation of God our own certainty. Through Him our self-knowledge and our knowledge of God are one. He allows us to know God in such a way that He calls us back to our origin. And because He calls us back to *our* origin, and leads us back to our home, we can believe, in such a way, that faith and certainty are one. Belief in Christ is home-coming, a re-discovery of the original truth, a home-coming to ourselves, in coming home to God. We perceive in Jesus the Original

"Word" in which we were created. Hence we know that He came unto His own. Since we know Him we see that we are placed at the point where we belong. So the knowledge of God in Christ is at the same time self-knowledge, and for that reason, and for that alone, can the knowledge of God be certainty.

Naturally this "home-coming", this recall to our Origin, means something quite different from the *anamnesis* of Platonism. For the theory of *anamnesis* says, in effect: "You already have the truth within you; all you need is to become aware of it." But Christ says to us: "You have lost the truth, therefore you cannot find it. You can only regain it if it returns to you, if it is *given* to you afresh, and that is what I will do." In faith, the lost truth, to which we no longer have access, comes back to us, and incorporates us into itself. But it is *our* truth, the truth which, on account of the Creation, is ours, which we now receive as a gift, as our original existence which has been restored, and, since we receive it afresh, we may know it as our own. Hence this truth, as self-knowledge which has been regained, is self-knowledge which brings certainty; therefore it is not heteronomous but autonomous, a knowledge of "our own". It is a truth of "our own", and yet it is a gift—this is faith, and this is the gift of the Holy Spirit.

10. Why do we believe that Jesus is the Christ? We believe it because this is so, and He is what He says He is, and we believe it because what He says agrees with His being, because in His being He reveals two things: God's being and ours, because since we know God in Him, at the same time we know ourselves, and therefore we know that this knowledge is true. Hence the "faith-knowledge" of Jesus the Christ is an autonomous and not a heteronomous truth. We do not believe that Jesus is the Christ because the Apostles say so. But we cannot know it apart from their witness. The picture which the Apostles give us of Jesus, and their witness that He is the Christ, are the means by which we learn to know Him, and in learning to know Him we come to know God. Therefore, because the historical element is interwoven with our knowledge of God, and of ourselves, the relativism which clings to all that is merely historical cannot touch us. The merely historical element, which, as such, is always subordinate to historical criticism, and is open to historical scepticism, has become in the act of faith more than historical—an organ of the revelation of the eternal God, and a moment of self-knowledge. Therefore

we can watch with confidence the oscillations of historical research; for we know what the final result will be—not in detail of course, but in its main outline; we know this by the same act of faith which creates in us both the knowledge of God and self-knowledge. The Historical has become the eternal Word of God.

(A) THE INTERPRETATION OF JESUS IN "CONSISTENT ESCHAT-
OLOGY"

IN the latest theological discussions in the sphere of Christology
there are two theories which deserve special mention, because,
owing to their extremism, they attack the centre of the Christian
Faith; the former is that of "consistent eschatology", and the
latter is the theory of the "de-mythologizing" of Christianity.
The former begins with problems of New Testament exegesis,
and finally ends in a complete destruction of the Christian
Faith—although this result is never wholly admitted. The
latter, although held by a New Testament scholar, starts from
philosophical premises, and a general philosophy of life; its
intention is to extract the ore of the Christian Faith from the
rock of time and space in which it is embedded. In this appendix
we shall be dealing with the former theory; in the second with
the latter.

The school of thought known as *"Konseqvente Fschatologie"*
or "consistent eschatology", represented to-day by two Bernese
theologians in particular, Martin Werner and Fritz Buri,
regards itself as a continuation of the *Leben-Jesu-Forschung* (or
the Quest of the Historical Jesus) of Albert Schweitzer. It
takes over from it, moreover, as its axiomatic starting point,
Albert Schweitzer's hypotheses: (*a*) that Jesus adopted a
Messianic dogma which he found in late Judaism and applied
to Himself; (*b*) that He regarded Himself as the Son of Man, in
the sense of a heavenly angelic being, that He expected the
transcendent Kingdom of God to break into history, and indeed
that history had already come to an end when He sent His
disciples forth; then, as this did not happen, He expected that
the Kingdom would appear after His entry into Jerusalem, as
the result of His vicarious sufferings.

In an imposing work of over 700 pages (*Die Entstehung des
christlichen Dogmas*) Martin Werner has tried to prove that
the whole dogma of Christology is a substitute for the failure
of the Immediate Coming of the Lord in Glory (so confidently
expected at first in the Primitive Church). He leaves it to the
reader to draw the final conclusion, namely, that consequently,
the whole Christian Faith is based upon an illusion, which can
be proved, and is therefore itself such an illusion. His pupil,

Fritz Buri, however, does explicitly draw this conclusion, and as a substitute for the Christian Faith which has thus been destroyed he offers a kind of existential philosophy from which not only Jesus Christ, but also God, as the object of faith, disappears; in spite of this, however, he claims that this view is "Christian", and may still be operative within the Christian Church. (Cf. his last article with the characteristic title: *Christus gestern und heute* (Christ Yesterday and To-day) in the *Schweizerische Theologische Umschau*, 1948, pp. 97 ff.)

Here then we are concerned with a central attack on the Christian Faith, with an "Either-Or", which shakes the whole Christian Faith, and not one part only. It is the task of theology to deal with this theory, all the more because it claims to be based on the scholarly and critical study and exposition of the New Testament itself. Primarily therefore New Testament scholars ought to deal with it; but in this one instance it becomes particularly clear that the whole of dogmatics is based upon the foundation of Biblical exegesis. If this theory is right, then the whole business of Christian dogmatics is over, for it could be nothing more than the orderly presentation of an illusion. New Testament scholars have already taken up this challenge, and it is of course only natural that the Swiss should be the first to deal seriously with this question. (W. Michaelis in Bern, *Zur Engelchristologie im Urchristentum, Abbau der Konstruktion Martin Werners*, 1942; O. Cullmann in Basel, *Christus und die Zeit, Die urchristliche Zeit—und Geschichtsauffassung*, 1946; W. Kümmel, in Zürich, *Verheissung und Erfüllung, Untersuchungen zur eschatologischen Verkündigung Jesu*, 1947. There are also a number of smaller publications.)

What is the result of these discussions?

To take the hypotheses of Albert Schweitzer and use them as if they were axiomatic propositions, truths which need no further examination, simply will not do. The great merit of Schweitzer remains undiminished, namely, that in developing the insights of Johannes Weiss, he proved, in a convincing manner, that the teaching and the activity of Jesus were absolutely determined by eschatological and Messianic motives. In so doing he dealt a death-blow to the older "liberal" view of Jesus, which regarded Him as a teacher of timeless, immanental, religious and ethical truths. "The Jesus of Nazareth who came forth as Messiah, proclaimed the ethics of the Kingdom of God, founded the Kingdom of God upon earth, and died, in order to give His work its consecration, has never existed at all" (*Geschichte der Leben-Jesu-Forschung*, p. 631). To-day we may regard this result of Schweitzer's work as established. But research did not come to an end with Albert Schweitzer. His particular hypotheses, which have just been mentioned, are by no means universally accepted by scholars; on the contrary, from very different quarters, and indeed by scholars of the most varied religious outlook, they have been decidedly rejected, in spite of the undoubted stimulus that they have given to the thought of other scholars. Their foundations are insecure.

(i) The wholesale acceptance of a Jewish Messianic dogma by Jesus is, *a priori*, extremely improbable; it does not fit into the Gospel picture of a man whose critical attitude towards Judaism, and whose spiritual freedom and originality are recognized by non-Christian scholars. For textual reasons, too, it is untenable; it must therefore be described as a purely artificial theory, an hypothesis, for which there is no proof.

(ii) The same may be said of the so-called "angel-Christology" which is supposed to have been common to the whole of Primitive Christianity. "The New Testament passages which are adduced by Werner cannot be regarded in themselves as illustrations of such a view in the doctrine of the Primitive Church, nor do such passages become illustrations of this theory in the framework of their connexion with the Apocalyptic of later Judaism, especially as even in this sphere there are no traces of such a Christology" (Michaelis, *op. cit.*, p. 121). "The view championed by Werner . . . is therefore untenable, because it cannot actually be proved that this idea existed at all, either in later Judaism or in Primitive Christianity" (Kümmel in the *Theologische Rundschau*, 1948, p. 111).

(iii) The third point, however, is the decisive one. Scholars of such a different outlook as Dodd, Kümmel, and Cullmann, have equally stressed the fact that the imminent expectation of the Parousia in the whole of the New Testament pales into insignificance before the belief that in Jesus Christ the New Age has already dawned—as indeed the message of Jesus Himself is permeated through and through with this conviction—and the New Testament itself proves that the "delay" of the Parousia did *not* have the effect which—according to the theories of the school of "Consistent Eschatology"—it should have had. The tension between the time of the End which had already dawned and the Hope of its fulfilment exists; it is an integral element—not only of Primitive Christianity, but also of all genuine Christian faith; but this tension was not weakened by the fact that the Second Coming was delayed, but by the incursion of a current of Hellenistic non-historical thought into the later development of Christian thought. To argue that the whole development of Christian dogma is based upon the fact that the Parousia was delayed, is an artificial theory, interesting enough in itself, but entirely unfounded on fact. "Neither to-day nor in the days of the Apostles did this delay contradict that characteristic blend of faith and hope; all that was altered was the expectation of an immediate 'Second Coming'" (Cullmann, *Theologische Zeitschrift*, Basel, 1947, p. 186). The greatest weakness of this Schweitzer-Werner theory, from the standpoint of scholarly exegesis, lies in the complete misunderstanding of the fact that Jesus Himself knew that the Kingdom of God had already come in His own Person—even though not completely—and that the New Testament witnesses see in that fact the main point in their confession of faith: *Kyrios Christos*. The problem of the imminent expectation of the Parousia remains a question which will be further discussed in the third volume of this work—in the section on Eschatology; it is also connected with the subject of the following appendix, with the ancient view of the world, which is that of the whole Bible. It belongs to the theme of Christology, to this extent, because it is connected with the fact that it is one element in the view that Jesus Himself confessed that His human knowledge was limited. But to argue from this one point that the Christian message of the New Testament, and thus that of the whole Church, is founded upon an illusion, can only enter the head of some one who cannot see the wood for the trees, who, above all, in the interests of a bewilderingly "simple" theory, misunderstands and misinterprets the witness to Christ of the whole of the New Testament.

(B) THE PROBLEM OF "DE-MYTHOLOGIZING" (*ENTMYTHOLOGI-SIERUNG*) THE MESSAGE OF THE NEW TESTAMENT

"No work which appeared during the years of the War, in the sphere of New Testament study, has caused so much discussion as Bultmann's book, *Neues Testament und Mythologie*" (H. W. Bartsch, in the Preface to the symposium entitled *Kerygma und Mythos*, 1948). Unfortunately, this discussion, and for the most part also Bultmann's book itself, has been inaccessible to the outside world, and only now (through the volume just mentioned), has it come into our hands. The theory of "de-mythologizing" is not new, but the extreme lengths to which Bultmann goes on this point, and above all, the fact that in so doing he does not wish to destroy the central point in the primitive Christian *kerygma* at the decisive point of Christology—unlike theological liberalism—gives it an outstanding importance, not only for New Testament exegesis but also for dogmatics.

Bultmann's theses are the following: "The world-view of the New Testament is a mythical one." Our view of the world has ceased to be mythical. But the Church continually tries to teach and to preach the message of the New Testament which is clothed in this mythical garment. In this effort she is trying to do the impossible. For the world-view of the ancients cannot be recreated, nor can that element of the message of the New Testament which belongs to that world-view be introduced into our present view of the world. Were a Christian to try to do so it would mean "that in his faith, in his religion, he accepts a view of the world which he rejects in the rest of his life". The only actual possibility therefore is to eliminate the element of myth from the Christian message; that is, the Christian message must be disentangled from its mythical folds. This is possible because the myth itself, in the last resort, wants to say something which concerns us. "The myth should not be interpreted cosmologically, but from the point of view of anthropology, or rather, existentially". It is indeed characteristic of myth that it speaks of the "unworldly in a worldly way, and of the gods in a human manner". Of course, this is not a new idea. What is new, however, is the expansion which Bultmann gives to the idea of the "mythical", and above all—and this is the weak point in Bultmann's contention—the way in which he confuses two questions: "Myth" and the world-view.

We see this at the very beginning of Bultmann's essay, where he runs through the points in the New Testament which belong to the mythical view of the Ancient World. In addition to the familiar cosmological idea of the three-story universe he mentions, in the same breath, the fact that "the earth is also the arena of the activity of supernatural powers", that this age is under the power of Satan, that "history does not move on its settled, law-abiding way, but that its movement and its direction are supported by supernatural powers". Above all, the confusion of the world-view with the question of myth comes out very plainly when Bultmann, in the next section, goes on to say that "the presentation of God's saving Act corresponds to the mythical world-view"; then, without further ado, all such ideas as the sending of the Son of God in the fullness of time, the pre-existence of the Son of God, His atoning death on the Cross, the despoiling of the "powers", the exaltation of Jesus, the coming Judgment, the Holy Spirit who works in the hearts of the faithful and guarantees their resurrection, etc., are reckoned as part of the mythical view of the world. It is obvious that here two subjects have been confused.

The question of the world-view is a truth of Natural Science; that is one point. The question of the interpretation of History, and the idea of the Nature and the Action of God is another, and a different point. The confusion of these two questions is a relic of the liberalism which in other respects Bultmann has abandoned. No religious discussion is needed on the question of the world-view. The fact that the earth is not a plate, but a ball, and therefore that we can no longer speak of "Heaven" as the "place" where God dwells, is a self-evident truth to anyone with even a smattering of science. But our thought of God and His working in History is a quite different matter, which has nothing to do with natural science. Now and again, however, when he is speaking of "History" Bultmann uses a causal idea which belongs to nineteenth century thought, and has no connexion with the scientific view of the world; it is simply part of a general view of life, prevailing at a certain time.

Then there is a further point, which is characteristic, at least, of the first part of Bultmann's essay. Sometimes he compares the statements of the New Testament with scientific truths which, in so far as they are real truths, (as, for instance, the fact that the earth is round) are absolutely final for us; then again, he contrasts the statements of the New Testament with the thinking of "modern man", whose understanding of man is either "biological" or "idealistic". Now it is a fact that "modern man" tends to accept one or other of these views, in other words, he inclines to "Naturalism" or to "Idealism"; hence it is obvious that the Christian understanding of man will be a stumbling-block to all who hold these views. Here, however, we are already dealing with *religious* questions, that is, with views of man's view of life as a whole, with views which, as Christians, we cannot accept, but which we must contest as mistaken. Bultmann is, of course, aware of the difference between the modern view of the world and the modern self-understanding of man. He adds, "What concerns us, however, is not only the criticism which is evoked by the world-view given to us by Natural Science but, equally, and at bottom still more, the criticism which is due to the self-understanding of modern man". What then is the value of this second type of criticism? Is, for instance, the "self-understanding of modern man", like his scientific view of the world, something final and settled?

The "self-understanding" of man is a religious matter, not an objective intellectual affair. Those who hold the Christian Faith must grapple with this "modern self-understanding" of man, and it will soon become plain that this view is simply that of "the natural man". Hence they must not accept this criticism of Biblical thought, but they must reject it as a misunderstanding of man's nature.

This is what Bultmann does in the second, positive part of his essay, but it then becomes evident that these two fundamentally different problems: that of the world-view, and that of the self-understanding of man, are not clearly differentiated in his mind. For instance, the fact that "neither the Naturalist nor the Idealist can understand death as the penalty of sin" does not in any way prove that this is an incorrect religious view. Again, the fact that modern man "cannot understand the doctrine of vicarious atonement through the Death of Christ", is simply what Paul calls "the offence of the Cross", which is the heart of his message of salvation. And when Bultmann says, evidently in agreement with the criticism, that "modern man does not understand that his salvation should consist in a condition in which he finds the fulfilment of his life, of his 'existence' (*Eigentlichkeit*)", he is using, not a naturalistic or an Idealistic conception, but a fundamental concept of Existential Philosophy, by which he measures what the New Testament means by "fulfilment of life" (*Eigentlichkeit*). Here then Bultmann makes a certain modern philosophical school of thought—and not "modern man"—the judge of what is valid in the New Testament or not.

In spite of all this, we cannot be sufficiently thankful to Bultmann for his attack, particularly because, in his more positive statements, he comes much closer than the first part of his essay would suggest to the real task of theology: To understand the New Testament in such a way that every statement it makes is questioned for its "existential" meaning.

This does not mean that a definite idea of *Eigentlichkeit*, taken from Heidegger's philosophy, is intended, but the interpretation of the New Testament in its own particular understanding of *Eigentlichkeit* in harmony with revelation, with that which we in our terminology call "truth as encounter", the understanding of the *Kerygma* as the Word of God which speaks to "me". Here I will permit myself to call attention once more to that passage of Luther which I have already quoted in my book *Revelation and Reason*, which clearly contains the programme of such a theology, and is at the same time genuinely Biblical, and also "existential". Since Luther is speaking of Justification by Faith, he says: "the other articles are rather far beyond us, and do not enter into our experience, nor do they touch us. . . . But the article on the Forgiveness of Sins is always part of our own experience, and a matter of daily exercise, and it touches you and me without ceasing. Of the other articles we speak of as matters outside our own experience, (for example: Creation, the fact that Jesus is the Son of God . . .). What is it to me that God has created heaven and earth if I do not believe in the Forgiveness of Sins?" . . . "But if they are to enter into our experience and touch us, they must come into this article, into our experience, and touch us, in order that we all, *I* for *myself*, and *thou* for *thyself*, and *each* for *himself*, may believe in the Forgiveness of Sins" (*WA.*, XXVIII, p. 271). This work of Dogmatics is an attempt to take this programme of Luther's seriously; this is also Bultmann's aim, when it is rightly understood.

In so far as Bultmann, in the positive part of his essay, carries out this programme, he achieves results which are extraordinarily fruitful for the understanding of the New Testament. At the same time, however, the confusion of the question of the world-view with that of Myth, and the effort to adapt the Christian Faith to "modern" views of life in general, and to the concepts of existential philosophy, comes out continually in the fact that he "cleanses" the message of the New Testament from ideas which necessarily belong to it, and do not conflict with the modern view of the world at all, but only with the "self-understanding", and in particular with the prejudices, of an Idealistic philosophy. In so far as Bultmann *also* does this, he is continuing the old Liberalism, which at other points he is able to describe so clearly, and to contrast with genuine Biblical thought.

This is not the place to prove this in detail. Only one point of special significance (which has already been emphasized by Schniewind in the *Symposium* above mentioned) should be mentioned here: Bultmann's conception of History. Right through he is lacking in insight into the significance of the New Testament ἐφ' ἅπαξ, of the "once-for-all-ness" (or uniqueness) of the Fact of Christ as an Event in the continuum of history. That there is a point in this historical continuum of which it is true to say that it is both an historic fact, and God's personal self-revelation—this is precisely the "foolishness" and the "offence" of the Gospel, and therefore the decisive element. Bultmann knows this, and yet he does not know it. Here there is still the lurking shadow of Lessing's phrase about "accidental facts of history". May I call attention to an article which I wrote in 1929 in the *Deutschen Blättern für Philosophie* on *Das Einmalige und der Existenzcharakter*. Recently, expanded and developed, it has appeared under the title: *La conception chrétienne du temps* in *Dieu Vivant*, 1949. Much of Bultmann's hypercritical abandonment of New Testament ideas is to be laid at the door of this lack of understanding of the *Einmalige* (that which has happened *once for all*). Coupled with that is an understanding of the Person which is still determined by Idealism. The standpoint of that which is not of this world, of that which is not given, dominates Bultmann's thinking to such an extent, that, measured by the truth of the Biblical revelation, he goes far beyond the mark—this too is an Idealistic *motif*. We would do well therefore to take Bultmann's postulate quite seriously, but to subject the presuppositions of his "de-mythologizing" to a strict examination, and accordingly to treat his conclusions with the necessary reserve.

This conception of the Mythical is one of these presuppositions which needs to be examined very thoroughly. In my book *Der Mittler* (1927) under the heading *Über die christliche Mythologie*[1] I have already called attention to the fact that, from two aspects, the Christian *kerygma* cannot be separated from Myth. Firstly, the Christian statement is necessarily and consciously "anthropomorphic" in the sense that it does and must do, what Bultmann conceives to be characteristic of the Mythical—it "speaks of God in a human way". To the extent in which Christian theology does not do so, it ceases to be Christian, and falls into the errors of Pantheism, or acosmism, an impersonal way of thinking about God. In so

[1] *The Mediator* (E.T.), pp. 377 ff. (TR.)

doing, however, it does not escape from symbolism; all that happens is that the neuter symbol, the "it", takes the place of the personal one. (Cf. my dissertation: *Das Symbolische in der religiösen Erkenntnis*, 1913.) No one has spoken more "anthropomorphically" of God than the Prophets of Israel, and Jesus Himself. We may even say: To the extent in which this happens the statement is a Christian one, presupposing that at the same time, through other symbols, the supra-mundane nature of God is expressed. With Jesus it is very simple: "Our Father, who art in Heaven." The anthropo-morphism which is so deliberate that, on the one hand, it is not afraid of crudeness of expression—cf. the Parables of Jesus, for instance, that of the Importunate Widow—and at the same time leaves no doubt of the fact that God does not belong to this world, and that He is far above and beyond it, is the only possibility of preserving Biblical personalism.

Secondly, the "Mythical", in the real sense of the word, is related to the historicity of the Divine revelation, to the history of Salvation. That our belief is based upon an intervention of God, indeed upon a *coming* of God into History, that this is both the object and the basis of our faith, can only be denied by someone who already regards the Gospel as a timeless metaphysic and thus misunderstands it—or, which comes to the same in the end—in the sense of an Idealistic conception of History. The specifically Biblical element is precisely this: the history of salvation, God's coming into History. Hence the mythical expression—"history of the gods" (Tillich)—is essential for Biblical religion. Therefore what matters is not, in the interest of a modern profoundly non-historical self-understanding of modern man, to replace this idea of "saving history" by something else (on this point cf. the excellent observations on Bultmann's book in Kümmel, *Mythische Rede und Heilsgeschehen im Neuen Testament*, Coniectanea Neotesta-mentica, Lund, 1947); all that matters is this: so to understand this "History" that it "touches us", to use Luther's phrase, that is, that when God is mentioned this always affects us too, and indeed in such a way that our untruth is exposed and God's gracious truth is given to us.

The second presupposition, which needs to be re-examined, is the idea of the world-view. Karl Heim in particular has been constantly and vigorously concerned with this problem. The science of the present day is now engaged in a radical transformation of some of the fundamental presuppositions which (above all in the 19th century) were regarded as essential elements in the "scientific view of the world". In so doing it acknowledges that in those unexamined axioms we are dealing with a "scientific mythology"—as, for instance, the infinity of space and time, as well as the absolute validity of the law of causality.

Modern psychology, likewise, is in the act of re-emphasizing certain truths of mythical thinking which had been "written off" by the Enlightenment, and in general to grant to the mythical element a limited right to exist, over against a merely rational scientific view of the world. In the scientific world-view of a particular period there are certain things which absolutely determine us like Fate, which simply are "so", and not otherwise, as for instance, the fact that the earth is round; but there are others, which indeed are still regarded as valid, and are generally accepted, but already belong to the sphere of a general philosophy of life, and therefore should only be used by us with the greatest caution. For all these reasons the idea of the Mythical should not be taken for granted and used in the way in which Bultmann does. If anyone wants to be critical, let him be above all critical in the use of his criteria! The fact that Bultmann does this too little is the reason why his work which is in itself so valuable, and achieves so much, has been so hotly opposed in certain circles; this is not fair to Bultmann's work, but some of the blame for it lies at his own door.

CHAPTER II

THE SAVING WORK OF GOD IN JESUS CHRIST

It is usual, and it seems natural, to deal first with the Person, and then with the Work of Jesus Christ. There are many important reasons for this procedure: mainly of course, because it seems natural and logical. Since, however, for reasons which have already been explained, in this section of the present work of Dogmatics we are going to use an inductive, and not—as is usual—a deductive method, we shall begin not with the Person, but with the Work of Christ. For the Person of Christ can be discerned from His work. In so doing we are following a line which has already been traced for us beforehand, by one of the most profound statements of Reformation theology: *Hoc est Christum cognoscere, beneficia ejus cognoscere.*[1]

In our short survey of the development of Christological statements in the New Testament we have already mentioned the fact that Paul, as the first theologian of the Church, differs from John, his great follower, in the fact that he speaks more about the Work of Christ than about His Person. In contrast to his numerous statements about the Work of Christ those about His Person are extremely few, and this is still more true of the Christology of the Primitive Church which preceded that of Paul. Here the work, the gift—and, if this word may be allowed—the "achievement" of Christ is always in the foreground, while the mystery of the Person is in the background. The Christology of the Primitive Church—as against the Johannine Christology—is determined more by the verb than by the substantive. Here Jesus Christ is contemplated in His action, or in God's operation through Him, in all that God does for us and in us through Jesus, in all that He gives us through Him, and has prepared for us through Him, not so much—as it *appears* at least in *John*, in His Hidden Being. The historical way which the knowledge of Jesus Christ has followed, leads from the Work to the Person.

This method of approach, from the Work to the Person, as the right way to reach the truth of the Person of Jesus, is supported by the fact that the titles given to Jesus in the New Testament, which are distinctive, are "verbal" and not

[1] Melanchthon, *Loci theologici*, Introduction

"substantive" in character; they all describe an event, a work of God, which He does through Jesus in or for humanity. Who and what Jesus *is*, can only be stated, at first at any rate, by what God *does*, and gives in Him. This is true, first of all of the first title given to Jesus, that of *Christos* or Messiah. The Christ is the One in whom and through whom God establishes His sovereignty. Christ is characterized not so much by His being as by His function. Whatever else Christ may "be", in any case He is the One who leads out of the "present age" into the "coming age",[1] who ends one period, and ushers in another, who realizes God's rule upon earth. The Synoptic Gospels scarcely ever go further than this—with one exception: in the doctrine of the Virgin Birth, which seems like a "foreign body" from another sphere, within the New Testament as a whole.

Even the title, "Son of God", which for instance in Peter's Confession occurs in close connexion with the title "Christ", must be understood here, as in the whole Synoptic record, in an entirely functional sense, suggesting His "office" rather than His being. The "Son of God" in the Synoptic record, that is, in the Semitic use of language, is the One to whom God hands over His sovereignty: this means, to use the language of the 110th Psalm: "this day have I begotten thee". Here there is no thought of "descent", or of a metaphysical relatedness. Jesus, as the Son of God, has authority to act in the place of God; He is the One to whom God transmits His whole power and His final authority. The same applies to that concept which, in the Greek-speaking Primitive Church, takes the place of that title which had already become a name: the *Kyrios*. By *Kyrios* the Greek Christian means exactly what the Hebrew means by "Christ"=Messiah. To the extent in which the name of "Christ" became the proper name of "Jesus", the functional meaning of the title of "Christ" was transferred to the name of the *Kyrios*. Jesus is the *Kyrios*, that is, He who rules over the Church: a right that belongs to God alone, and which God alone is able to exercise.

This functional verbal meaning comes out quite clearly in some other titles. The title "Emmanuel" is an example in the linguistic sense. "God with us" says exactly what Paul states in a whole sentence (2 Cor. 5: 19)—a central clause in his theology—"God was in Christ reconciling the world . . ." That is the precise meaning of the term "Emmanuel" in Messianic

---

[1] Matt. 12: 32

terms. Still more clearly names like "Saviour", "Rescuer", "Mediator", (which linguistically are verbal nouns) mean the same thing. One of the most beautiful and fitting names for Jesus, which belongs entirely to this category, is the German title of *Heiland*, the one who brings *healing* or salvation, the *Healer* (or Saviour). All this expresses the fact that Jesus is first of all understood by the Church through His work, His function, His significance for salvation. The Christology of the New Testament—which, as we shall see, is also that of the Gospel of John—is determined throughout by *saving history* (*Heilsgeschichte*) and not by metaphysics. Anything to do with metaphysical being and substance is the background, not the foreground, of the message of the New Testament. To speak of Jesus is to speak of His work: *hoc est Christum cognoscere, beneficia ejus cognoscere.*

It is no accident that it was Reformed theology which, in its doctrine of the "offices" of Christ, re-emphasized this original Biblical stress on *saving history*, which, in the period of medieval scholasticism, had been lost.[1] The work of Jesus is the fulfilment of the Old Covenant. In the doctrine of the Three "Offices" of Christ we are again reminded of the truth that we know Jesus through God's action in Him; this had already been suggested in the various titles given to Jesus in the Primitive Church, all of which have a "functional" character and suggest His Work rather than His Person.

The fact that the Reformed theologians speak of the three-fold "office" or "work" of Christ, is due to the fact that under the Old Covenant there were three theocratic figures: the Prophet, the Priest, and the King; in Jesus all that these three represented was fulfilled since they all merged into a complete unity in His Person. Whereas in the Old Testament these three functions were divided among three different persons, which accounts both for their limitations, and for their provisional character—in Jesus Christ they are blended into a unity; only then is their full and real significance perceived. In the Old Testament indeed, there is an evident tension, if not an absolute contrast, between these three. The Prophet, at least in the days of the great Prophets, is deliberately and consciously on the defensive against the priesthood and the Temple; more than once this attitude developed into fierce hostility.[2] The Priestly element, from the Prophetic point of view, is something

---

[1] Cf. Visser't Hooft, *The Kingship of Christ*, p. 11
[2] As in the case of Amos, Isaiah and Jeremiah

which, at its best, can barely be tolerated, and often seems an utter impossibility. It is indeed that element in which the religion of the Old Testament is least differentiated from the pagan religion of the surrounding nations; therefore it is also the point from which paganism continually penetrated into the life of Israel or Judah.

But from the point of view of the theocratic idea, the King is also a very ambiguous phenomenon. On the one hand, from the time of David the Monarchy was always closely connected with the Messianic Hope of the future, so that the Messiah is expected to issue from the House of David, and to be a powerful and righteous King. On the other hand, from the time of Moses and the Judges, from the classical period of Yahwist religion, there was a very critical attitude towards the Monarchy, because it seemed to interfere with the direct divine guidance of the nation. Israel, in contrast to the surrounding Eastern nations, was not originally a monarchy nor a hierocracy, but a *"pneumatocracy"*. The ruler of Israel is to be a leader called and empowered by God, not an hereditary sovereign. Saul, as the first King, as an elected King and as a "Nabi"[1] is evidently a transitional phenomenon. Thus the monarchy exists in a kind of twilight between God's highest will for His people, and that which is in direct opposition to His Will, owing to the blurring of the distinction between Israel and the surrounding nations, reducing it to the merely human level.

Both tensions: that between Prophet and Priest, and that between Prophet and King, could not be overcome under the old dispensation. It is only Jesus the Messiah, whose Kingship is totally different in kind from that of the Davidic dynasty, and whose Priesthood is so entirely different from that of the Jerusalem priesthood, and, still more, who was not a Prophet of the Old Testament kind at all, who can eliminate these tensions and contradictions because He gathers up these three "offices" in His own Person. In His Word He is both Reconciler and King; in His sovereignty, He is both Revealer and the Sacrificial Lamb; in His Priesthood, He is both the One who proclaims the Name of God, and asserts God's glory and God's Sovereignty. We shall now proceed to deal in more detail with this threefold "office", with this threefold gift of God in Jesus.

[1] I.e. the Hebrew word for prophet (TR.)

(A) THE PROPHETIC OFFICE

1. We have to begin with what Jesus did in His historical life upon earth. Jesus began His active ministry in such a way that the people immediately came to the conclusion: "He is a Prophet." His first appearance in the synagogue was primarily that of a Rabbi,[1] a Teacher, a Man who expounds the Scriptures, and in so doing makes known the will of God. But from the very beginning it was plain that there was a great difference between His method of expounding the law and that of the rabbis: "He taught them as one that had authority, and not as the scribes."[2] But even the title of Prophet was not sufficient for Him. Like the Prophet, it is true, He had to proclaim new truth about the will of God. He had to say something to men which no human being had ever been able to say before—truth derived from the super-human sphere. Was He not One like John the Baptist, whom indeed He followed, and whose message "Repent! for the Kingdom of Heaven is at hand," was almost exactly like His own?

No, He was not a Prophet. He never claimed, as they did, that His authority was derived from a Divine Call: nor did He ever appeal to the "Word" which had been given to Him to utter with the preface: "Thus saith the Lord!" On the contrary, He says quite plainly that He is not a Prophet, that the time of the prophets is past, that here is One who is "more than a prophet".[3] It is true that Jesus says of John the Baptist that he is "more than a prophet"—because, in contrast to the Prophets, he is the immediate forerunner of the final revelation.[4] But Jesus is more than John, although He says of him: "among them that are born of women there hath not arisen a greater than John the Baptist" (Matt. 11: 11). He still belongs to the old dispensation. But now the new day has dawned, the new era has begun, because Jesus is here. He brings in the New Age, the Kingdom of God. Where Jesus is, "in the midst of you",[5] there is the Kingdom of God. Hence His Word cannot be severed from His Person; whereas for the Prophet all that matters is the "Word" given him by God, but his personality does not matter at all. This is why Jesus speaks with such absolute authority: "*I* say unto you"; hence He does not claim to be "inspired"; on the contrary, in His words He often points to Himself as the One who ushers in

---

[1] Mark 1:21 ff.; Luke 4: 31 ff.   [2] Mark 1: 22
[3] Matt. 12: 39; 13: 17   [4] Matt. 11: 9   [5] Luke 17: 21

the new Day, the day that points to the End, the heavenly world. Hence He could say—as no prophet could ever do—"I am come" . . . That is why He summons men to trust in Himself; this, too, is the reason for the new category which designates Jesus, in contrast to all the prophets whom he describes as "servants of God", by the claim which is alone fitting for Him: that of the Son.[1] This too is why He hinted (even though not very clearly and obviously) at His coming Death and its meaning—although His disciples did not understand what He was saying. This, in contrast to the "Word" of the Prophets, is a new stage of revelation, and by its very nature, final and complete: here the Word and the Person are one: the Word is no longer a pointer to something beyond, but the "Word" actually expresses the presence of that world beyond, for this is the category of "Emmanuel"—God Himself acting and speaking in the action and the speech of this Unique Person: Jesus.

2. Now what is the relation of all this to the fact of the "*Teaching of Jesus*"? We must first of all get rid of two opposite misunderstandings. One is the rationalist view of the "teaching" of Jesus as something which can be understood apart from His Person altogether. This misunderstanding claims to be based chiefly on the records of the message of Jesus in the Synoptic Gospels. Jesus is regarded as one of the many religious teachers who proclaim eternal religious truths. "So", says Harnack, "the whole message of Jesus may be reduced to these two heads, God as the Father, and the human soul, so ennobled that it can and does unite with Him."[2] This is "the permanent element", whereas everything else is "historically changing form". Negatively this means—and this is the main thesis, not only of Harnack's book, but also of the whole of "liberal" theology—"Not the Son, but only the Father belongs to the Gospel as Jesus proclaimed it".[3]

Even into the second decade of this century Harnack believed that these statements constituted a true account of the historical reality of the teaching of Jesus: since then, however, New Testament scholarship has demolished the very foundations of this conception. This is most decidedly *not* the teaching of Jesus.[4] This "teaching" is not the formulation of eternal truths which Jesus was "the first" to perceive and to teach or "the first" to do so "in power and purity"; it is rather a

[1] Matt. 21: 33 ff.　[2] *Wesen des Christentums*, p. 41 (E.T., p. 63)
[3] *Ibid.*, p. 91　[4] Cf. A. Schweitzer, *op. cit.*, and Kümmel, *Jesus und Paulus*

message which is most intimately connected with His Coming, with the *Kairos* in which it was spoken, with the new age which had dawned in and with Jesus; therefore it contradicts the historical view that only the Father has a place in it and not the Son. Indeed the truth is the very opposite: No saying of Jesus is based—as in the case of "eternal truths"—in itself, but every statement is related to Him, the Speaker. The words "But *I* say unto you", even if they are not always explicitly pronounced, are always presupposed.

In many passages, which have been handed down by tradition as His Sayings, this is quite clear. When Jesus tells the Parable of the Lost Sheep, He does so in order to justify his own action against the opposition of the Pharisees. *He* deals with sinners as the Father in the parable deals with his sinful son—and it is precisely this which offends the Pharisees so much.[1] He is the Good Shepherd, who goes out into the desert to find His sheep, as the story of Zacchaeus shows us.[2] It is He, by His own authority, who forgives sins, to the horror of the Scribes.[3] It is because with and in Him the "new age" has actually dawned that the Kingdom of God has not merely "come near"—but has "come upon" them—it is everywhere present[4]—because He is "amongst you" not "within you";[5] this is why He has things to say which no one could ever have said before. All the Sayings of Jesus are fully of this Messianic authority and actuality. It is because they would not admit this that the Jewish religious leaders were like those "wicked husbandmen" who not only killed the "servants", but also the "Son" whom the Father sent "last of all" in order to receive from them the fruit of the vineyard. What they rejected is not His "Word" but "Himself"; He is the "stone which the builders rejected".[6] Moreover, it is in His Blood that the new Covenant is founded.[7] Anyone who eliminates the Son from the Synoptic Gospels is not dealing faithfully with the historical tradition, but—even if he is not aware of this—he is falsifying it.

The other misunderstanding is more subtle, and is therefore perhaps more dangerous. It comes from the exactly opposite direction. It consists in the tendency to turn the teaching of Jesus into pure Christology, and in so doing into an "exposition", which is itself a falsification, reading a meaning into it which it does not possess, and suppressing the real meaning. Even if Jesus is everywhere the secret point of reference, the

---

[1] Luke 15: 2   [2] Luke 19: 1 ff.   [3] Mark 2: 10
[4] Matt. 12: 28   [5] Luke 17: 21   [6] Matt. 21: 42   [7] Mark 14: 24

presupposition for the understanding of His Sayings, He is not their content.[1] The Sermon on the Mount does not really deal with what Jesus has done for us, but with what the disciples, who acknowledge Him as their Lord, and who are therefore already living in the "new age", ought to do. Even if the "better righteousness" which Jesus requires is not simply an intensified legal demand, but a new life, derived from participating in the new age, yet it is still the "better righteousness" of the *disciples*, existence in the love of God, to which they are summoned, because the way to this new life has been opened up for them. The former misunderstanding may produce a wrong kind of "synoptic" Gospel, but the latter leads to a mistaken "Paulinism". In this view, all that God does for us in Jesus is stressed to such an extent that the new way of life to which Jesus calls His disciples disappears altogether, while the distinctive element in the teaching of Jesus is either wholly or partially obscured by a doctrinaire kind of theology. What is this distinctive element in the teaching of Jesus? It *has* a content; and although we must never forget that the One who speaks is the Source of the teaching, yet His "content" cannot merely be labelled "Christology". Jesus teaches two things—both can only be rightly understood in reference to Himself: the new demand for righteousness, which is required of those who belong to the new age, and is the condition upon which they are able to share in His life; and forgiveness and the coming of the new age in its fullness as the gift of God.

3. It is not simply wrong to say that the claim of Jesus, owing to its radical character, is utterly different from all other claims. Jesus does not abrogate the law of the Old Testament; but since He sums it all up in one: the summons to absolute love, He simplifies the law to an incredible extent. This love is the one thing that matters in every commandment. No mere external observance of the Law therefore can satisfy the demand of God; what matters is the inner attitude, the relation of the heart to God and to our neighbour. God requires nothing but love; that is what all the commandments mean. This love is the "better" righteousness. But this love is *not* a legal demand, although it may be the quintessence of all laws; it is only possible where the heart is filled with God, where man is already living in the new existence, in the Kingdom of God which has "come" in Jesus. But for the disciple, who has already received the forgiveness of God, it is an absolute and

[1] Against E. Thurneysen, *Die Bergpredigt*

urgent commandment. Here then we are not concerned with an "ethic of Jesus", a system of requirements, which exist in themselves, in timeless validity; here we are confronted with the imperative aspect of the gift of God, of the Kingdom of God which has "come". The message of the Kingdom and of its coming, however, is the exact opposite of an eternal truth. It is to the highest degree historical. It does not speak of a Kingdom of inwardness which can be entered or perceived by everyone, as the mystics and the religious rationalists have always thought. Rather, it is the message of that which "now" comes, and "henceforth" will come, because Jesus, the Messiah, is now here and will come. This Kingdom or Rule of God, promised by the Prophets, ushered in by Jesus, and through Him to be finally completed, is the essence of the message of Jesus. Here *God* alone matters: the will of God, the sovereignty of God, the gift of God, the truth about life, its meaning and its aim, which lies within this divine sovereignty and this divine gift. There is no other meaning. In comparison with this one meaning everything else is of accidental, secondary, peripheral significance; indeed it only has any meaning because it is connected with this one centre. The final goal alone decides the meaning and direction of the course. He who loses sight of this final goal loses his life. Jesus came to say this "one thing". All that He says is part of this "one thing".

Forgiveness is part of this "one thing", because this "one thing" alone is the act, gift, and creation of God. Only one who knows that he needs forgiveness is capable of taking part in the Kingdom.[1] For only in this does man show himself as one who knows that he lives solely on the gift of God. And through forgiveness he has a share in this gift. But the forgiveness which Jesus offers combines inseparably the gift and the task (*Gabe und Aufgabe*). Only one who himself forgives preserves the forgiveness which has been given to him; he who does not forgive loses it.[2] The Kingdom of God comes from God alone; but he alone receives a share in it who "seeks first the Kingdom of God", who is ready to give up everything for it. There is no reception of the divine gift which is not at the same time, to the highest degree, an act of personal surrender to God, and an act of obedience.

This Kingdom of God is not only something which Jesus proclaims, but something which is inseparably connected with His Person. Hence the attitude to Jesus cannot be separated

[1] Matt. 9: 13   [2] Matt. 18: 21 ff.

from the attitude to the Kingdom. In His action, in His life, in His sufferings and His death He brings in the Kingdom, and is the representative of the Kingdom. In Him we see what it is, and through Him it becomes real to us. The Kingdom is not "something" but it is God's Presence in Person. The Kingdom is where Jesus is, and if He is not present, the Kingdom is not present. During His earthly life, before Good Friday and Easter, a great deal could not possibly be said which became possible afterwards. In so far as there is something temporary even about the teaching of Jesus, it can only disappear when the depth and richness of the message of the Kingdom is fully disclosed in the message of the Crucified and Risen Lord. In this sense the teaching of the Apostles is more than the teaching of Jesus. But the teaching of the Apostles cannot be understood, or it is misunderstood, apart from the teaching of Jesus.

4. The Prophetic work of Jesus therefore does not end with His own teaching. From the very beginning it points beyond itself to Himself, to His Person, to "Emmanuel", to Him in whom God is present in person, and who establishes communion with Himself. But it is not the whole, because His death on the Cross and His Resurrection are not the content of His own teaching. The highest revelation of God is Jesus Himself. The Johannine saying, "He that hath seen Me hath seen the Father",[1] even if it is not the actual word of Jesus, expresses this truth. In His life He reveals the mystery of the incomprehensible unity of God's holiness and God's love. In Jesus' life and action God reveals Himself as One who receiveth sinners. Since Jesus Christ has come, we human beings can know who God is. In the stories of Jesus the holy merciful God meets us Himself. "I have revealed unto them Thy Name"[2]—that is really the summary of the life of Jesus. But the same John who reveals Jesus in this saying as the sumtotal of His activity, allows us also, from the very beginning of his narrative, to see through it that it is the Jesus whose highest revelation is the Cross and the Resurrection, the "Lamb of God who taketh away the sin of the world".[3] There, where Jesus went down into the depths for our sake, the revelation reaches its highest point, because God can only really meet man in the depths of humanity, because this depth of man is reality. It is necessary to unveil this reality of man in order to be able to perceive the reality of God. At the point

[1] John 14: 9; 12: 45   [2] John 17: 6   [3] John 1: 29

where Jesus completes His life He reveals these three things: the Reality of God as Holy and Merciful, the reality of man as sinner, and the genuine reality of man in God. Thus the revealing work of Jesus culminates in His priestly work of reconciliation.

(B) THE PRIESTLY WORK

1. The priestly work of Christ, the Atonement, the grace of God in Jesus Christ which justifies the sinner, culminates, it is true, in the death of Jesus on the Cross, but it does not begin there. The whole life of Jesus, including His teaching, is the Merciful God stretching out His hands to His rebellious, lost creation. The whole life of Jesus is the self-giving of the Holy for sinful humanity. "The Son of Man came not to be ministered unto but to minister, and to give His life a ransom for many".[1] In wonderful simplicity, in the story of the Feet-Washing, John has shown us that the life and the death of Jesus are one. The whole life and activity of the Saviour is God stooping down to sinful, lost humanity, God reconciling sinful man, alienated by his sin, to Himself, through the "coming" of the Son, through whom God has "visited and redeemed His People". All that Jesus does and all that He teaches is directed towards man, who is "lost", not in order to judge him or to "lecture" him, but in order to save him, to bring him back to God, in order that the broken fellowship between God and man may be restored. Jesus Himself has described this with incomparable power in the parable of the Good Shepherd who goes forth into the wilderness to find His sheep "which is lost". Jesus is not concerned with "them that are whole", but only with "them that are sick"; hence anyone who regards himself as "whole" has no share in Him and His gift. The poverty of Jesus, His renunciation of success and human reputation, is the outpouring of this love to sinful man as such; it springs naturally out of this movement of His whole life towards this world of ours; His one aim is to lift man who is "down there" upwards into communion with God. From this standpoint we can understand that constant opposition to self-righteous Pharisaism, which runs right through the life of Jesus upon earth. Nothing excludes us from saving communion with Jesus except the conviction that we do not need to be "saved". Harlots and publicans are not excluded[2]—

[1] Matt. 20: 28   [2] Matt. 21: 31

on the contrary, Jesus included them in His action and in
His teaching—but the self-righteousness of the lawyers and the
religious leaders did shut them out from communion with the
saving presence of Jesus. Therefore the whole life and action
of Jesus proclaims "justification through faith alone". Indeed,
this central feature of Pauline theology, which is supposed to
be exclusively "Pauline", is explicitly used by Jesus Himself
when He makes the sharp contrast between the repentant
publican and the self-righteous Pharisee in His well-known
Parable.[1]

Because men rebel—with a feeling of hurt pride—against
God's loving will to bring them home to Himself, Jesus knew
that His life must end in catastrophe. He knew that His life,
which was a "descent" from the very beginning, would end
in a final abyss of desolation, and in this very act would find
complete fulfilment. He knew—and told His disciples so, as a
secret—that the way of God, which He must follow, is the
Way of the Cross.[2] And on the very eve of death He interpreted the meaning of His death to His disciples; He told them
that this event which, from the human point of view, was a
desperate tragedy, was the real meaning and completion of
His life-work, the establishment of the New Covenant.[3] Those
who would eliminate the prophecy of the Passion, and the
establishment of the Covenant in the Lord's Supper, as non-
historical, from the life of Jesus, destroy its whole inner unity.
The whole historical life of Jesus is the Way to the Cross.

2. Hence the doctrine formulated in later Protestant orthodoxy,[4] that it was not the *oboedientia activa* but only the
oboedientia passiva Christi which has atoning value, is not
only intolerably pedantic, but it is also a complete misunderstanding. The statement that He "was obedient unto death,
even the death of the Cross", is the shortest summary of the
whole life of Jesus. He actively fulfilled the Law, because He
fulfilled its meaning, which is *agape*. But *agape* is generous
love, love which serves, as in the Feet-washing, when the Lord
bent down to serve. Only those who do not see this unity of
the life and death of Jesus can fall into the error of thinking
that there is any truth in that distinction between an *oboedientia
activa* (which has no saving significance) and an *oboedientia
passiva* (which alone has atoning worth). In a story like that
of the Feet-washing, which took place on the very eve of the

---

[1] Luke 18: 10 ff.   [2] Matt. 16: 21 ff.   [3] Mark 14: 24
[4] Cf. Schmid, *Die Dogmatik der evang. Luth. Kirche*, pp. 267 ff.

Passion, we see how utterly impossible it is to make such a distinction.

The view that[1] because our one aim is to proclaim "Christ Crucified" the story of His life does not actually belong to the Gospel, is equally mistaken. The Early Church, rightly, held the opposite opinion, when she called the four books which tell the story of the life of Jesus, "the Four Gospels". As the life of Jesus can only be rightly understood from the point of view of the Cross—the object of the Fourth Gospel is to show this—so, conversely, the Cross of Jesus can only be understood in the light of His life, as its culmination. The highest point in the "work" of Jesus, is that which, from the human point of view, is its lowest point: the death of a criminal on the gallows. So the death of Jesus on the Cross is a "shewing . . . of His righteousness".[2]

3. From the very outset the Primitive Church felt that it was necessary to reflect upon the meaning of the death of Christ on the Cross, and to gain a positive view of this event which seemed so terribly negative. Indeed, from the first Easter Day they saw clearly the positive meaning of the Cross. Those who had seen Jesus as the Risen Lord could never believe that He was merely the helpless victim of the blind obstinacy of the Jewish people. If the Crucified is the Messiah— and this was absolutely proved from the day of the Resurrection—then the death of Jesus on the Cross must have saving significance. It is highly probable that the conversation of Jesus with the disciples on the road to Emmaus reflects the thoughts of the earliest Christian community: Jesus had died "according to the Scriptures" and here "the Scriptures" means primarily Isa. 53. But a developed theory of the meaning of Christ's death on the Cross only came into being very gradually, or, rather, several parallel interpretations appeared, which, as we look back on them in all their variety, we can now see to be a whole.

The first method of interpretation was offered by the sacrificial cultus of the Old Testament, which indeed was still a living and present fact for the Early Church, before the destruction of Jerusalem; at first indeed, it was a sacred custom which was still followed without question. For us this interpretation is only intelligible indirectly through historical reflection. The Jewish sacrificial system is not specifically Biblical, but it is an element common to almost all religions. The specifically

---

[1] 1 Cor. 2: 2   [2] Rom. 3: 26 (R.V.)

Old Testament element was the connexion of the sacrificial system with the knowledge of the Holy God; that is why sacrifice was regarded as the means of atonement for the injury done by man to the Holiness of God. It contained the truth—still valid for us to-day—that sin is a reality, which can only be removed by a real event. The atoning sacrifice represents the truth that something must *happen*, if there is to be peace between God and man, if the communion which has been broken by sin is to be restored. Indeed, there is a further truth behind the shedding of blood in the atoning sacrifices: blood must actually flow, for man has forfeited his life by his rebellion against his Creator and Lord. This real truth was, however, heavily obscured in the atoning sacrifices of the Old Testament. For one thing, here it is not *human* blood that flows, and yet it is man, who, through his sacrifice— far too easily—achieves atonement. Thus for the Christian Church it was first clearly expressed in the Epistle to the Hebrews[1] that the true atoning sacrifice is the death of Jesus on the Cross. It is highly probable that the picture of the vicarious suffering of the "Servant of the Lord" in Isa. 53 was the link between Christ's death on the Cross and the atoning sacrifice, although here—as in the Prophetic message as a whole—the sacrificial system and the idea of "atoning *sacrifice*" is not strongly emphasized.

A second conception which was used for the interpretation of Christ's death on the Cross, was, on the other hand, directly suggested by this wonderful chapter in the Book of Isaiah: that of penal suffering. The idea of punishment does not belong, like that of sacrifice, to the sphere of the *cultus*, but to that of public law. Man, through sin, has become liable to punishment. Through sin he has forfeited his life. The holy Law of God requires his death. But in his place the obedient Servant of the Lord willingly suffers death. That is the meaning of the Cross: "The chastisement of our peace was upon Him" and "the Lord hath laid on Him the iniquity of us all". It is a verdict, a sentence of condemnation—κατάκριμα[2]—a curse, which not only separates us from the love of God, but when it is fully accomplished must mean annihilation. This "curse",[3] this condemnation, Christ has borne for us: "for the transgression of My People was He stricken, and they made His grave with the wicked, and with the rich in His death."

There was, however, a third view which was different from

[1] Heb. 9: 26   [2] Rom. 8: 1 ff.   [3] Gal. 3: 13

that of the sacrificial system and from that of legal penalty:
that of guilt, and the idea of a "bond": the "bond written in
ordinances . . . against us":[1] a figure taken from the sphere of
civil law—the "law of contract" as we would say to-day. The
creditor can, as Jesus says in His parable, tear up the "bond"
and in so doing cancel the debt. This third conception is suggested in the chapter on the Suffering Servant: He, the "Righteous
Servant" shall "bear their iniquities". He "goes bail" for
them; he covers the deficit which they owe with something of
His own and in so doing the "bond . . . which was against us"
is cancelled.[2] He "redeems us",[3] and indeed He "pays" at the
cost of His life, and in this act He sets us free,[4] through "the
blood of the covenant shed for many unto remission of sins".

Now, however, this conception drawn from the sphere of
ideas connected with the law of contract opens the way into
a fourth sphere, where the idea of *atonement* is replaced by
that of *redemption*. Here the idea is that of a struggle for power
between God and the hostile powers of darkness which enslave
and corrupt man, from which, however, God through Christ
rescues the booty, by delivering man from "the power of
darkness" and "translating" him "into the Kingdom of the
Son of His love".[5] The Cross achieves a real *spoliatio hostium*,
which ends in a triumphal procession of the victor.[6] In this
process sinful man is simply an object of struggle which
changes hands in the conflict. He is snatched away from the
powers of darkness into God's keeping, but in the process he
experiences his own liberation—that is, redemption. Jesus
Himself had already connected this fourth series of ideas with
the third by His Saying: "The Son of Man came . . . to give His
life a ransom for many."[7]

Finally, there is a fifth conception, which is connected with
the interpretation of the Old Testament: Christ's Death on the
Cross is the true Paschal sacrifice; in the blood of Jesus the
New Covenant is established, which ends the Old Dispensation,
and at the same time fulfils it. Jesus is the true Passover Lamb;
like the lamb of the first Passover, the thought here is that of
being set free from slavery—not from that of Egypt but from
sin, from enmity towards God. The "Blood of the New
Covenant", the blood shed on the Cross, is not only the sign,
but also the means by which the new relation with God, the
new communion with God is created.

[1] Matt. 18: 21 ff.; Col. 2: 14   [2] Col. 2: 14   [3] 1 Peter 1: 18
[4] Matt. 26: 28   [5] Col. 1: 13   [6] Col. 2: 15   [7] Matt. 20: 28

4. All these conceptions, in themselves very different from one another, are to a large extent interwoven in the New Testament; they have become blended, and thus in spite of their great variety and difference of content, they form a concrete whole; they are also so closely interwoven in our Christian thought that we find it difficult to disentangle them from their different sources, and to distinguish them from one another. How important this variety of ideas is, we shall see immediately, in contrast to Anselm's theory of Satisfaction which has become the classical formula of orthodoxy. First of all, however, we must note that all these conceptions are trying to express one truth. They are all *a posteriori* ideas; their one aim is to clarify, in the light of faith, the historical fact of the Cross of Jesus Christ, which at first sight seemed to be something completely irrational and obscure. In their different ways they all want to say two things: owing to Sin, man's situation in relation to God is dangerous, sinister, and disastrous. But man cannot alter this situation. God alone can do this; and He has done it in Jesus Christ, through His death on the Cross. There is a kind of inevitable connexion between this Event, and that dangerous, disastrous human situation, a sense that "this *had* to happen". If man is to be brought back into contact with God, if he is to be able to receive the salvation which God has provided for him, then the Cross of Jesus Christ "*must*" happen. It is the necessary condition for God's reconciling work. It is only because the Cross "must be", that what seems to be an unintelligible tragedy becomes a significant saving fact. The knowledge of such a necessity, of the feeling that "it could not be otherwise", was identical with the knowledge that the death on the Cross was no accident, no thwarting of the divine plan of salvation, no frustration of the divine government of the world, but, on the contrary, was itself an integral part of the divine saving history. "Therefore Christ *had* to suffer"—the whole liberating truth is based upon this "must".

This sense of necessity refers to the transformation of the human situation from evil into good, from a state of separation from God into one of communion with Him, from the way which leads to death, and indeed to eternal death, to the way which leads on the one hand to eternal life, and on the other to the death of Jesus on the Cross. If that transformation is to be achieved then this death on the Cross must be, and indeed is an act of God; for the One who suffers is the One who is in all

things empowered by God, One in whom God Himself is present
and acting. The fact that this transformation has taken place
is due to the death of Jesus Christ on the Cross; apart from the
Cross it would not, and could not happen. This is what all these
different interpretations are/ trying to say; for they are not
"theories"—like Anselm's view, but "pictures", through which
they are trying to show the meaning of the Cross for salvation
and for revelation. The fact that they are not theories, like
the "Satisfaction" theory of Anselm, comes out in the way in
which these four or five series of ideas are blended and inter-
mingled. None of these conceptions, by itself, is adequate;
and even when they are all combined they do not constitute a
clear intellectual unity. But, all of them combined,—while
each one is regarded as a parable, or an inadequate expression
of the truth they are trying to expound—do form the foundation
upon which we base our understanding of the meaning of the
Cross, as God's "mighty act" of Salvation; this, again, leads
us to the heart of the central doctrine of revelation and salvation in the New Testament as a whole.

The essential point, because it is common to all these ideas,
is evidently that "must", that necessity, which connects that
transformation of the human situation from evil to good, from
tragedy to victory, with the Death of Jesus on the Cross, as
the revealing, atoning, and redeeming act of God. Why "must"
Jesus suffer in order to establish or to create the salvation of
the world? All these ideas of sacrifice and atonement, of
vicarious punishment, of the payment of a debt, the rescue of
man from slavery to the powers of darkness, of the establishment of the new Covenant by the true Passover Lamb, are
pointing to "something" beyond—what is it? How can we
understand this without being dependent on those various
"pictures", either as a whole or on one in particular? The
mystery of that "must", of that necessity, is the mystery of
the Cross as God's Saving Act.

5. In order to find the right answer to this question, we will
start with two famous theories which have acquired a canonical
importance in the history of theology, both of which, when
more closely examined, prove to be insufficient: (a) the subjective view of Abelard, which constitutes the model for the
conceptions of modern liberal theology; and (b) the objective
doctrine of Anselm—the theory of Satisfaction—which was
adopted both by Protestant and Catholic thinkers, and thus
became the standard one.

The main idea in Abelard's doctrine is this: that the death of Jesus on the Cross gives us a supreme demonstration of the Love of God, which should kindle a corresponding love in our hearts. Nothing can convince us more deeply of the reality and the greatness of the divine love than the Sufferings and the Death of our Lord. It is, of course, quite clear that there is an element of truth in this view. Indeed, it has the witness of Scripture on its side: "God commendeth His own love towards us, in that, while we were yet sinners, Christ died for us";[1] "Greater love hath no man than this, that a man lay down his life for his friends".[2] The Cross is the manifestation, the highest "proof" of the love of God, which convinces us of its reality and greatness as nothing else can do. And yet the very words in the Epistle to the Romans that Christ died "for us" presuppose the decisive element which has not yet been explained. What Abelard says is true, but it is not the whole truth, nor indeed is it the fundamental truth: it does not answer the question of that "must". The sinner, so it says, evidently has difficulty in believing in the love of God, certain hindrances exist, one might almost call them "difficulties" which "arrest" man's development. A change of disposition, or at least some divine help is needed, in order to overcome these inner psychological hindrances, and to attain to full trust, to true responsive love; this "help" is the proof of God's love on the Cross, the "difficulty" which Christ takes upon Himself, in order to open our eyes, in order to awaken trust in our hearts. But this doctrine does not tell us why it was necessary for this terrible event to take place, *why* this *had* to be. In the further development of the Abelardian type of doctrine as we see it in Schleiermacher and Ritschl, this comes out still more plainly. According to Schleiermacher, reconciliation through Christ consists in the fact that under the influence of Jesus the "frustrations of life" which are caused by sin, are increasingly overcome, and that "the longer and the more continuously we are led by Christ the more we forget sin".[3] Thus in this view reconciliation (or atonement) consists in the removal of the difficulties and frustrations of ordinary life. Guilt is something which is best forgotten. We only need to take one further step and we would reach that idea of Fichte[4] who would eliminate repentance altogether, as a mistaken clinging to the past, as a futile occupation with something which we cannot

---

[1] Rom. 5: 8   [2] John 15: 13
[3] *Glaubenslehre*, II, para. 108, 12   [4] *System der Sittenlehre*, 1798

alter. He claims that if man is to give himself wholly to the work of the present he must leave his past entirely behind him. It is not guilt which needs to be eradicated, but the sense of guilt. It is not man's separation from God which needs to be overcome, but merely the—mistaken—opinion that he is separated from God. Reconciliation (or atonement) consists in clearing up a misunderstanding, namely, that man is not from the very outset already united with God. Certainly it is a long way from Abelard to this modern Idealistic argument, but this way is continuous, the idea itself is implicit in the view of Abelard. If the Atonement were simply what Abelard says it is, then the doctrinal development would necessarily lead to this conclusion.

With Anselm the situation is the exact opposite. Here the question which predominates in his thought is this "must". It is already suggested in the title of the standard work on this subject: *Cur Deus homo?* Not only the Cross, but the Incarnation of the Son of God, as such, as well as its culmination, the vicarious suffering on the Cross, *had* to be. And this "must" is not, as is suggested in Scripture, a necessary *condition*, but it is absolute. God *must* go this way,[1] if He is not either to annihilate humanity, and thus be forced to give up His plan of Creation, or to lose His Glory, both of which are unthinkable, and objectively impossible. The Incarnation and the vicarious penal sufferings of the Son of God are proved, by way of deduction, to be an absolute necessity. It is only the sacrificial death of the Son of God, which as such possesses infinite value, that is sufficient to vindicate God's honour, and to expiate the guilt of humanity, which is infinite. This is the meaning of the book, *Cur Deus homo?*

In spite of the fact that Anselm's theory was adopted not only by the Catholic Church, but also by the theology of the Reformation, and by orthodox Protestantism, and in spite of the fact that it contains important elements of truth, it is not in accordance with the teaching of the New Testament. It is true that it does preserve the main concern of the different ways in which the writers of the New Testament present this truth, and in which they give their interpretations of the event of the Cross: what matters is this "must"; but in the thought of Anselm this "must" is not, as in the New Testament, *a posteriori* and therefore conditioned, but *a priori*, and therefore unconditioned necessity. Anselm does not say: "we can

[1] *Cur Deus homo?*, I, 15

understand the event in this way," but: "God could not do otherwise". Then there is a further difference: Anselm's theory of "satisfaction" claims to be an adequate, completely sufficient expression, which does not need to be complemented by any other ideas—it does not even allow for them—whereas for the writers of the New Testament the variety of conceptions and expressions points to the fact that none of these expressions in themselves are regarded as sufficient, but that all, as figurative expressions, are intended to point to a fact which by its very nature can never be fully understood. Further, the rationalistic form of the proof, and the spirit of calculation, is contrary to the outlook of the Bible. Finally, and this is by far the most important point—the theory of Anselm is purely objective in character. Whereas Abelard lays all the emphasis upon the subjective reaction of man, Anselm's theory does not mention man's faith at all, whereas the New Testament always regards both the atoning event and faith as indissolubly united. "For God so loved the world, that He gave His only begotten Son, that whosoever believeth on Him should not perish, but have eternal life."[1] "Whom God set forth to be a propitiation, through faith, by His blood . . . that He might Himself be just and the Justifier of him that hath faith in Jesus."[2] In the New Testament reconciliation in Christ is "truth as encounter"— just as much as every other part of the Faith; with Anselm, on the contrary, it is rational objective truth, which can be understood. If we look at this question from the opposite end, from God's standpoint, it means: that whereas in Anselm's view *God is the Object* of the Atonement (or reconciliation)— it is *God* who is reconciled—this is certainly *not* the teaching of the New Testament. Here it is *men* who are reconciled, not God; God alone is the Reconciler, the One who makes peace, who restores man to communion with Himself.

This contrast between two opposing classical theories shows us the way for our own interpretation. On the one hand, certainly, with Anselm, we are concerned about this "must"— how are we to understand it?—not as an *a priori*, deductive, unconditioned, truth, but as *a posteriori*, and conditioned—but we are likewise dealing with an Event which includes faith, as in the view of Abelard. We are not dealing with a purely subjective or a purely objective process, but with an Event which is both objective and subjective at the same time, a truth of "encounter".

[1] John 3: 16   [2] Rom. 3: 25 ff.

6. We ask first of all: Why "must" it be? What is the reason for this common necessity, which appears in all the records and ideas of the New Testament, in which the whole meaning of reconciliation (or Atonement) is implied? Paul wrestled with this question, and he succeeded in giving an answer in which all those different ideas are blended into a unity, by his doctrine of the curse of the Law, an answer which comes nearer to our own questions and our own powers of understanding than any other. Communion with God has been destroyed by sin. But while man is in this state of separation he is still firmly held by God—not by a "misunderstanding", not by means of an error which needs to be removed, but by a fact which man cannot evade because the strength and the burden of this separation is derived from God Himself—by the Law. Man, who has become guilty, cannot work his own way out of the state of separation into which he has fallen. All that he undertakes in his own strength comes under the curse of the Law, because he is never able to comply with the divine command. Between us and God lies the burden of guilt, which is an objective separating fact, the burden of our sinful past, over which we have no power, and which we cannot shake off without falling into still deeper guilt. The superficial or light-hearted method of "forgetting" (Schleiermacher), the courageous act of casting the past behind you (Fichte), the explanation that God is never angry, and thus that our separation from God is based upon a misunderstanding (Ritschl), the suggestion of lack of trust in God (Abelard)—all these views are not solutions, for they all amount to this: that guilt is glossed over, and this breeds a still greater guilt. The separation can only be removed by God, and it must be removed, if there is to be a restoration of fellowship between man and God. But this can only happen if God actually removes that which constitutes the separation. This removal must be as real an act as the reality of guilt. An act of restoration must take place, if there is to be a real restoration, and this must be God's doing.

We see this when we are faced by the Cross of Jesus Christ. It is not a rational truth, which is at our own disposal, it is not something which everyone, if he only examines it sufficiently carefully, can know; to "see" this, we need divine revelation. That great saying of Anselm in *Cur Deus homo?*, "*Nondum considerasti quanti ponderis sit peccatum*", is true of everyone who does not know Jesus Christ. Even a mere glimpse of the danger and inevitability of our situation is an effect of the revelation of Christ. It is only in the light of the greatness of the divine Act that we perceive the greatness of the obstacle which it removes. Anselm is right when he answers Boso thus: *"Nondum considerasti quanti ponderis sit peccatum"*,[1] but he is not right in thinking that the "exceeding gravity of sin" is something which can be perceived by the human reason. The true perception of sin is a gift of revelation, a religious truth, never the object of a rational demonstration. But faith recognizes guilt as a fact of unfathomable gravity, and the necessity of atonement is based upon this fact. The human situation is desperate, and it cannot be transformed, fellowship with God is impossible, save through an intervention in the human situation, a re-establishment of man's relation to God, by God Himself.

7. This transforming intervention, however, many people maintain, is simply the divine forgiveness. The idea of a sacrificial death, of an expiatory atonement, is a return to a pre-Christian, and indeed even to a pre-prophetic understanding of the relation between God and man, a crude anthropomorphism, which infects the idea of God with the all-too-human attribute of wrath—forgiveness certainly, but not atonement. This line of argument is supported by two appeals to historical exegesis. The Old Testament, in its prophetic passages, speaks of forgiveness without any reference to sacrifice, or to a special act which "makes" reconciliation. The idea of forgiveness, from Hosea onwards, is a firm element in the prophetic message. Jesus, too, in the Parable of the Prodigal Son, speaks of forgiveness without any hint of an act of reconciliation, without any connexion with the death of Jesus. It was Paul who first connected the two elements, the death of Jesus and the forgiveness of sins; in so doing the purely "spiritual" prophetic religion of the genuine Gospel of Jesus was saddled with priestly sacrificial ideas from the Old Testament, and thus its meaning was obscured.

At first sight there is something attractive about this line of thought, both in its principle, and in its Biblical and theological arguments. But if we examine it more closely, we soon perceive that it is the basis of that rationalism which begins with the ideas of Abelard, and ends with those of Fichte. Let us first of all examine the biblical "proofs". It is true that the Prophets and the 103rd Psalm do speak very wonderfully about the forgiving goodness of God, without any allusion to a

---

[1] *Cur Deus homo?*, I, 21

process of atonement. But it is the prophets who, by a special divine commission, are empowered to do this. The message of the forgiveness of God is part of their transcendent revelation, coming to them from a sphere beyond the possibility of human perception, given to them through inspiration. The 103rd Psalm appeals explicitly to that which God has disclosed to us through "Moses". Forgiveness is offered to man by God Himself, through His Prophetic Word of revelation. Thus it is God's historical gift, not a truth which man can acquire by the use of his reason. It has nothing to do with that mocking phrase: *Dieu pardonnera, c'est son métier.* Forgiveness is part of the special, Covenant-revelation.

This is still more true of Jesus' message of forgiveness. Not only has He Himself explicitly expressed the connexion between forgiveness as the sign of the New Covenant—according to Jer. 31: 31—and His own Passion, but even where, as in the Parable of the Prodigal Son, He does not do this, His message is connected with His Messianic commission, and His Messianic authority. He Himself, to the horror of the Scribes, who regarded this as blasphemy, forgave sins in His own Name, by His own authority,[1] and He told the Parable of the Prodigal Son in order to make clear to the Jews what He was doing as "the Friend of Sinners". As we have already laid down in principle, His sayings are never to be separated from His action. They are the commentary on His action, they are part of His Messianic work and commission. He may say it, because He is the Christ. What He says about forgiveness, like all His other Sayings, is "an act of His Messianic consciousness."

Hence the connexion between God's free forgiveness and the Death of Jesus was intuitively perceived by the Christian Church from the very outset, although it was Paul who gave this insight clear expression. In the thought of Paul there is no suggestion of a "pre-prophetic", "ritual" point of view. The ritual image of the atoning sacrifice is indeed only one among others, and one which he uses least. Paul does, it is true, sometimes use the language of the sacrificial system of worship (with which otherwise his thought shows no other particular affinity), although at other times he expresses himself in quite different terms. Far more important for his thought than the image of the atoning sacrifice is that of the curse of the Law, and of man's enslavement by the powers of darkness. But all these expressions are only "images", by means of

[1] Mark 2: 10

which he is emphasizing the one truth: it is only through God's reconciling action that man can be forgiven. But this "reconciling action" is God's gift, Jesus Christ, the Crucified. Is there anything "primitive" about this? Is it a reactionary idea? All these apparently convincing Biblical arguments break down completely when they are examined in closer detail.

They are also not decisive. People have been glad to make use of them because they seemed to provide Biblical support for something which they thought they had already independently recognized as true. Such thinkers do not *want* to admit that Atonement has taken place, because they believe that forgiveness is a truth which we can discover for ourselves. Otherwise, indeed, they would be faced by the question: How do we know that God forgives? If they were to take this question seriously, and thus not regard forgiveness as something which is a "matter of course", they would be immediately confronted by the problem of authority, of the transcendent revelation. But forgiveness as revelation is simply that intervention on the part of God which fundamentally changes the human situation, which man himself cannot possibly alter. Forgiveness, then, is an historical event, something which man cannot achieve or know by his own efforts. Forgiveness is then perceived to be that which sinful man cannot pronounce for himself; it is a verdict which must be pronounced by God. Whether this message from "beyond" comes through the Prophetic Word of revelation, or the authoritative Messianic Word of Jesus, or through His death on the Cross, is primarily less important than the other fact: that in each case it is something which must *happen* in a region beyond and outside of all human effort. In any case, forgiveness can never be taken for granted; it is something incomparable, which can only be granted on God's authority.

8. The difference between the message of forgiveness in the Prophets of the Old Testament, in the message of Jesus, and in that of the Apostles, corresponds exactly to that which we perceived earlier about the relation between these three stages of revelation. The Old Testament is the temporary revelation which only finds its fulfilment in the New Testament. The teaching of Jesus is always related to His Messianic authority and to God's action in Him, but its relation to His life and death still lacks the full clarity which could only be perceived after His life on earth had been closed by death. Every later stage of revelation brings out still more clearly the essential

truth, namely, that the event in which forgiveness takes place
cannot be taken for granted, as something quite natural, but
that it is something unheard of, incredible, that is, this historical
event bears the marks of a transcendent divine intervention.
Just as the full revelation in Jesus Himself is distinct from
revelation through the Word of the Prophets, so too the
reconciliation through the Cross, in which God forgives man's
sin, is to be distinguished from the prophetic message of
forgiveness. Thus the message of the Cross is the highest
expression of the fact that forgiveness cannot be taken for
granted; forgiveness is God's act of reconciliation.

9. The message of the Cross is first of all the revelation of
the incomprehensible, unconditional love of God. God loves
man, in spite of the fact that he is a sinner, a rebel. The love
of God is not, as it must be in legalistic thinking, conditioned
by the love of man, but it is entirely without conditions, and
reveals itself as pure *Agape*. But how can this unconditioned
love of His show itself more plainly than in the fact that He
takes the guilt of man upon Himself, that He Himself, in His
Son, experiences the curse which clings to sinful existence as
its law, that He not only humbles Himself to take on Him
"the form of a servant", but to the low estate of one who has
lost his glory and forfeited his life, and therefore dies a death
of shame as a criminal? Moreover, in Jesus Christ God has
penetrated to the depths of human existence, in order to *find*
man. Secondly, the revelation of righteousness is combined
with love. God takes His own law seriously. Forgiveness *sans
phrase*, without further ado, is exposed to a terrible misunderstanding, namely, that "it doesn't matter" if we do break the
law, because God can easily overlook it! Forgiveness is not
only something undeserved, but it is "unjust". Everything
that shakes the idea of merit, shakes that of righteousness too,
it throws doubt on moral earnestness, on responsibility. The
moral shock which the idea of acquittal from all guilt evokes
in the ethically "serious" person is justified. "Mere" forgiveness
may lead to a careless disregard of moral obligation. Hence
the Atoning death of His Son is a "sign" that God sees this
moral danger, and thus gives us a "proof of His righteousness",[1]
lest we should doubt His Wisdom. But this "proof" is not—as
with Anselm—something objective, the fulfilment of an
objective requirement, but it is something which is both
subjective and objective: it is effective as this "proof of

[1] Rom. 3: 25

righteousness" only where man, in faith, identifies himself with Christ the Crucified, and understands that it is really he who ought to be condemned to death and executed as a criminal, and that Christ is suffering in his stead, and bearing the penalty which he had deserved.

Thirdly, the Cross becomes the disclosure of the human situation. This is where you are! This is your rightful place, which you have deserved. The *pondus peccati* is, so to speak, weighed before our eyes, and the weight is called: Jesus Christ the Crucified. Introspection alone is not sufficient to show us the full extent of our sin. For this we have need of a divine act of revelation. It is the mystery of the divine wisdom, that the same event which reveals to us love and righteousness, also discloses to us our own actual situation. But since faith is kindled by the Death of Jesus, it leads to one final act, the justification of the sinner, atonement as a subjective happening, "having peace with God." In this act of "making peace" man is restored to his original position in the purpose of creation, since he is placed once more in his original attitude to God, which constitutes his true nature. The Atonement is also the *restitutio imaginis*. Since man sees himself judged and justified at the Cross of Jesus Christ, he is at the same time born again and sanctified. He becomes what God intends him to be. The true man is one, who, through Jesus Christ, lives in the love of God. The curse of legalism has been removed; the Law no longer weighs upon his mind. The man who perceives and accepts the forgiving love of God from the Cross of Christ, will, however, no longer try to create a right relation to God through a legalistic "righteousness of works". He has now received it as a gift; he lives no longer on his own efforts, but upon grace.

10. It is superfluous to ask whether all this could not have been attained otherwise than through the Cross. We will not try to prove with Anselm that the death of Jesus on the Cross was an *a priori* necessity. The New Testament message of the Cross is indeed no *a priori* deduction, but an *a posteriori* interpretation. This "must" cannot be proved logically, it can only be believed. It is not an objective fact "in itself", but it is a fact which includes faith. Looking back, the believer knows that there was no other way for him, in order to attain the renewal of fellowship with God. On the basis of the fact of the Cross, and only thus, we may say that the wrath of God is not an objective reality, but "subjective-objective", a reality

of "encounter", a reality for everyone who is not in the realm of faith. God's wrath cannot be compared with God's love; for God's love is His nature, but His wrath is never, and in no sense, His nature. It is His relation to the sinner so long as the sinner does not believe. It is not an error about which man needs to be "enlightened", it is not the product of a primitive "anthropomorphic" idea of God, but it is something real, which can only be removed by the real event of the death of Christ on the Cross, and by faith in Him. It is the reality in which sinful man lives, until through faith in the Cross of the Son of God he is actually led out of it. It has the same reality as the law, as the guilt and the curse of the law. It is as real as the Passion of Jesus. It is the effect of sin, that God must seem to the sinner to be angry, that he comes under the curse of the law. Sin creates a reality, which lies between the love of God and man, and man cannot remove this real obstacle; God alone can do this. This removal of the reality of wrath is the Atonement.

In the Atonement both the love and the righteousness of God, and the reality and the truth of man are revealed; hence the atoning work of Jesus Christ is the centre of the New Testament message. This, too, distinguishes the Christian Faith most sharply and clearly from all other religions. The fact that God reveals Himself in the criminal's death of an historical human being—this is something which no religion has ever dared to assert; on the contrary, for all men it is at first pure folly, and a great stumbling-block. The Cross has therefore rightly become the Sign of Christianity. The Passion narrative has become the climax of the story of Jesus, and it is significant that this is the most consistent and detailed part of the gospel narrative as a whole. It is also one that no historical scepticism has been able to affect. "Crucified under Pontius Pilate" points to the fact that from the very beginning the Christian Church was conscious that its most sacred possession is contained in this period of human—and world—history, with all its shame. This story is in very deed: the Gospel. "For God so loved the world, that He gave His only begotten Son, that whosoever believeth on Him should not perish, but have eternal life." It is only from this standpoint that we can rightly understand what the New Testament, and particularly the teaching of Jesus, means by the Kingdom, or the Rule of God. The third part of the doctrine of the work of Jesus deals with this point: His "office" as King.

(C) THE ROYAL WORK OF JESUS

1. It is all the more surprising that this third theme has been less fully treated in the doctrine of the Christian Church,[1] because the message of the Lord Himself is the proclamation of the coming Kingdom or Rule of God. With the cry: "Repent, for the Kingdom of Heaven is at hand!" the preaching of Jesus literally joins that of John the Baptist; we can also say: with this message of the coming Kingdom of God Jesus places Himself on the foundation of the Old Testament. For everywhere in the message of the Prophets this is their main concern, the Rule of God. The clause in the Lord's Prayer: "Thy will be done, on earth as it is in heaven," is wholly in the spirit of the prophets. The fact that the Rule of God is not identified with what now actually exists, but is in contrast to it, is the element which distinguishes the Old Testament doctrine of God from the nature religions of the surrounding nations. The "Kingdom" has not yet actually "come" in human life, but is only "coming", in judgment and in mercy, in the creation of a new perfect order, in a new age, which differs from the present world-order whose distinctive signs are unrighteousness and disorder, by its true righteousness, and peace.

When Jesus began to preach, His message was linked with these simple fundamental ideas of the message of the Prophets, which had been intensified and made more urgent through the preaching of John the Baptist. The content of His discourses, with all their variety of subjects and ideas, is this one conviction: The coming Kingdom of God, the new age, in its contrast to the present age. This is the reason why, in many of His parables, the subject is a King, or the Master of a household. This is the goal of all history, that at last the will of God shall be done, that at last the King will have an obedient people. "Ye are my people; I am your God." This is the personalistic fundamental feature of the Biblical view of God. Certainly, as in every religion, "salvation" is important, but this "salvation" consists in unity of will with, and personal communion between, God and man. Everything else is secondary, or is merely a conclusion drawn from this truth.

2. If Jesus had merely proclaimed the coming of this Kingdom of God, and obedience to the will of God as the condition of sharing in the Kingdom, then He would have been one of the Prophets. But Jesus did not merely proclaim this coming

---

[1] Cf. Visser't Hooft, *The Kingship of Jesus Christ*, p. 13

Kingdom of God, at the same time He inaugurated this new age and represented it in His own Person. He Himself, in His own Person, is therefore already the dawn of this Kingdom of God.[1] In Jesus the sovereign authority of God is present in an entirely new way; hence it has become impossible to evade it. Not only His Word, but also His Person, confronts man with the final decision. Anyone who stands before Him is aware of the claim of God to rule, in a wholly different way from that in which he is aware when he hears the word of a Prophet. Here, over against him, stands the holy sovereign will of God in person. Here the divine authority becomes visible, in person. The phrase, "But *I* say unto you", which confronts the whole of the legalistic teaching of the Old Testament, creates a new situation. These words "But I . . ." are implicit in everything that Jesus says. One who encounters Him encounters the Will of God incarnate.

But the divine Kingdom which Jesus, as present, sets up, is not merely, and not primarily, a demand for obedience, but a gift. The divine kingdom which Jesus inaugurates, is God's liberating, restoring, forgiving presence, which creates communion. Here is One whom, because He is Holy Love incarnate, we can trust utterly, and whom we can love in return without losing ourselves. Hence the idea of the Rule or the Kingdom of God here gains a new meaning. It is not the rule of One who in austere and royal majesty simply demands our obedience, but of One who, through His Holy Love, overcomes the resistance of the Evil One. It is the rule of One who pours out His life in loving service, who breaks down resistance by an inward victory. It is the Kingdom which consists in liberating man from the power of the demons; "Jesus is Lord", who wins our trust, love and service by what He gives. Jesus is a new kind of King, who exercises His royal power through the forgiveness of sins, and by re-creating the formerly rebellious human heart, making it one which is full of the will to serve.

Therefore this King actually exercises His power in that act which is the exact opposite of all that we mean by "grasping power": the death on the Cross, vicarious suffering for sinful humanity. There, in that event, which, humanly understood, represents the complete deprivation of power and glory, Jesus conquers the forces hostile to God. The Cross is His triumph

[1] Cf. Kümmel, *Verheissung und Erfüllung*; Cullmann, *Christus und die Zeit*, pp. 130 ff.

over the enemies of God's kingdom,[1] and therefore the actual establishment of the Kingdom of God. Correspondingly the human experience of sharing in the Cross works itself out through faith, as liberation from the tyranny of evil, and as the beginning of that true freedom which is identical with willing obedience to the Will of God. For in sinful humanity, the centre of resistance to God is the Self which seeks to be its own master and to be entirely independent. In faith in the atoning act of Jesus Christ on the Cross this self-determining "I" is broken down, and in its place there comes the "I" which accepts its life from the hands of God and dedicates himself to the service of God. Through the word of the Cross received in faith, the new man, the man who serves God, is created,[2] who no longer lives on himself and for himself, but on and for the love of God. This alone is true divine rule, where God rules through the free obedience of those who trust and love Him. Where the love of God actually reigns in the human heart the opposition between God's will and the self-will of the creature has been overcome; there it has become true: "I will be your God, and ye shall be My people."

3. Of late there has been some discussion of a theory about the "rule" of Jesus Christ outside the circle of those who have become subject to Him through faith.[3] This theory is based on sayings like those in Matthew 28: 18 and in Ephesians 1: 20 ff., which speak of an unlimited sovereignty of Jesus Christ over all creation: "To Me has been given all authority in heaven and upon earth." There can be no doubt at all about this statement, and its central significance within the confession of faith of the Primitive Church. The question is only, how are we to understand it? If since Good Friday and Easter Jesus is Lord of all and over all men, He is not King over them in the same way. This comes out very clearly in the Christological passage in the Epistle to the Philippians: "Wherefore also God highly exalted Him, and gave unto Him the Name which is above every name, that in the Name of Jesus every knee should bow, of things in heaven and things on earth and things under the earth and that every tongue should confess that Jesus Christ is Lord, to the glory of God the Father." Here there are two points: Jesus is Lord over all, because He has been appointed to this. It is that kind of dominion which is not only outward submission but the most

---

[1] Col. 2: 15   [2] Rom. 12: 1 ff.
[3] Cullmann, *Königsherrschaft Christi u. Kirche im N.T.*, 1941

inward surrender in the confidence of obedience, as we can now see it—although incompletely—in the Church. But just because it is this true dominion which is meant, it cannot mean a purely external exercise of power, where this inner consent is lacking. Merely external submission is not the rule of Christ of which the New Testament speaks. In so far as His dominion over all people and all things is expressed, this can only mean a "potential" but not an "actual" dominion. The hostile forces have been thoroughly deprived of their power by the Cross and the Resurrection, it is true, but their actual resistance still continues. It continues in those who do not "bow the knee" to Jesus, who do not believe in Him, who do not obey Him; it also continues in those invisible regions which form the background of human sin; it continues most evidently in the still unbroken dominion of death, the Last Enemy. Jesus is indeed appointed to be Ruler over all, but His dominion will not be fully established until "the end, when He shall deliver up the kingdom to God, even the Father; when He shall have abolished all rule and all authority and power".[1]

If therefore we are to sing and say that "Jesus is Lord", and that He "rules as King", we must make a distinction between the potential, prospective dominion of the *imperator designatus* Jesus, which includes all people and all things, and the actual present dominion which everywhere has begun, where, in point of fact, people actually do "bow the knee" before Him, and where men actually "confess that Jesus Christ is Lord, to the Glory of God the Father". That potential prospective appointment to dominion is universally valid as the claim to sovereignty, but it is not universally a fact as the exercise of power. It is like the decisive victory of an army over the enemy, which for everyone who really understands, guarantees the final victory, whereas the beaten enemy is still capable for a long time of active resistance, to such an extent, that no traces of a victory can be seen.

This question: how are we to understand the Dominion of Jesus Christ over all men? is of direct practical importance in the sphere of social ethics. If, for instance, as often happens to-day, people speak of the "sovereignty of Jesus Christ over the State", from the point of view of the New Testament this must mean the *claim* of Jesus Christ to be recognized everywhere, even in the State, as Lord. This expression, which is so often used to-day, is not a very happy one, even when

[1] I Cor. 15: 24

it is understood in the sense of a "claim to sovereignty". What does it mean when we say that Christ claims to be Lord in the State? The State is an institution of compulsory Law. The nature of the State is in opposition to the nature of the *Agape* of Jesus. Where there are police, whose duty it is to arrest criminals, and armies, arsenals of weapons of war, penitentiaries, etc.—and where would a State be without these necessary aids to its rule?—evidently Jesus Christ is not "ruling", save in the hearts of individual persons, who as believing Christians, want to serve Christ within this State. The existence of the State as an institution is itself a sign of the fact that Christ's rule over men is not yet realized. We human beings need an order of the State, with police, soldiers, and compulsory laws, precisely because, and in so far as Christ does not rule over us. For the true rule of Christ is identical with free and generous love, free obedience to God, while the necessity for the dominion of the State always and everywhere points to the fact that men do not willingly do what is necessary for the well-being of all. The true dominion of Christ, and what we call the State, are fundamentally opposed.

But there is some sense in saying that Christ wills to be Lord over all men wherever they are and whatever they do. Thus He wills to rule over every citizen of the State, and over every one of its officials. And He wills that each person who knows Him as Lord should also in his political service know himself to be a servant of Jesus, and to the best of his knowledge, and in harmony with his conscience, give Him obedience in the sphere of state action, which is so far from the spirit of Christ. So even in the best conditions the Lordship of Christ in the State is only expressed in a broken and imperfect manner, which will be still more imperfect, the fewer convinced and serious Christians there are in this particular political sphere. Hence the formula "Jesus Christ is Lord of the State" should only be used with great caution, because otherwise it leads to confusion and does more harm than good.

4. It must be admitted, however, that in the course of its history the Church has taken the office of Christ as King far too lightly. This is due, in the first place, to the fact, that a false distinction or separation has been made between faith and service, or between faith and love. The real Lordship of Jesus Christ is shown in the fact that human beings serve God and their neighbour in love. For this service is the will

of God. Where love and service are true and real, there God's will is being done "as in heaven so on earth". There God's commandment is fulfilled, which commands nothing else but love. Love—and nothing else—is the fulfilling of the Law. Without love faith is dead. The Lordship of Christ is only real where "the knee" is really "bowed", and where "the heart" really "confesses that Jesus Christ is Lord," thus where men really live in obedience to Jesus Christ.

Further, we must admit that Christendom has failed in this respect, that all too often Christians have thought that obedience to Jesus Christ refers only to their private life. One who belongs to Christ, belongs to Him wholly, and therefore in all sections and parts of his life. Christ the Lord wills that His disciples should be truly His disciples both in public and in private life. Even if the will of Christ in public life can only be expressed indirectly and imperfectly, yet that is no reason for making a distinction between the service of Christ and the service of the State, any more than the fact that in both spheres "Jesus is Lord" should deceive us into ignoring the fact that very different demands are made upon us in these different spheres.

5. The Lordship of Jesus Christ is therefore only a reality where men actually "bow the knee" to Him, that is, in the *Church*. The community of the disciples, the fellowship of those who through the obedience of faith have become the property of Jesus, is the correlate of the Lordship of Christ. The Church consists of those who acknowledge Jesus Christ as their Lord, and in the obedience of faith, and in love, serve Him as their Lord. Conversely, the Lordship of Christ means that through His Word and His Spirit He actually rules over men. Jesus is not a King who simply claims His rights, but to whom no one actually submits, He is the Head of the Body, the Church.[1] He is *actually* the authority in a community of persons who *actually* obey His will. The fact that His authority is so utterly different from that of secular rulers does not alter the fact that He really *is* Ruler and Lord. On the contrary, all secular "lords", in comparison with Jesus Christ are only "pseudo-rulers", because although they can force external obedience, they cannot gain or command that inner obedience which can only come from confidence and love. This actual obedience and willing submission to the will of the Lord is that which distinguishes the Church from the world. If there are

[1] Col. 1: 18

those in the Church who are only pretending to be subject to Jesus, because they only acknowledge His Lordship out of hypocrisy, they are the "tares among the wheat"; this does not alter the fact that the true Church is the true real sphere of the Lordship of Christ. As the Head actually rules the body—and where this does not happen the death of the body ensues—so also Jesus is the actual Head of the Body, of the Church, and where this actual Lordship ceases to be exercised, the life of the Body also ceases: then it is not the "Body of Christ", but the world.

But the Lordship which Jesus actually exercises now in the Church, even in the true living members of the Church, is not perfect, but it is only gradually coming into being. The members of His Body are, it is true, those who have accepted His claim on them for the obedience of faith, and they daily submit to Him, but they are also human beings "in the flesh," in whom the claim of Jesus Christ to rule over them is constantly shaken by the claims of the "Self" and of the world. The perfect Lordship of Jesus Christ is therefore something which is still unrealized, something for which we wait and hope. Even the Church is still connected with the world, not merely externally and physically, but also inwardly, through the "old man", the "flesh", through the sinful desires which are continually re-asserting themselves. We wait for the perfect Lordship of Christ, not merely in the world as a whole, but also in the Church itself.

Only when "He hath put all His enemies under His feet"[1] only then, when not only in principle, but also in actual experience, all resistance will have been broken, all that has not willingly submitted to Him as the true Lord will have been purged away, and the contradiction between flesh and spirit, between the will of God and self-will shall have been removed by the perfect and totally effective influence of the Holy Spirit, and "the last enemy, death," shall have been "abolished",[2] only then will that actually become real, which since Good Friday and Easter has happened in principle and decisively: that to Him every knee shall bow, and He will really have all authority in heaven and on earth. Until then, however, the conflict between the Kingdom of the Son and the Kingdom of darkness will still go on, as a struggle which is, it is true, decided, but whose violence in the visible sphere of the earthly historical reality does not decrease, but rather

[1] 1 Cor. 15: 26 ff.   [2] 1 Cor. 15: 26

increases. Certainly we may look forward in faith to the day
of the victory of Jesus, and from this point of view we can
look back to Good Friday and Easter as the point at which
the decision was made, once for all. But we are not living in
harmony with the New Testament message, and with Christian
experience, if we behave as though this conflict were no longer
a real conflict, but a sham one. Our confidence in the certainty
of final victory must not allow us to deceive ourselves about
the seriousness of the struggle for each individual: "wherefore
let him that thinketh he standeth take heed lest he fall",[1]
and we are told that the severest struggles lie ahead. In spite
of all this, however, to believe in Jesus is also to believe in
Christ, the Victor, because Easter is the guarantee of final
victory.

(D) THE THREEFOLD OFFICE OF JESUS CHRIST AS A WHOLE

Revelation, Atonement, and Lordship are three aspects of
one and the same reality, of what God in Jesus Christ has
done, and will do for us. In the New Testament these three
aspects are sharply separated from one another, but to a
large extent they merge into one another. Both in looking
back on what has already happened, and also in view of the
future fulfilment, the expressions which describe the threefold
work of Christ appear to be interchangeable.

Revelation, as such, is both Atonement and Lordship.
Revelation is indeed the disclosure of the divine will for
communion, indeed it is the achievement of the establishment
of community. Thus—in the Johannine summary of His life
and death—Jesus gathers up His work in the phrase: "I have
manifested Thy Name unto the men which Thou gavest me
out of the world";[2] by this He means the union of the faithful
with God and with one another. And indeed should not the
Incarnation of the Word, the supreme revelation, also be the
union between God and His creatures? Indeed, in the passage
where the Atonement is spoken of as a sacrifice, does it not
say that here the "righteousness of God" has been "revealed"?[3]
Likewise, the revelation of Jesus in word, work, and suffering,
is the beginning and the establishment of God's rule upon
earth, which previously had only been expected, but now—in
Him—has been realized. But the end of the whole story of
salvation, the ushering in of the perfect rule of God, is

[1] I Cor. 10: 12   [2] John 17: 16   [3] Rom. 3: 21 ff.

preferably described by the expression the "revelation of the Lord Jesus".

Dogmatic theologians have often made a sharp distinction between Atonement and Redemption, but in so doing they have left out of account the characteristic element in the view of the New Testament. For there one and the same fact, the death of Jesus on the Cross, is regarded sometimes from the standpoint of "Atonement" and sometimes from that of "redemption". A powerful passage like that of Col. 2: 15 owes its strength precisely to the fact that in it revelation, atonement and the establishment of lordship are blended into a complete unity. We are reconciled "through the Blood" of Jesus Christ, redeemed from the power of darkness, and transferred into "the Kingdom of the Son of His Love", and in faith we receive the highest revelation of His merciful Will. We were obliged, first of all, to look at the three aspects of the Work of Christ in their distinctive character, in order to see them clearly. But the more deeply we penetrate into this truth the more we perceive at the same time, that each implies the others; we cannot speak aright about revelation without at the same time speaking of redemption, and we cannot speak rightly about Atonement without at the same time thinking of Redemption, as the overcoming of resistance and the restoration of the rule of God. The dogmatic pedantry which clings to these distinctions, fails in the most important task of theological reflection: the vision of unity, which had previously been concealed.

We ought also to look at this from the human standpoint. The Coming of God in Jesus Christ removed something out of man's way which prevented him from fulfilling his destiny. This "something" was, firstly, his blindness, his groping in the dark, his "walking in darkness"; Jesus Christ, as the Revealer, is the light of the world;[1] who brings the darkness to an end. Night is turned to day, blindness to sight, uncertainty to certainty—both of the way, and of the goal. The hindrance which the Bible shows to be central is the guilt of man's sin, his separation from God, the fact that he is living under the wrath of God! Jesus Christ, as the Reconciler, heals the rent and restores the broken communion. Distance from God becomes most evident as the sinful will, as disobedience and self-will, as sinful self-seeking and love of the world. Jesus Christ as the Redeemer breaks the power of sin, which sets

[1] John 8: 12

man in opposition to God; He creates the new, obedient heart.

These "three" hindrances are at bottom one and the same. Blindness, like guilt, is the effect of sin. Since Jesus Christ reveals the gracious will of God, He breaks the power of darkness and establishes communion with God. As the sinful heart is that which is separated from God, blind to God, and opposed to God, so faith—which is the opposite of sin—is the inward eye which is opened to the reality of God, the heart which is reconciled to God, and the will which is united to God in obedience. And this threefold unity is the new creation in Christ Jesus, which will be completed when faith passes into sight.

(A) THE HISTORY OF THE DOCTRINE OF THE THREEFOLD OFFICE
OF CHRIST

IN the Primitive Church, reflection upon "saving history"
(*Heilsgeschichte*) ceased very early; nothing shows this more
clearly than the fact that in the development of dogma the
doctrine of the "threefold office" of Christ, and indeed His
Work as a whole, plays a very subordinate part. Not only
is the doctrine of a "threefold office" practically absent, but
the work of Christ as a whole is obscured by the development
of the doctrine of His Person. This does not mean, of course,
that the Early Fathers did not think or speak about the Work
of Christ at all; but—we may even say, down to the time of
Anselm—these ideas are only developed "by-the-way" and
never doctrinally.

This statement should be modified, however, at least to this
extent, by saying that the central doctrine of the Person of
Jesus Christ, the doctrine of the Incarnation of the Logos, must
itself be regarded both as an answer to the question, *Cur
Deus homo?* and also as a doctrine of Atonement and Redemp-
tion. Athanasius, at least, developed the doctrine further,
from this point of view (in his work: *Of the Incarnation of
Christ*). The Incarnation of the Logos—and the fact that
"the Word became flesh"—is at the same time the Atonement.
The Person of the God-Man, as such, is the Mediator, who in
Himself reconciles God and Man. In this view, not only the
Incarnation, as such, but even the Death of Jesus on the
Cross, as the final consequence—so to speak—of the Incarnation,
should rather be regarded from the point of view of Christ's
victory over death through the Resurrection, than from that
of Atonement and Expiation. If God's plan for the world is
not to be frustrated by the doom of death, due to sin, which
hangs menacingly over humanity, through the Incarnation
of the Logos mankind must again be united with God and led
into the fulfilment of its destiny.

Irenaeus was not only the first to develop this idea, through
his doctrine of *recapitulatio*, but the first to make it the central
point of his theological thought. On this point, as at all others,
we see how close Irenaeus is to Biblical thought and the idea

of "saving history"; we see this in the way in which, as he works out his doctrine of "recapitulation", he is far more interested in the story of Jesus than other thinkers; he is therefore able to interpret the Gospel story in detail, as "recapitulation"; in so doing 'he united the doctrine of the Person and the Work of Christ in a way no later theologian was able to do. The interest of the theologians of the Early Church was centred almost exclusively in the doctrine of the Person of Christ, and all that they said about the fact of the Incarnation, as such, also expressed what they had to say about the work of Atonement.

Alongside of this main line of development there runs a second current of thought: the theory of the "ransom". Strangely enough, this is almost the only idea drawn from the whole range of ideas in the New Testament, which the Early Church laid hold of and used in order to describe the significance of the Work of Jesus, and on which it based its characteristic theory of the death of Jesus as a "ransom" paid to the Devil in exchange for the souls of men. The one to whom the "ransom" had to be paid could be no other than Satan. From the time of Origen it was taken for granted that this ransom *had* to be paid—and therefore that the Death of Jesus was a necessity —because the Devil had a claim to compensation[1] which the "righteousness" (or "justice") of God could not ignore. This theory, first propounded by Origen in its strongly mythological and detailed form, was adopted by many of the later Fathers, and expressed in a variety of ways, without, however, adding any essentially new idea to it. This did not take place until Anselm published his book, *Cur Deus homo?* The importance of this work, both as an achievement in the sphere of theology and on account of its influence on the whole of theological thought—both Catholic and Protestant—cannot be over-estimated.

The epoch-making achievement of Anselm is based, first of all, on the fact that the idea of *guilt* became central in his doctrine; in the doctrine of the Early Church, on the other hand—both in its main line of development which is determined by the Incarnation, as well as in the "by-pass" road of the "mythological" doctrine of the necessity to "ransom" man from the power of Satan which borders on dualism—the idea

---

[1] I.e. because through the sin of Adam the Devil had acquired certain semi-legal "rights" over humanity, which the "justice" of God could not ignore (TR.)

of guilt was quite secondary, whereas in the New Testament it is central. Anselm re-discovered the Biblical centre, the forgiveness of sins, and, in addition, he united it firmly and clearly with the idea of the Glory and the Sovereignty of God. The fact that he did this in such a way that he outstripped all previous Christian thinkers (on this subject), by the intellectual coherence and clarity of his thought, is not only an admirable intellectual achievement, but a fact of particular theological significance, namely: that in this way alone was he able to bring out the inner concrete necessity for Atonement. In so doing Anselm had also got rid of the mythological notions connected with the "ransom" theory, and the still more unpleasant one "of a trick played by God upon the Devil, in offering him Christ's humanity as his prey without telling him that it veiled the Godhead"[1]—a magnificent instance of "de-mythologizing" which, however, like later attempts, did not altogether escape the opposite danger of rationalization. Another great merit of Anselm's achievement consists in the fact that he was able to unite his main thesis, the removal of guilt, with the leading doctrine of early theology, the Incarnation. In his thought "Satisfaction" and "Incarnation" form an indissoluble unity. God became man, because only thus could guilt be expiated, and humanity reconciled to God.

In comparison with these great achievements, it does not much matter that Anselm used certain ideas which are foreign to the message of the Bible, such as that of "Satisfaction", which is doubtless derived from the legal practice of the Middle Ages, and is further connected with the medieval theory of repentance and the practice of penitence; then there was the idea of the *laesa majestas* and the *majestas Dei*, to which he gives a twist which is not in complete accord with the genuinely Biblical and central conception of the Divine Glory and the Divine Wrath. The criticism which fastens on these points—here I regard Cremer's excellent critical treatment as an exception—is often due only to a reluctance, characteristic of the spirit of the Enlightenment, to accept the notions of the Glory of God and of the Divine Wrath; therefore, measured by the standard of the New Testament, it falls below the level of Anselm's genuine insight into Biblical truth, which he nevertheless attained with the aid of such ideas.

We have already shown why, in spite of all these great, we might almost say unparalleled, merits, Anselm's theory does

[1] N. P. Williams, *The Ideas of the Fall and of Original Sin*, p. 293 (TR.)

not do justice to the message of the Bible. It is therefore not surprising that in spite of its great success it was not received without modification. The first volume of Ritschl's *Rechtfertigung und Versöhnung* gives the best account of this process; this volume is indeed that part of Ritschl's great work which has the most permanent value. We can well understand why the Enlightenment, which began with Socinianism, began by criticizing the ecclesiastical dogma, and Anselm's theory of "Satisfaction" in particular; for although it may not have been adequate, it expressed the real heart of the New Testament: the forgiveness of sins, as the reconciling act of God in the Cross of Jesus Christ, as the ultimate meaning of the Incarnation of the Word.

All that was later on brought against the doctrine of Satisfaction from the rationalist quarter—in which Kant should certainly be included—was already explicitly contained in the Socinian criticism. The Socinians deny the necessity for "Atonement", because they regard the idea of the wrath of God as contrary to the love of God, therefore they reject it; and also because they regard sin as a mere matter of ethics, affecting the will, but not something which taints and infects the existence of man as a whole. Their criticism of Anselm's doctrine, however, does discover the weak points in his theory, and picks it to pieces by a process of intellectual argument, without taking into account his original intention. They maintain, with some Scriptural support, that the Bible does not say that *God* is reconciled by the death of Christ, but that He reconciles Himself to mankind; but their criticism attacks the view of God's Nature as just and merciful: both are not a *qualitas* of God, but only an *effectus voluntatis eius* (Socinus, *Prael. theol.*, p. 566). Further, they feel that there is a contradiction between "atonement" and "forgiveness"; either God forgives sin—and then there is no need for atonement, or He allows someone else to pay the penalty, and then the punishment remains with him. Rightly, they call attention to the inadequacy of the idea of "satisfaction"; guilt is something personal, not something which can be objectified, therefore it is not something which can be transferred. From this they draw the conclusion that an objective "Atonement", as an act of God, cannot even be considered. The paradox of the unity of Mercy and Justice they solve intellectually: Either God is merciful, then He will not punish, or He is just, and He cannot forgive (*op. cit.*, p. 571). Likewise they rightly point out that the logical reckoning of atonement (expiation) which Anselm presents does not hold water: for sin required as punishment eternal death, but Christ is risen. They also say— with good scriptural justification—that for Christ suffering was not a punishment, but this leads them to the conclusion that it cannot have any significance for the forgiveness of sins. So that precisely that which seems to be the strength of Anselm's view, namely, the logical stringency of proof, is that which partly justifies the Socinian criticism, yet at the same time it provides the occasion for them to throw over the doctrine itself, as well as the unsatisfactory form in which it is expressed. Here "de-mythologizing" ends in complete disintegration. This is true, however, not only of rationalistic theology in the narrower sense, but also of all "liberal" theology influenced by Idealism. Even the doctrine of Schleiermacher is no exception, owing to his Idealistic conception of Sin:— Sin is merely the absence of something, it is "not-yet-spirit", his theology has no room either for the idea of the Wrath of God—which is rejected as an "anthropomorphism"—or for an act of forgiveness on the part of God, an atonement which actually posits an objective act of forgiveness. In modern liberal theology, in addition to these dogmatic objections to the doctrine of the Atonement, there is one which appears to be based on the New Testament, namely: that God through Jesus pronounced forgiveness without connecting it with an act of atonement, and that the sacrificial theory of Paul is a retrogression into more or less pagan thought—which requires that the blood of a victim should be shed in order to placate an angry God. It is strange that these modern liberal critics fail to observe that Paul is also able to express his doctrine of atonement without the aid of the sacrificial theory, by means of ideas derived from other spheres of thought. All these modern rationalists need to be confronted by the phrase of Anselm: *nondum considerasti quanti ponderis sit peccatum.*

The Reformers, like the Catholic theologians, adopted Anselm's theory, but in so doing they expanded, and in various ways modified it. Luther, in particular, was very fond of proclaiming the mythological view of the Early Church—that the devil was outwitted by the "bait" of the death of Christ; here, however, it is clear that he is only using a central Biblical idea in mythological terms; it is only another way of expressing the "folly" of the Cross. Luther implicitly criticized Anselm's view in the fact that he used a great variety of images (all of

which have been used in the New Testament) in order to
express this one truth, and by this very fact he emphasized
their figurative and inadequate character. As in the thought
of Paul, in Luther's doctrine of the Atonement the dialectic
of the Law is central. So long as we are in a legal relation to
God, we are under the wrath of God. But in Christ the Law is
both fulfilled and abrogated, and—in the justification of the
sinner—the new life, life in the love of God, is offered and
given to those who believe. Like Irenaeus, Luther also sees
the Incarnation completed upon the Cross; there the God of
love, the true God, approaches us and offers us communion
with Himself. But for that very reason the Incarnation is not
only connected with the justification of the sinner, but it
constitutes its real personal meaning: living communion with
the God of love. But this is only possible through the objective
act of God, the Cross of Christ. This is the "cost" which God
Himself "pays", in order that we may be set free from the
law, and thus redeemed from the wrath of God, and that we
may share in the love of God. In a word: in Luther's thought
the whole New Testament message of the Cross, in its fullness
and its depth, as well as in the way it transcends all human
calculations, has been rediscovered, and in so doing the doctrine
of Anselm, with its apparent tendency to "calculate" (or
estimate) the act of God, is corrected. Because faith cannot be
severed from the event of the Cross the purely personal meaning
of the Atonement is restored, which transcends the contrast
between objectivism and subjectivism.

Lutheran theology soon allowed all this wealth of Luther's
thought to become re-entangled in the pseudo-rational form of
Anselm's Theory. Melanchthon's *Apology*, it is true, is still
free from this rationalistic tendency; on the contrary, it keeps
strictly to the simple Biblical formulae, and emphasizes the
close connexion, and indeed the unity between reconciliation
through Christ and justifying faith—*reconciliatio* and *justificatio*
are interchangeable ideas. But with Johann Gerhard the period
of exact logical juridical distinctions began, which became
intolerable during the scholastic period which followed.

In this whole question, so far as I can see, there is complete
agreement between the Swiss Reformers and Luther, with the
one difference, that Zwingli and Calvin seem to be rather more
tied to the terminology of Anselm, and do not use the various
New Testament images with the same freedom as Luther.
Their feeling for intellectual clarity makes them unable to

see the necessity for mythical language and the use of images, and they strive for a logical clarity which will satisfy the intellect. But in the main, for them as well as for Luther, the mistaken "objectivism" of Anselm's doctrine of Atonement has been overcome by the close connexion between Atonement and Justification by Faith. The Heidelberg Catechism expresses this very beautifully: "The satisfaction, righteousness and holiness of Christ is my sole righteousness before God, (provided that) I can only accept this and appropriate it for myself through faith" (61st question). Especially we must oppose the Lutheran legend which suggests that Calvin makes a sharp distinction between the "active" and the "passive" obedience of Christ. The very opposite is the case: it is precisely the Reformed theologians who lay particular stress upon the unity of both. Ritschl sums up Calvin's doctrine in these words: "Christ's acquirement of righteousness for us is based upon the whole course of His obedience; the basis of forgiveness, which frees us from the curse of the law, extends to the whole of the life of Christ; since He took on Himself the 'form of a servant' He began to discharge the debt by paying the price for our liberation. Death is only the final link in this chain of achievements" (*op. cit.*, p. 234; cf. above all the *Institutio*, II, 16, 5). The distinction between both goes back to Osiander, and was adopted by the *Formula Concordiae* (*sol. decl.*, III, 14). It also appears, at least from the time of Polan,[1] in the Scholasticism of Reformed theology.

The threefold Office, the *Munus triplex*, was first introduced into dogmatics by Calvin (*Institutio*, II, 15), yet it was not unknown to Luther. (Cf. the chapter on *Das dreifache Amt Christi* in Th. Harnack's book, *Luthers Theologie*, Chapter 16.) Yet although Luther taught that Christ was Prophet, Priest and King, he never spoke of a "threefold office." It was Calvin's interest in the connexion between the Old and the New Covenant, as well as his way of thought which was permeated with the idea of saving history (*Heilsgeschichte*) which led him to present the Work of Christ under this threefold aspect. The fact that in his presentation the largest part is given to the office of King, is in harmony with the whole of Calvin's outlook, and also with that of the earliest creed of the Church: *Kyrios Christos*. In the rest of Reformed theology the same end is sought by means of another idea, which binds the Old and the New Testament together, and also emphasizes a central

[1] 1561–1610 (Tr.)

idea of the New Testament, that of the "covenant", while the doctrine of the threefold office is rather forgotten. At first, Lutheran dogmatics like Catholic dogmatics—had no particular doctrine of the Work of Christ. It was only after Gerhard that the work of Atonement at least was dealt with in particular—probably on account of the Socinian attack—and in this connexion it develops something like a doctrine of the *munus*—or as it is here called *officium—triplex. Officium Christi vulgo* (?) *triplex statuitur—quod tamen revocari potest ad duo membra, ita ut duplex statuitur officium, sacerdotale et regium* (Hollaz, *Examen Theologiae Acroamaticae*, 729). Of modern theologians Ritschl and Frank have rejected the distinction of a *munus triplex*, the former because he wishes to include everything under the heading of royal sovereignty, the latter because "neither the prophetic office nor the kingly office stands on the same level as the priestly" (*System der christlichen Wahrheit*, II, 194). As though Jesus Christ, as the Light of the world, or as the Lord of Lords, were less than the High Priest who reconciles us to God!

It is significant that in modern theology the doctrine of the Work of Christ has been developed to a considerable extent by British theologians. Thus in the middle of the nineteenth century John Macleod Campbell wrote an excellent book on *The Nature of the Atonement*, from which we can still learn to-day. Following him, at the beginning of this century, came Peter Taylor Forsyth, with a valuable book on *The Work of Christ*, in which he discusses, with genuine Biblical understanding, various alternative modern theories; and finally, quite recently, D. M. Baillie, in an extremely original work, *God Was In Christ*, has tried to combine historical criticism with the fundamental doctrines of the New Testament, by an absolutely independent interpretation. If I understand him aright, the view expressed in the present work is in almost entire agreement with his line of thought.

(B) THE KINGSHIP OF CHRIST AND "CHRISTOLOGICAL SOCIAL ETHICS"

Visser 't Hooft, in his interesting book *The Kingship of Christ*, aims at filling a gap which he, rightly, sees, in the previous treatment of the *munus regium Christi*. He rightly stresses the fact that the doctrine of the threefold office of Christ was first introduced into theology by Calvin (p. 11);

also that neither he, nor the other Reformers gave that central place to the Kingship of Christ, which would have been in harmony with the witness of the New Testament (p. 16). To-day, he says, we ought to proclaim the Kingship of Christ over the whole world; and it is at this very point that he finds a certain weakness in the theology of the Reformers; he supports his contention by quoting the view of Karl Barth, *K.D.*, II, I, 712. In Barth's opinion the Reformers are especially concerned with the basis and origin of salvation . . . rather than with its fruit and goal. The result is that the world is not sufficiently regarded in the light of the victory of Christ. The orders of creation come to occupy a larger place than they had in the New Testament (p. 14). In support of this contention he might also have appealed to an earlier work of Karl Barth, *Rechtfertigung und Recht* (Justification and Justice) where the Reformers are directly reproached for the fact that in their social ethics—especially in the doctrine of the State—they had abandoned their Christological basis and had simply proclaimed Natural Theology.

Now when Visser 't Hooft, in a very detailed examination of the New Testament passages, comes to the conclusion that the witness to Jesus the *Kyrios* is the dominating centre of the message of the New Testament, he certainly need fear no serious opposition from any quarter. Visser 't Hooft feels obliged, it is true, to remind us of the two aspects of this question: (*a*) that the powers of darkness were defeated and despoiled on Good Friday and at Easter; (*b*) that on the other hand, and even in the New Testament, it is constantly stressed, and most decidedly, that there will be a continual conflict between Jesus Christ (in His Church) and the hostile powers of darkness. He sees, rightly, that this twofold fact reveals the tension which pervades the whole of the New Testament; that in Christ we already have a share in His final victory, but that on the other hand we must wait for the completion of His final victory. But when Visser 't Hooft draws from this truth the conclusion that we ought to have "an optimistic hope in the gradual penetration of the world by the forces of the Church and the Kingdom", this "progressive optimism" sounds very questionable. He cannot support this statement by any passages from the New Testament, nor from any leaders of the Church, but he confines himself to appealing to the younger Blumhardt as witness for the Crown (p. 31), whereas we all know that his views were a mixture of an optimistic belief in "progress", and his expectation of the Kingdom of God. Does this mean the beginning of a new "social gospel" on a different theological foundation? In any case, it is perplexing to be told that this proclamation of the real Kingship of Jesus Christ will "provide the basis for a social gospel which is truly a gospel" (p. 95).

It is natural that Visser 't Hooft should not have much sympathy for Luther's doctrine of the Two Realms, and also that he has no use for Calvin's sharp distinction between the *ordo civilis* and the Kingdom of Christ. So he maintains that in Calvin's teaching about the "world" there are "two distinct trends: one in which the accent falls on the orders of creation", and the other, in which "the main accent falls on the universal sovereignty of Christ"; here "the world and the State are conceived in a definitely Christocentric manner" (p. 16). To this I would reply: none of the Reformers, even when speaking of the world or of the "orders of creation", ever intended anything other than Christian, and even "Christocentric" theology, and that their doctrine of the orders of creation has no connexion with natural theology, but is part of their "Christocentric" or "Christological" view. They have an absolutely Christocentric doctrine of the orders of creation. Luther's doctrine of the Two Realms is not, as Visser 't Hooft thinks, a denial of their belief in the exclusive Kingship of Christ, but is the expression of their Biblical and realistic doctrine, that in the world and in the State Christ must reign in a different way from that in which He rules in the Church. Visser 't Hooft himself suggests the reason for this: The Kingdom of Christ in the direct sense of the word is established exclusively through the Word, and thus not by the method of compulsory law by which the State imposes its rule. Christ's *opus proprium*, to use Luther's phrase, takes place only where man listens to the Word of Christ and the Gospel of His saving grace, that is, where people believe in Christ. Where rule is exercised on lines other than that of this Word, the "spiritual" realm ceases, and what he calls the "secular" begins. That is why there is such a vast difference—emphasized by Calvin in an important passage in his works—between the *ordo civilis* (or civil government) and the *regnum Christi* (spiritual Kingdom of Christ) in the direct sense of the word (*Inst.*, IV, 20, I). The State is not, and cannot be governed by the Gospel of God's forgiving grace, but by "the Law".

Now it is a mistake, often committed by those who take this line in theology, to maintain that in the theory of the Two Realms—that is, in their distinction between the Gospel and the Law—the Reformers proclaimed that the world, and above all the State, is "autonomous". This could only be the case if they did not declare the law of God to be binding on the State; Luther certainly never said this; at the most, the only people who might have said something of this kind would be neo-Lutheran romantics and nationalists. On the other hand, these "Christological" theologians would only be justified in their reproach, if they believed in a State which could be governed by the Gospel of Grace, and not by means of compulsory law—which would be pure fanaticism, or if they gave up saying that the real Kingdom of Christ is only achieved through the Word. For the State will never, never be governed by the Word—in the sense of the Gospel—but exclusively by the word of the Law, quite simply by the Decalogue, which is not the actual "Word" of Christ.

Visser 't Hooft is right when he says that the doctrine of the orders of creation plays a very subordinate part in the New Testament. Only he has forgotten to say that the other statement is equally correct, that social ethics and the doctrine of the State play a very small part in the New Testament. Both statements are co-extensive. Where the State or the Family are mentioned (and this is not often), the New Testament does not speak of Christ, as ruling through His Word of reconciliation, but simply of the "ordinances of God".

Attempts have recently been made to meet this awkward situation by arguing—and Visser 't Hooft also gives his full approval to this theory, (pp. 93 ff.)—that behind the "authorities" (ἐξουσίαι) of Rom. 13 there are cosmic forces, and it is asserted that, through the death of Christ, these have become forces in His service, rather than hostile forces. This theory is, obviously, an attempt to turn this *locus classicus*—which is *against* a directly "Christological" theory—into a Christological one. But this whole theory has very weak exegetical support. It is rejected absolutely by all present-day New Testament scholars, even by those who are most decidedly Christian in their outlook. The main argument against it is this: that nowhere in the New Testament is there any mention of Christ taking formerly hostile forces into His service—it is said rather, that He has deprived them of their power—still less is there any trace of an idea that Christians are to be "subject" to cosmic forces. The witness of the New Testament is the exact opposite.

But even supposing that this exegesis were correct—what would be gained? Would it mean that because we serve the servants of Jesus Christ in the State, the usual norms of the law of good and evil would be set aside by other norms derived from the atoning act of Jesus Christ? What does Paul say about this? He says quite plainly, that the State must be judged by a law which makes a clear distinction between "good and evil"; by this he obviously means the *Roman* State—the only one then paramount—and Roman Law, which is based upon the Moral Law, and not upon the Atonement or upon the Gospel. He praises the State—Rome—and calls it an "order" which has been "constituted by God", because, and in so far as it upholds this Moral Law, rewarding some and punishing others. It is from this clear, unshakable exegesis of Rom. 13 that the Reformers derived their doctrine of the Two Realms, or like Calvin, their *maximum discrimen inter rem publicam et regnum Christi*. It cannot indeed be otherwise, if it be true that only in the Church, that is, in faith, the real word of Christ can be received, whereas in the State we have to take into account that many, indeed most, of its subjects will not know or will not believe, the *verbum proprium Christi*.

Thus when we ask, how, in the view of Visser 't Hooft, a "Christological" social ethic, based upon the Gospel, can be developed, we are left completely in the air. The conclusion is the same as that reached by Barth in his first attempt in *Rechtfertigung und Recht* (with which he himself was evidently so dissatisfied that he has recently made a second attempt—*Christengemeinde und Bürgergemeinde*)—where, in the embarrassment which ensues when he tries to move from Christology to concrete norms for the State, he seizes a new principle, by the aid of which he hopes to fill up the awkward gap, the principle of—analogy! *Per analogiam*, Barth now derives norms from the Christian Church for the civil community, but he evidently does not notice that anything and everything can be derived from the same principle of analogy: a monarchy just as much as a republic (Christ the King), the totalitarian State, just as much as a state with civil liberties (Christ the Lord of all; man a servant, indeed a slave of Jesus Christ).

Visser 't Hooft, for his part, feeds us with empty promises. He is not able to provide us with even a glimmer of light by which we can make distinctions, according to which, for instance, we can differentiate a good law from a bad one, a good penal system from a bad one. He simply reiterates: we must proclaim Christ to the State—as though the State were a "person" who could believe and be converted—we must proclaim Christ's kingship in all spheres of life (p. 40). If this means that the Christian who is determined to listen to the voice of his Lord, knows that he is the servant of Jesus Christ in all spheres of life, that is a truth generally accepted in Reformation doctrine. But if he means, that it is sufficient to know the Gospel of Jesus, the Saviour, in order to lay down norms of conduct for the State, education, law, culture, then Visser 't Hooft gives us no proof of this statement at all. What for instance does it mean for a lawyer, who is working on a new penal code, to acknowledge the Kingship of Christ? In the light of the atoning act of Jesus, who has borne the sin of all men *equally*, and who has taken the penalty upon Himself, is there anything to tell us which criminals ought to be more heavily punished than others? and which ought to be let off more lightly? and indeed whether anyone should be punished at all? When we ask these questions we see that this whole "Christological ethic" is pure fantasy; at its best it would have no result; and at its worst it would lead to that ancient Utopian mixture of "spiritual" and "secular" elements, of the Kingdom of Christ and the State, or to the no less unpleasant confusion between Church and State which occurs in some of the efforts which have been made to unite theocracy with "ecclesiocracy". This whole line of thought is, in fact, simply a new edition of the "Social Gospel", on a different theological foundation.

The Reformers, in their struggle against fanaticism on the one hand and against Catholic "ecclesiocracy" on the other, were well aware why they based their social ethic not upon Christology, but upon the Law—or, (and this comes to the same thing)—upon the orders of creation. From this point of view it is possible to lay down norms for the State and for civilization; for here there are concrete orders to be followed. But none of these theologians who want to "improve" upon the theology of the Reformers has been able to say what a legal system derived from norms based on the message of the Cross, would be like. The only result which has plainly emerged up to the present is that it has fostered a terrible arrogance on the part of the ministers who take this view: they think they understand everything, and that they can and should interfere with everything "in the name of the Church", even where they understand and know nothing at all.

The Kingship of Christ—yes, in all things and first of all! But this slogan, which the Reformers used (rightly) with caution, will produce something very different from Utopia or "ecclesiocracy", if we add: the direct Kingship of Christ through the Gospel, in the Church, the indirect Kingship of Christ through the Law in the world. And this is exactly what the Reformers meant, and carried out; in this respect they are "streets ahead" of those who try to pick a quarrel with them; this comes out very plainly in the seriousness with which—on the basis of this distinction—they were able to carry out some actual practical reforms in political and social life, instead of being content with uttering high-sounding phrases.

CHAPTER 12

THE PERSON OF JESUS CHRIST

(A) THE MYSTERY OF THE PERSON OF JESUS

THE way to the knowledge of Jesus leads from the human Jesus to the Son of God and to the Godhead. "The Scripture beginneth very gently and leadeth us to Christ as to a man, and after that to a Lord of all Creation, and after that to a God. Thus I come into it gently, and thus I learn to know God. . . . We must begin at the bottom, and afterwards rise to the heights."[1] It is the miracle of the divine condescension towards us that He wills to meet us in a human being. If *God* has opened this way to Himself for us, we ought to follow it too; we have no right to try to reverse the process. That is why the Gospels, the records of the human life of Jesus, are placed first in the New Testament, in order that, meeting the Man Christ Jesus, we may, through this encounter, come to the knowledge of God. Only so can our Christian faith become our "own". We must see for ourselves—certainly not apart from the witness of the Apostles—who this Jesus really is.

1. "When the fullness of the time came, God sent forth His Son born of a woman, born under the law".[2] The words "born of a woman" express the fact that He shares our common humanity; He is a creature, just as we are. The fact that He was born of a woman, just as we are, shows that He was true Man. "Born under the law" means: He was born as a Jewish child. He was educated, as Jewish children were educated, He lived in the tradition of the Jewish people.[3] As one who was "born of a woman" He was subject to all the natural laws of growth. Of Him too, as of the young Samuel, it was said: "He advanced in wisdom and stature, and in favour with God and man".[4] He shared the limitations common to humanity. This comes out clearly in the Gospel story: He eats and drinks; He is tired; He sleeps; He feels physical pain; He is exposed to ill-treatment; He suffers the agony in the Garden of Gethsemane, being "sore troubled and amazed" . . . He dies of exhaustion on the Cross.

[1] EA[2], 12, 412   [2] Gal. 4: 4
[3] Cf. Kümmel, *Jesus und die Tradition*   [4] Luke 2: 52

He grew up in the school of the "Law", the Old Testament deposit of revelation. He was not only a Jew by descent but by education. By constant reading of the Scriptures He learned to know the Bible well; He had mastered the Scriptures and He could quote them freely and accurately. He became a religious Jew, that is, one who prays to the God of the Old Testament revelation. It seems probable that He was a practising craftsman; He is not only called the "son" of the carpenter, but *the* Carpenter.[1] The sources give us practically no material for an external or internal biography of Jesus. We know nothing about His inner development. He emerges into the light of the historical tradition as a mature man, at the moment when He permits Himself to be baptized by John the Baptist. The interpretation of this act in the Scriptures themselves, and still more in the history of exposition and of Christian theology, is very varied. We shall be dealing with this later on. The fact itself, however, is firmly established. The second fact that is recorded about Him is that He was tempted of the devil. Whatever the divine aspect of these first two recorded incidents in His life as an adult may be: in any case they are also extremely human. To accept baptism for the forgiveness of sins, and to be tempted of the devil, are events which presuppose a truly human person. The next thing that we learn about Him is the beginning of His public activity, with the summons (like that of John the Baptist) "Repent! for the Kingdom of Heaven is at hand", coupled with His first appearance in the synagogue at Capernaum which caused great excitement; here He appears in the guise of a wandering rabbi, able to expound the Scriptures.

2. Was Jesus "a man like ourselves"? This question must immediately be answered, quite definitely, in the affirmative; even the Christological dogma of the fifth century, which was above all concerned to maintain His divinity, expressed this with the utmost clarity: *Vere homo.* But was Jesus really a man like ourselves—and thus a sinful man? The apostle Paul, speaking of the real humanity of Jesus goes as far as possible when he says that God sent His Son "in the likeness of sinful flesh".[2] The Epistle to the Hebrews adds: "One that hath been in all points tempted like as we are, yet without sin".[3] Does this perhaps mean the same thing as the strong Pauline expression? We cannot know for certain, but there is no reason to suppose that Paul wanted to go further than this. This—

1 Mark 6: 3   2 Rom. 8: 3   3 Heb. 4: 15

but no more—was involved in being "in the form of a servant", in which He had to "learn obedience".[1] We only possess one saying of Jesus Himself about His sinlessness, in the tradition of the Fourth Gospel: "Which of you convicteth Me of sin?"[2]

But this is precisely what the historical picture of Jesus— which everyone can see—shows us. It shows us Jesus as One who was tempted just as we are, and nowhere does it show us a man who was defeated by temptation. The decisive element in the story of His threefold temptation is the sureness and naturalness with which Jesus repels the suggestions of the Tempter. Even if ultimately the verdict "without sin" goes further than anything that can be grasped empirically, and thus carries us into the sphere of faith, yet we know of no situation which could shake the truth of these words: "yet without sin". The second question which is often raised is rather different: Was the knowledge of Jesus limited by human conditions? In the light of the evidence given us in the Bible we must answer decidedly: "Yes". As we have already said, as a human being Jesus developed in the normal way from a child to an adult; He "advanced in wisdom and stature".[3] But we have a still more important testimony from the lips of Jesus Himself. "But of that day or that hour knoweth no one, not even the angels in heaven, neither the Son, but the Father."[4] Jesus in Gethsemane prays that this Cup may pass from Him. Jesus at prayer places Himself on the level of those who are limited in their knowledge of future events. Jesus would not be True Man if this were not the case.

3. Yet the picture of Jesus in the Gospels leads us, so to speak at every point, precisely where the narrative is most simple and straightforward—and not interpreted theologically —beyond this borderline, so that while we agree with the verdict "He is a Man like ourselves", we are also obliged to come to the exactly opposite view and say: He is *not* a Man like ourselves. Not only can no one accuse Him of sin, but He stands before us as One who, at every point in His life, is wholly one with the will of God; who really does not allow Himself to be ministered unto, but who "ministers, and gives His life a ransom for many". His life flows on harmoniously in an unbroken series of acts, in which, in Holy Love, in free obedience to God, He does and says what only a man could do and say whose will is wholly surrendered to the will of God. The story of His life shows us a human being who is the

[1] Heb. 5: 8   [2] John 8: 46   [3] Luke 2: 52 (R.V.)   [4] Mark 13: 32

personification of the Holy Love of God. Even unbelievers bow in reverence before this Man. They try, it is true, to make His "otherness" a relative matter, by comparing Him with other "holy men". But these comparisons will not bear strict examination. We know of no other man in whose life sin plays no part, whose life is pure and unstained, reflecting the holy love of God; who, therefore, without hypocrisy or self-assertion could come forth to meet man as One coming from God.

Two further facts must be mentioned, which are on the borderline of our Lord's human experience: His miracles and His "Messianic consciousness". Whether the former should really be regarded as a sign of this "borderline" is, however, somewhat questionable. Did not Jesus Himself promise His disciples—according to the saying in the Gospel of John— that they should "do greater works" than He Himself?[1] And, in point of fact, the Book of Acts recounts stories (told in such a way that they seem credible even to the critical reader) of particular miracles worked by the apostles, which seem little different from those of Jesus: at any rate they are not different in principle.

The other point, however, is absolutely decisive: the "Messianic authority" which Jesus claims. This is indeed the new element in His message, not in degree, but in principle, namely, that He definitely distinguishes Himself from all the Prophets as One who no longer merely *promises* the coming of the Kingdom of God, but who proclaims that the new age has actually dawned in His own Person; He does this over and over again, in different ways.[2] If we understand the Messianic claim as the unique and ultimate category, the presence of the New Age, of the divine authority, connected with His Person, and not merely with His teaching or His Word, then this Messianic claim of Jesus is an historic fact which can be proved: and can only be denied or ignored by those who are full of prejudice.[3]

This is as far as we can go in the mere collection of evidence; beyond this the only possibilities are: faith or unbelief. It is, of course, most ill-advised to maintain that we can *prove* that Jesus was Messiah. All that we can prove is merely that He claimed to be the Messiah; it does not matter whether He actually used the *title* of Messiah or not. Even if we are not ready to step over the borderline of all that can be empirically

[1] John 14: 12   [2] Cf. Duncan, *Jesus, Son of Man*, pp. 119 f
[3] Cf. Buri, *Christus gestern und heute. Schw th. Umschau* 1948, p. 102

perceived, we cannot remain on this side without being profoundly disturbed and embarrassed. A person in this situation
has to choose, either to regard Jesus as a visionary, who
believed something about Himself which was quite untrue,[1]
or to believe in Him. Albert Schweitzer's formula, which seems
to provide a way out of this dilemma: Jesus had already found
a "Messianic theology" in Judaism, and had applied it to
Himself,[2] is only an apparent solution. For, firstly, to say this
does not solve the problem, it simply states it in a different
way. Certainly if a mere man were to apply to himself the
"Messianic theology" of Judaism, he would be a "visionary",
and almost what we would to-day call a "psychopath". Secondly,
if we do not interpret the sources in an arbitrary way, Jesus
certainly did not do this, but in order to avoid this misinterpre-
tation He expressed His Messiahship in such a guarded and
veiled way that even during the Entry into Jerusalem on Palm
Sunday the general opinion was only: "he is a prophet".[3]
On the other hand, the glimpses Jesus gives us of His Messianic
authority are, to some extent, in evident opposition to the
"Messianic theology" of contemporary Judaism. The Messiah
that Jesus claimed to be, was quite different from the one that
the Jews were expecting. It was precisely because His way of
being Messiah and the Jewish theology of the Messiah were so
utterly different that He was arraigned by the Jewish religious
authorities.

4. Thus in fact there is only the choice between two possibilities; either, although Jesus was a man like ourselves, He
regarded Himself as the "Son of God", which was not true; or,
in fact, Jesus is what He says He is. We cannot *prove* that the
first statement is false; it is still a possibility for the unbeliever.
But so much we can say: the unbeliever is confronted by an
enigma which does not exist for the believer: How was such
self-deception possible for a human being whose truthfulness,
sincerity and clarity of thought were so real and so outstanding?
Does the statement (which for an unbeliever is unavoidable)
that Jesus was a victim of an almost psychopathic self-delusion
and fantasy, fit the actual picture of Jesus? The historical
evidence supports the believer, not the unbeliever; although
the verdict: "Jesus is the Son of God" is a verdict of faith, and
not of mere historical insight. The man who believes in Christ

---

[1] Cf. Buri, *op. cit.*, p. 103
[2] *Quest of the Historical Jesus*, Ch. 21
[3] Matt. 21: 11, 46

can say with a good conscience: at this central point faith proves to be the only true historical perception. From the standpoint of historical science there is no objection to the verdict of faith; on the contrary, the unprejudiced historical verdict agrees absolutely, as far as it can go, with that of faith.

5. In Chapter 10 we tried to answer the question: Why do we believe in Jesus Christ ? Our answer was: we believe in Him because He meets us as the Christ, first of all in the historical picture of His life. The historical Jesus is no other than the Christ to whom the Apostles bear witness. In His action and His speech He stands before us as the Only One, the Man, who, with divine authority—both in His demands and His gifts—claims us for Himself. Those who do not close their eyes to the actual Jesus of History, who do not evade Him, but respond to His claim, can do no other than confess with Peter: "Thou art the Christ, the Son of the living God".[1] Those who refuse to bear this witness cannot appeal to *historical* reasons. The refusal of this witness can only be based on one's general "philosophy of life", not on history. But if this frequently occurs then it can only be that our "world-view" unconsciously affects our historical judgment, and obscures our historical insight. What is really at stake is not the claim of historical truth against dogmatic prejudice—as will be maintained—but, quite simply, faith or unbelief. The fact that this is so will, however, only be recognized by faith; unbelief will always find excuses for this state of affairs, and will feel obliged to justify itself on "intellectual" grounds.

In His historical reality Jesus proves that He is the Christ; but it is only faith which perceives this full historical reality. To see the true Jesus of History and to believe in Him as the Christ, is the same thing. Faith in Jesus the Christ is identical with the true perception of the historical reality of Jesus.[2] Faith is the act of "grasping reality", faith is the open eye for the true historical actuality of Jesus—namely, for the reality that Jesus IS the Christ. But what does this mean? "that Jesus is the Christ"? What kind of reality is it that faith knows? The answer to this question is the witness of the Apostles to Jesus as the Christ and the Son of God, and this answer is the subject of the doctrine of the Church, which we call "Christology", the doctrine of Jesus who is not only true Man but also True God.

6. Hitherto, we have been speaking only of the picture of

[1] Matt. 16: 16   [2] Cf. Kähler, *op. cit.*

the life of Jesus, as it is given to us in the New Testament tradition, in the "records" of the Apostles. The second objective fact, upon which faith depends, is, as we have already said, the witness of the Apostles to Jesus as the Christ. This witness is linked on the one hand wholly with the record of His life, as it has been handed down to us, but it also goes much further, since it speaks of that which is revealed in the historical figure of Jesus, of His supra-historical existence, which became clear to the Apostles chiefly through the Fact of Easter.

The life of Jesus, as the disciples narrate it, is a summary of actual facts, which, to some extent, are also accessible to the unbeliever. Even the non-Christian historian[1] recognizes Jesus as an historical personality, and describes the course of His life and the main points of His teaching in terms which are not essentially different from the records of the disciples in the Gospels. But there is one fact recorded by the disciples which does not exist for the non-Christian historian: the Resurrection of Jesus. What Jesus said and did, unbelievers also saw and heard: that is the part of the historical *continuum* which, on the whole, is the same for both the non-Christian historian and for the evangelists. But the final section of the story of Jesus in the Apostles' narrative, which we call the Resurrection of Jesus, is an event, which no unbeliever has perceived. The appearances of the Risen Lord were only granted to believers. On this point all the accounts of the Apostles, which otherwise vary greatly, are agreed. Indeed, they were conscious of this themselves. "Him God raised up the third day and gave Him to be made manifest, not to all the people, but unto witnesses that were chosen before of God, even to us, who did eat and drink with Him after He rose from the dead".[2] And this is the proof that here we are dealing with history of a different kind from that of the events recorded of the life of Jesus. It is not wrong, but it is at least liable to misunderstanding to designate the event of Easter simply as an "historical event"; for it is not historical in the same way as other events, because the historical event, in the usual sense, is something which, in principle, everyone can perceive. But Easter is *not* an event of this kind. Historically it is for believers only. It is not part of the historical *continuum*, but at this point the Beyond "breaks into" history.

[1] As, for instance, the Oriental scholar, Ed. Meyer, *Ursprung und Anfänge des Christentums*, 3 vols., 1920–23

[2] Acts 10: 40–41

Now this event of Easter is the standpoint from which the Apostles teach about Jesus. In the light of Easter the life of Jesus, and above all the Cross, became intelligible. Peter, it is true, had already, during the earthly life of Jesus, confessed Him as "Son of God" and "Messiah". But the apostolic witness to Jesus in its fullness and depth was only made possible by meeting with the Risen Lord. Therefore for us too the apostolic witness about Jesus the Son of God cannot be understood from the Life of Jesus alone, but only from the Life of Jesus of which Easter is the culmination. It is not impossible, it is true, but it is not very probable, that a person could become a Christian simply on the basis of the Synoptic Gospels, and reach the statements about Jesus which form the teaching about the Person of Christ which the Apostles give in their testimony. The full encounter with Christ which is the basis for the doctrine of Christ includes the encounter with the Risen Lord, which—for us—is mediated through the witness of the Apostles, whereas for the Apostles themselves it was direct. We can only teach "the Christology of the New Testament" as we speak of Him who was crucified, *and* who rose again from the dead.

On the other hand, the basis of this doctrine of Jesus, the Christ, does not include the tradition of the way in which Jesus came into the world, which we call the "Virgin Birth", narrated by Matthew and Luke alone. Apostles never mention this; still less does it form part of the content of the original Christian *kerygma*. As we shall see, it is highly probable that the fullest doctrine of Jesus the Christ, as we have it in the writings of Paul and John, took shape without any knowledge of that event recorded by Matthew and Luke. The basis of the apostolic doctrine of Jesus does not contain special historical information about the wonderful way in which Jesus came into the world; if it were otherwise, then the Church, and especially the apostolic teachers of the Church, would have had the greatest possible interest in making this knowledge part of the content of the Christian message. Obviously this was not the case. On the contrary, other Biblical writers simply do not mention it at all. The Apostolic doctrine of Jesus expounds the Nature of Him who rose from the dead, but not of Him who was born of the Virgin Mary.

(B) THE DIVINITY OF CHRIST

1. *Non-Christian Interpretations of the Person of Jesus*

Our previous course of reflection has been primarily concerned with the fact of the Humanity of Jesus, which is admitted by those who confess Jesus as the Christ, as well as by
those who do not do so. Before we go more fully into the
meaning of the Christian Confession for those who believe, we
must briefly consider the interpretations of the Person of Jesus
given by those who do not believe in Him as Christ. We cannot
conscientiously represent the witness of the Apostles without
having examined these alternatives.[1] The first answer to the
question: *Who is Jesus?* is this: Jesus is one of the great
religious teachers of mankind. He was the first to perceive
certain eternal religious and ethical truths, or the first to
express them with particular clarity and purity. Here the
Person of Jesus has no constitutive significance, for these
eternal truths are independent of His Person; their truth, once
they have been uttered, is no longer connected with His
Person. Just as Pythagoras was the first to formulate the
geometrical proposition which bears his name, but which,
once it has been expressed, can be understood by any public-
schoolboy who knows nothing about Pythagoras, so also the
truths of the Fatherhood of God, and the infinite value of the
human soul are, in principle, independent of the Person of
Jesus. Jesus, however, remains worthy of reverence as the one
who first uttered these truths, and expressed them most
clearly. This view lies behind the rationalistic idea that in the
Gospel we are dealing with religious truths which—in principle
—can be known by everyone, religious and ethical truths to
which, in principle, everyone has access. For this reason alone
the question of the authority of Jesus here plays no part.
Jesus is the "Teacher", whose highest aim is to make the
pupil independent of himself.

Sometimes, but not always, this view includes a second idea:
Jesus as our Example. Jesus did not only teach these truths,
but He exemplified them in a very real way in His life. It is of
course true that others after Him have done the same. If He
has an advantage over them it consists in His being *primus
inter pares*. Hence to know something about Him is a help in

[1] Cf. H. Weinel, *Das Jesusbild in den geistigen Strömungen der letzten* 150
Jahre, 1928

understanding these truths and particularly for their practical realization, but it is certainly not indispensable.

This conception of Jesus as an Example (*Vorbild*) differs little from that in which He is regarded as the Perfect Ideal (*Urbild*) of religious truth.[1] Here, it is true, a perfection of personal incorporation of truth is asserted, which seems to go further than a question of degree, and to lead to a difference in principle. The view of Jesus as the perfect Ideal of ethical or religious truth would then correspond to one part of the Christian creed, namely, the statement that Jesus is not only *a* true man, but that He is *the* true Man. But the exceptional position assigned to Jesus—an absolute and not a relative one—which is implied in the Christian doctrine of the Real Humanity of Jesus, presupposes that Jesus, True Man, the Sinless One, could only be True Man because He was more than man; because He was also—God.

But the protagonists of this doctrine of the *Urbild* (perfect Ideal) do not mean this. If you ask them: "How then can a man like ourselves be sinless and thus perfectly, ideally, good?" they can only say: "It is so!" Evidently this does not cause them any difficulty: this is because—as is evident in the writings of Schleiermacher—they regard sin as something merely relative. Hence for them, in principle, there is no difference between Perfection and the maximum of ethico-religious goodness which man can attain. Here too there is no necessary connexion with the Person of Jesus. Ethico-religious perfection is, in principle, a human possibility, and can therefore be attained without relation to Jesus, even if the "impulse" which proceeds from Jesus, the Ideal, is a great help.

A special variant of this conception—though at bottom it is exactly the same view—is the theory of Jesus as the supreme religious genius. The superlative attribute suggests that here we are only dealing with a relative difference. It is, of course, true that the expression "genius", as against that of "teacher", suggests that here there is an exceptional quality, and moreover a qualitative difference of degree. But, firstly, the difference between a genius and a non-genius is fluid—who can say where the borderline runs between talent and genius, and who will deny that every human being, in some degree, though possibly not to a very great extent, is talented? Secondly, however, "genius" is a purely anthropological category, which does not

[1] Schleiermacher, *Der Christliche Glaube*, § 93

extend beyond the sphere of man's inherent possibilities. The genius is the first to discover something, but once it has been discovered it becomes the common possession of all men, and it is not connected with his person. There is no essential difference between the notion of the supreme Teacher and that of the Genius.

Neither the Genius nor the Teacher, neither the Example nor the Ideal has authority, in the strict sense of the word. The truth which they teach or incorporate is not connected with their person; this is because, by its very nature, it is imminent, not transcendent, thus because at least in principle, as a possibility, it is inherent in man himself.

All these interpretations are contrary not only to what the Apostles teach about Jesus, but to all that Jesus claims for Himself, which as we have already seen, cannot be separated from His teaching and His life as a whole: His Messianic authority. They can only be harmonized with the teaching of Jesus if we first of all denude this teaching of all its transcendental, authoritative meaning. Then we would be obliged to formulate it thus: Jesus, as a Teacher of genius, did discover, it is true, certain religious and ethical truths; He proclaimed them, and embodied them in His life. Unfortunately He did this in such a way that it is no guide for us; indeed, He did it all in a very mistaken way, since He claimed for Himself a transcendental authority which was quite unfitting, and He cast His teaching in a transcendental, authoritative form which is contrary to its timeless valid content. This, speaking roughly, is the conception of Jesus of the Liberal Theology of the nineteenth century: the eternal core is the teaching of Jesus; the temporal veil under which it is concealed is the Messianic self-consciousness of Jesus. Thus we must disregard these temporal elements and peel off the outer covering in order to reach the eterna core. But after this process of "peeling off" the outer skin has been accomplished almost nothing remains of the real teaching, and the actual historical Person of Jesus. This attempt to reach the "heart" of the mystery ends in a perversion of the truth itself Those "eternal truths" of religion are fundamentally different from the teaching of Jesus Himself which cannot be separated from the Messianic claim. This "interpretation" of Jesus is only possible so long as we do not see the vast difference between the Biblical Jesus and this rationalisti immanental theory.

The idea that Jesus was the greatest of the Prophets seems

to be far nearer to the Biblical *kerygma* and the Life of Jesus.[1] "Prophet" is a transcendent category. The prophet does not proclaim "eternal truths", but something which man could not know by his own efforts, something whose validity cannot be verified by men, a "Word" which has authority, because it has been revealed by God. Here, in place of "immanental truths", that is, something which, in principle, man has at his own disposal, is the Transcendent, which does not lie within the human sphere. In any case this is the *Biblical* view of the Prophet.

But this interpretation is diametrically opposed to the testimony of Jesus to Himself, that He is not a Prophet but "more than a prophet", and not only to His witness to Himself, but to His whole message, which is inseparable from this self-testimony. What matters is the coming of the Kingdom of God, which, in His Person, is already present, which is present because He Himself as Person possesses that authority of revelation which, in the time of the prophets, was granted to their Word. When Jesus says that He is "more than a prophet", He means that in contrast to the many prophets of the old dispensation He stands alone; He alone is the One in whom the transcendent authority of the Word is identical with that of the Person. In the following pages we shall show in what sense this is to be understood. One point, however, is plain from the outset: the conception of the Prophet, as a category for the interpretation of Jesus, is entirely ruled out.

Then there is a further point. As a rule modern theologians who speak of Jesus as a Prophet do not use the idea in the strict categorical sense of the Old Testament; to them the idea of the prophetic element is simply a way of describing what others mean by the "religious genius". Thus they do not mean the transcendent authority of the Word, but something immanent, that is, something which in principle is a human possibility. Jesus Himself, as He stands before us in the Gospels, stands upon the foundation of the revelation of the Old Testament. For Him the Prophets are not merely pioneers and sages who proclaim religious and ethical truths of an essentially immanent character, but they are the bearers of the divine Word of revelation. In the history of revelation He regards Himself, in this sense, as part of a series, in the fact that He contrasts Himself, at the same time, with the earlier

[1] Cf. Weinel, *Biblische Theologie des Neuen Testamentes*, § 37, and in R.G.G.[1], *Das Jesusbild der Gegenwart*, III, Sp. 108 ff.

prophetic revelation as the Other, as something New, namely, as the Fulfiller of their promises, as "Son" over against the "slave", as the One who has the personal authority which they lacked. This understanding of Himself cannot be separated from His teaching as a whole; we must either accept both or reject both. But what is meant by the phrase "more than a prophet"? or the "Son"? or the "Messiah"? or the Fulfiller of the promises foretold by the Prophets?

2. The Son of God, the Messiah

Henceforth it is our task to prove the meaning and the truth of our earlier thesis, that we come to know the Person of Jesus through His Work. We have seen how the first titles given to Him by the Primitive Church, which expressed what Jesus was for them, were functional in character. They all express what Jesus *does* in and for men. Jesus is the Revealer, Redeemer, and Lord. The question now is: Does this threefold description of His Work, or of His Office, contain a fundamental truth about His mysterious being as Person?

(a) *The Revealer*. The prophets are revealers of the will of God, and of God's nature, because they receive a Word of particular, transcendent revelation, a Word of God, which no human being could attain by his own efforts, and this "Word" is wholly independent of their personality. God chooses whom He will, as the instrument of His revelation. No human being, as such, is qualified to be a prophet; a prophet becomes one through something that happens, a call and an enabling from God. From time to time he receives a Word of God, which he has to proclaim with divine authority, not thanks to anything that he is, but thanks to God's free communication. The authority lies wholly in the divine communication. The Word of the prophets contains, of course, also "general ethical truth" but it is not this, but something outside this sphere of what is common to man, which makes their Word a "revealed" Word. The moral laws, as such, are also known to the heathen; the new element of special revelation is their message of judgment and of promise. The Prophets are not teachers of true morals and piety, but they are men who proclaim the will of God, until then unknown to men, as men, here and now. Hence the Prophets speak with divine authority, but with an authority which does not belong to their personality, but to the Word given to them. It really does not matter who they are; their "revelation authority" refers exclusively to the divine Word which they have received.

Jesus, as we have seen, is Revealer in another sense. His Word of revelation is inseparable from His Person, the authority or power with which He speaks is at the same time the authority of His Person. Therefore He reveals the will of God, unknown to men, as much in His actions as in His speech. What He does is as revealing as His speech; His action is just as much and in the same sense God's action as His speech is God's speech. His speech often has no other meaning than that of a commentary on His action.

His action was not—as in the immanental interpretation it is thought to be—merely the exemplary incorporation of an ethico-religious truth, which, in principle, is at man's disposal, but something which was completely new to men, something which was particularly offensive to those who revered the Law; to them it seemed blasphemous. Both His action and His speech reveal a divine mystery; indeed it is all a mystery, in so far as it points to an authority of revelation which is inherent in the Person of the Revealer. As Person He is revealing subject in His action as well as in His speech. In Him God Himself acts and speaks.

This means first of all, negatively, that in Jesus that very event which is constitutive for the Prophets, the experience of the Call, and the reception of the divine Word, is absent. In His experience there is not that characteristic glance behind his personality to the Word which alone authorizes him to utter the Word which he has received, with the preface: "Thus saith the Lord." Instead of this gesture, which points away from the personality of the prophet, He explicitly points to Himself as the source and the seat of authority: "But I say unto you". Secondly, this means, positively, the explicit declaration of why, and in what sense, He Himself, Jesus, in His Person, is the bearer of divine authority. Whereas the prophets merely foretell the coming of the Messianic Kingdom as a future event, Jesus explains this Messianic Kingdom in the sense of the personal presence of God as already "come", in His own person. Between the prophetic period and the Messianic era which has now dawned stands John the Baptist who is therefore more than all other prophets, because he is the immediate forerunner and herald of the Messiah, and yet at the same time he does not belong to the New Age, and is therefore "less" than those who are members and sharers of

the New Age.[1] But Jesus is the contemporary Messiah proclaimed by John the Baptist. Not only does the perfect revelation of God, the personal presence of God Himself "come"
"with" but "in" Jesus. In Jesus Himself, speaking and acting
in His person God Himself is present, as the Subject of this
action and this speech. The "revelation-authority" of God is
the personal authority of Jesus. The transcendence of the Word
of revelation is now the transcendence of the Person who
reveals. He Himself, Jesus, is "from above", as in the days of
the prophets, the Word came down "from above". The mystery
of the divine Nature and the divine Will becomes evident in
all that Jesus speaks, does, and is, revealed as it had never
been revealed before.

"He that hath seen Me hath seen the Father".[2] Even if
Jesus did not actually say these words, even if they only
represent a word of faith formulated by the apostle later on,
as he looked back at the Cross and the Resurrection, yet it
expresses something which *is*. In Jesus, as we gaze at Him,
we look believingly into the very Nature of the Father. We
do this when we let the life of Jesus as recorded by the
evangelists, the story of His life on earth, speak to us; we do
it still more truly when, with the Gospel of John, we see this
Life in the light of the Resurrection. Only one who knew Jesus
before His death and His Resurrection as the Revealer can
believe in the Risen Lord, but the fullness of the truth of the
unity of Jesus with God only dawns on those who believe in
Him as the Risen Lord. But only those who know Him not
only as Revealer, but also as Redeemer and Lord, know who
the Revealer is.

(b) *The Redeemer.* In Jesus Christ, in His action, teaching,
suffering and death we perceive the God who seeks the lost,
who restores communion between Himself and sinners who
were alienated from Him, and through this makes them new
creatures who know for themselves what it is to be children
of God. The unreserved self-surrender of Jesus is not only a
symbolical act, a parabolic action, as we know it in the prophets.
When Jesus enters the house of Zacchaeus as his guest something actually *happens*: "To-day is salvation come to this
house." The divine reality of this event is reflected in the act
of restitution in which the publican shows that he has really
become a different person. The Parables of the Lost Sheep and
of the Lost Son, or, rather, of the Good Shepherd and the

[1] Matt. 11: 11   [2] John 14: 9

THE PERSON OF JESUS CHRIST

Forgiving Father, are simply a commentary on what actually happens in Jesus' action, because God is working "in" Him. Jesus *is* the Good Shepherd, who seeks and saves the lost sheep; He does not merely *say* that God forgives, but He grants forgiveness; Jesus does not merely *speak* of reconciliation, He effects it, with divine authority. His whole life is the establishment of fellowship between God and man.

This reconciling action of God in the life of Jesus culminates in the sufferings and death of Jesus on the Cross. His death on the Cross is not only a parabolic suggestion of the divine reconciliation, *it is* this reconciliation, its completion, its reality. In this event, as it is grasped by faith, God passes judgment on sinful man, and proves His absolute will of love; through the Cross God makes manifest to men His holiness and His mercy; but this is only realized where men see God Himself acting in this "Mighty Act" of Jesus, who is suffering vicariously for the sins of all men. The mediatorial significance of the Cross is only understood by one who sees in it the twofold movement of divine and human action, thus only where the Mediator, the God-Man, is perceived in the Crucified. But this can only happen because Jesus' whole life already had this mediatorial significance and reality, and because, on the other hand, the Cross is illuminated by the Resurrection. Apart from the Resurrection Christ's death on the Cross is a catastrophe, not a saving fact. The faith of the disciples in the Messiah was shaken by the crucifixion, until the appearance of the Risen Lord gave them back their faith in Christ, and at the same time fulfilled it. Then they were able to say, "God was in Christ, reconciling the world unto Himself", and this confession of faith fulfilled what they had already seen in the life of the Lord as the divine activity of the Saviour.

The disciples may have first begun to see in Him the divine power of reconciliation when they saw Jesus, on His own authority, forgiving the sins of a man, while those who were looking on protested that this was "blasphemy". Here there was a clear choice: *Either* this act was an act of blasphemy, *or* Jesus was acting with personal divine authority. As they saw His Work they began to understand the mystery of His Person. A person can only act like this who is not like us, sinful, needing forgiveness: he must be One who comes to us "from the other side" with authority to forgive. The disciples' understanding of Jesus' own words about His sacrificial surrender was, however, so limited and imperfect that they could not bear

Him to speak about the suffering He *must* endure in order to complete God's work.[1] Peter had confessed Him as the Messiah, as the Son of God; but only after the Resurrection of the Crucified Lord did the disciples understand the Messiah as the Suffering Servant of the Lord.

But if Jesus is only a man, then His death on the Cross, and indeed His whole life, has no reconciling significance, and "we are yet in our sins".[2] If Jesus is only a man, then His word of forgiveness has no value for us. No *man* can know whether God forgives. Either Jesus could say this in virtue of a prophetic revelation, or He could say it because He Himself knew it, because He Himself came to us out of the mystery of the Father. Jesus' whole life, which is fulfilled in His Passion and Death and does not merely *end* there, is full of the authority of Him, who, in the very authority and power of God, not only proclaimed reconciliation but accomplished it, and His resurrection, moreover, revealed His divine power of reconciliation. To know this, and thus to know the action and sufferings of Jesus as God's reconciling Act, means to believe in Jesus, the God-Man.

3. *Jesus the Lord*

Here indeed, where we are concerned with the origins of the Christian Faith, this third point should really come first. Not only for the disciples, but also for us to-day, probably the first awareness of a superhuman mystery in the Person of Jesus is connected with the perception of His authority as Lord. When this Man confronts us, we know we are confronting One possessing absolute authority. It is not merely the authority which attaches to His Speech, to His word, but to His Person. In Him there meets us One who is "Our Lord", One whom we cannot evade, in whose Presence self-assertion is impossible. It is thus that Jesus describes Himself in the Parable of the Wicked Husbandmen: as the Master's Son, the Heir, who challenges the tenants' will to mastery and independence far more strongly than those other "servants" who had previously been sent to them.

His personal authority as Lord, which inheres in His Person, is so indissolubly connected with His relation to the Sovereignty of God that we may say they are identical. As He proclaims the royal sovereignty of God so it is present in His Person. Here Being and Message are one. He *is* what He preaches, and

[1] Matt. 16: 22   [2] I Cor. 15: 17

He *preaches* what He Himself is: the Presence of God as Lord, in Person. It was this which made the disciples obey His call; they felt: "we must obey this man as we must obey God". Above all this will to obedience which His Person awakened was not an obedience in fear but an obedience in trust, ὑπακοή πίστεως. He is Lord, as God is Lord; He is Lord in a quite different way from that in which men are "lords" and "masters". The new element in His "Lordship" is not only its absolute character, but the security it gives to His obedient disciples. As Lord, He not only demands obedience, but He gives to His followers a share in the blessedness (or salvation) of the Messianic future.

The disciples, however, only learned very slowly how very different this Kingship of Jesus was from human royalty, because it was God's Lordship. Since Jesus not only summoned them to obedience, but *made* them obedient servants, they experienced the divine "otherness" of His sovereignty, that kind which the Fourth Gospel expresses with the one word "friends".[1] The message of the Kingdom of God is Good News, and this Kingdom which makes men glad is that which the disciples experienced every day. But it is plain that at first they were very slow indeed to realize fully the "otherness" of His Kingship. In the Fourth Gospel, when Peter refuses to allow Jesus to wash his feet this is a sign of this misunderstanding.[2] Therefore the death of Jesus on the Cross was at first for them an "offence", which shook their faith in the Messianic Lord, almost to the verge of despair. And again, it was the encounter with the Risen Lord, which once more, and moreover in new depth and wonder, drew from their lips the confession: "*Kyrios* Jesus!" Only now could they understand Jesus fully as the divine Lord, as Him who "sits at the right hand of God", to whom is given "all authority in heaven and on earth". Here too the reverse is true: only when they understood Him as this absolute Lord, to whom the full divine sovereignty belongs, did Easter as victory, and Good Friday as a saving Fact, become intelligible. Only when they knew Jesus as the present Heavenly Lord, did they know themselves to be sharers in the Messianic Kingdom as men of the new, the Messianic era.[3]

Is Jesus the Lord? Can we call Him, in the full sense of the word, "our Lord"? Can we speak of His "absolute authority"? If we say "yes" in answer to these questions this "yes" expresses

[1] John 15: 15   [2] John 13   [3] 1 Pet. 2: 9

our confession of faith in this Man who is more than man, who comes to us "from the other side" and confronts us, as God alone can confront us. There is only one *Kyrios* who has absolute authority, only One before whom we can and must bow in absolute obedience. It is the marvel of revelation that we shall never understand, that this authority which is the authority of God, meets us in a human being. That indeed is the meaning of the expression the "God-Man". If anyone can express it better, let him do so. The word does not matter, but everything that does matter lies in the knowledge that here is "Emmanuel", the God-with-us, the God who has chosen to meet us not only in His Word, but in a Person of supernatural authority and power.

In His revealing, reconciling, redeeming, and royal work we feel compelled to express the mystery of His divine Person. Because He reveals God to us, as no human being could reveal Him, because He reconciles us to God, as no human being could reconcile us to God, because He makes us trustful servants of God, as no human being could do, we know that we must confess Him to be the *God-Man*, we must confess Him as the One who is not only True Man, but at the same time—whether we understand it or not—True God.

4. *The Eternal Godhead of the Son*

"And finally to Jesus as to a God . . ." Beginning with the Man Jesus, in the Man Jesus perceiving the Christ and His royal authority, finally through faith we are impelled to believe in Jesus as the Son of God from all eternity. This is the way of knowledge which lies before us plainly in the testimony of the New Testament. The earliest testimonies of primitive Christian faith do not yet say anything about the eternal pre-existent Son of God. The early letters of Paul are confined to the confession of the Risen Lord, and their main theme is the work of the Redeemer. It is only the later Epistles which, with some clearness, show the background of this work of salvation, the fact that Jesus is the Eternal Son of God, but even they do so in such a way that the historic work of salvation is still in the foreground of interest. The eternal Sonship of Christ only becomes the main theme of the Christian message in the Gospel of John. This way of primitive Christian knowledge is also the way of every individual Christian, and therefore too the way marked out for dogmatic Christology: from the historical foreground to the "super-historical" background. Only thus does living personal Christian faith arise.

The Church, however, in its formation of dogma, and in its doctrinal practice, very soon took the opposite line, which is not the way of knowledge but the way of logical order. If Jesus really is the eternal Son of God, why not begin there? And end with the Incarnation and the Humanity of Jesus? We certainly cannot say that this second way is wrong. But we must certainly point out that this line has its own particular dangers, and that historically it has been, to some extent at least, influenced by a mistaken view of "faith". It is evident, that where "faith" is understood as belief in an authoritative doctrine, this second, deductive line seems the best. The Church knows who Christ is; it already stands at the end of this path, in the Jesus of History it sees the Son of God who has become Man. It has to communicate this knowledge to men, above all to those who were baptized as children, and therefore without faith already belong to the Church, and these children must believe that this doctrine is divinely revealed. Here the question, "How then does faith in Jesus as the Christ arise?" is never raised. Faith amounts to no more than the obedient acceptance of what the Church teaches.[1] It "arises" through submission to the doctrinal authority of the Church.

The situation is not essentially different, where instead of the authority of the Church there is the authority of the Bible. The question, how then does faith in Jesus as the Christ arise? is here answered by saying that the Bible teaches us that Jesus is the Christ, the Son of God become Man, and that we have to submit to the authority of the Scriptures. We believe in Jesus the Eternal Son of God, because the Bible testifies that this is who He is. We believe in Jesus because we first of all believe in the Bible. Faith in the Bible, as Johann Gerhard puts it, is not an article of faith, but a principle, that is, an "axiomatic presupposition of all the articles of faith".[2] The authority of the Bible precedes the authority of Jesus. Like everything else we must believe, we have to believe in the divinity of Christ, because the Scriptures—among other things—also teach the Godhead of Christ. There is no essential difference between the Catholic and the orthodox Protestant conception of faith; they are both types of authoritative doctrinal faith.

[1] *Credendum proponit* . . . (in the statements of the Vatican Council, *Denzinger*, 1792)
[2] *Loci theologici*, I, 9

But if we understand faith in the New Testament sense as "meeting" (or encounter) it rules out this other conception of faith. According to the Biblical conception of faith we believe in Jesus as the Christ not because it is taught to us by the Church or in the Bible, but because He, Jesus, the Christ, meets us as the true Word of God in the witness of the Scriptures. We do not believe in Jesus the Son of God because the Bible teaches this, but we believe in the Bible because, and in so far as, through it we have come to know Jesus as the Christ. The Bible is not the authority, on the basis of which we believe in Christ, but the Bible is the means, which shows us and gives us the Christ. We cannot believe in Jesus the Christ without the Bible; but we should not believe in Jesus the Son of God *because* the Bible says so. Because, and in so far as, the Bible communicates Christ to us, it is the Word of God, and it has a share in the authority of Jesus Christ. But it is never the axiomatic basis of our Christian Faith. This situation *must* not, it is true, be obscured by a doctrine about Jesus Christ which begins at the top instead of at the bottom, but this *may* very easily happen. The way that God Himself has shown us in the New Testament is the opposite, the way that God has taken with men, in that He allowed His Son to become Man. The disciples of Jesus did not believe in Him on account of any doctrine that Jesus was the Christ. Because God, through His Spirit, opened their eyes, they "discovered" Jesus as the Christ. After they had discovered the Son of God in Jesus Christ the Lord, gradually they also came to see what lay "behind" or "in" this knowledge of Jesus: that He who is really the Messiah, the Son of God, the Lord and the Redeemer, is the God-Man, who can only be this because He is the Eternal Son. That is the reason why the doctrine of the Eternal Son of God and its testimonies come last, in the Gospel of John. Henceforth we ourselves have to follow this way which the Apostles also followed to the end. We must now consider why this way *must* lead to this end.

We begin at the point where our previous course of reflection ended: In Jesus we meet Him who is endowed in His Person with the divine authority of revelation, with reconciling redeeming power and with divine Lordship. Jesus is the Man in whom God Himself meets us as the One who reveals Himself, as the Reconciler, and as the Lord, personally present. That disturbing mystery of the Person of Jesus which even unbelievers feel, becomes evident to faith as the mystery of the unity of the divine and the human Subject in the action and speech, in the suffering and in the death of Jesus. "God was in Christ, reconciling the world unto Himself."

But what does this mean: *God was in Christ?*[1] The Early Church was not clear about the exact meaning of this confession from the very beginning. The view which was known later on as Adoptionism,[2] and was rejected by the Church, was probably not actively ruled out from the outset. We cannot be sure whether the Gospel narratives of the Baptism of Jesus, of His Transfiguration, and finally of His Resurrection, were coloured by later Adoptionist doctrine. According to this view Jesus would have been at first a ψιλὸς ἄνθρωπος, an ordinary (or "bare") man, who, at His Baptism, was filled with the Holy Spirit to an extraordinary degree, and was appointed to be Son of God, or, it was only at the Resurrection that He became the Son of God, who sits at the right hand of God, and thus has a share in His glory. The Messianic Psalm 110, in which it is said explicitly: "Thou art My Son, to-day have I begotten thee," might at first sight seem to favour such a conception. For the phrase "to-day—begotten"—meant—and from the beginning there was no doubt about this—not a kind of divine-physical conception, but the appointment of a human being to the dignity of the Messiah and Son of God Whether this conception was present in the Primitive Church or not, we cannot decide; we can only say for certain that it does not come out plainly in the Scriptures, as it did later on in the second century in the form of Adoptionism.

In any case those words at the beginning of the Epistle to the Romans might be thought to support such a conception: "Concerning His Son, who was born of the seed of David according to the flesh, who was declared to be the Son of God with power, according to the Spirit of Holiness, by the resurrection of the dead . . ."[3] Literally this would not be impossible, but it would not harmonize with the rest of the statements of the Apostle, both in his earlier and his later writings. Not only the Epistles to the Philippians and to the Colossians, but even the first Epistle to the Corinthians contain statements about the eternal Son of God[4] which cannot be reconciled with any Adoptionist view of that kind. But why is this, actually, in itself, impossible?

[1] Cf. the excellent book by Dr. D. M. Baillie, *God was in Christ*
[2] Or Dynamic Monarchianism (Tr.)
[3] Rom. 1: 3 ff.
[4] I Cor. 8: 6

So far as the argument just quoted is concerned, based on the experience of Jesus at His Baptism, it places Him on a level with the Old Testament prophets. If this were correct, then the basis of His authority would be the experience of a "call". But in that case His authority would not be that of His Person, but merely that of a special divine inspiration. In that case Jesus would not differ from the Prophets in principle, but only in degree. Thus this conception contradicts what we found to be the result of our reflection on the Messianic authority of Jesus: that its distinctive characteristic, in contrast to that of the prophets, consists precisely in that union of "person" and "authority", and not in that of a "call" and the inspiration which this involves. Adoptionist Christology contradicts the historical facts.

If possible, however, the variant of Adoptionist doctrine based upon the Resurrection goes still further astray, based as it is supposed to be on the passage just quoted from the Epistle to the Romans. If Jesus only *becomes* the Son of God through the Resurrection, then the unity of His Messianic activity before and after the Resurrection is severed. Then what was Jesus before the Resurrection? What was the basis of His authority which He exerted and possessed before His death, during His whole historical ministry? Logically, we would have to say: previously He had no authority, or at the most, His authority was only that of a prophet: that means, not a personal authority but simply that of the message entrusted to Him. But the facts are too much for this theory. Thus Luther's translation of the passage in Romans "mightily proved to be a Son of God" is apt, even if literally it is impossible, yet it is actually correct, and it agrees with Paul's other Christological statements. Thus the Church was right in rejecting Adoptionism as an explanation of the mystery of the Person of Jesus.

The Church, however, had to fight against another alternative in the form of Sabellianism, which it fought and rejected. In Sabellianism, it is true, the statement that "God was in Christ" was accepted in the full sense of the divine authority, but the difference between God the Father and God the Son was ignored—if the Sabellians really taught what the Church said they did; but we have not enough to go upon to be sure of this. The fact that we only know Monarchianism "through its enemies should never be forgotten" (Loofs).[1] Here we must

[1] Loofs, *Dogmengeschichte*, p. 187

say first of all that the witness of the New Testament is diametrically opposed to such a "Patripassian" understanding of Jesus. It is true that there is a Pauline passage (the one which we have already frequently quoted from the Second Epistle to the Corinthians): "God was in Christ", which could be interpreted in a Sabellian sense; if isolated from the context of Pauline doctrine it could be expounded along these lines. But, after all, the New Testament as a whole, as well as the Pauline doctrine, leaves no room for the Sabellian interpretation of the mystery of the Person of Jesus. Jesus is always, and quite definitely, designated, not only in His historical existence, but also in His pre-existence, as the Son of God and set over against the Father. A sentence like that of Thomas in the Gospel of John, "My Lord and My God!"[1] is an absolute exception in the New Testament, although in the Gospel of John of course its meaning is not Sabellian. The Gospel of John as a whole is the witness to the Eternal Son of God.

We must now examine the actual argument against this Sabellian interpretation, and ask why it is impossible to combine it with the doctrine of the Apostles? Why, and in what sense, is the authority of Jesus that of the *Son* of God, and not that of "God" absolutely, thus not that of the Father? Why do the Apostles—even when they are not speaking of the historical man Jesus, but of the supra-historical eternal subject of revelation—speak of the "Son", and not simply of "God"? It would, of course, be too easy to reply: because the Son always differentiates Himself from the Father. For we might answer: this applies only to the historical personality of Jesus, but it proves nothing in favour of the acceptance of an eternal Son. Certainly, Jesus the man of prayer, stands over against the Father, certainly He makes a distinction between His knowledge of the divine mystery and that of the Father, certainly as the Son He subordinates Himself to the Father; but all that, we might say, is indeed true of the God-Man, and is natural for Him. But it is not true of the divine authority present in this historical man, of "God in Christ". Why must He too be distinguished from God the Father?

The objection to the Sabellian doctrine is this: that it separates the personal being of Jesus and His Godhead from one another, so that only as Man would He be person, whereas as *God* His being would become that of impersonal divinity. The mystery of Jesus is this: that as the Person whom we know

[1] John 20: 28

historically, He has divine authority, so that His being as Person and His divinity are one. His personal being does not belong to the flesh which He assumed, but it is precisely His personal being which is identical with His divine authority, to reveal, to reconcile, and to rule. Precisely in His *relation* to the Father is He Revealer, Reconciler, and Lord.[1] We can therefore well understand the horror which the Patripassian heresy aroused in the Church. The Son is the revealer of the Father, as the Son. His Eternal Sonship derived from the Father, identical with His authority, is the revelation of the Father.

He who knows the Jesus of History from His work as Revealer, Redeemer, and Lord, cannot doubt, that the Son is indeed the One who reveals the Father, but not the Father whom he reveals, and that precisely in that in which, *as the Son*, He reveals the Father, in His personal being He has divine authority.

Can we then speak of the Godhead" of Jesus? Are we allowed, are we obliged, to take the step from the historical into the supra-historical, and to speak of the Eternal Son of God? We have already seen how reluctantly this assertion, this doctrine of the pre-existent Son of God emerges in the New Testament. Should this step, perhaps, after all, never have been taken? First of all, we can answer this question indirectly: if we do not dare to make this assertion, what other possibility is there save Adoptionism, since Sabellianism, for another reason, is impossible? But Adoptionism, like Sabellianism, only in another way, destroys the unity of "revelation-authority" and the Person. We have therefore already rejected it as an impossible interpretation of the mystery of the Person of Jesus. Thus all that remains is the possibility provided by the witness of the New Testament.

But this indirect argument, however correct, is not satisfactory. We hold firmly to this truth: that in His being as Person Jesus has divine authority, that is, true, transcendental authority, which is not given to Him as in the experience of the Call of a prophet, but is inherent in His Person, and is identical with it. If this be so, how can we evade the further truth that this Personal being of Jesus, as truly divine, like God Himself, is from eternity? Is Jesus really the Son of God? and not merely a particular kind of prophet? then from all eternity He is "the Son", even if from all eternity

[1] This is the theme of John 17

He is not the Son in human form. Once this step has been taken, two further points emerge: the pre-existence of the Son, and the Incarnation of the Son. Or can there be a third possibility?

After both the Adoptionist and Sabellian misunderstandings had been rejected, another interpretation of the mystery of the Person of Jesus arose, which the Church regarded as the most dangerous of all Christological misinterpretations, and rejected as arch-heresy: Arianism. This claims: that if the Son be identical with the Jesus of History, and, as such, is distinguished from the Father, then He may be "divine", but not in the sense in which the Father is Divine, for though He may be greater than the Angels, He is not really "God". Arianism no longer asks whether the Son of God as Person has an existence beyond the sphere of history; but it maintains that this pre-existent Son is not "true God", that although He is very great and much more than man, "there was when He was not"—in other words, He is a "created Being" and therefore not "True God".

In spite of the unanimous condemnation of Arianism by all the great Fathers of the Church—and not only in the early days of the Church but also by the Reformers—we cannot reject it without having examined it more carefully. This obligation is all the more urgent since this heresy appeals to many passages of Scripture in support of its theory. These are all passages which teach a subordination of the Son to the Father, and indeed suggest that the Son arose out of the Father. The Biblical witness to the subjection of the Son, and thus of "subordination" as the traditional idea is called, is clear and unambiguous. The Son is from the Father; He has received what He has and what He is from the Father. Yes, even according to the classical doctrine of the Church there is a relation of subordination. *Pater est fons totius trinitatis.* The Son is from the Father, but the Father is not from the Son. The Church, however, provides against Arian "Subordinationism" by the distinction: not created, but begotten, not a creature, but God from all eternity, of the very Nature of God. This actually exposes the heart of the Arian heresy.

The ecclesiastical rejection of this doctrine is therefore justified and necessary, because Arianism posits a created being, the Son, who is divine, and because it implies a divine Being whose divinity is not genuine, but who is only partially divine, a semi-divine being, mid-way between the creature and God. This, however, is simply the fundamental idea of all paganism: the deification of creatures, continuity between God and the creation, the semi-divine, a transcendence which is not genuine transcendence. The Son may be "divine", but He is not God; He may stand over against us men as One who comes to us from "the other side", from "above", but He comes from a higher region which is not God. Thus since we men meet the Son in Jesus, we do not really meet God, but an "interim-being", who comes "from above", it is true, but is a "creature" just as we are.

It is very interesting to note the arguments used by the anti-Arian Fathers of the Church to controvert the doctrine of their opponent. Naturally the proof from Scripture plays the leading part. But since Arius also appeals to Scripture, the proof from Scripture is not sufficient. They use arguments drawn from the subject itself, and these are practically entirely drawn from the truth of the Work of Christ. Since God Himself alone can reveal God, the Revealer must be God. How could a creature, even if it were semi-divine, be able to reveal the true God through its Being?[1] God alone can reconcile the sinful creature with Himself. If the act and the sufferings of Jesus are really revelation and reconciliation, then it can only be the acts and the sufferings of God Himself. If Jesus be really Lord, there can be no other being between Him and God. If, as the Church has done from the beginning, we really may invoke Him as "Lord", then He must be "God", in the full sense of the word; for to call upon any other than God in prayer would be to worship idols.

With this retrospective glance at the Work of Christ, with the early doctors of the Church, we have reached the primitive Christian, New Testament line of thought and belief. If Jesus be the Revealer, in a different sense from that of the prophets, that is, not merely in His Word, but in His being, in His Person, then He must be God. If Jesus be really Reconciler and Lord, then He is God. Faith knows that this is what He is. "God was in Christ, reconciling the world unto Himself." And this divine existence, this truly revealing, truly reconciling, and truly ruling force, is not an impersonal Word, given by God, a power inspired by God, but it is the Person of Jesus Himself. This is

[1] "Such restoration cannot be effected by any creature, but only by Him who as Man is at the same time essentially one with God. Only God can unite creature with creature" (Athanasius, *C. Ar.*, I, 43)

the very heart of the truth of Jesus as the Christ, that in Him God really meets us, and that this meeting with God is itself based upon the personal being of Jesus, and is one with Him. Jesus is the One in whom God meets us personally—not impersonally.

That is why the Apostles were impelled to go beyond the sphere of history. Jesus can only be the true Revealer, Reconciler, and Lord, if He is "from above", from the sphere of true transcendence, from the un-created sphere, from God, and this transcendence, this absolute authority is vested in His Person. Hence this Person, in spite of the fact that He meets us as a human person, is at the same time divine Person, the Son from all eternity, the "Son of the same substance with the Father", and yet distinct from the Father. This is what John teaches, and this is also, though less explicitly, what Paul teaches, and this doctrine of theirs only expresses what was already—although not then explicit, and therefore scarcely conscious—implicit in the very earliest confession of faith: Jesus, the Messiah, the Son of God, the Lord.

But there is still something more to be said. The aim of this doctrine is not that it may solve the mystery of Jesus. We know that when we confess Him as the God-Man, and must so confess Him, we are saying something which goes far beyond anything we can understand. We have no right to claim that we have *explained* the mystery of the Person of Jesus. Indeed this *is* the mystery of Jesus, of the Man whom we meet in the pages of the Gospels, that in Him we meet *the* Man in whom God Himself meets us. Why then cannot we stop there, and simply accept the divine-human *mystery*? What gives us the right to go further than that which is actually given on the plane of history, and to speak of the eternal Son? There are two things to be said in answer to this question. First of all, in saying this we are not going beyond what has been given in History, for the story of the Resurrection is part of the story of Jesus. It belongs to it just as much as the Messianic character of Jesus, the truly divine authority of Jesus, which can be discerned by faith alone. This is what happens when we believe in the Jesus of History: in Him we meet the One who "has come", who comes from "beyond" this world, and we experience His revealing, reconciling influence and His power as Lord, in exactly the same way as that in which we recognize Him as the One who comes from "beyond".

We have no words to express what we mean by all these references to the "beyond" and to "coming from beyond". But we know that when we use these expressions we are simply stammering. But—and this is the second point—not all our stammering attempts to express something of the truth we see in this question, are of equal value. There *are* attempts to understand the mystery of the Person of Jesus, which contradict its very meaning, and there are others, which, although they are inadequate, do not contradict the subject itself, but—at least for us—they do express it adequately. We must say it precisely in this way if we are to express it aright, and yet we know that whatever we say, we are stammering about a mystery which we can never fathom. We must say it, however, and we must say it in this way, because if we do not do so, something else will be said which is quite wrong. That is why the Apostles, after a period when the simplest creed seemed to suffice—Jesus the Messiah, Jesus the Lord, Jesus the Son of God—had to go further, and had to make fuller theological definitions in order to prevent these very expressions from being misunderstood. The distinctive element in the apostolic language about the Divine Son is this: that it never—as was the case in later periods of the development of doctrine in the Church—was regarded as an isolated doctrine, but always as one which was in direct and immediate connexion with the Work of Jesus, with the salvation given us in Him, with the revelation, reconciliation and royal Lordship of God. Christological doctrine in the narrower sense, the doctrine of the Person of Jesus, is also "truth as encounter".

(C) THE INCARNATION OF THE ETERNAL SON OF GOD

The truth that the Eternal Son of God meets us in the Man, Jesus, necessarily leads to the doctrine of the Incarnation of the Son of God. This doctrine, however, is also directly connected with what Jesus says about Himself. He speaks of His own Coming in a way which no prophet has ever done: "I am come", He says, "to call sinners to repentance."[1] The Son of Man "is come" not to be ministered unto but to minister.[2] No prophet ever said that *he* had "come"; he says that the Word of God has "come" to him; by this he means the divine transcendence, which is from "above", the sphere

---

[1] Matt. 9: 13
[2] Matt. 20: 28; cf. Matt. 5: 17, 10: 34, 18: 11

which lies beyond all human possibilities, the divine world, God Himself. The fact that "God comes" is one of the fundamental facts of the Biblical revelation. This revelation deals always and everywhere with God's coming to man, and is in harmony with the idea of the "coming" Kingdom of God. The Kingdom of God, the Rule of God, is not at first "present", because men are living in separation from God, in sin. The coming of the Kingdom of God is the coming of the self-revelation and sovereignty of God, and of the redemption of man. Therefore the Promise proclaimed by the Prophets culminates in the announcement of the Messiah, in whom alone God's saving presence culminates as the dwelling of God with His people: "I will be your God and ye shall be My people"— "I am with you", "Emmanuel".

Thus the fact that Jesus speaks of Himself as "having come", and as One who "will come", is in accordance with His message, that in Him the Kingdom of God has already "come"—although in its open glory it will only be present when the Son of Man shall come again in His glory. That is Jesus' own testimony, which is historically tangible. According to the Synoptists He does not say more than this. His reserve on this point corresponds to His reserve in everything that concerns His Messianic authority. He suggests only as much as is necessary in order that men may know Him to be the true Revealer, Lord and Reconciler, so far as that is possible before the end of His life on earth, and before His Resurrection. But not only Jesus Himself, but also His Apostles, do not say much about the Incarnation. The passage in the Epistle to the Romans, "God sending His own Son in the likeness of sinful flesh";[1] the passage in the Second Epistle to the Corinthians (which possibly should not be expounded in the same sense) "Ye know the grace of our Lord Jesus Christ, that though He was rich, yet for your sake, He became poor, that ye through His poverty might become rich",[2] and the two *loci classici* of the Epistle to the Philippians[3] and of the Prologue to the Fourth Gospel[4] are the sole testimonies. None of them says anything about "how" the Incarnation took place: they simply witness to the fact of the Incarnation.

This might serve as a hint to the theologian not to want to know too much about "how" these things can be, and to abandon all subtle considerations and distinctions. It will be sufficient for us to say that the order of knowledge—that in

[1] Rom. 8: 3   [2] 2 Cor. 8: 9   [3] Phil. 2: 6   [4] John 1: 14

the historical Revealer, we know the Eternal Son of God—
corresponds to an order of being, which goes in the opposite
direction: that the Eternal Son became man, that He who is
from everlasting entered into human history, that it is precisely
this entrance into history which constitutes the basis of His
threefold work. All that goes further than this is useless speculation. On the other hand, we must deal in greater detail with a
New Testament tradition which seems to be concerned with
the question: *How* did the Incarnation take place? I mean
the question of the so-called "Virgin Birth" of Jesus, which
some theologians, and above all certain ecclesiastical circles,
regard as a central doctrine of the Christian Faith.

The two introductory narratives of the life of Jesus in
Matthew[1] and Luke[2] go further than the other four Bible
passages which have been mentioned, in this, that in contrast
to them, they deal with the way in which the divine-human
Person came into the world. But this does not mean that they
throw any light on the Incarnation of the Eternal Son. As a
rule we do not notice that these passages *do not* refer to the
Incarnation of the Eternal Son, but that they deal with the
origin of the Person of Jesus Christ. When the doctrine of the
Incarnation of the Eternal Son of God was read into these two
Synoptic introductory narratives, this was itself an attempt on
the part of the Church to "harmonize" its doctrines; as if this
part of the Gospel record were only concerned to explain *how*
the Eternal Son of God could become *man*. These early chapters
of the Gospels of Matthew and Luke do not mention an Eternal
Son of God, who became Man; they simply tell us how the Son
of God, Jesus Christ, was begotten.

The doctrine of the Incarnation of the Eternal Son of God
in Paul and John, and the doctrine of the conception of Jesus
through the Holy Spirit, in the womb of the Virgin Mary, are
two independent parallel attempts to interpret the mystery of
Jesus. Whether they can be combined with one another, is at
least an open question. At first in any case, so far as the literal
meaning of the passages is concerned, they present two different
conceptions of the relation of the divine-human Person to
historical existence. Luke and Matthew still know nothing of
an Eternal Son; the starting-point of their narrative is that
stage in the growth of Christology in which the thought of
the "Eternal Son" and of the "Incarnation" had not yet
become explicit. But they were evidently already aware of the

[1] Matt. 1: 18 ff.   [2] Luke 1: 26 ff.

necessity to say something about the origin of the Son of God, Christ Jesus. Their idea of a parthenogenesis is an attempt to answer this question of "whence", and an attempt to interpret the "I am come" of Jesus. Their answer amounts to this: Jesus the Son of God—whom the Church confesses as Lord—has "come", through the fact that without a human father, He was begotten of God in the womb of the Virgin Mary, through the operation of the Holy Spirit. This is all that both Evangelists say. They do not say that this is the way in which the Eternal Son became Man. On the contrary, if we take their record literally, it excludes the pre-temporal existence of a Son of God who at a definite point in time became Man. The view of a parthenogenesis, presented in the narratives of Matthew and Luke, deals with the fact of how the Son of God came into existence—and with nothing else at all. It certainly does not deal with the doctrine of the *assumptio carnis Verbi aeterni* introduced by orthodox theology later on, in order to make the doctrine of the Incarnation of the Son of God agree with the doctrine of the Virgin Birth. The doctrine of Matthew and Luke is an alternative to the doctrine of the Eternal Son of God and of the Incarnation, not a more exact formulation of the doctrine of the Incarnation. Of course, as the theology of the Church has done for centuries, we can interpret the narratives of Matthew and Luke in such a way that their statement can be brought into harmony with that of the Gospel of John; but apart from this re-interpretation there is a clear contradiction. It is therefore not wholly improbable that the Johannine Prologue was deliberately placed where it is, in opposition to the doctrine of the Virgin Birth.

If it be true that Matthew and Luke are simply dealing with the question: how did the Person of the Redeemer come into existence? and not with the Incarnation of the Eternal Son of God, this is a Christological view which the Church cannot accept. In point of fact, the Church never *has* accepted this view, but it has re-interpreted it in a sense which alone could make it acceptable. The idea that Jesus Christ as Person was "procreated" (*erzeugt*) is an idea which belongs to the sphere of Arian thought. If the expression "generated" (*gezeugt*) does not sound Arian but Athanasian, it is an illusion. According to Matthew and Luke Jesus Christ was created in time through procreation in the womb of the Virgin. That is the theological content of the narratives of the parthenogenesis literally understood. Is it allowable to expound them in such a way that "procreation" does not mean creation in time, but *assumptio carnis?*

One thing cannot be gainsaid: The Apostles never mention the Virgin Birth. In the preaching of the Apostles, in the preaching of Paul and of John, as well as of the other writers of the New Testament, this idea does not play even a small part—it plays no part at all. Thus the doctrine of the Virgin Birth does not belong to the *Kerygma* of the Church of the New Testament, for which we have documentary evidence. When the Apostles preach and teach about Jesus the Son of God, they never even mention the Virgin Birth. Thus we must assume, either, that the Apostles were unaware of this view, or, that they considered it unimportant, or even mistaken. It can scarcely be thought that if Paul had known it and accepted it, he would have expressed himself as he does in Romans I: 3: "born of the seed of David according to the flesh". It is highly improbable that he who wrote the Prologue to the Fourth Gospel, concerning the Incarnation of the Son of God, would not have mentioned that idea, if he had known or accepted this view. Whether he does not mention it because he does not know it, or because, although he knows it, he does not accept it, we cannot be certain, although the fact that in the Gospel of John Jesus is several times called the son of Joseph[1] seems to suggest that the latter rather than the former is the most probable answer.

The fact that the doctrine of the Virgin Birth of Jesus[2] was either unknown or ignored by the leading thinkers in the Church of the New Testament, that in any case it plays no part in the teaching of the Apostles, not even the minutest, is in strange contrast to the other fact, that through its inclusion in the so-called "Apostles'" Creed it became part of the doctrinal norm of the Church, and from then onwards was regarded as part of the message and doctrine of the Church, and thus was taken for granted.

On the other hand, the view which is often suggested, that the doctrine of the Virgin Birth is a special protection for the central doctrine of the New Testament, the doctrine of the Incarnation, is obviously wrong. All the Christological heresies,

---

[1] John I: 45, 6: 42
[2] When Schlatter, *op. cit.*, calls the word "parthenogenesis" "childish", because what is concerned is not the Virgin Mother but God's "Mighty Act", he misses the point. Everyone who believes in the Incarnate Son of God believes in the wonder of the Birth of Jesus; the question here is: is it necessary that this "wonderful" Birth of Jesus should be the *Virgin* Birth?

even the Adoptionism of a man like Paul of Samosata, and Arianism, accepted this tenet; it was no protection against any of these errors—even those heresies which rejected the divinity of Christ believed in the Virgin Birth. Hence there is no justification for making it the criterion of true faith in the divinity of Christ—as is the case with a certain type of Fundamentalism. We cannot believe in the divinity of Jesus, as the Eternal Son of God, on account of, but only in spite of, the doctrine of the Virgin Birth, as it is recorded in the Gospels of Matthew and Luke.

Not only is there considerable tension between it and the doctrine of the Incarnation of the Son of God, but also between it and the doctrine of the true Humanity of our Lord. Is a man who is born without a human father a "true man"? Does he not lack the most essential thing for a human being, the fact that he has been born in exactly the same way as we all are? There is a strongly docetic trait in this idea, and a negative valuation of sex procreation as such, which is more in accordance with a Hellenistic ascetic view, than with that of the Biblical doctrine of Creation. It has therefore frequently served to strengthen ascetic anti-sex tendencies, quite apart from the fact that it has become a main support of Mariolatry, which is so entirely foreign to the Bible.[1]

But what do all these *a posteriori* considerations mean if the Virgin Birth is, after all, an historical fact? If it is, then it must come from the Mother of Jesus, who alone could know whether her Son had been born without a human husband or not. That, too, is what the two Evangelists record. The historical credibility of this narrative, however, is not such that of itself theological misgivings would be silenced. Although we cannot say absolutely that the narrative of both Synoptists is evidently non-historical, yet we must admit that the historical basis is uncertain. The genealogies of Jesus which point to forbears on the male side, the incidents (which cannot have been invented) which show the attitude of His family to Jesus,[2] the silence of all other Biblical witnesses, the probability of the influence of the mistaken translation of Isa. 7 in the Septuagint, the Pauline phrase "born of the seed of David according to

[1] When K. Barth, *K.D.*, I, 2, p. 200, quotes with approval Berdyaev's criticism of my rejection of the Virgin Birth, he has forgotten to add the continuation of the passage by B. where it becomes plain that Berdyaev's passionate rejection of my view is due to the fact that it destroys the foundation of the worship of the Virgin, of Mariolatry
[2] Mark 3: 21

the flesh", the fact that this incident occurs exclusively in the two introductory sections of the Gospels which contain legendary features to a larger extent than anywhere else in the New Testament, the absence of this tradition from the Gospels of Mark and of John—all these negative indications are significant for a historical judgment, and they make it difficult for the conscientious historian to maintain the historical credibility of this tradition.[1] We have no right to say, however, that on account of the historical credibility of the story all theological misgivings disappear. Once more: We believe in the divinity of Jesus and in the Incarnation of the Eternal Son of God, in spite of Matthew 1 and Luke 1, but *not* because of these two passages. Therefore we have no occasion to re-interpret these two passages in order to make them agree with the doctrine of the Eternal Son of God and of His Incarnation.

The great, unthinkable, unimaginable miracle of the Incarnation which the Apostles proclaim, is not that the Son of God was born as the son of a virgin, but that the Eternal Son of God, who from all eternity was in the bosom of the Father, uncreated, Himself proceeding from the Being of God Himself, became Man; that He, the eternal and personal Word of God, meets us in Jesus Christ as man, of our flesh and blood, as our Lord, who in His existence manifests to us the Being of His Father, and as the Redeemer, in whom we have reconciliation and free access to God and are true sons of God, if we believe in Him. In spite of this, it cannot be denied that the idea of parthenogenesis does express an important religious idea: Jesus IS "by nature" God, He receives His divine authority not through divine inspiration but He possesses it in His Nature. In this sense this doctrine has exercised a very wholesome influence, and as the first attempt of Primitive Christianity to proclaim the mystery of the Person of Jesus it deserves our utmost respect.[2] The fight against this view is usually carried on by those who do not believe in the divinity of Christ, by modern Adoptionism, which in theological terms is called "Liberalism". It should be clear from the tenor of these remarks, that our rejection of the doctrine of the Virgin Birth has nothing to do with this view, but comes from the very opposite angle.

[1] The arguments here suggested, which are further developed by K. L. Schmidt in his article, *Jesus Christ*, R.G.G², III, Sp. 119–121, have not been put out of action by his later article, *Die jungfräuliche Geburt Jesu Christi*, Theol. Bl., 1935, Sp. 289–97

[2] Cf. Schlatter, *Das Christliche Dogma*, p. 355

(D) THE DOCTRINE OF THE TWO NATURES[1]

Let us look back once more at the narrative of the Virgin Birth in the two Synoptic Gospels. Is not this doctrine the necessary presupposition for all that the doctrine of the Two Natures is trying to express: *vere Deus vere homo*? Can Jesus be true Man otherwise than as one who is not tainted with Original Sin? Is not sex procreation, as such, the source of inherited corruption? The Apostle Paul, at any rate, is of a different opinion. He emphasizes, on the contrary, that God's Son came to us "in the likeness of sinful flesh", that the miracle of the Person of Jesus actually consists in the very fact that in Him the "sinful flesh" which He assumed did not become sin, but that the curse which lies over all human existence from birth is removed in Him. It might even be possible that this passage (quoted from the Epistle to the Romans) is intended to be an explicit correction of the doctrine of the Virgin Birth. For the Incarnation of the Son of God is fulfilled in the fact that He assumed the "likeness of sinful flesh", without Himself being infected by sin.

With the doctrine that Jesus is the God-Man, theological thought returns from the sphere "beyond history" to the Historical. We only spoke of the Eternal Son, the Logos, and of the Incarnation, because Jesus is the historical man, the God-Man. We only see Him as a figure in history aright when we see Him as the God-Man, when we see Him as the One who is the Eternal Son become Man, true God, of one substance with the Father. But also we only see him aright as He really is when, while insisting that He is "True God", we do not forget the other point—which, indeed, from the historical point of view comes first—that at the same time He is "True Man". This is what the doctrine of the Two Natures is trying to express, and which was expressed, in lapidary simplicity, for the first time, by the *Confessio Augustana: "Vere Deus, vere homo."* The great controversies—which later on became so terrible—about the doctrine of the Two Natures were all fought over this simple, yet profoundly mysterious truth.

The more we study the documents of that period, the more strong does the impression of discord become. On the one hand, there was the passionateness of those (to some extent) really great theologians of the *centrum evangelicum*, who urged that both the *vere Deus* and the *vere homo* must be taken

[1] As it is usually called

seriously, that in Jesus we are faced by one Fact, to which both refer, and that both must be stressed with equal emphasis if the whole fullness of the evangelical message of salvation is not to be lost. On the other hand, this controversy was carried on in such intellectual terms, and with the aid of such arguments and discussions, that it really makes us wonder whether the point at issue was served by all this debate. As soon as the idea of "Nature" emerges in theology we have occasion to be disturbed, and in any case we must be on our guard. For us at the present day indeed the ancient idea of "Nature" has become almost wholly foreign; for us it has been almost hopelessly "naturalized". We find it difficult to understand what they meant by the "divine Nature". But quite apart from this change in language and its use—which must have taken place somewhere during the time of the later Renaissance—we cannot view the application of such an abstract philosophical idea to theology without considerable misgiving.

Certainly, this was a real problem and one that had to be faced: How can we, without losing sight of the unity of the Person of Jesus, say both these things at the same time: *vere Deus* and *vere homo*? The question, however, is this:—and this question never seems to have troubled the minds of those early Fathers: Is it possible to throw light on the mystery of the unity of both statements by an effort of thought? Must not every attempt to define the "togetherness" of divinity and humanity in the Person of Jesus break down? Is it not a fact, that all such attempts, of whatever kind, are disastrous, because they inevitably lead man to go further than is allowable in trying to transcend the limitations of human thought? When we think of the arguments and mutual anathemas of men like Cyril and Nestorius is it not the fact that something like this nearly always happens: both are concerned to defend religious views which, as soon as they are formulated in intellectual terms, lead to irreconcilable contradictions? Do we not see the same thing happening in the experience of our great Reformers? one of whom with a genuine passion for Biblical truth, comes very near to the Nestorian diophysitic view, while the other, with equal religious passion, is nearer to Cyrillic Monophysitism? And the fact that the Chalcedonian Definition is the final result of these controversies, seems to justify our doubts of the usefulness of such discussion, since it simply places two irreconcilable contradictions side by side? We may, of course, reply: In order to attain this result it was necessary to have these long conflicts, which were carried on with all the theological acumen possible. This may be right. But then, if we admit that this result is the only possible one, ought we to draw the conclusion that we can scarcely hope to get any further with the consideration of the "Two Natures" than this final result, which indeed simply means that at this point we have reached the limits of human understanding? We might perhaps have learned this lesson directly from the Bible, which certainly does not explain the mystery of the divine Humanity, but sets it before us as a mystery. The idea of "Nature" raises questions which can only be answered in a controversial manner. Once we begin asking about the "Two Natures" we are both Monophysites and Diophysites. Just as all speculation about the way in which the Incarnation came to be is fruitless—and therefore dangerous—so also is it fruitless to speculate about the "Two Natures".

The verdict on the historical figure of Jesus which seems forced upon us in the light of the apostolic testimony is True Man, True God. It is a legitimate and necessary task of theology to examine this verdict again and again, above all in the light of the Gospel narrative. We have taken this examination for granted. The result of the examination is this: After the critics have done their work, there is nothing in the story of Jesus, or in His Sayings, which have been examined according to all the rules of historical and literary criticism, which contradicts this twofold verdict, that Jesus is True God and True Man. In the early period of New Testament criticism, especially of the Gospel narrative, people did believe, it is true, that the verdict "True God" could not stand the critical examination of the Gospel tradition, especially when the Fourth Gospel was eliminated as a source for the genuine Sayings of Jesus. But the progress of literary and historical criticism in particular has convinced us that this supposedly scientific argument, which is really only a general "philosophy of life", is untenable. We do not need the Johannine Sayings of Jesus, which in the usual sense of the word are regarded as "unhistorical", we do not need certain Synoptic Sayings of Jesus which have been fiercely attacked by the extreme critical school as non-historical, in order to be able to hold to the verdict of the Church. On the contrary we now see that the objections to this critical separation between the Johannine interpretation of Christ and the Jesus-tradition of the Synoptists was due to a certain docetic tendency, in spite of the rejection of the docetic theory in principle which had been in the Church from the earliest days down to the present time. We say: even if Jesus had only said and done what the most extreme school of radical criticism leaves us as credible, even then there is nothing to alter in this verdict, that this Jesus is the Christ, and therefore the Gospel of John has rightly presented this "Jesus of History" as the Christ and the Son of God, although it is possible that He never really uttered those words which "John" put into His mouth. From this point of view, Liberal Theology, with its confusion of historical and religious knowledge, seems to be primitive Ebionism, just as the orthodox refusal to accept criticism of the Gospel tradition turns out to be unconscious Docetism.

But the real intellectual problem of the doctrine of the Two Natures, that is, how to conceive the union of the two natures in Jesus at the same time, is beyond us. We must certainly hold firmly to both statements without reduction: True God, true Man. Thus, for instance, we must not make the attempt, which many people thought they could discern in my work on *The Mediator*, to deny to Jesus full human personality. A man who prays to God is "True Man" even in the sense of the human historical personality. On the other hand, because in Jesus we find neither divine omnipotence nor omniscience we ought not to deny His divinity. It is, of course, obvious that the *Kenosis* which belongs to the Incarnation, constitutes a self-limitation of God whose limits cannot possibly be defined by us. We cannot say how God became Man. But we can and must say, that God, as He confronts us in the Man Jesus, and especially as He is manifested to us as the Crucified, has divested Himself of His attributes of majesty. It is, however, quite useless to desire to examine the extent of the possible or necessary self-emptying of God by an artificial model which we have constructed for the purpose, by asking for instance: to what extent and in what way did God have to "empty" Himself, in order to meet us in a God-Man, of whom it would be actually true to call Him *vere Deus, vere homo*? We do not possess the necessary presuppositions for the construction of such an intellectual model. Our verdict is purely *a posteriori*: we see the True God present in the Man Jesus. All the questions concerning the different elements in the life of Jesus—which belong to His divine, and which to His human nature, are beside the point. And all schemes of thought which theology has produced, both before and after Chalcedon, in order to make it clear how both the divine and the human nature could exist together in the Person of Jesus, do not in reality make anything clearer, therefore they do not help us at all. The only thing we can do here has already been done. We have to show why we are not simply content to say "true Man", but feel that we must proceed to the second unthinkable statement, "true God". But how we can do this without destroying the unity of the Person, or how the one can be combined with the other, is utterly beyond the power of human understanding, and it is also beyond all that really concerns faith.

Monophysitism is right in stressing the truth that Jesus, in the wholeness of His Person, is revelation. The very thing which seems to conceal His Godhead, His flesh, the weakness of earthly creatureliness, is an essential element in the divine glory of revelation. It is the Crucified of whom it is said: "We beheld His glory".[1] It is not in spite of the Cross, in spite of its evident "weakness", in spite of human impotence and frailty, that He reveals Himself to us as the Son of God, but particularly on the Cross. It is precisely the folly of the Cross which is the wisdom of God, it is precisely the *exinanitio*, the extreme point of the *kenosis*, which is the supreme height of the self-manifestation of God. When Clement of Alexandria says: "It would be ridiculous to imagine that the body of the Redeemer, in order to exist, had the usual needs of man. He only took food and ate it in order that we should not teach about Him in a docetic fashion, He was not driven in a passive manner",[2] then from the point of view of Biblical truth, the exact opposite must be said, as Athanasius puts it: "The Word bore the weakness of the flesh as His own, for it was His own flesh, and the flesh was serviceable to the working of the Godhead, for it was in the Godhead, it was God's body".[3] Luther too, with his passionate, monophysitic tendency, also took this line.

But there is justification also for the Diophysitic view, when it rejects the view that the Logos was transformed into flesh, and on this account rejects the Θεοτόκος of Cyril. Its protagonists are right when they urge that the human nature which the Logos assumed is genuine, creaturely human nature, and that we ought not to describe it in the terms we would

---

[1] The whole Gospel of John, with its strong accent on the δόξα χριστοῦ, must be read *sub specie crucis*. That is what John means by the exaltation of the Crucifixion (3: 14)

[2] *Cl. Al. Str.*, VI, 9   [3] *Orationes*, 3, 45

use for the divine nature. They are right when they dwell upon the truth that *Deo quae Dei sunt, et homini quae hominis sunt, non deputanda esse.* But does not this precisely show that both are defending a real concern? but that within the formulation of a doctrine of the Two Natures it is inevitably connected with logical impossibilities, and that this doctrine of the Two Natures deals in abstractions which do not aid reflection on the mystery of the divine-human Person? Once we begin to think in terms of the abstract schema of "Natures" then all we can say is this: Even in Jesus Christ the human element is human, and the divine element divine, and the human and the divine are never the same.

Again, once we begin to think in abstract terms of the *schema* of the Two Natures, then we cannot hold the unity of the divine-human Person save through the denial of duality, thus, through the assertion of the unity of the divine nature. But why need we think in such abstractions? How do they help us to understand the true, insoluble mystery, that at this one point in the world and in history it is true that the borderline between the Creator and the creature has been crossed, that from the standpoint of natural knowledge, there is a human creature who is God, and that it has pleased God to identify Himself with a definite, localized finite given entity, with the historical Person Jesus of Nazareth? Let anyone who can, go further than the dilemmas raised by the representatives of Monophysitism and diophysitism and still have more to say than the paradoxical statements which place alongside one another that which cannot be logically combined, as in the Chalcedonian Definition, and show it to us! We will gladly listen to him. I do not feel myself in a position to do this, and at the present time I have no cause to complain of this incapacity, since I must suppose that every so-called "solution" would only raise further difficulties.

Yet perhaps, without following the great Fathers of that period too closely, we could say that the whole complex of problems raised by the doctrine of the Two Natures is the result of a question which is wrongly posed, of a question which wants to know something which we simply cannot know, namely, how divinity and humanity are united in the Person Jesus Christ. There is still something else to say: This whole problem with all the passionate emotion it arouses, is not thinkable apart from the question of the Virgin Birth, and of the Θεοτόκος, and its denial. The theory of parthenogenesis is itself a first attempt to say how the Person of Jesus came into existence, the first attempt to give an explanation of the mystery of the divine-humanity. The teaching of the Apostles does not lead us to such an attempt. It confronts us with the mystery of the Person of Jesus Himself. Not because we hold this or that theory on this point, not because we believe that this Person came into being in this or that way, should and can we believe in the God-Man. The Jesus Christ shown to us in the Scriptures accredits Himself to us as the God-Man. One who meets Him with that openness to truth which the Bible calls "faith", meets in Him One who, in the unity of His Person, is both true God and true Man. It would be good for the Church to be content with this, and not wish to know more than we can know, or more than we need, if we are to trust Him and obey Him as we should.

(E) THE RISEN AND EXALTED LORD

The final point of the *kenosis* of the God-Man is His death on the Cross. That is where Paul draws the line. The assumption of the "form of a servant", and the way of obedience, ends in the death on the Cross. The coming of God to us ends in the event of the Crucifixion. There He "meets" us, there He takes "what is ours" upon Himself, in order that "He may give us Himself." Christ's death on the Cross is the completion of the Incarnation. He was born like any one of us—according to the flesh—He died too, like any one of us, but He did not die *merely* as we do, for in His dying He sank into greater depths than any other human being had ever done; He fell into that abyss into which we deserve to fall. In His death the Son of God, who comes to us, does not only empty Himself of all His royal and divine attributes, but also of all that could distinguish the one from the other. No one can sink to greater depths, indeed no one has ever fallen so far, for no one as a dying man anticipated Hell as He did.

That is indeed "our desert", yet by the mercy of God, even one who dies most wretchedly is spared this final torment. This extreme humiliation is the culmination of God's love as He stoops down to our level; here we see it completely manifested as absolute, all-embracing self-surrender for our sakes.

And yet here the victorious power of God is manifested as nowhere else. The impotence of the Son of God is the *spoliatio diaboli*. Over against this love the Devil's hatred of God is powerless; this supreme proof of the divine self-surrender disarms him. Through this death on the Cross a "place" is cleared within this world where the ban of human sin is broken, where unfettered communion between God and Man can be established. When we enter this "place", we are free from the accusations of the Law and from its curse, and at the same time we are also set free from the inmost core of resistance against God, from our arrogant self-assertion. Outside this "place", God and man are at a distance from one another. This "place" is the meeting-point of God and man. Here the "meeting" really takes place—at this point: this means, however, that here, through faith in Jesus Christ the Crucified, man accepts God's judgment on himself, and becomes nothing, and that in faith he believes in God's incomprehensible, self-giving love, manifested in this utmost humiliation. God had to stoop so low, in order that man might abandon his self-delusion, and live in the love of God.

The question may, however, be raised: is the death of Jesus on the Cross, with all its shame and torment, really the end of the divine condescension? On the fringe of the New Testament there emerges the idea of Christ's "descent into hell".[1] This idea was accepted, and inserted into the (so-called) Apostles' Creed. The exposition of the relevant passages in the Bible, 1 Pet. 3: 19 and 4: 6, has given rise to a controversy within Protestantism. Lutheran theology understands the *descensus ad inferos* as the beginning of the *status exaltationis*, as the point at which Jesus begins "to take His Power", and moreover as the first stage in His exaltation.[2] Reformed theology, on the other hand, interprets it in the opposite sense, as the deepest point in His humiliation, interpreting it spiritually as the suffering, not merely of human anguish, but also of diabolical despair.[3] Has this idea still any significance for us?

It is no sign of theological insight to say bluntly that our present view of the universe makes nonsense of the idea of a "descent into Hell", because it is based upon the ancient three-storey view of the universe, which we have discarded. The question cannot be settled quite so simply. We no longer believe in a "place under the earth", it is true. any more than we believe in a "place above the earth". But just as the New Testament picture of "heaven"—"Our Father, who art in

---

[1] 1 Pet. 3: 19, 4: 6   [2] Hollaz, *Examen theol.*, p. 778
[3] Polan, *Syntagma*, VI, 21

heaven"—is not equated with the ancient view of space, and is therefore not discarded, so also, when we discard the idea of a "place under the earth", we do not then abandon the idea of "Hell", or of a "realm of the departed".

It is not the change in our cosmological views which raises difficulties about the statements in 1 Peter, but the religious and metaphysical idea of a "realm of the dead" as such. But we can only deal with this in detail in the whole context of the problems of eschatology. The article in the Apostles' Creed still raises problems because it speaks of "Hell", whereas the Petrine passages speak of Hades, the "realm of the dead". Christ's preaching to "the souls in prison", in that passage in Peter, contains, it is true, a precious thought—which we must emphasize later—the glimpse of a possibility of a meeting with Jesus Christ for those who did not meet Him during their life on earth. But it will be better to deal with this point in another connexion. So far as we are concerned, within Christology the only interpretation of the *descensus ad inferos* which we can consider is that of Reformed theology; namely, as the expression of the fact that Jesus did not merely take upon Himself, and drink to the dregs, the bitter cup of human suffering, but that He also endured a measure of spiritual suffering, in the sense of feeling utterly forsaken by God, which no other person has ever suffered, and which we can only imagine as a foretaste of Hell—not as the "realm of the dead" but as the horror of being separated from God. The significance of the article of the *descensus ad inferos* in the Apostles' Creed, is above all that it calls our attention to the fact that the point of the deepest humiliation of Christ is at the same time the beginning of His exaltation, of the Resurrection.

Apart from these two passages, the New Testament does not speak of the descent into Hades, but from beginning to end it is full of the witness to Jesus Christ, the Risen Lord. Even from the temporal point of view this is true, from the very outset. In contrast to several other points in Christology which do not stand out so clearly, in the early days and years of the preaching of the Gospel, the witness to the Resurrection of the Lord is the centre, the decisive content of the preaching of the first Apostles and disciples, from the first moment that they come out into the open.[1] The Christ Jesus whom they proclaim to the Jews in Jerusalem is He whom the Jews had crucified, whom God, however, had raised from the dead, and therefore

[1] Cf. Bultmann, *Theol. d. N.T.*, p. 43

vindicated as the true Messiah and Lord. This fact—that the message of the Primitive Church is the witness to the Resurrection of Jesus, that it was the appearances of the Risen Lord which brought the shattered and scattered disciples together again after the catastrophe of Good Friday, and formed the real foundation of the Christian Church—stands upon such firm ground, that even the unbelieving historian cannot get away from it. He may judge these "appearances" to be purely subjective; he may call them "hallucinations" or whatever he will; but he cannot shake the actual fact of belief in the Resurrection as the basis of the Christian Church.

But further: since Paul first expressed it, the Christian Church knows that everything depends on belief in the Resurrection. "If Christ hath not been raised, your faith is vain; ye are yet in your sins."[1] A Jesus who had not risen, who had remained in the grave, could not be the Christ. The Resurrection is the necessary vindication of His Messiahship. It is true that the disciples believed in Him as Messiah before His Resurrection; this comes out very clearly in Peter's Confession at Caesarea Philippi. But this faith did not survive the terrible shock of Calvary. Without the fact of Easter the world would scarcely have heard either of a Church, or of Jesus Himself. It was the encounter with the Risen Lord which rescued the disciples from their perplexity and hopelessness, restored their broken faith, and more than this, filled them with jubilant certainty of victory, which was, and remained, the vital element in the Primitive Church, and gave the first Christians the power to be in the full difficult sense of the word "martyrs" for the truth of Christ.

In strange contrast to this historically indubitable fundamental fact, and to the absolute unanimity of the New Testament witness in reference to this fundamental tradition, there is the other point, which also cannot be denied: that on points of detail concerning time and place, etc., these narratives disagree at many points. With the best will in the world the five Resurrection narratives of the four evangelists and of the Apostle Paul cannot be harmonized into a coherent picture, and the traditional method of harmonizing them often allows the most reliable witnesses to be overlooked at the expense of others of less importance. The most ancient and most reliable testimony is that of the Apostle Paul from the year 56—in the first Epistle to the Corinthians—which, with its

[1] I Cor. 15: 17

mention of the fact that "He hath been raised on the third day . . . and that He appeared to Cephas; then to the Twelve; then to above five hundred brethren at once", takes us right back to the event itself. The witnesses to whom Paul appeals some twenty years after the first Easter, must have mostly been alive when this letter was written and circulated; they were thus in a position either to confirm what he says or to deny it. This earliest and—according to the most reliable criteria of historical criticism—most reliable narrative, differs, however, at several points from the narratives in the Gospels, which were added later at different times; the further they are in time from the events recorded the more do they show the influence of the growth of legend. On the other hand, the Pauline account is in agreement with certain conclusions which the historical critic is obliged to draw from the gospel sources. What is the result of this critical examination of the source material for a picture of what really happened?

There is no reason to disturb the indication of time given in the words "raised on the third day", for the addition of the words "according to the Scriptures", to which the historian might object—as if here perhaps as at other points, the actual history could be corrected by the prophecies of the Old Testament—proves to arouse, on closer examination, no suspicion. There is indeed no passage in the Scriptures from which this indication of time would have to be removed. We can evidently remain sure of this indication of time, which belongs to the very oldest strand of tradition. But when we come to the question of place the situation is very different. Here there are plainly two different traditions: one of which points to Galilee, the other to Jerusalem and its neighbourhood, as the place where the appearances of the Risen Lord took place. This question, in itself unimportant, acquires importance by its connexion with the third question, the question of "how" the Resurrection took place, and the whole problem of the so-called "Empty Tomb". Paul's account mentions a quite definite series of appearances of the Risen Lord: to Peter, the Twelve, the Five Hundred brethren, which contradicts the Gospel narratives, and suggests that these are not very reliable. Paul's narrative, however, says nothing about an Empty Tomb. While in the Gospel narratives the sight of the Empty Tomb is a matter of independent significance, in the mind of Paul it obviously played no part at all. And more than this: Paul places his own encounter with the Risen Lord on the same level as that of the other Apostles. Even if we ought not to press these parallels too far, and should not draw too extensive conclusions from them, yet there is one result which comes out of this, namely, that to him who was the earliest and most reliable of the witnesses to the Resurrection, the thing that mattered most was not the Empty Tomb, but the meeting with the Risen Lord, as a spiritual personal reality.

Another point leads us in the same direction. According to the agreed narrative of all the witnesses, the meeting with the Risen Lord was only granted to those who believed in Him; "Him God raised up the third day, and gave Him to be made manifest, not to all the people, but unto witnesses that were chosen before of God" (Acts 10: 40–41). The knowledge of the Risen Lord had to be one which was granted to faith alone. But the Empty Tomb is a world-fact, which everyone, whether they believe in Christ or not, could have perceived. According to the Gospel narratives it was the pagans who were guarding the Tomb, who certainly did not belong to the Church, who, being aware that something wonderful was happening as Christ left the grave, became witnesses of His resurrection, and were only prevented by bribes from spreading the news of this event far and wide. In connexion with these narratives, which are full of legendary touches, the testimony to the Resurrection becomes quite different from the account given by Paul. Further, according to the earliest account in the Gospels—in Mark and Matthew—the meetings with the Risen Lord do not take place in Jerusalem but in Galilee, thus without any connexion with the Empty Tomb, while the later stories in the Gospels of Luke and John combine both. All this suggests that the original testimony to the Resurrection did not contain any reference to the Empty Tomb, but was solely concerned with the appearances of the Risen Lord to His disciples.

Nevertheless, we must admit that there is a circumstance which gives some historical weight to the tradition of the Empty Tomb. In the Primitive Christian period there is no trace of a Tomb of Jesus which was present and well known, but on the contrary, very soon the impious legend was being spread by the enemies of Jesus that the disciples had stolen His Body in order to be able to assert that He had risen from the dead. This certainly makes us think; though it is not a proof. Rather, in view of the scanty and contradictory nature of the source-material we must say: *Non liquet*. One point, however, does emerge with certainty from the earliest narratives, in Paul, Mark and Matthew, and that is, that the original witness to the Resurrection of Jesus referred to the appearances of Jesus to His disciples, and not to the "world-fact" of the Empty Tomb; it is extremely probable that these appearances did not take place in Jerusalem but in Galilee. So much for the historical element. But what is the relation of faith to the historical element? Is not the whole situation very precarious if faith has to be based on a historical fact which is supported by such uncertain and contradictory testimony?

Let us be quite clear what this means. The position is not that which Fundamentalism of a certain type, and theological traditionalism, would like to maintain, namely: that "believers" are those who believe in the historical sources as "the Word of God", while others, who lack such faith, simply prove their unbelief. This is the situation: the sources contradict one another, and only a "harmonizing" process which is not too much concerned about truth, could patch up a fairly connected account of the events, in which it is only too manifest that the later and less credible witnesses appear more important than the earlier, and more reliable ones. Such a dishonest way of dealing with the subject really has nothing to do with "faith in the Word of God"; it only serves to support the disastrous prejudice that Christian faith is only possible in connexion with historical dishonesty. What "historical criticism" does is simply to present, honestly and simply, the result of the tradition recorded in the New Testament; from this honest procedure, which for everyone who is willing to see things as they are, is inescapable—the conclusion is drawn that things are not very happy in this historical tradition, so far as questions of the manner and place of the Resurrection-appearances are concerned. But no reliable historian would object to the *fact* of the appearances of the Risen Lord as such—however he may try to explain them.

But the question which confronts faith is far more radical. On the basis of what we know already, ought we, at this one point, to set aside our usual method of establishing facts, namely, that faith is not primarily faith in a record, in a written word of Scripture, but that the word of Scripture is only the medium through which Jesus Christ authenticates Himself to us as the Word of God? In this question of the Resurrection must we look at the matter the other way round?

That is, are we obliged, first of all, to put our trust in the narrative of the Apostles, and are we then to base our faith in the Resurrection solely on their report of their encounter with the Risen Lord? Thus, is our belief in the Resurrection, belief in the fact that the Apostles saw the Risen Lord? If we go on to answer this question in the negative, obviously, we do not take this line, because as we have seen, as a record of historical fact, this story is not well supported. On the contrary, so far as faith is concerned, and the question of the Resurrection as such—apart from particular details of place, etc.—the position, historically speaking, is very good. Every reliable historian will admit that very soon after Good Friday the Apostles did see the Risen Lord. The interpretation of this fact, that they actually *saw Him*, does not belong to the sphere of history, but either to that of one's general philosophy of life, or to that of faith. So far as the honest historian is concerned no objection can be raised to the testimony to the Resurrection as such; it must authenticate itself, even if the individual historian explains it as a "subjective vision" or even as an "hallucination". That is not the reason why we refuse to make the historical record, as such, the primary object of faith, but because to do so would destroy all that we have known hitherto about the nature of faith, and its relation to revelation. We remain true to our canon at this particular point, because only so do we gain a real understanding of belief in the Resurrection.

We believe in the Resurrection of Jesus because through the whole witness of the Scriptures He attests Himself to us as the Christ and as the Living Lord. The Apostles' account of their meetings with the Risen Lord are not the basis of, but an element in, the testimony of revelation, which is the basis of our faith in Christ, and therefore of our faith in His Resurrection. He who manifests Himself to us as the Christ through the testimony of the Scriptures as the Son of the Living God, as the God-Man, is no other than the Risen Lord. The question whether we could believe in Him as the Risen Lord if there were no special testimonies to His resurrection is an idle one, since these testimonies do, in fact, exist. It has at least this justification, however, that it draws our attention to the fact that our belief in the Resurrection of Jesus is not only, and not primarily, based upon the Apostles' testimony to the Resurrection. The Christ, whom we know through their witness; cannot be other than the Risen Lord Himself.

The significance of the Apostles' experiences of the Resurrection is not the same for the Apostles, and for ourselves. The Apostles needed these appearances in order to restore their faith in Him, the Christ, which had been shattered by the catastrophe of Good Friday, and to bring them to full certainty of faith. Through these appearances, of which they alone, and not we, are witnesses, they were enabled to know Him, and to be sure who, and what, He is. These Resurrection experiences alone ensure our knowledge of their witness to Christ, and through this witness of theirs, we also, on our part, can know Him to be who and what He is. Through their witness as a whole He authenticates Himself to us as the Living and Present Lord; through their witness He has become living and present to us too. Through the faith which He creates by means of the witness of the Apostles—by means of that witness, which contains both the story of His life and the doctrine of His Person—He is "with us all the days, even unto the end of the world." We are thus ourselves enabled, from our own knowledge, to be His witnesses, although we have not experienced those appearances of the Risen Lord. He *had* to attest Himself thus to the Apostles by those appearances as the Risen Lord, in order that they should believe in Him, see Him again, and really see Him as He is. He does not make Himself known to us in the same way. He makes Himself known to us through the collective witness of the Apostles, through the story of His life (in the Gospels), and the explanation of this story which the Apostles give us, through which we see Himself, and can ourselves learn to know Him as they saw Him and knew Him.

Hence our faith is not based upon the record of their experiences of the Resurrection. Every believing Christian knows this. He believes in the Risen Lord not because the Resurrection is told as a narrative of something that happened, but because he knows Christ as the living present Lord. Indeed, we might say: we would believe in Him as the Risen Lord, even if there were no narratives of the Resurrection at all; we must only add it is not an accident that there *are* accounts of the Resurrection given us by the Apostles. Only because they met the Risen Lord, as Paul and others tell us, is there an apostolic witness to Jesus, the Christ, and only because there is this apostolic witness, can we ourselves know Him.

Hence all questions of "how" and "where" the Resurrection

took place, including the question of the Empty Tomb and the physical Resurrection understood in this sense, are secondary. This is so because we who, in view of our own resurrection, are called "His brethren", among whom He is the First-born, do not believe in our physical resurrection in the sense of an empty tomb. Here again we see the significance of the original Pauline account of the Resurrection. Just as Paul lays no stress upon the Empty Tomb, so, on the other hand, he lays decisive emphasis upon the parallels between the Resurrection of Jesus and our own, on the fact that "He is the first-born among many brethren". Even if Paul (which we simply do not know) did know anything about the Empty Tomb, it was not for him a fact of central importance, because for *us* there will not be an empty grave.

Emphasis upon the Empty Tomb led to the medieval conception of the "resurrection of the body", with its drama of the Last Day, and the opening of the graves, which has also been inserted into the Apostles' Creed. Paul's teaching about a "spiritual body" is in opposition to such a conception; in any case it can only be combined with such a view with great difficulty. Resurrection of the body, yes: Resurrection of the *flesh*, no! The "Resurrection of the body" does not mean the identity of the resurrection body with the material (although already transformed) body of flesh; but the resurrection of the body means the continuity of the individual personality on this side, and on that, of death.

Jesus Christ is Victor over death and the grave, not only because He is the Risen Lord, but because He is the Christ, the God-Man, who, as such, could not remain subject to death. It has usually been too little noticed that the witness of Paul to the victory of Jesus over all hostile powers is connected not so much with the fact of Easter as with the fact of Good Friday. There, on the Cross, the decisive thing happened, for there the Incarnation of the Son of God—paradoxically— reached its climax. That which, from the world's point of view, was the absolute *nadir*, the "zero-hour" in the ministry of Jesus, is from the spiritual point of view the absolute zenith, the fulfilment of the revelation of God in the "form of a servant", and in that very fact His victory over the powers of death. John expresses this in his use of the term "exaltation". In his Gospel being "lifted up" always means being "lifted up" on the Cross.

This brings us to a final problem of the doctrine of the

"States" of Christ;[1] the question of the Ascension and the Exaltation of Christ. The Church teaches, in Luke's twofold account, the "Ascension" of Jesus as a particular historical event. Behind this narrative lies the idea that the period of the appearances of the Risen Lord, the "forty days", was ended by a special act, by the Ascension, a wonderful event, seen by the Apostles. Within the New Testament writings, however, Luke is the only one to give this account, which is entirely isolated. No other apostle mentions such an event; further, this conception is irreconcilable with that of Paul. For Paul there are no "forty days", within which the appearances of the Risen Lord took place. Paul indeed sets the appearance of the Risen Lord, which was granted to him as the last of the Apostles, on exactly the same level as those granted to Peter, the Twelve, and the Five Hundred brethren. But this event, which happened on the Damascus road, took place long after the "forty days" were over, indeed after the first persecutions—whose active leader was the Pharisee Saul at that time—had swept over the Church. Once more we stand at a point where theology must have the courage to be ready to abandon the ecclesiastical tradition. For Paul the Exaltation of Jesus is identical with His Resurrection, and the same is true of John: only in John, still more plainly than in Paul, resurrection and crucifixion, and therefore crucifixion and exaltation are regarded as a unity. While the exaltation of Christ and His session at the Right Hand of God belong to the fundamental *kerygma* of the witnesses in the New Testament, the exaltation as "Ascension" plays no part in the teaching of the Apostles.

Thus it is not for reasons connected with our present world-view that we abandon the tradition of the Church at this point, but for reasons inherent in the Biblical witness itself. It is true that many modern preachers have been aware of the scientific difficulties connected with the Lucan story of a physical ascension; this cannot be denied. The idea of "going up" to "heaven" fits into a picture of the world for which Heaven is a region which is actually "above" in space, but does not fit into ours, which has no such conception. These difficulties are not at all decisive. Those who wish to believe in the Ascension will certainly be able to go on doing so within

---

[1] The "*Ständelehre*", or the old Lutheran doctrine of the two "States" of Christ: the state of humiliation, or *exinanitio.* and the state of exaltation. Cf. Horst Stephan, *Glaubenslehre* (p. 170) (TR.)

our present views of time and space. What is alone decisive is the fact that there is an irreconcilable contradiction between this idea and Paul's conception, and that the New Testament, in its message and its doctrine, makes no use of this particular isolated idea of the Lucan narrative.

But the idea of "Exaltation", which is absolutely central for faith, has nothing to do with this question. For faith Jesus Christ is the "Exalted Lord", who "sitteth at the Right Hand of God". We know, of course, that when we say this we are using the language of parable. God, who is Lord of Space, is not "in space" but is "beyond" all spatial categories. Therefore there is no "right hand". But we cannot speak about Him and His Being otherwise than in spatial terms; but when we do this we know that we are speaking "improperly", or in a parabolic manner. Perhaps this reminder of the inadequateness of such language has become clearer to us than to the ancients, because our spatial idea of Heaven has been removed by our view of the world which no longer knows any "above" or "below", while they, with their cosmological ideas, which were at bottom those of the ancient Babylonian view of the world, could more easily forget the parabolic character of their theological language.

The idea of "Exaltation" is of central significance for us because it expresses the truth that through the Resurrection of Jesus humanity and divinity are henceforth bound together "in Heaven". In the Person of the Risen Lord humanity has entered heaven, the transcendent existence of God. He who sits at the Right Hand of God is not the Eternal Son before the Incarnation, but the God-Man. As such He is the Mediator between God and man, not only in His earthly historical existence, He not only "has been", but is now, to the very end of time, Mediator between God and man. He is therefore our Advocate, who takes our part, and speaks for us. He is the One who guarantees the fulfilment of human history. The "Exaltation" is the return to the pure transcendence of His pre-historical existence. The Exalted Lord is the guarantor of Saving History, which cannot be reversed, of history which is moving towards a goal, of a history which is not returning to its eternal beginning, but is moving to an end, which is different from the beginning. Belief in the Exaltation, and in the Exalted Lord, is therefore a final decisive protest against all mythology, whose fundamental formula is that of eternal recurrence.

The Church rightly connects the belief in the Exalted Lord with the *munus regium Christi*; He who is exalted at the Right Hand of God, is appointed to dominion over humanity. His exaltation is the ideal of the aim of humanity, which he ushers in by His Government. He is, it is true, the "first-born among many brethren"; He IS, what "we may become". But that is not all. He does not simply wait until we reach this goal. It is He who, in the power and the purpose of God, leads humanity to this goal.

To this extent the idea of the *regnum Christi* as a universal sphere, which does, of course, include the community of the faithful as its innermost centre, but goes further and takes in unbelieving humanity, is justified.[1] Because Jesus Christ leads the whole of humanity to its goal, His sovereignty is not confined to the circle of those who believe in Him. Because He has been commissioned to do this, "all power has been given unto Him in heaven and on earth". But His Lordship outside the Church is exercised in a wholly hidden way, which we cannot follow. It is only visible to us *sub contraria specie*, namely, as non-sovereignty, as the resistance of those who are disobedient to their rightful Lord. His real direct Lordship is only achieved where, through His Word and His Spirit, He makes the hearts of men obedient unto Himself.

The exaltation of the Risen Lord to the "Right Hand of God" is not only the guarantee of the goal of human history, but also of the cosmos. Not only humanity, but the creation as such is represented in the heavenly world, by the exaltation of the Lord who was born as a creature. Death is indeed not only a human and historical phenomenon, but a phenomenon of all creation. The conquest of death by the Resurrection of Jesus has also a cosmic significance. As all power is given unto Him in Heaven and on earth, the whole cosmos is, in principle, subordinated to Him. It is, however, in harmony with the whole attitude of the Scriptures that this cosmic character of the Lordship of Christ is emphasized far less than His Lordship over human history. The Bible tells us nothing about what this cosmos will become when "heaven and earth pass away"; the Lordship of Christ over the universe as a whole is asserted negatively rather than positively: nothing is to be excepted from the Lordship of Christ; the Universe as a whole depends upon Him for its life; He is also its *Telos*, its goal and its End.

At the time of the Reformation, as we know, there were

[1] See App. B, Ch. 11

many doctrinal controversies about the question of the exaltation of the Risen Lord to the Right Hand of God, which were
so hot because they were directly connected with a fundamental article of faith; the Presence of Jesus Christ in the
Holy Communion. Jesus Christ is risen in bodily form, therefore
He is also exalted in the same form; that was the common
thesis. But opinions differed on the following points: whether
the presence of Jesus with His own in the Lord's Supper is a
bodily or a spiritual one. Luther's monophysite tendency led
to a passionate emphasis upon the bodily Presence; for in the
Supper the whole Christ is present. What matters is that the
whole God-Man is really present with us, not merely His
Spirit. With no less determination Calvin defended the view
that the bodily presence meant spatial limitation, and, therefore, that a body which can be everywhere is no longer a
body, since it would not have that decisive characteristic of
corporeality that it is "here and not there", localized within
space.

Naturally for both conflicting parties the physical resurrection was understood in the sense of the Empty Tomb. The fact
that the witness of the Bible on this very point, so far as the
Exalted Lord is concerned, has nothing to say about a
"corporeality" of Jesus Christ, seemed not to disturb these
theologians, who were so sure of their ground. Since they did
not doubt the traditional conception of the physical Resurrection, they did not feel obliged to carry the original Pauline
line any further, and they also overlooked the fact that whenever
Paul speaks of the Body of Christ he means the Church, and
nothing but the Church, and that the New Testament knows
nothing of a Christ transferred to heaven in bodily form—save
for those two passages of Luke in connexion with the story of
the Ascension. But the fact that both the Lutheran *Pro* and
the Calvinistic *Contra* were defended with the same intense
religious passion, should warn us that here they had ventured
into a region of theological speculation where a clear statement
of faith is no longer possible, but opposing "truths" can be
maintained and "proved" with equal reason. The silence of
the Bible on these controversial questions must make us more
careful than they were. Perhaps the controversy about the
Eucharist would never have assumed such disastrous propor-
tions if there had not been behind it pseudo-problems of
Christology, due to an uncritical adoption of traditional views
on the Resurrection of the Lord. If in this respect the Reformers

had remained as "Pauline" as they were on the doctrine of Justification, then probably these controversies would never have been necessary. Thus, as we look back, we can see that the further Christological development of the doctrine of the physical Resurrection confirms our view, based upon the testimony of Paul, that the traditional view of the physical Resurrection is not based upon the testimony of the first witnesses, but upon a later, cruder, view, which for its part led to the medieval belief in the Resurrection of the flesh, to that dramatical mythical vision of the dead arising at the sound of the trumpet.

The "Body" of the Risen Lord, according to the Bible—where it is mentioned theologically—is always and only the Church. Jesus Christ is the Head of this Body, and he who belongs to Him in faith belongs to the Church; and conversely, in belonging to the Church he must show that he is really united with Him, the Head. The danger of a false "spiritualization", which Luther rightly saw in Zwingli, is not to be opposed as Luther thought, by a doctrine of the heavenly body of Christ, but much more by taking seriously the concrete historical Word of the message, and the historically concrete "body" of the Church of Christ. False spirituality does not consist in the fact that we think in one way or another about the heavenly Body of Christ; but it is due to the fact that we turn away from the historic Mediator and the historical concrete form of the Christian message, and pay attention to speculative or mystical theology, rather than to the theology of the historical revelation. Is not this the deepest meaning of that Johannine mystery, that the Fourth Gospel always speaks of the exaltation in such a way that at the same time it means the exaltation of the Cross? And is not this also the meaning of the Pauline doctrine of the victory of Christ over death, which sees this victory—and also the exaltation of Christ—in the fact of Good Friday?[1]

Through faith we are "in Christ", and thus we have a share in His Body. But being in Christ through faith is not the final word of faith. Faith points beyond itself to an ultimate future, when we shall "see" Him "face to face". Our part in the life of Jesus Christ, so long as we are in the flesh, is a hidden one. Hence our victory, which we have in faith, is hidden *sub contraria specie*, as the glory of the Son of God on the Cross is only visible *sub contraria specie*. We wait, therefore, for a final

[1] Col. 2: 15

revelation in which this veil will be removed, which now conceals the glory, the glory of Christ in the veil of the Crucified, and the glory of victory in the veil of involvement in the world and death. As we look on our Exalted Lord we are sure of this final coming event; but as we look at Him we also notice that "we are absent from the Lord".[1] He is there, we are here. The fact that He, the "firstborn among many brethren", *is* there, gives us the certainty that He "will draw us all unto Himself".[2] But the fact that He is there, where we are not yet, allows us to wait in longing expectation for that which "is not yet made manifest". But when "He shall be manifested" we know that "we shall be like Him."[3]

[1] 2 Cor. 5: 6   [2] John 12: 32   [3] 1 John 3: 2

INDEX OF SUBJECTS

INDEX OF NAMES

INDEX OF SCRIPTURE REFERENCES